THE DISSIDENTS

The Dissidents

A MEMOIR OF WORKING WITH THE RESISTANCE IN RUSSIA, 1960–1990

PETER REDDAWAY

BROOKINGS INSTITUTION PRESS
Washington, D.C.

1775 Massachusetts Avenue, N.W., Washington, D.C. 20036
www.brookings.edu

Library of Congress Cataloging-in-Publication Data
Names: Reddaway, Peter, author.
Title: The dissidents : a memoir of working with the resistance in Russia, 1960–1990 / Peter Reddaway.
Description: Washington, DC : Brookings Institution Press, 2020. | Includes bibliographical references and index.
Identifiers: LCCN 2019018087 (print) | LCCN 2019980856 (ebook) | ISBN 9780815737735 (hardcover) | ISBN 9780815737742 (epub)
Subjects: LCSH: Dissenters—Soviet Union—Biography. | Human rights—Soviet Union. | Civil rights—Soviet Union. | Reddaway, Peter—Friends and associates. | Soviet Union—Politics and government—1953–1985. | Soviet Union—Politics and government—1985–1991.
Classification: LCC JC599.S58 R45 2020 (print) | LCC JC599.S58 (ebook) | DDC 323.092/247—dc23
LC record available at https://lccn.loc.gov/2019018087
LC ebook record available at https://lccn.loc.gov/2019980856

9 8 7 6 5 4 3 2 1

Typeset in Adobe Caslon

Composition by Elliott Beard

CONTENTS

Introduction 1

ONE
First Steps 5

TWO
Graduate Studies 28
A Double Miracle

THREE
Immersion 38
Daily Life in Khrushchev's Russia

FOUR
Expulsion 69
Cultural Trends, Literary Friends, and the Sharp Edges of the Soviet State

FIVE
The Emergence of Dissent 103
Bringing Dissidents and the Emerging Human Rights Movement to the World's Attention

SIX
The Other '68 120
Upheaval in the Soviet Bloc and the Chronicle of Current Events

SEVEN
Two Early Giants of Soviet Dissent 132
Marchenko and Grigorenko

EIGHT
Confronting the Naysayers in the West 150

NINE
"The Mental State of Such People Is Not Normal" 164
Exposing the Political Abuse of Psychiatry

TEN
Dignity under Persecution 185
Dissent among the Ethnic Minorities

ELEVEN
Religious Persecution, Religious Dissent 196

TWELVE
Fighting on Old and New Fronts 203
1968 to 1983

THIRTEEN
Publishing Samizdat in the West 215

FOURTEEN
Dissent and Reform under Gorbachev 220
Uncertain Terrain

FIFTEEN
Upending Manufactured Schizophrenia 242

SIXTEEN
The End: RIP USSR, 1917 to 1991 257

Some Conclusions 289

Works by Peter Reddaway Cited in This Volume, by Year 295

Notes 301

Subject Index 319

Names Index 329

THE DISSIDENTS

Introduction

This book is a memoir, primarily a chronicle of my personal experiences regarding the Union of Soviet Socialist Republics (USSR) from the late 1950s to the collapse of the country in 1991. Starting at Cambridge University, at the age of nineteen, I was attracted to Soviet studies, an interest I fed with an eight-month stay in the USSR in 1963–1964, and with my work with dissidents and on *samizdat*—literally "self-published" writings of typescripts by dissidents—from 1965 to the late 1980s. This book's reflections on Russia's political, social, economic, and historical background throughout the thirty-odd years are part of this story.

In the period from 1956 to 1964, the most notable political events in the USSR were Nikita Khrushchev's denunciations of Joseph Stalin in 1956 and 1961 and his easing of party and KGB controls; the fanciful utopianism of the new party program of 1961; and the pushing of all of these trends into reverse from 1962 on by a growing opposition to the self-aggrandizing Khrushchev by his colleagues on the Politburo. This led to his removal from power in a Kremlin coup in 1964.

Meanwhile, my own involvement with the fate of the USSR was developing as my education concentrated on learning Russian and studying Russian history and politics at Cambridge University (1958–1962), Harvard University (1962–1963), Moscow University (1963–1964), and the London School of Economics (1964–1965). As a student, I took three trips to the Soviet Union, two for five to six weeks and one for eight months. In

May 1964, I was arbitrarily expelled from the country and not allowed to return for twenty-four years.

After Khrushchev's ouster, in 1964, the collective Soviet leadership hesitated in settling on its policy regarding dissent, but eventually it opted for a relatively hardline position until 1968, both domestically and vis-à-vis the West. The arrest of the writers Andrei Sinyavsky and Yuli Daniel occurred in 1965 and the trial against them in 1966.

In 1965, I started to teach Russian and Soviet politics and history at the London School of Economics with Professor Leonard Schapiro. Also I began to write for both academia and the press about politics and human rights in the USSR. With Schapiro, I edited *Lenin: The Man, the Theorist, the Leader; a Reappraisal* (Pall Mall Press, 1967), and I wrote articles for *Peace News* and *The Times*. Gradually I became involved in Amnesty International and human rights activity related to the Soviet Union, sometimes with my friend Martin Dewhirst.

Between 1968 and 1986, the USSR had four leaders, first Brezhnev, for fourteen years, after he had established a first-among-equals position, and then three others in rapid succession. These leaders adopted varying stances toward the West and dissidents: under Brezhnev, a harder line from 1971 to 1973 and a softer one from 1974 to 1978; under Brezhnev, Yuri Andropov, and Konstantin Chernenko a quite harder line from 1979 to 1985.

During this period, I wrote regularly on human rights for *The Times*, *The Observer*, *The Guardian*, the *New York Review of Books*, and elsewhere. I also edited translations of Moscow's samizdat periodical *Chronicle of Current Events* from 1968 on, first for typewritten distribution, and from 1972 to 1983 for Amnesty International. I also wrote a book on the *Chronicle*, titled *Uncensored Russia* (Cape, London, 1972) and, with the psychiatrist Sidney Bloch, two further books on psychiatric abuse.

In addition to teaching political science at the London School of Economics, I produced occasional academic articles, papers, and radio and TV broadcasts on Soviet politics and human rights. I was a source for the BBC and Radio Liberty, sending the latter samizdat, reviewing some broadcasts, and participating in conferences on the subject of samizdat. To gain a wide distribution of samizdat, I helped to get it out of the USSR via tourists, journalists, diplomats, and others.

Starting in 1971, I was one of the creators and active members of a U.K.-based group, the Working Group on the Abuse of Psychiatry for

Political Purposes, whose purpose was to combat the misuse of psychiatry to persecute dissidents, also writing its "Information Bulletin" and developing links with similar groups in other countries. Eventually we helped to form an international coordinating group. I also collaborated with Michael Bourdeaux, an Anglican priest, to form Keston College in 1970 in the U.K., whose mission was to publicize religious persecution (I served on its board until 1985). In addition, I assisted Karel van het Reve in creating and running the Amsterdam-based Alexander Herzen Foundation (1969–1988), which published smuggled samizdat books, and I helped some of the few dissidents who came out of the USSR to publish and settle down in the West.

Academically, I spent sabbatical years at Columbia University in New York (1973–1974) and with the Kennan Institute for Advanced Russian Studies (1983–1984) in Washington, D.C. In January 1986, I left the London School of Economics to direct the Kennan Institute, carrying on my journalism activities in the United States.

From 1986 to 1991, Mikhail Gorbachev liberalized the Soviet regime with increasing resolve until the hardline opposition forced him to compromise and then reverse course. He survived a coup attempt—just barely—in August 1991, but the USSR collapsed in December of that year and dissolved into fifteen independent states.

In the immediate aftermath of these ground-shaking events, I continued to direct the Kennan Institute, while giving more lectures, attending more conferences at other institutions, and being approached as a consultant by a wider variety of entities in Washington, elsewhere in the United States, and abroad.

In early 1989, I moved to become a professor of political science at George Washington University, while continuing my other activities. Most of my publications were now on Soviet politics under Gorbachev and appeared in the *New York Review of Books* and occasionally in the *Washington Post* and the *New York Times.*

In 1988, I was able to travel to Russia again after being excluded from the country since 1964. Until 2003, I made more or less annual trips for research and to attend conferences.

In 2014, I decided to ease off on my absorption in Russian politics in favor of finishing my book on Putin's fomentation of war between two groups of his hard-line allies (*Russia's Domestic Security Wars* [Palgrave Macmillan, 2018]), and then embarking on writing the present volume.

Getting started involved sorting through my enormous collection of books, papers, documents, and letters to cull what I needed to write this book.

In 2012, I donated much of my collection of samizdat documents, books, and materials to the Gelman Library of George Washington University, and three-quarters of my library on Russian and Soviet history and politics to Kaunas University in Lithuania. In both cases, I resolved to give the rest on the completion of this book. This I have almost completed doing, and soon all of my books, documents, and other sources will be available for study.

For their support while I wrote *The Dissidents,* I would like to express my warm thanks to friends and colleagues, above all Ben Nathans and Martin Dewhirst, who have been kind enough to read this book in draft and make invaluable corrections and comments. They have enabled me to avoid numerous errors large and small.

Let me also thank my wife, Betsy, whose unfailing moral and practical support has kept me on an even keel.

ONE

First Steps

In 1958, at eighteen years of age, I was about to enter university and, ultimately, make lasting decisions as to how I would spend the rest of my life. It just so happened that this period coincided with a dynamic era in the history of the Soviet Union that saw Nikita Khrushchev at the apex of his power—and led to my lifelong commitment to studying and understanding the Communist state, its peoples, and its leaders. I soon developed a consuming commitment to Soviet dissidents—their aims, their methods, their fates.

After ordering the release of a couple of million people from forced-labor camps and exile, Khrushchev, since 1953 the first secretary of the Communist Party, partially but strongly denounced Stalin in 1956 and 1961 and eased the controls over the population exercised by the Communist Party and the secret police, the KGB (Komitet Gosudarstvennoy Bezopasnosti, the Committee for State Security). However, Khrushchev's new party program of 1961 was viewed by more conservative colleagues as fanciful utopianism, and all was pushed into reverse from 1962 on by growing opposition to the self-aggrandizing Khrushchev from these conservative colleagues in the Politburo.

Khrushchev felt compelled to respond with a risky move: placing missiles in Cuba in fall 1962, a rash venture that was soon thwarted by the skillful diplomatic and military maneuvering of President John Kennedy. But Khrushchev kept up his more innovative tendency by further easing cultural controls at home, and allowing the publication of a frank short story by Alexander Solzhenitsyn on the heretofore forbidden theme of the labor camps, "One Day in the Life of Ivan Denisovich," in November. The next month his opponents riposted by pushing him into going along with a big meeting of party leaders with prominent liberal writers that was designed to knock the latter into line. This led to a party-sponsored attack on them by conservative writers in March 1963.

Meanwhile, Soviet-Chinese relations had taken a further turn for the worse in the wake of Khrushchev's 1961 assault on Stalin. The Chinese leaders, inspired by Mao Zedong, expressed abhorrence of this assault and didn't give up until, in October 1964; after much maneuvering in the Politburo, this top Soviet political body removed its colleague Khrushchev from power in a carefully staged, nonviolent Kremlin coup. Khrushchev was allowed to live out his days under a relatively mild form of house arrest (which gave him the opportunity to secretly dictate some quite revealing memoirs and have them smuggled out to the West, where they appeared in English in 1971). At the same time the Politburo adopted a more benevolent attitude to Stalin, thus somewhat appeasing the Maoists in China.

In Khrushchev's stead a collective party leadership troika of Leonid Brezhnev, Aleksei Kosygin, and Nikolai Podgorny emerged in which Brezhnev became a clear first among equals from 1968 on. In 1964–65, this troika eased the reins a little: for example, they released from labor camps and exile most of the few hundred political and religious prisoners whose punishment for peaceful dissent Khrushchev had commissioned or endorsed. But in fall 1965 they tightened the reins again, including in the reversal of the less hostile attitudes toward the West that they had shown in their first year.

Why Learn Russian, and Why Do It in Ireland?

"Welcome to Collon!" said a smiling Captain Nikolai Couriss, as I arrived at his remote home in Ireland in September 1958 to start learning Russian. Thus began two weeks of exhilarating, idiosyncratic instruction that I shall never forget.

Disaster had just struck the inhabitants of the modest house in the sleepy little town of Collon, to the north of Dublin, near Drogheda. Their entire mushroom crop had been wiped out by blight. The annual sale of this crop made up a large part of their income. Nonetheless, Captain Couriss, a former tsarist diplomat; his wife, Elizaveta, a former nurse who had been her husband's colleague in General Anton Denikin's White Army (which the Bolsheviks eventually pushed out of Russia in 1921); and their aged friend Prince Pavel Lieven, who was about eighty and the grandfather of my future colleague Dominic ("Chai") Lieven, set cheerfully to work earning the rest of their living: instructing students in the Russian language who also paid them for lodging and board.

There were not many of us—only one or two at a time, and then not year-round. Two cadets from the military college of Sandhurst departed as I arrived, and a student from Cambridge University came just before me and was assigned to the one spare room in the Courisses' modest dwelling. I was placed in a house across the road, as a lodger.

Why, you may wonder, had I decided to learn Russian? In 1956, when the Soviet leader Khrushchev gave his acclaimed speech denouncing Stalin for monstrous crimes against humanity and the Soviet people, I was sixteen and oblivious to Khrushchev. But the next year, a young Hungarian refugee, Paul Magyar, came to my school and gave a talk to a small group of advanced students of modern languages, my own field being French and German. I was much impressed by Magyar's quiet, low-key description of the horrifying events he had witnessed the previous year during the Hungarian Revolution: the violent suppression of the Hungarian anti-Communist revolutionaries by the tanks of the USSR and some of its allies in the Eastern Bloc. Tens of thousands of people had been killed or imprisoned, and many more thousands driven abroad.

Magyar's presentation inspired trust. He aroused feelings of sympathy for the victims of Stalin and his successors, thus creating fertile soil for a suggestion that my father made to me soon after. This was that at Cambridge University I might do better than just become one of hundreds of graduates in the commonly studied languages of French and German. Instead, I might embrace a neglected language that showed signs of becoming more important and, therefore, more in demand. Given the Soviet Union's arsenal of nuclear weapons and its aggressive ideology, and Khrushchev's partial reversal of course in cautiously opening his country to the outside world, Dad suggested that Russian might be a good choice.

He also reminded me that he had published a book in 1935, *The Russian Financial System*, based on the research that he and a senior colleague at the Bank of England had done in Moscow. In addition, he stressed that his own father, a Cambridge historian of modern Europe, had been moved by the weak understanding and neglect of Russia and Eastern Europe by Western historians to teach himself Russian and Polish quite late in life and to write a few books about this part of the world, including one about Russia's eighteenth-century monarch, the formidable Catherine the Great.[1] Finally, Dad mentioned that Frank Reddaway, a distant cousin of his father's, had opened a hose-making factory on the edge of Moscow in about 1880 and developed a thriving business in Russia, which diversified his core activities in Lancashire. Frank had also married a Russian woman and spent sizable chunks of time in Moscow, until the Bolshevik revolution put a nasty end to his whole eastern adventure. These various historical snippets made me more inclined to consider learning Russian.

My next step was to talk with the university's director of Slavic studies, Elizabeth Hill, a lady as formidable in her way as Catherine. She spoke fluent, expressive Russian, having been brought up by a Russian mother. She also possessed a strong and cheerful personality that welcomed challenges. Her appointment to the university had been assisted by my grandfather. Liza, as she was widely known, with the name pronounced à la russe—Leeza—said that normally a couple of years' study of Russian was a requirement for acceptance into her department. But she made exceptions for motivated beginners. So she accepted me and urged me to study with her friends the Courisses, before starting at university in October 1958.

So that's how I ended up studying beginning Russian in Ireland. My study program involved five to six hours of Russian a day: sessions of Russian grammar with Nikolai and vocabulary with Elizaveta, and—when I was ready—a further session of conversational Russian with Prince Pavel. The problem with the latter session was that it came after lunch, and usually, after a while, assisted by my halting efforts at conversation, the charming and dignified prince would drift away into a rewarding snooze.

However, the work with the Courisses and the chance to listen to, and occasionally take part in, the continuous Russian spoken at meals were enormously helpful. Probably in their mid-sixties, the Courisses were talented teachers. As I wrote to my parents from Collon: "I certainly can't imagine a much more enjoyable or efficient way of learning a language."

In addition to the "formal" study program with the Courisses and the prince, I worked for two or three hours a day in my room across the street, where I played my 78 rpm records of Assimil's "Teach Yourself Russian" on the gramophone I'd brought with me. The Courisses were impressed by these, which were new to them, and much preferred them to their own Linguaphone discs.

For recreation, I played chess in the evening with Captain Couriss. This was fun, because we were equally bad and each of us had a similar number of wins and losses. Also, he introduced me to a couple of nearby families, both of which had private squash courts. I greatly appreciated the chance to play a number of games with good opponents. One of the houses was owned by a Count Tolstoy, whom Nikolai regarded as a Soviet fellow-traveler. At the Tolstoys' I could also take a bath. This aroused envy in the Couriss household, which owned neither a bathtub nor a shower! Ireland appeared to contain very few Russians, and these few had lively suspicions of each other.

Alas, after that summer I never returned to Collon to learn more from the Courisses. Soon after I left, Nikolai trained to become a priest in the Russian Orthodox Church Abroad, and was sent to run a parish in Liverpool.

Off to Cambridge

These years of undergraduate education ended with my earning a degree in modern languages that could more accurately have been called a Russian studies degree because I had focused virtually all of my energy on Russian language, literature, and history.

My most colorful professor was Elizabeth Hill, whose course on spoken Russian I attended with great benefit in my first year. The course was designed for students in the government-sponsored two-year program to train selected military officers performing their regular "national service." I didn't know about this course until it was too late for me to consider applying for it. The program's goal was to train not just eavesdroppers for listening in to Soviet communications, but also interpreters and translators who would quickly be available if war with the Soviet Union should threaten or break out. Hill's course was too advanced for me, but she allowed me to sit in. But by sitting through it and trying to understand the exuberant, often humorous, Hill in her give and take with the budding interpreters, I learned a lot that was hard to absorb in other ways. In particular, apart from vocabulary, I learned how Russian words are pronounced and how remarks and sentences are typically inflected.

Another professor—almost equally colorful—was Nikolai Andreyev, a fine medievalist whose English was sometimes delightfully quirky because he had only spent some fifteen years in the West. I much enjoyed his lectures on history and my tutorials with him in his home.

The precise opposite of Hill and Andreyev in terms of colorfulness was a scholar and teacher whom I greatly respected and saw often. This was my main academic supervisor, Alexis Vlasto, who spoke softly and seemed intent on not being noticed. His two quiet passions were Russian studies, especially early Slavic history, and gardening. The fine garden behind his house on Adams Road was the product of his untiring labors. He often tended its soil with his own bare hands, as he planted or uprooted particular vegetables and flowers. This I deduced from sitting near him during supervisions, when his muscular hands bore plenty of garden dirt visible in their creases.

Once one got used to his extreme modesty and low-key style, he was a good and interesting teacher and an exceptional scholar. For his finely written and well-received book *The Entry of the Slavs into Christendom: An Introduction to the Medieval History of the Slavs* (1968), on which he worked for many years, he used contemporary medieval sources in, among other languages, Arabic, Persian, ancient Greek, and Church Slavonic, some of which, to the best of my knowledge, he learned especially in order to research the book.

One teacher whose lectures on Russian history I attended assiduously, Mr. Young, was not a well-known scholar, because he had not, as far as I'm aware, published anything. But he knew a lot about different aspects of Russian history from the eighteenth to the twentieth century, and was good at explaining it in straightforward terms. I recall with particular interest his analyses of Catherine the Great's foreign policy and of the Bolsheviks' struggle to take power throughout Russia from 1917 to 1921.

Summer 1960: First Trip to the USSR

My studies profited from the two trips I made to the Soviet Union during my time at Cambridge. In August 1960 I departed for a five-week trip on which I acted as an inadequate but just viable interpreter for a group of twenty medical students who planned to visit hospitals in Sweden, Finland, Poland, and the Soviet Union, traveling in a convoy of four cars. I knew four or five of the students already, and all of them turned out to be pleasant to travel with. They had been invited by a senior Moscow doctor to visit some mental hospitals in Leningrad and Moscow. This relaxed and charming man evidently wanted to open up the especially backward—indeed, corrupted—field of psychiatry to some healthy outside influences.

I embarked on the trip as someone with a critical view of Soviet Communism, developed by my meetings with Paul Magyar, my friendship with the Courisses, and my first two years of study of Russian culture and history at Cambridge University. The reality that I found on the ground in Russia—the low standard of living, the omnipresence of the official ideology of Marxism-Leninism, the reticence of ordinary people who were frightened to be more open—was of huge interest, but was more or less what I had expected.

We took ferries from England to Sweden, then from Sweden to Finland, then drove on to Leningrad and Moscow and back home through Poland, Czechoslovakia, Germany, and Belgium. It was only the second year that foreigners had been allowed to travel in their own cars around the Soviet Union. All but a few roads were closed to us, these being on the western side of the country. My parents kindly lent us their Austin A-70, which performed valiantly on the often badly paved Soviet roads.

We slept in cheap campsites used by both Russians and foreigners, which were usually quite well set up, some having big pitched tents and boarded floors. The food was mostly mediocre, but outstanding local dairy products were available: kefir (fermented milk), slivki (cream), smetana (sour cream), and tvorog (white farmer's cheese). For our food supply we had successfully solicited sizable contributions from firms that wanted to be associated with a big trip to the largely unknown Soviet Union, so in the campsites we enjoyed powdered coffee, Ovaltine, Marmite, jams, apple dumplings, steak and kidney pie, and so on, all in tins or bottles. In other countries, if memory serves, such campsites were nonexistent and we always had to find spots to pitch our own tents.

Our biggest source of cash was an impressive stack of rubles that we had bought from a firm called Brown, Shipley in London at a price five times as favorable as the official exchange rate in the USSR. Changing money on the black market also turned out to be surprisingly easy, if done carefully, and at about the same rate as in London.

On leaving Finland, the only real problem with our first Soviet camp, in Repino, was that it was about thirty miles short of Leningrad. Furthermore, the road into the city was a mass of potholes. The Leningrad–Moscow highway was not nearly as bad. That road took us through Novgorod, where we stopped for a few hours to admire the ancient churches and other buildings dating from centuries as distant as the twelfth.

The impressions I got of the mental institutions in the two major cities were rather general. All of the buildings were gray and rundown, with little ornament, and the institutions were largely silent places. We were received politely but not warmly, and except for a "receiving doctor" in each institution, who showed us some wards, we had very few chances to talk with patients, doctors, or nurses. Electroshock therapy appeared to be the prevalent form of treatment. To my knowledge, no Soviet doctor showed any interest in establishing ties with us or the outside world by, for example, arranging to exchange publications or future visits.

One evening in Leningrad we went to an enjoyable performance of some short ballets set to the music of Ravel. We also made time during the day for some shopping. I was in constant demand for linguistic help with this and other enterprises. One of the highlights of our whole trip was our visit to Pushkin—earlier called Tsarskoe Selo, the Tsar's Village—and the magnificent eighteenth-century palace of Peterhof, a little way outside the city.

But most interesting to me were some social friendships that I was able to strike up outside the hospitals. At a gas station in Leningrad I met a friendly Russian of our age, Valery Lebedev, who was driving a clean and stylish Volga and spoke better English than I did Russian. After we had all moved on to Moscow Valery drove a few of us to visit his aunt, Natalya Ferdinandovna Irteneva. She spoke English as well as her nephew, which wasn't surprising because she taught English to students at the Moscow Pedagogical State University in Moscow. She was a gracious hostess, and both she and her nephew were not afraid to behave naturally and show us that they did not support Communism.

Natalya's late husband had been one of the main design engineers for the Volga car and received generous pay. Since they had no children, there was plenty of money to spend on a fine dacha and an equally fine "cooperative apartment"—that is, privately owned—in Moscow. They could also pay for a maid, whom they called by her patronymic surname, Petrovna. In her mid-sixties, like Natalya, she had a quirky, engaging sense of humor. Valery's real mother had died when he was young, and he and Natalya lived in the city apartment during the teaching year, Natalya serving as a foster mother for her nephew. Later, when I spent much of 1963–64 as a graduate student at Moscow University, in some ways she played this role for me too. She and Petrovna often cooked delicious meals for Valery and me, and we chatted about a wide range of subjects for hours. (I would encounter all three—Natalya, Valery, and Petrovna—again in later visits in 1961 and 1963–1964.)

The other Russian of our age whom it was a pleasure to get to know was Boris Kudashev, a fourth-year student of medicine in Moscow. He had volunteered to help us after learning of our planned visit through the USSR–Great Britain Society. Although he was a leader of the Young Communist League in one of the top medical colleges in Moscow, and behaved in orthodox fashion in public, he, like Valery, let a few of us know that actually he had a politically critical mind. In addition, he initiated a serious book exchange with me that continued for three years. We gave each other lists of books we would like to receive through the mail. Among Boris's mailings were some valuable books from the eighteenth and nineteenth centuries that he had bought in secondhand bookstores and thought I would like either to keep or to sell. Most of them I did sell or donated to the Cambridge University Library. Boris was also a kind and helpful person, and made sure to take us to two or three nice restaurants.

Our Moscow campsite, at Butovo, was nearer to the city than our Leningrad one, and the road was better. Our hospital visits were more rewarding than those in Leningrad, and we still had time to complete a basic sightseeing program: We visited massive Red Square, the extravagant St. Basil's Cathedral, and its architectural opposite, Lenin's austere, unadorned tomb, with one of whose designers, Alexander Pasternak, the brother of the writer Boris Pasternak, I later became friendly. We also enjoyed a performance at the Bolshoi Theater of the ballet *Romeo and Juliet*, set to the music of Prokofiev.

Less enjoyable was a very lucky escape from what might have been an appalling car crash just outside Moscow. To avoid it, our driver instinctively drove straight into the ditch rather than collide head-on with a motorbike doing about 100 m.p.h. None of us was hurt, but our car was pretty much a write-off. We left it behind in Russia and squeezed into three cars for the rest of the trip.

Summer 1961: The USSR by Land Rover

A year later, a very different sort of trip took shape, as I and four others, traveling in a long-wheel-base Land Rover, drove to Moscow and then sped south for a seven-week tour of the Black Sea region and Georgia, driving back west through Kiev and Lvov.

Four of us were friends from King's College, and the fifth, Duncan Noel-Paton of Emmanuel College, a close friend of mine, was proclaimed an honorary Kingsman, at least for the summer. Soon, Duncan, Anthony Figgis, Jonathan Steele, our mechanic, Patrick Finn, and I became a cheerful and resourceful fivesome. My father made the trip possible by lending us the money to buy the secondhand 1958 Land Rover—later we sold it and repaid him. We each scrounged up enough cash to cover the modest costs along the way. In addition to our sleeping bags and camping gear, we brought along a lot of food, some of it supplied to us free, as in 1960, by food companies.

To raise interest among ordinary Russians, we painted a board a light Cambridge blue, wrote on it in bold Cyrillic letters "Cambridge—Moscow—Black Sea" ("Kembridzh–Moskva–Chernoe More"), and attached it to the car above the windscreen. (This device would pay off, we would later learn, when we reached what was then Georgia.)

Fitting five people into a heavily loaded car proved surprisingly easy. Three sat in the front, while the other two took turns lying behind on comfortable sleeping bags and pillows, their heads against the back of the cab, enjoying the three-sided view provided by rolling up the car's canvas surrounds.

Thus prepared, we set off at the end of June 1961 for Tilbury to catch a well-appointed Swedish ferry to Gothenberg. From there we drove to Stockholm, where, after exploring the intriguing downtown for a few hours, we took another ferry to Turku in Finland and proceeded to Helsinki. Then we followed the route I knew from 1960 to the Soviet border and, beyond it, the campsite at Repino.

This time, with East-West relations deteriorating, we were discreetly followed most of the time by beefy KGB men in civilian clothes. Occasionally we couldn't resist annoying them—for example, by making a sudden U-turn and forcing them to drive past us, and then, when they were out of view, to make their own U-turn and hope to catch up with us. Their task of keeping an eye on us was made easier by the fact that we were not allowed to depart by more than a few yards from the handful of approved roads that connected major cities.

Another way in which we felt the cooler Kremlin attitudes was when it came to changing dollars for rubles on the black market. Recently a new law had prescribed the death penalty for Soviet citizens indulging in currency exchanges. In fact, two people had promptly been executed, retroactively, for actions taken before the new law came into force. Thus, the number of people changing money had drastically declined and the exchange rate we could get in Leningrad was only twice, not five times, the official one. Moscow was even worse: we couldn't find anyone prepared to do business.

Selling our clothes was a much better proposition. What sold best, we found, were new, brightly colored nylon shirts and socks, bright woolen sweaters, and new plastic raincoats. These yielded the equivalent of five or six times their cost to us in London. Transactions needed to be conducted out of the view of observers.

LENINGRAD

On this trip I reveled in the historic district of Leningrad, dominated by eighteenth-century Baroque buildings. For sightseeing we linked up successfully with my friend from 1960, Elena Topchiy. She was still, to my pleasant surprise, working for the USSR–Great Britain Society, itself a member of the Society for Friendship with Foreign Countries. Elena was generous and critically minded, and had a keen sense of humor, which she no doubt concealed from her bosses, who would instead have been impressed by her outstanding English.

The weather was beautiful, and Elena took us to lots of magnificent and interesting places: Peterhof and Pushkin, and parts of the famous Hermitage palace and museum. For its formidable size, range of subject matter, the beauty of its collections, and the stunning style of its interior, the Hermitage can only be compared to the British Museum and the Louvre. Its collection of French impressionists, along with that of the Pushkin Museum of Fine Arts, is inferior only to that of the Jeu de Paume in Paris. Cézanne and Gauguin are particularly well represented, as are Rembrandt, van Dyck, Picasso, Matisse, Bonnard, and da Vinci.

We also explored the huge collection of art from all periods of Russian history that is held in the State Russian Museum in Leningrad and the

Tretyakov Gallery in Moscow. Perhaps the latter has the edge, because it contains many first-class works by Andrei Rublev, an extraordinary early-fifteenth-century icon painter. Otherwise, my favorite artists in the Tretyakov Gallery and the Russian Museum are Ilya Repin (1844–1930), a brilliant portrait painter, especially of his wife, who was from the Caucasus region, and Isaak Levitan (1860–1900), a serene and moving painter of Russian landscapes, and some of the early-twentieth-century Expressionists.

Elena also took us to the Alexander Nevsky Lavra, an impressive monastery-cum-cathedral-cum-cemetery complex where many famous Russians are buried, including Tchaikovsky, Dostoevsky, and considerable royalty. She also introduced us to the Museum of the History of Religion and Atheism, housed in the former Kazan Cathedral, where the exhibits not surprisingly denigrated religion and idealized atheism, but the museum nonetheless was well worth a visit.

We spent many pleasant hours wandering round the streets by car and on foot, looking at spacious gardens, the Smolny Institute, the cathedral, and small palaces turned into offices. Elena was the perfect guide: informative, cheerful, witty, playful, interested in our opinions as well as her own, and always sensitive to our feelings and needs.

Finally, there was a leisurely, sun-soaked visit to the dacha outside the city belonging to my friend Sergei Repin, a scientist who had recently spent a year in Cambridge on an academic exchange. The charm of this visit is best conveyed in a letter I wrote soon afterward:

> *The five of us arrived at 3:00, and soon all present—including Sergei's charming wife and small son, his mother-in-law and his aunt—launched into a three-hour dinner in the open air. The long pauses between unfailingly delicious courses were filled with smoking, conversation in Russian, English or German (Sergei's wife spoke the latter well, and taught it), and lots of drink—vodka, then Armenian or Russian wine.*
>
> *Finally, at 6:30, we staggered upright and went for a walk through the village at a sleepy pace, drinking in an atmosphere so residential and non-productive—except for a few gardens—that we could have been in the nineteenth century. All the houses were wooden dachas in a galaxy of styles, almost all with carved balconies, some painted in exotic colors. Then we sipped tea in the twilight, using a silver samovar from Tula for the hot water, and ate mouth-watering confectioneries. At 11:00 the balmy July air*

still invited us to continue lingering and chatting beneath the birch trees, but, reluctantly, we felt it was time to leave.

TO MOSCOW VIA NOVGOROD

Our next destination was Novgorod, the famous ancient city, rather small, about halfway between Leningrad and Moscow, and the home of Alexander Nevsky. Founded in 859 as an increasingly important station on the trade route from the Baltic Sea to Constantinople, it is unique among the surviving towns of that period in that it was not ravaged by the Mongol invaders who in 1220 reached Kievan Rus'. The old buildings and their contents were not destroyed and are remarkably well preserved. By far the worst damage was done by the Germans in the Second World War, when about half the churches were bombed to the ground. A delightful and knowledgeable young guide took us round the most outstanding of the surviving churches, built in about the twelfth century in the Russian Byzantine style.

Equally engaging was the art museum, which, in addition to its exceptional Rublevs, had a fine historical section that offered an explanation as to why the Mongols didn't manage to reach Novgorod.

In Moscow our sightseeing guide, provided free by the government, was an Armenian from Georgia, Julietta Shakhbagova, who also worked for the USSR–Great Britain Society. She was friendly and reasonably knowledgeable, but professionally not on Elena Topchiy's level and much less spontaneous than Elena. Increasingly I felt that she was being paid to watch us (especially when she turned up unexpectedly in Georgia's capital, Tbilisi, when we arrived there, and again acted as our guide).[2]

In Moscow she took us to the well-known sights that I had seen in 1960, and also to the Permanent Exhibition of Economic Achievements, which we did not find absorbing. However, we ate at an Uzbek restaurant that served us a superb dinner of lamb shashlik.

For me, one of the highlights of our Moscow stay included a couple of marathon late-night walks through the streets of Moscow with Boris Kudashev, the medical student with whom I had been corresponding since we had become friends the previous year. Walking for three or four hours in the late evening ensured that no one could overhear our conversations.

We talked about politics and all the other sensitive issues that we both found compelling, and discovered that our views were rather similar.[3] In particular, Boris's understanding and experience of Soviet politics coincided closely with my own opinions and observations. We both felt that the ideology of Marxism-Leninism that permeated the Soviet system and society was a false construct. It was based loosely on Marxism, but had been adapted over time to function as a monopolistic means for justifying the rule of a handful of men and their party, and for manipulating society to serve their ends. All this was done by using a powerful Communist Party, a widely feared secret police, and other coercive organizations.

Boris rejected many Communist principles, such as the following:

- Individualism must always be suppressed in the interests of collectivism and "dialectical materialism."
- The arts must be practiced exclusively in tune with "socialist realism," because only then are they socially "useful."
- The Communist Youth League, or Komsomol, should police and record the personal and public behavior of all its members, to ensure orthodoxy and to determine whether each student, on graduating, should be dispatched nearby or faraway for his first job.
- A tourist trip abroad is a rare privilege beyond the reach of almost everyone.
- A socialist economy requires the state to own and administer nearly every component.
- Lenin and the party should be constantly adulated as the source from which all blessings flow.
- The West is consistently aggressive, and only thanks to the USSR's heroic efforts is the peace kept.

Boris had come to reject these positions largely through his work as a leading member of the Komsomol in his medical institute (Komsomol is from Kommunisticheskiy Soyuz Molodyozhi, meaning literally Communist Union of Youth). He had become active in the Komsomol because this was a good way to advance academically and professionally. But the manipulation of his fellow students and his growing perception of the falseness of the ideology had gradually taken him to an inwardly critical position. He could not now talk about his true opinions with anyone, not even, it seems, his intelligent wife. And he could not afford to do anything that might redound against his father, who was a senior official of the regime. So it was a relief to be able to talk freely with me, in the instinctive knowledge that I would respond honestly to his questions and would also be discreet and not betray him.

Actually, he felt that quite a few of his fellow students held views that were critical of authority to one degree or another, but he had no idea how many. Also, he thought that political change for the better would come only slowly and inconsistently, and its nature—that is, would it emerge from neo-Leninism or from liberalism—was unpredictable. Certainly, the party would hold on to its power at all costs, if it could.

Our Moscow visit also included a drawn-out dinner at a dacha outside the city that belonged to Natalya Irteneva, whom I had also met the previous summer through her nephew Valery. He was as gentle and cultured as Natalya and studied English and German at the Moscow Pedagogical Institute. Relaxing after our trip from Moscow, we absorbed the unpretentious beauty of the dacha and its perfect setting under the birch trees in the warm sun. As soon as Valery had seated us in nice old wicker chairs beneath the birches, he began to ply us and his aunt with cognac, beer, and a brand of port. Duncan Noel-Paton, meanwhile, gave all of us a treat by quoting T. S. Eliot by the yard and talking in his most inspired way about English poetry.

After the drinking began the eating ensued and went on for two hours: stuffed peppers, smoked meats, and fresh tomatoes, some of them prepared by Natalya's eccentric, Dostoevskian servant, Petrovna. Petrovna told us that she had married for a second time specifically to inherit her new husband's apartment and money. Much to her delight, he had died a year later! This was especially good for her, because her monthly pension was no more than a pittance of twenty-five rubles.

She also asked us repeatedly to bring her a bulldog from England the next time we came, so that she could replace a beloved pet that had died. She had a shriveled, dark-skinned face, with vivacious, mischievous eyes encircled by wire-rim glasses. And she enjoyed a most unusual relationship with her employer. Natalya seemed to find her irresistibly and eternally a source of amusement as well as companionship, something on which Petrovna clearly thrived.

However, Natalya herself is my most cherished memory of our entire trip. She only allowed her sadness about the early death of her husband to show in rare glimpses through the gracious, all-enveloping smile that came over her face at frequent intervals, a smile of spontaneous warmth and love. In general, her features displayed an open, honest, and movingly humble sensitivity, in strong contrast to the guarded, often aggressive facial expressions of the majority of her generation, all of whose surviving members had been brought up as the tempo of Stalin's terror rose. The graceful dignity of Natalya's movements never threatened to inhibit the emergence of her irrepressible playfulness. The latter, I felt, had calmly refused to be crushed by the cruel pressures of each new twist in Soviet history. I was glad that no historical quirk had deprived her of her most natural setting: an old-world dacha with a wild and entrancing garden—and an endearing old-world companion.

As we motored on south from Moscow, we came to the home of Leo Tolstoy in Yasnaya Polyana, about which Anthony Figgis wrote in his memoir:

> The house is not grand, and the garden not well kept. The whole place was like us—scruffy. But it sits in gentle countryside, unhurried, unpretentious, patient, permanent. Tolstoy's life there was sometimes tempestuous, especially his relations with his wife. But the place meant so much to him that it breathes his spirit. You half expect to see him tilling the fields in bare feet, as he did, or hear his pen scratching out another chapter of 'War and Peace' in his study. We left the place feeling refreshed.

We crossed the Russian steppe on a long straight road and then drove east along the enticing Black Sea coast, called the Soviet Riviera, arriving at last in Georgia. Alas, we largely rushed through the towns of Novorossiisk, Sochi, and Sukhumi. The disintegrating, bone-rattling roads reduced our speed so much that we had very little time to stop and recline on the tempting beaches if we were to complete our tour on schedule.

A NOTE ON SOVIET ROADS

It is hard to say anything kind about the USSR's best roads in 1961. They were still suffering from the severe damage they endured during the Second World War, and from excessive neglect by Stalin and Khrushchev. The surfaces varied from just reasonable to deplorable, and often included a multitude of yawning potholes and alarming corrugations, especially on hills. Bridges had to be approached and exited with great caution: their surfaces and those of the approach roads were usually of notably different heights. Bridges—like military barracks, power stations, and radio masts—were never to be photographed, since they usually rated as objects of military significance, although this was nowhere spelled out.

After dark, cars and trucks turned their lights off completely when approaching within fifty yards of oncoming vehicles. If you failed to do the same, you would be the object of intense anger and deliberately dazzling, blinding headlights. Also, bicycles, carts, and roadworks were rarely provided with lights of any sort. Traffic lights—some horizontal, some vertical in design—were located indiscriminately. For example, some were wholly absent when they were needed, others hung above the road, and others were located on posts of varying heights on the side of the road. City maps were regarded as almost military objects, and could not be obtained in most cities. Apparently there were many rules, but some were not written down, while others appeared on signs only irregularly. And the traffic police were either lazy and inattentive, or, sometimes, officious and seemingly intent on getting a bribe. That was the reality of Soviet roads.

GEORGIA

As we approached Sukhumi, we entered what was then Georgia, but is now part of the Russia-controlled separatist entity of Abkhazia. Turning inland on still-dreadful roads, we came eventually to Stalin's birthplace of Gori. We stopped to eat spicy Georgian food in a garden restaurant, and enjoyed listening to a fine local band playing and singing with verve in the warm evening air.

Then we moved on to the capital city, Tbilisi, where for two days we visited ancient churches, wandered in the dilapidated but picturesque Old Quarter, gazed at the narrow but dignified River Kura, and learned how to drive in a city with few traffic lights. Julietta Shakhbagova, from Moscow, mysteriously reappeared and attached herself to us. The ancient churches were mostly in two places just outside the city, at the former capital of Mtskheta, where the oldest church dated from the fifth century, and on a small, grassy, sharply peaked nearby mountain that was topped by the Jvari Church, which looked down on Mtskheta and even on Tbilisi. It was built in the sixth century on numerous vast, chunky blocks of off-white stone and, amazingly enough, has not been altered since. The pointed roofs, which looked like half-open umbrellas, a shape that has been embraced by Georgian church architects to the present day, and also the imaginative icons inside made the church well worth the climb.

A highlight of our time in Tbilisi started off on a low note. The manager of the USSR–Great Britain Society had, in our presence, booked a table on the balcony of a famous hilltop restaurant that commanded a stunning view of the city. When we arrived at the appointed hour, the manager claimed to have no knowledge of us, and said that all the balcony tables were occupied. When he rudely ignored all our representations, we said we would wait for a table to come free. An hour later nothing had happened. So we grumpily accepted an inferior table.

The menu occupied some fifty pages, but when we tried to order what we wanted, the surly waiter announced that everything on the menu had been finished except for two dishes that we did not want.

At this point a burly man from a neighboring table strode over to us and plonked down two magnums of champagne. He smiled, said nothing, and quickly returned to his group. We were flummoxed, but opened the first bottle, filled our glasses, and took them over to thank him and toast his whole table of five. He explained that he had observed how badly we were being treated and that this was especially outrageous, since we were foreigners. Foreigners should always be received with gracious hospitality.

So we pulled our tables together and launched into a discussion of many topics, some of them politically sensitive. Our new friends' waiter appeared, and it turned out that plenty of menu items were available after all, including the ones that we had selected. Drinks flowed, and by the end of the evening there were eleven empty bottles on the floor—for ten people.

Our host was the champion toast maker, proclaiming in stentorian tones for the whole restaurant to hear: "Democracy—yes! Communism—no!" followed by "Georgia—yes! Russia—no!" and "England—yes! Georgia—yes!" After each negative declaration, he spat on the floor with a demonstrative lurch of his whole body. The guests in the restaurant appeared to enjoy these bold proclamations as much as we did.

He explained to us that the manager must have accepted a hefty bribe to give our table away to someone else, and thought he could just hardnose us without difficulty. Also, our friend flatly refused to let us pay our share of the bill, on the grounds that we were respected visitors who should be treated with special courtesy.

We concluded that the sum of his behavior showed him to be a man of influence, whose friends could easily outpunch those of the manager, and who had no fear of the KGB. We also got a useful lesson in how strongly Communism and Russia were disliked among many Georgians.

We had already gained some idea of this when we stopped the car several times in Tbilisi squares. The prominent sign above our windscreen aroused a strong curiosity among the crowds that gathered round. The question "Otkuda?" ("Where are they from?") could be heard from many people to whom "Kembridzh" meant nothing. Eventually I gave a short explanation in Russian that we were students from Cambridge University in England and were taking a holiday by car in the Soviet Union. This led to other questions, a few delivered in English. Before long, all five of us were busy trying to answer them. Jonathan Steele, who knew some Russian and had also spent hard time in the car immersed in *Teach Yourself Georgian*, profoundly impressed many people with his Georgian.

The Georgian language is unique, possessing its own alphabet and no known connections to any other language, except possibly Basque. The reasons for this are many, and relate to the country's history. The first Georgian dynasty is thought to have appeared in about 300 BCE, with its capital at Mtskheta. But the most important and definite development came in the fourth century CE, when Greek missionaries arrived and converted the people to Christianity. The Georgian Orthodox Church was subsequently autocephalous from the fifth century until early in the nineteenth, soon after the Russian empire had conquered the country and taken away the autocephaly.

Meanwhile, Georgia had been assailed from the fourth to the seventh centuries by Persian Sassanians from the east and the Byzantines from the west. Then it had undergone Muslim rule from the seventh to the tenth centuries, before enjoying its most glorious period—two hundred years of union under a Georgian dynasty. The language, religion, and culture blossomed, the capital moved to Tbilisi, and a Georgian empire was established.

From 1220 to 1400, however, the Mongols savagely destroyed the country and maintained control by force. The Georgians, though helped by their language and religion, could not quickly recover from the Mongol devastation. Moreover, from the fifteenth to the eighteenth centuries they were harassed and often lost land or sovereignty to the constantly warring Ottomans to the west and the Persian Safavids to the east.

In 1783, Catherine the Great's Russian armies descended, and independence was lost until 1990. One brief respite came in the exciting three years 1918 to 1921, while the Russians fought a long and violent civil war.

Since the Soviet collapse in 1990–91, Georgia has reestablished full independence, and foreign tourists, attracted by the magnificent Caucasus mountain ranges and Georgian hospitality, are arriving in ever-greater numbers. However, the country has lost two provinces, Abkhazia and South Ossetia, in effect to the Russians, who fought a five-day war against Georgia in 2008.

It is hard to see how a people of 2 million or 3 million (today 4 million) could have survived all this battering and foreign occupation if it had not had its own unique language and its own church. Today these cultural assets make the country strong, even though it has few raw materials (manganese and coal mainly), its economy is weak, and many of its people are poor. Clearly its future depends heavily on Russia's intentions and economic power, and on the West's uncertain level of interest in defending the small country.

From sunny Tbilisi we followed the one road north over the Caucasus directly into Russia, pounded now by unforgiving, tempestuous rain. This route took us via the Krestovyi Pass, at 7,800 feet the lowest of the three passes that allow passage over the Caucasus Mountains. In a few places the rain had washed away the asphalt completely and we were glad to be in a Land Rover, which could cope with hazardous conditions and an appalling road. When we stopped, we were greeted by tribesmen who mostly spoke no Russian, so Jonathan's Georgian, though basic, came in handy. Wildly bearded and dressed in thick coats that kept out the rain, they were happy to see us and were intrigued by the sign mounted above our windscreen.

KIEV, LVOV, AND UZHGOROD

Once we came down to a normal height above sea level, we had a long slog north, then made a ninety-degree turn to the west, and with persistence made it to the Kiev campsite. Kiev, on the mighty Dnieper River, became an organized town in the tenth century, not long before two Greek monks, Cyril and Methodius, arrived to convert the emerging nation known as Kievan Rus' to Christianity. Prince Vladimir, the prince of Novgorod who ruled Kievan Rus' from 980 to 1015, was converted in 988. Originally a practitioner of Slavic paganism, he chose Christianity from several religions that he considered.

Like the other towns of Kievan Rus' except for Novgorod, Kiev was first cruelly sacked by the Mongols in the early thirteenth century, and then had to pay them regular tribute. In 1961 Kiev was a large city and the capital of the USSR's Ukrainian Soviet Socialist Republic. We spent two days in early August seeing the sights, and on Sunday I attended a service in the Orthodox cathedral, built in about the fifteenth century and one of the few churches that the Communist regime allowed to remain open. It was a moving occasion with a large congregation—which did not surprise me. Even though I was fully aware of the Soviet regime's openly expressed determination to eliminate religion completely, I believed that human nature would make this impossible.

When the service ended I had no difficulty in finding a charming young woman who was grateful to receive from me, unobtrusively, two small-format bibles in Russian that a friend had given me for distribution. She recounted how she and a single co-believer were often subjected to severe hostility for their steadfast refusal to renounce their faith. My motivation was primarily to help out good people in the USSR whom the regime deprived of necessities, in this case religious ones. My own faith at this time was not strong, but was strengthened whenever I attended a Russian service. Then I felt uplifted by the Christians' dignified resistance to oppression.

On our last evening in Kiev we decided to dispose of a large chunk of our store of rubles by having dinner in a good restaurant. Afterward we were feeling cheerful from the wine and decided, stupidly, to provoke the man who was following us by splitting into two groups and going in different directions. I saw him rush into a phone booth to tell his boss what was happening and, no doubt, ask for help. But it was too late. Both groups escaped official surveillance and enjoyed feeling that much freer for what remained of the evening.

The next day we made our way west to Lvov, where we briefly enjoyed the imposing cathedral and the other beautiful remains of the old city, much of which had been destroyed by the Germans in the Second World War. It had been ruled at different times by the Poles, the Lithuanians, and the Germans. The KGB kept a tight watch on us, perhaps because of our trickery in Kiev, perhaps because Lvov was one of the most Western-oriented cities in the Soviet Union and thus likely to be especially friendly to Westerners, as indeed it was, and hence would attract more than the normal number of Westerners to be closely observed.

But we had to press on to the Soviet border beyond Uzhgorod, which was where the KGB really took its revenge. While a Russian group returning from abroad jumped from their cars, some of whom kissed the Motherland's soil, we were confronted by armed officials. They took the Land Rover away with them, emptied it of all of our belongings, and drove it over a deep pit to inspect it for any Russians who might be clinging to its chassis. We were taken one by one into a small room and in some cases made to strip (by chance I escaped this); then our bags were examined in excruciating detail and anything suspicious was confiscated. Our films were either developed and printed or confiscated, and we were not allowed to depart until many hours had passed and we had developed visions of perhaps being thrown into prison. We were then told to get out of the Soviet Union and never to return.

Only when we got home did I realize that an album of photos of my family, showing typical English family life, had not been returned to me. Naively I wrote to the customs office in Uzhgorod, explaining what had happened, and asking for the album, when located, to be mailed to me. Rather promptly, I received a polite but doubtless mendacious reply to the effect that a careful search had been conducted, but the album had not been found.

When we arrived in Vienna late that night we learned that the Berlin Wall had started to go up the previous day. That tightened the screws of East-West tension a few more notches.

From there we hurried on to the place in Austria where Duncan and I would learn where we should go in order to begin the work we had contracted to do for a rich Italian family. We were to teach the three young children English and Latin, and generally look after them in the absence of their parents. It turned out that our goal was to go to the family's home in the Dolomite mountains—an imposing, ancient castle, to which our friends kindly delivered us

The 1960 visit had laid valuable groundwork for the second one, so that I had been able to learn a lot more on this absorbing, exciting, and instructive second trip. We had all of our time to ourselves, and could pursue a wide range of activities of our own choosing. Thus we became knowledgeable about Russians, Georgians, and Ukrainians and their countries. Two interpreters—Jonathan and I—for three others was a lot better than my being one for a score of travelers, as in 1960. We were also lucky not to experience any serious mishaps, and not to develop any major frictions in our own ranks.

On our return to England, we all plunged into our final year of undergraduate studies. The outcome for me in June 1962 was—in a grading system of four degree classes—a class 2, upper division. Jonathan was the only one of us to get a highly valued and well-deserved class 1.

Influenced by my trips to the Soviet Union, I found myself in this last year concentrating increasingly on Russian language and history, and decreasingly on literature. At the same time, I felt frustrated that Cambridge taught Russian and Soviet Russian history only up to 1941. This didn't give me enough background to understand the USSR that I had experienced at first hand in 1960 and 1961. During the next academic year, I started to fill in that background, and also began to launch my public writing career with three fairly solid articles for serious student magazines, one of them called "How Socialist Is the Soviet Union?" By my definition of socialism, the answer was "Not very much."

TWO

Graduate Studies

A Double Miracle

The years from 1962 to 1965 ended up determining the future outline of my career. First, I became committed to studying the history and politics of the Soviet Union. And second, a deep ingrown interest in issues of human rights began to emerge in parallel to that commitment. I was intrigued by the ways the Soviet system denied human rights to its citizens, yet left open a few gaps in which the more thoughtful people could exercise some limited freedoms. I wanted to understand how this came about and how the various parts of the system worked. I also wanted to be useful to any Soviet citizen who might seek my help.

These thoughts had been encouraged by several outstanding books: Robert Conquest's *Common Sense about Russia* (1960); *The Captive Mind*, by Czeslaw Milosz (1960); Edward Crankshaw's *Khrushchev's Russia* (1961); Vladimir Dudintsev's *Not by Bread Alone* (1958); and a special issue of the journal *Daedalus* (Summer 1960), "The Russian Intelligentsia," that included articles by Richard Pipes, Leopold Haimson, Max Hayward, David Joravsky, Leopold Labedz, and Leonard Schapiro.

In early 1962 I spent a week in the Foreign Office in London as an intern, to help me decide whether to apply for a position there. Martin Dewhirst, from Oxford, was a fellow intern with whom I quickly became friends. It turned out that we had similar views on many matters, and a common interest in the burning question of where the Soviet Union was going under the unpredictable leadership of First Party Secretary Nikita Khrushchev. Our frequent communications soon led to my being invited by Martin's adviser, Max Hayward, to attend as an observer a high-powered conference on Soviet literature at St. Antony's College, Oxford. The conference included several discussions of the interactions of literature and politics, which especially interested me, and also enabled me to meet personally some smart and attractive American and British academics, which was exciting and potentially helpful for the future.

I had gone ahead and taken the Foreign Office entrance exams, but failed them. So instead of becoming a diplomat, as I had hoped (but I soon realized would not have suited me), or a journalist, I focused on academia. I applied to the government-funded British Council for a ten-month studentship for graduate work in the social aspects of Soviet literature at Moscow State University. Shortly afterward, I was looking through the notices pinned to the board of the Modern Languages Department in Cambridge and spied a sheet of paper that hung precariously askew on a single pushpin, announcing that Frank Knox Fellowships, of which I had never heard, were available for British graduates to study for a year at Harvard University. I didn't think my chances were good, but nonetheless decided to apply. In a double miracle, I was offered a Knox fellowship, and also a British Council studentship to Moscow. I decided to go to Harvard, and then, in 1963–1964, to Moscow.

When I read through the catalog of Harvard graduate programs, I was delighted to find that scholars whose names I knew, such as Merle Fainsod (specializing in Soviet government), Adam Ulam (Soviet foreign policy), and Richard Pipes (Russian history), were professors at Harvard. I resolved to sign up for the Master's Program in Soviet Area Studies as soon as I arrived in Cambridge, Massachusetts.

September 1962 to June 1963: Harvard

My ship docked in New York, and I stayed a few days there with a friend before proceeding to Cambridge. His brother-in-law, an attorney named Bob Goodman, held pro-Stalin views on the nature of the USSR that differed more from mine than those of anyone else I had ever met. He had long been a devoted supporter of the Stalinist Communist system, and, like the Chinese Communists, sharply disapproved of Khrushchev for making partial denunciations of the longtime Soviet leader. A couple of trips to the Soviet Union had confirmed him in his views, and none of my numerous objections to his position moved him a single inch.

My choice of Soviet area studies was a fortunate decision from several viewpoints. Most of the teachers in my program, as well as professors from other universities, had offices in the Russian Research Center.[1] During their lunch hours and at other times most of them were open to including graduate students in their conversations and faculty seminars. Luring all comers was the center's Mrs. Black, who served a splendid lunch every weekday for a mere ninety-nine cents. This lunch attracted most of the people in the building and served as the forum for numerous conversations and discussions of exactly the sort to which I needed to listen and, occasionally, nervously, contribute.

The most absorbing of all my classes was the graduate seminar of Professor Merle Fainsod. He had written two influential books on Soviet government, *How Russia Is Ruled* (1953; a heavily revised edition came out in 1963) and *Smolensk under Soviet Rule* (1958). The first benefited from his training and writing on topics of comparative government, and the second from the fact that he alone had access to the Smolensk Archive, the archives of the Smolensk Oblast Committee of the Communist Party, which had been abandoned by the Soviets, captured by the German forces when they overran the western regions of the USSR in 1941, and eventually came into American hands. In this archive Fainsod found numerous internal documents that were not available in any other source accessible to Americans.

Fainsod's teaching method was to have us sit around a table, introduce the day's subject in a quiet voice, then draw each of us out gently, to answer his questions; he graded our papers himself. I wrote my master's thesis for him: "Yevtushenko and Kochetov in the Soviet Literary Struggle since 1956," on the politics of Soviet literature from 1956 to 1963. This was my first serious academic work; it had 60 pages and 150 notes and earned Fainsod's enthusiastic appraisal, and he later supported me when, after I had met the charming, erudite scholar Leonard Schapiro of the London School of Economics and Political Science, I applied for a graduate fellowship there. Fainsod kindly did the same when I subsequently sought a job, and later a promotion.

My thesis highlighted the contrasting careers of Vsevolod Kochetov, a hard-line pro-Stalinist writer and journal editor, and Yevgeny Yevtushenko, a mostly freelance writer of liberal persuasion.[2] In some writings Kochetov saw the West as ready to violently overthrow Soviet Communism should the Moscow leadership weaken its autocratic rule even briefly. In one novel, *The Yershov Brothers*, a character asks his friend, "Are we, then, going to sit around and wait while they start hanging us by the ankles from the very trees that we ourselves planted?" "Who is going to be hanging us?" says his friend. "Well, who is hanging the Hungarian comrades?" comes the reply, along with the claim that the West sent its special forces in to do the job during the 1956 revolution.

Meanwhile, Yevtushenko called for an end to the Cold War and for friendly relations with Western countries.[3]

Also enjoyable and highly instructive were the courses I took from Adam Ulam, on Soviet foreign policy, Melvin Croan, on Eastern European politics, and Abram Bergson, on Soviet economics. Ulam had a keen, wry sense of humor, and an attractive personality, and I always looked forward to his classes.

Bergson was an eminent economist who as a professional colleague of my father knew some of his writings. But Dad had kept quiet at home about his work and had never encouraged me to take a course on economics. Thus it was truly mortifying when Bergson, wanting to start a discussion on "the factors of production," turned to me to ask what these were. He clearly thought that the son of an economist would be able to give a good answer. Alas, I had not the slightest idea what to say! I just sat there while Bergson patiently waited, until eventually I got up the nerve to admit the awful truth. Bergson was kind enough not to say anything and moved on calmly to someone else.

My Russian language skills were thoroughly tested and earned top grades, but in the end I failed to earn a Harvard degree because I failed to finish my paper for Croan's course within the requisite two years.

Among the people at the Russian Center who were not employed by Harvard but taught me the most, and whom I most liked, were Priscilla Johnson (after her marriage she wrote under the name Priscilla Johnson McMillan), Edward Keenan, and Michael Rywkin. Priscilla was a highbrow journalist who returned in October 1962 from a reporting stint in Moscow to gather material for three articles on the regime and the intellectuals for *The Reporter*.[4] Before she left the Soviet Union the KGB had confiscated her eighteen notebooks, creating a thorny situation for people she had met while preparing her articles. Since her subject overlapped with my thesis topic, we often exchanged notes and references. Thanks to her sense of humor and a range of interests similar to mine, we formed a strong friendship that has lasted to the present day.

Edward Keenan was an advanced Ph.D. student in early Slavic history who returned from the USSR during the academic year after being expelled, basically for having an excessive number of free-thinking Russian friends. He, too, had a sharp, endearing sense of humor and was a genius for telling engaging stories. Although his subject was very different from mine, we became friends and remained so virtually for the rest of his life (he died in 2015).

Michael Rywkin, a professor on a year's leave from New York University, was a Pole who had been forced to live in the USSR for many years. Michael liked to tell stories. He must have found my company at least somewhat tolerable, since he agreed to have lunch with me most days at the center and to speak only Russian with me. This helped my efforts to become fluent in spoken Russian immensely, for which I shall always be grateful to him.

One of the exciting aspects of the Russian Research Center was that it invited eminent outside speakers to come and give talks. Among those whom I had the good fortune to hear were the future West German chancellor Willy Brandt; the eminent British politician Anthony Crosland; the political counselor of the Soviet embassy; a Yugoslav diplomat; the British diplomat Thomas Brimelow; the Russian writer Valentin Katayev; the prominent scholars Isaiah Berlin, Zbigniew Brzezinski, Alec Nove, Georges Florovsky, and Leopold Labedz; and the well-known journalists Marvin Kalb, Richard Lowenthal, and Wolfgang Leonhard.

I set down my impressions of these eminent men in letters to my friends: Leonhard was "absolutely brilliant" on Soviet politics, Labedz "demolished Isaac Deutscher, a British journalist, completely," and Nove was good on Soviet economics, but faced fierce criticism from Alexander Gerschenkron for being overly optimistic in his assessments. Also, I was lucky enough to be included in a dinner for Isaiah Berlin, with whom, I immodestly reported, "my rapport . . . was amazing and sparkling."

Kalb recounted to a seminar group a revealing story about Soviet officialdom. When he arrived in Moscow at the beginning of a two-year assignment in about 1960, he was invited to visit the official responsible for Western journalists. This official, after explaining to Kalb that he should be guided in his reporting by the principles of "socialist realism," took him to a window overlooking Red Square and pointed to an old woman sweeping up snow and depositing it in a cart. His comment: "Socialist realism decrees that for your purposes she does not exist, because that form of manual work belongs to the past and will soon disappear. Socialist realism is about the future, that is, what we are building today. That is the subject matter we expect you to write about."

Of course, Harvard scholars also gave talks at the institute. Both the historian Richard Pipes and the lawyer Harold Berman, on their return from a few weeks on academic exchanges in the Soviet Union, reported that their colleagues in the USSR were pessimistic about Soviet political trends. This view gained support from the news we got a little later that the Harvard exchange with Leningrad University had been canceled from the Soviet side, as had the Soviet exchange with West Germany.

In reporting Berman's account to my friend, I wrote: "Soviet legal thinking essentially believes that criminal law equals political law, and therefore criminal statistics are state secrets. This fits in with civil offences being treated as a result of mental illness." Also, at a meeting to discuss the recent 22nd Party Congress, "A well-known lawyer called Ginsburg got his colleagues to stand in silence for a minute in memory of the innocent people who died at the hands of Stalin. There was much embarrassment, but all complied."

During my time at Harvard, an event occurred that shook the institution to its core: the twelve-day crisis from October 16 to 28 when American spy planes discovered that the Soviets were secretly installing ballistic missiles in Cuba. This provoked an American blockade of Cuba and the most varied and intense protests all over the United States. In liberal Harvard the protests were mostly aimed at signs that the Kennedy administration might overreact and set in motion a process that would lead to the catastrophe of nuclear war. The administration was accused of making overly aggressive statements, for example, about its continuing intention to "get rid of Castro." This was partly because, as it turned out, Castro had sparked the crisis by asking Khrushchev to provide him with a missile defense. This would protect him from being overthrown in the way the United States had tried to do through the Bay of Pigs attack by Cuban exiles the previous year.

Three of the professors of courses I was taking—Fainsod, Henry Kissinger, and Croan—decided to devote whole classes to discussion of the ongoing events around Cuba. One special meeting I attended took place in a huge hall that was packed to the walls. The most powerful speaker was Barrington Moore Jr., a formidable political sociologist and student of comparative government systems, some of whose writings I had read. He repeated the accusations aimed at President Kennedy and called for the exercise of wisdom in the White House in concert with consultations with experts. In fact, Fainsod was one of the experts Kennedy did summon to Washington.

My own view on the crisis was that the alarmism that prevailed at Harvard was somewhat overblown. I felt that Khrushchev would never risk an actual war with the United States, because this would probably result in the removal of him and the Communist Party from power, and perhaps his death. I also had faith in Kennedy and his administration, which I saw as rational and thoughtful, and as having learned some lessons from the Bay of Pigs fiasco. So I was not surprised at the sensible compromise that Kennedy and Khrushchev came up with: a Soviet withdrawal of its missiles in return for an American "no Cuba invasion" promise and a secret undertaking to remove U.S. missiles from Turkey.

In October 1962, I wrote to Martin Dewhirst to note that even though the communist parties of Poland, Yugoslavia, and Hungary were successfully easing their systems in small ways, we still shared negative views about current Soviet political trends. "Ultimately," I wrote, "I'm afraid, I see a new revolution as the only outcome—in thirty years' time?—after a long internal liberation movement (underground, of course)." As things turned out, a largely peaceful revolution took place twenty-nine years later, after free thinking had developed in an underground way for twenty-five of those years in the form of increasingly widespread samizdat journals and other writings.

Meanwhile, contradictory events were occurring. Liberal developments in the literary world from September to December 1962 had raised hopes that Khrushchev's reformist side was still alive. In September, the Party in effect forgave the young writers their sins by allowing them to publish again. Yevgeny Yevtushenko's long poem, "The Heirs of Stalin," was published on October 21, and an editorial praising the de-Stalinization of literature appeared in *Pravda* on November 23. In November came the dramatic publication of the first work to deal honestly with the Soviet concentration camp system, Alexander Solzhenitsyn's novel *One Day in the Life of Ivan Denisovich*, in the monthly journal *Novyi mir*, to worldwide acclaim.

But then, in mid-December, Khrushchev and his ideological sidekick Leonid Il'ichev warned the liberal intelligentsia in person that it had gone too far. As mentioned earlier, after several more warning signals, on March 28, 1963, the hard-liners launched attacks at a plenary meeting of the Writers' Union that obliterated most of the recent gains of the liberal writers. Yevtushenko's attempt to save himself by recanting his liberal errors failed, with the result that he had difficulty getting his work published.

But the political leadership seemed to be divided: in spring 1963 three pioneering dissidents—the philosopher and samizdat innovator Alexander Yesenin-Volpin and the writers Valentin Ovechkin, an idealistic neo-Leninist, and Valery Tarsis, an uninhibited anti-Soviet realist—were released from mental institutions. It seemed likely that a mixture of hardline and softer-line policies should be expected for the time being.

Summer 1963: A Classic American Road Trip

In Washington, after my time in Cambridge, I met up with Mark Elvin, a friend from both King's College and Harvard who was earning a doctorate in Chinese history, and his fiancée, the American-British poet Anne Stevenson. In Cambridge I had gone on numerous runs with Mark along the Charles River; he made generous allowance for my inferior running ability.

Anne gave me invaluable help with the poetic problems I encountered in translating a forty-page narrative poem, "The Driver," by the Russian writer Vladimir Kornilov (1928–2002), set in the virgin lands of Kazakhstan.[5] Although quickly published in a book in the United States, this "enormously long poem . . . had little chance of appearing in Russia in the foreseeable future," I wrote to a friend.

In mid-June, I spent a remarkable and unforgettable three hours chatting with the famous American political writer I. F. Stone (1907–1989), known as Izzy. He was a lifelong radical who had had a strong interest in the Soviet Union ever since, at various times in the 1930s and 1940s, he had met for news-gathering lunches with Soviet officials in Washington. However, the Molotov-Ribbentrop Pact of 1939–1941 and Khrushchev's denunciation of Stalin in 1956 put an end to his indulgent view of Communism (although he approved of the executions of hundreds of civilians and military loyal to Batista under the direction of Che Guevara immediately following the Cuban Revolution, in 1958). Subsequently he was best known for editing, from 1953 to 1971, his exactingly documented magazine *I. F. Stone's Weekly*, in which he was rivetingly critical of all forms of authoritarianism in all countries. Izzy grilled me on my views of what was currently happening in the USSR, but his prime target was his own country, the United States. He was a warm and exceptionally engaging man.

A little later, Mark, Anne, and I set off on a long road trip that took us by stages to El Paso, Texas. From there I flew to California, visited friends, then drove back across the country. In New York I visited a friend of Priscilla Johnson's, Patricia Blake, at her fashionable address on Washington Square in Greenwich Village. She had recently had painful experiences in the Soviet Union, having earlier edited, with Max Hayward, *Dissonant Voices in Soviet Literature* (Pantheon, 1962). She had also written a lengthy essay, "New Voices in Russian Writing," in the journal *Encounter* (April 1963).[6] She possessed a good understanding of the literary situation in the USSR—which coincided quite closely with my own views—and was glad that I would soon be off to Moscow for a year.

Russian Ripples in England

After spending two weeks on the East Coast, I boarded the majestic RMS *Queen Elizabeth* in New York in August and arrived back in the U.K. a week later. I was due to leave for Moscow in September. Martin Dewhirst and I spent many hours pursuing Russian themes that we had raised in our long correspondence. Martin gave me numerous leads on how to contact friends of his in Moscow and introduced me to a couple of Russian expatriates who were active in a small European political group, the People's Labor Union, or NTS, for its Russian name, Narodno-Trudovoi Soyuz. The group collected as much unofficial and "underground" information as possible about developments in the USSR, and published it through various channels, with the aim of showing that the regime was much less powerful and more porous than was widely thought and that a small underground, assisted by the NTS, was already active. The group's ultimate goal was to help lay the groundwork for replacing the Communist system with a democratic, pro-Western one. The group raised money by its own efforts, but was also thought to receive a subsidy from the American government and perhaps also from the British. Some Western specialists thought, plausibly enough, that parts of it had probably been infiltrated by the KGB.

The group's one full-time member in the U.K. was Boris Miller, who lived modestly in Kent with his hospitable wife, Kira, and their young family. Here Martin and I were received and generously fed. I told Boris that I could not help his group actively or openly during my upcoming year at Moscow University, but I would write via a secure channel to Martin, who could pass on anything of special interest.

To arrange the secure channel I contacted a friend from Cambridge, Tony Bishop, who had joined the Foreign Office and was about to be sent to Moscow for a tour of two or three years. Tony kindly agreed to my request to forward through the diplomatic bag letters I wrote to Martin and didn't want read by the KGB. Later, after my return to the U.K., I quietly supported the NTS by anonymously editing its magazine, *The Bell*, which appeared annually four times, starting in 1965.

In early September 1963, I attended a conference on Soviet literature near Schliersee, Bavaria, and then boarded a train for Berlin, then Moscow.

THREE

Immersion

Daily Life in Khrushchev's Russia

Throughout the eight months that I was a graduate student at Moscow State University I wrote long, detailed letters to several friends about all that I was experiencing, from new friendships and intellectual stimuli to my fellow Muscovites and other foreign students to my observations regarding Soviet domestic and foreign policy to my personal relations with Soviet officials. It was an immensely rich chapter in my life—one that came to a sudden and dramatic end.

Getting Settled

My train from Berlin arrived in Moscow on September 6. I went directly to the university's main building atop the Lenin Hills on the edge of the city, a solidly constructed "wedding cake"–style structure that dated from the post–World War II period, where I had been assigned a room. The building was located an inconvenient seven miles from the center of town. Nonresidents found it almost impossible to enter and visit a friend or attend a party, but it was better than the hostel downtown, which had just one bathroom and one kitchen for the residents of all five floors!

My wing, called Zone B, had eighteen floors, and my room was on the twelfth, giving me a good view over the eastern side of the city. There were four elevators, but two or three of them were usually out of commission, awaiting repair. At certain times of the day enormous queues would form at the bottom, and anyone living on the sixth floor or lower was not allowed to board. If someone broke this unwritten rule and pushed buttons two through six, they would be rudely ejected from the elevator amid shouts of "To the sixth floor on foot!"

I had a room to myself in a two-room block and didn't have to share my room with two or three others, as was the norm for Soviets unless they were privileged. The only problems were a too-short bed for my tall frame and heating that could not cope with the winter cold when the wind blew from the east. In about 1960 a near revolt had occurred when the enormous building, which housed eight thousand students, had been divided into different sections for men and women. The sexes were not allowed to enter each other's rooms—on paper at least.

A privileged Russian, Tolya Arkhipov, lived in the other room of the two-room block. He was cheerful and friendly and did not, as far as I could see, spy on me. We two shared a tiny bathroom and there was an open kitchen for us and our neighbors across the corridor. Tolya probably enjoyed this privilege thanks to being an older student—he was twenty-nine, in his third year—and also to being the head of the Young Communist League (Komsomol) in the Geography Department. After leaving high school, he had done his military service and then worked for a few years in a factory. One time he took me to the Sandunovy public baths, which had been well maintained since tsarist times and proved to be a lot of fun. We had a cubicle to ourselves, swam in a big, inviting pool, and whipped each other in traditional Russian style with birch branches to stimulate our circulation.

Tolya made no pretense of valuing ideology and had some flaming rows with his slippery dean. He refused, for example, to submit his annual report for any censorship by the dean that he, Tolya, would not agree to. It was noticeable that most young Komsomol officials on his level came from poor families and thus really had something to be grateful for, even if they had no time for ideology. By contrast, children from rich families were usually the most anti-regime.

Also absent in Tolya was what I soon found was a common defensiveness among Soviet citizens regarding their peasant origins, inviting me to join him when his mother came to visit. She had no husband, had worked in an unpleasant factory job for forty rubles a month for several decades, was illiterate and poorly dressed, and looked haggard and completely worn out. Though subdued, she tried to be nice to me. Having a successful son may have been one of her few consolations. In the years to come, I learned that Tolya died in his thirties, from causes unknown to me. By then his mother had probably predeceased him.

For income, we foreign graduate students (known as *stazhery*, or "temporary students") received a monthly allowance of 157 rubles, which was adequate if we avoided eating in expensive restaurants. Soviet university students got about 30, if their family's average monthly income per head was under 40. If it was under 70, the grant was 18 rubles, and if it was over 70, the student got nothing.

Not surprisingly, many students had to work at outside jobs to get by. Across the corridor from me lived a student who was also a full-time metalworker earning 100 rubles a month on top of his scholarship of 30. How he managed to study I couldn't imagine. Tolya told me that the dropout rate in the Geography Department for financial reasons was rather high.

Many nonstudent employees of the university also made pitiful incomes. Some cleaning women I became friendly with earned only 47 rubles, and were understandably upset by this. In Leningrad, a young sign painter who made 100 rubles wondered whether he could ever afford to go over the border to Finland, even if this became politically possible in twenty-five years' time. He knew that the Finnish government sent back Soviet citizens who escaped the USSR illegally.

There were a number of potential ways to spy on students. We British *stazhery* were invited to the USSR–Great Britain Society, which was secretly run by the KGB, and I agreed to give an unpaid weekly class in advanced English conversation for Soviet citizens. I was also offered free singing lessons once a week by a pleasant young woman who was about to graduate in singing from the Moscow Conservatory, which turned out to be enjoyable and did improve my singing voice.

One of the university's channels for spying on the students, especially foreigners, was a desk in the middle of each floor, next to the elevators that was always occupied by an inquisitive woman or a student who earned some money for keeping an eye on things, both of whom undoubtedly reported to the KGB.

Another channel for potential spying was the university's Department for Foreigners (known in Russian as the Inotdel). British *stazhery* had to report to a fortyish woman named Lilya Pavlovna.[1] Generally she was not unpleasant, but she could become so when a directive she received from higher up conflicted with our wishes, in which case she was the typical Soviet bureaucrat, made worse by a high degree of emotional instability. I had been chosen as one of two leaders of the British cohort, so I had to deal with her quite often and experienced this directly.

Each graduate student had an academic supervisor who was probably also a KGB official and whose function was to oversee the students' academic work. One of Lilya Pavlovna's first tasks was to tell each of us who our academic supervisor was, and when and where we had to meet him. Aleksei Metchenko, a typical Soviet apparatchik who headed the Soviet literature department, was a bossy, unattractive man in his sixties. The department was located in a university building in the center of Moscow, and getting there from the Main Moscow University Building in the Lenin Hills involved inserting myself into one of the heaving masses of humanity that inhabited all buses and metro-trains. I told Metchenko that my research subject was the role of literary journals in the development of Soviet literature since 1956. Luckily, he assigned me for the first three months to an academic adviser, Boris Mikhailovsky, who was a scholar, not a KGB official. A quiet, rather timid man probably also in his sixties, he looked as though he had either gone through the labor camp system under Stalin or had been thoroughly scared by its existence and successfully kept his head down. He was helpful and kind to me, and only saw me when I called him to ask for a meeting. However, this was not to last, as Metchenko himself soon became my academic adviser, but I kept out of his way if at all possible, and only occasionally did he bother me.

To pursue my research, I usually went to the Lenin Library in central Moscow, where foreign graduate students were allowed to use the quite large professors' reading room, which had a few librarians whose job it was to fetch books that we ordered. A couple of times there I saw Vyacheslav Molotov, Stalin's longtime right-hand man who had been dismissed from the party Politburo, the top political body, a couple of years earlier for failing to recant his Stalinism. He looked very old, although he was only seventy-three.

Making Friends

Perhaps the most rewarding aspect of my experience in Moscow was the time I spent with many Russian friends, some of whom I knew from previous visits and some I had come to know through my daily life. Martin and other colleagues introduced me to new friends by letter

My most treasured friends of all were Natalya Ferdinandovna Irteneva, now sixty-seven, and her nephew, Valery, who lived with her during the academic year, whom I had met in 1960–1961. As mentioned earlier, Natalya came to treat me as a second son, like Valery. She frequently invited me to large tasty meals and lengthy, relaxed conversations about matters of common interest, with or without Valery. Valery spoke less than his aunt but seemed always to agree with her. My friendship with Valery endured, and I met his wife, Svetlana, a doctor, when she and Val took a trip to England and visited us in London.

From Natalya's conversation I learned a lot about many aspects of life in the Soviet Union. One day, she told me that political jokes (*anekdoty*) had been produced continuously throughout Soviet times, in reaction to and despite the strict official censorship. Her husband had collected them in a book, but during the worst of Stalin's terror they had reluctantly burned it as a precautionary measure. Born in 1896, she also recalled nostalgically the safeness of the pre-revolutionary countryside, and the "charm and honesty" of the peasants she had known. Since the 1917 revolution, she lamented, "There have been no friends anymore."

During the Second World War she had been working with a peasant in a field when an air raid had caused them to throw themselves to the ground. She turned to the peasant and said that she had heard that the Red Army had just broken through on the Romanian front. The peasant responded, "Those poor people," meaning the Romanians.

On occasion, Natalya would tell me a bit about her dealings with her "special department," the KGB department in her institute at the Moscow Pedagogical State University, where she taught English. They knew she went to great lengths to avoid any sort of politics during her work, and were not happy about it. She hinted to me that she managed to explain her relationship with me by reference to my love of Russian culture.

Natalya introduced me to a nice group of her students, who ironically egged me on to become a Soviet citizen. They mocked officialdom's questionnaires and regretted that I wouldn't be able to read Freud, who was banned in the USSR, although huge interest surrounded his name and work, nor attend exhibitions of abstract art, which was likewise banned.

Natalya lamented the terrible lack of opportunities for the young to find some real purpose in life, and also to let off steam in healthy ways—so they would not let it off in "unhealthy" ways: extreme sexual promiscuity, homosexuality, and the terrible obsession with clothes. More positively, one student dabbled in religion, but had no one to guide her, and others were attracted to foreign radio stations. She regarded the young generation as still very cautious in expressing their views, rightly so, and she worried that perhaps I talked to them too openly.

Only once did Natalya surprise me, when she came out with some virulent anti-Semitism, a view she shared with a large number of Russians I met. She also thought there had now been enough criticism of Stalin. She hadn't read Solzhenitsyn's groundbreaking short novel about the concentration camps, *One Day in the Life of Ivan Denisovich* (1962), and she disliked the new anti-Stalin poem by Alexander Tvardovsky, "Vasili Terkin," about a Soviet soldier in the Second World War. This discomfort with coming to grips with the Stalinist era stemmed mainly, I think, from her desire not to be reminded of the horrendous aspects of that time and of the permanent disappearance into the Gulag of a beloved brother. More broadly, her rejection of Communism probably came at least in part, she hinted, from her having grown up before the revolution in a comfortable middle-class family.

My other particularly good friend from 1960–1961 was Boris Kudashev, the medical student and Komsomol official who had been one of our guides. He had gotten married (his wife, Valya, was also a doctor) and graduated from his institute, and as an outstanding student and senior Komsomol official he'd been assigned to teach medicine at Moscow University. We took to meeting for good solid dinners à deux in decent restaurants, and continuing our long talks of 1961.

In 1963–1964 he developed some of these themes in interesting ways. He felt that the West tended to overestimate the Soviet intelligentsia's desire for more intellectual freedom, which could not realistically be achieved, and to underestimate its desire for greater freedom of action, as consumer, traveler, professional—in short, for greater economic efficiency. In all spheres except heavy industry, the present economic system seemed increasingly inappropriate: not geared to the consumer society that most people wanted, including, now, most party members. The "New Class"—to use the dissident Yugoslav Milovan Djilas's phrase for the newly privileged class in Yugoslavia—now was happy when things didn't break down.

In these circumstances, Boris said, good Western radio broadcasts were becoming more important than ever. They should concentrate on providing detailed refutations of official Soviet statements, particularly on economic issues. These touched people's everyday experiences and would be talked about at work, unlike the Pope's travels or American supermarkets, types of lifestyle topics commonly covered by Western broadcasters that just aroused envy. The broad strategy should be to build up the pressure of informed public opinion that would push the party toward making radical reforms in institutional structure, especially economic (and indirectly political), that were needed if it was to have a chance of surviving.

But Boris was pessimistic that the party would manage to transform itself fast enough. He foresaw the possibility of terrible upheavals when the people came out of their post-Stalin daze and began to organize themselves. The possibility of achieving anything meaningful in the USSR at present seemed nonexistent. Evidence of this pessimism was his five friends who trusted him enough to tell him that if they could suddenly go and live in the West, they would leave at once, even though they hadn't thought about the difficulties of cultural adaptation.

Boris thought that no-one joined the Communist Party now with the aim of trying to reform it from the inside. The West should not be deceived by the many references to "fervent applause" that appeared in press accounts of party meetings. If someone at such a meeting proclaimed "Long live the Communist Party!" he said sardonically, "You try not cheering, too!"

He recounted one example of the present infuriating economic inefficiency: A Soviet printing plant bought a large lithography machine from the Germans, at great expense. They installed it with only one week's supply of ink, because the economic plan didn't provide for more. When the German ink ran out the operators used an inferior Soviet ink and a red warning light came on. They unscrewed the bulb and continued printing in order to fulfill the output plan. Result: the machine broke down, no one in the USSR could mend it, there was no budget to pay the Germans to repair it, and the money to purchase the machine was wasted.

Boris didn't lack for other examples of the gross inefficiency of Soviet industry: the failure of the much-touted Zaporozhets car, which quickly turned out to be so badly designed that it was unfixable; the renowned tractor factory in Minsk that was working only two shifts a day, owing to an inadequate supply of certain parts from shops that were already putting in three shifts. Boris's general impression was of widespread inefficiency, huge labor wastage, and a paralyzing reluctance to innovate.

Svetlana Semyonova and her husband, Georgy Gachev, were new friends I remained close to. The daughter of a general who was posted to eastern Siberia, Svetlana was a kind, sensitive, strong-minded young woman who had no time for Communism or the Soviet regime, and rightly took it for granted that the same was true about me. She taught me a great deal about Russian literature and philosophy, and confided to me that the KGB had called her in to ask her about me, but she had succeeded in brushing them off by saying that I was deeply interested in Soviet culture and that was why we became friends.

Svetlana had started as a student of French language and literature, but later was attracted to the work of Nikolai Fedorov (1829–1903), a writer and cosmologist of the late nineteenth century. While working on her research as an employee at the Gorky Institute of World Literature, part of the Russian Academy of Sciences, she wrote three original, penetrating, and readable books and scores of articles and booklets not only about him, but also about the moderate nationalist author Valentin Rasputin and her own detailed personal philosophical conclusions.[2] In the late Soviet period Svetlana also became a leading member of a strong association of women scholars.

Georgy, a Bulgarian, was a charmingly eccentric intellectual who studied in a quasi-anthropological way some of the main peoples of the world and wrote highly readable books about each of them. However, since the books exuded a free spirit and said nothing of consequence about Communism, they could not be published until after Gorbachev relaxed censorship in 1987. Before that, Georgy gave copies to a few trusted people to read, thus turning them into a form of samizdat. His finances had miraculously been secured when he alighted on the Institute of Slavic and Balkan Studies, whose secretly liberal director was prepared to pay him a salary for twenty-five years while he published nothing and did no teaching. In this way he avoided being arrested and exiled as a "social parasite," and able to do the writing he enjoyed. He was one of a minuscule number of people who had the great good luck to be thus supported—almost furtively—from the 1960s on.

Through Svetlana I met Volodya Kharitonov, who had as little interest in Communism and Sovietism as she and, like her, a kind and sensitive disposition, but was less outgoing than Svetlana. He eked out a living translating works of literature from English into Russian. He also lent me a thin, self-made booklet of underground poems, an early example of samizdat. His wife, Ella, a cultured person who worked in a research institute as an administrator, kindly invited me to their home for dinner.

I shall never forget when Volodya's mother, who lived with them for some years, was cautiously introduced to me. She was about fifty but looked seventy, and had been released from a concentration camp in the late 1950s after a long imprisonment on a fabricated charge of anti-Sovietism. This experience had shattered her. She could only just walk. In general, she didn't want to talk to people, and just stayed in her room all day, staring out of the window. She talked very little to me, slowly and quietly, without affect and apparently with some difficulty. She was as pleasant as she could be, but said nothing of substance. I said little, and after five minutes my visit with her was over. I think that Volodya and Ella wanted me to see at first hand the awful things that Stalin's Gulag had done to many of the estimated 10 million innocent people it had not simply killed. They did not tell me more about her, no doubt because to do so would have been too painful for them.

Dmitry Shestakov and his wife, whose mother was a well-known actress, Vera Maretskaya, invited me often to their spacious apartment, and his wife sometimes cooked us a meal. Through his contacts, his extensive reading, and his position as an assistant professor in Moscow University's Literature Department, Dmitry was extraordinarily well informed about Soviet culture and politics, and was willing to talk freely about them.[3] But in April 1964 he suddenly informed me that he would have to turn me over to an acquaintance of his, because he himself would now be too busy to see me. This seemed odd, and caused me to recall his wife's having several times come into the room, heard what we were discussing, and reproached Dmitry with a sigh for talking with me "about those things." Later I had reason to reflect on those sighs, and their cause.

A decade or so later, some tragic but not wholly surprising news reached me. Dmitry had committed suicide by wading into the Baltic Sea and drowning himself. In my opinion, he had been caught on a KGB hook, probably through getting to know Westerners too well. In fact, I might have helped set the hook. A British friend of his, a professor named Tony Cross, had brought to me in England about fifty books that were prohibited or unavailable in the USSR and I had delivered them to Dmitry. He was far from being a bad person, but I had made a serious error in trusting him, and this mistake may have been a factor in my expulsion from Russia.

Khrushchev's Power

During the period of my graduate studies in Moscow the general political trend was from a mild thaw, after the tightening of March 1963, to a gradually less liberal situation, though with many waverings and uncertainties. Brezhnev gradually emerged as a potential leader of the anti-Khrushchev forces that were seemingly probing for the leader's vulnerabilities. Meanwhile, Khrushchev was reliably reported to have had a three-hour conversation during this period with Stalin's earlier disgraced loyal lieutenant Vyacheslav Molotov, but it evidently came to naught. My speculation is that Khrushchev may have offered political rehabilitation to Molotov in return for his help against Khrushchev's opponents. Economically, the main trend was more clearly for the worse, due in the main to the increasingly serious agricultural crisis.

In a number of spheres a marked dualism was evident as to what was officially allowed, and a number of policies seemed to be in flux. For example, in September, hard-line critics were attacking Alexander Tvardovsky and Solzhenitsyn for their literary heterodoxy, while at the same time liberal writers who had been punished in a crackdown the previous March were beginning to publish again, though not yet reappearing widely. In political commentary, one could read both positive and negative analyses of the work of the prominent American specialist on the USSR, Marshall Shulman.[4] On the hard-line side, no new films from the West were shown, and plays in theaters were still dull. Directors of public lecture halls had to present official lectures on the ideology that the party's Central Committee prescribed for the arts. Conservative publications continued to be given excessive circulations and generous funds with which to pay authors. In general, though, to my surprise, officialdom appeared to impose no set fees for works by authors of left or right. In this way they facilitated editorial favoritism, but also free bidding for the best authors.

On the liberal side, the literary magazine *Novyi mir* (New world), now under the editor Alexander Tvardovsky, spread hope by announcing a more interesting array of writings to be published in 1964, including the Kiev writer Viktor Nekrasov's free-spirited *Putevye zametki* (Travel notes), about his tour to the United States in 1963.[5] Tvardovsky was also collecting biographical materials for a big survey of the life of Pope John XXIII. Dmitry Shestakov saw Tvardovsky as aiming at freedom of expression by taking a gradualist approach to loosening the reins, although what wider *type* of freedom was left unclear. To facilitate this—that is, to keep a foot on the brakes—the work of "formalists" such Albert Camus was not published, and the journal's outdated but familiar cover and page layout were left unchanged. The full editorial board almost never met, because Tvardovsky did not trust one of its members, Konstantin Fedin. Instead, decisions were made behind the scenes—often in the evening over glasses of vodka—by various individuals from a small number of like-minded people, namely, Tvardovsky, Vladimir Lakshin, head of the criticism department, A. G. Dementiev, head of long-term planning, and Boris Zaks, A. M. Maryamov, and Valentin Ovechkin. The atmosphere was not very "European," partly because few of these individuals spoke a foreign language.

Tvardovksy had a special relationship with Khrushchev that evidently stemmed from the latter's being attracted to his personality, but despite his skill at bureaucratic maneuvering, Tvardovsky was not regarded as exploiting his opportunities to the full in the service of Russian and Soviet literature. Part of the problem was his heavy drinking, but this was just one of the factors that prevented the emergence of a powerful combination of famous older writers that would have made a stronger impact on Khrushchev and possibly increased liberal support for him. Other factors lay with the writers themselves: Konstantin Fedin was easily manipulable; Kornei Chukovsky was too satisfied with his own popularity; Konstantin Paustovsky only emerged from Tarusa occasionally, and then to be aggressive about some personal matter; and Mikhail Sholokhov was simply irresponsible.

In order to retain or regain liberal support in the wider political context, Khrushchev, after watching a screening of the film made from *Sekretar' obkoma* (the regional party committee secretary), written by the conservative leader and Stalinist hard-liner Vsevolod Kochetov mentioned earlier, banned it outright.[6] He accused Kochetov of trying to provoke a quarrel between him and "the creative intelligentsia."

In the economic sphere, policy included an attempt to "buy off" Muscovites with such window dressing as creating some gaily decorated cafés, putting more up-to-date clothes in the stores, and minimizing price increases. Unfortunately, these measures led to super-long queues outside the stores, even though many people simply could not afford such clothes and cafés.[7] Meanwhile, continuing shortages of retail goods, especially agricultural products, were beginning to arouse "real indignation and feelings of shame," one friend reported.

Nevertheless, when it came to political action to achieve needed change, one skeptical and often angry friend believed it was still right to expect change to come from within the system and to work for it wholly within the system, as advocated by the relatively liberal writer Daniil Granin. She believed, as I noted later, that "many young people entering the Communist Party are *not* in fact irretrievably corrupted, and do not allow themselves to be morally destroyed." I could believe this about some people, but the question was, how many?

Among my young friends the general feeling about the most desirable speed of change and the durability of Khrushchev's own regime seemed to be relief that the negative trend begun in March 1963 had ended, combined with considerable caution about the present and guarded optimism about the future. The clock couldn't be turned back radically, they felt, and should continue to advance in a "three steps forward, two steps back" fashion. Although most young people didn't think much about politics, this seemed to be their overly optimistic attitude about evolution in general.

A definite step back was a new rule that the graduation certificates of new graduates would be mailed only to the location that the authorities had chosen for them to work for the first two years after graduation. For those completing their studies at Moscow institutions this could be a remote village thousands of miles away in eastern Siberia. This measure came at about the same time as the highly unpopular requirement that all citizens of working age must have an official work book in which to keep a full record of their employment history.

Neo-Leninist ideas about the centrality of political action persisted, but they were hardly held with much conviction. Most people turned away from politics to self-expression and absorption in their private lives: drinking, smoking, sex, dress, makeup, and the adulation of cosmonauts or film-stars. Some men were even fast learning how to make themselves look attractive.

As a result of these changes in the level of young people's commitment to maintaining the current system, a friend told me, the KGB was having difficulty recruiting enough trustworthy graduates, and another friend said that almost all the students in their graduating year in Moscow University's Literary Department were approached by a somewhat desperate KGB. He added that about two-thirds of the personnel who staffed the KGB's "special sections" (*spetschasti*) in university dormitories and departments were volunteers who regarded it as a form of "social work" for which they would before long be rewarded.

The ever-bolder political jokes that were told appeared to engender the attitude "If you allow us *this* level of freedom, we must give you the benefit of the doubt and support you 'within the system,' if only passively." Several times I heard Khrushchev's de-Stalinization described as "sincere," and the ambiguities of his March 8, 1963, speech were either unrecognized or forgiven. Cynical older friends told me that people who didn't live as adults under Stalin had no right to denounce or be indignant about that period; some even felt that virtually everything had already been said, and why did Tvardovsky rake it all up again? However, a few of them believed that a return to full Stalinism still could not be ruled out.

Of course, my generation in Russia often thought that while the passive support for Khrushchev might dwindle over time, in the short term nothing short of some major disaster could seriously jolt it. A determined clampdown on the intelligentsia would probably not be enough. It would have to be something like a war with China; the regime's resorting to terroristic methods of rule; a crude, chaos-causing power struggle in the Kremlin; a sharp decline in living standards; or a sudden collapse of the Eastern European empire. At present, only the threatening agricultural situation came near to this level. Khrushchev's common sense in buying food abroad and thus not risking massive discontent kept that danger in check and also earned him marks for "sincerity": he admitted the predicament in public. Also, he undoubtedly remembered that in June 1962 the lack of food in southern Russia had led to riots and the "Novocherkassk massacre" of several hundred protesters in a city near Rostov.

The View from the Street

Nevertheless, implicitly critical jokes about Khrushchev circulated. There was the one about his search for advice in the wake of the serious food situation and other setbacks. First he asks Lenin for advice. Lenin replies, "Sorry, 'fraid I can't help. I worked to liberate peoples, but you hold them in chains"—a reference to the national minorities and the peoples in the Eastern European satellite countries. Then he asks Stalin, who says, "Sorry, I raised you up from the depths of society, but now you've buried me deep"—a reference to Khrushchev's removing Stalin's corpse from Lenin's mausoleum and putting him in a deep grave. Then he asks Peter the Great. Peter replies, "Regret I can't help. I brought experts and goods into Russia to benefit the people, but you just take them out"—a reference to Soviet foreign aid.

Some jokes were more pointed:

What does Khrushchev's head look like?
Answer: The harvest of 1963.

What sort of a year was 1963?
Answer: Oh, pretty average. Worse than
last year's, better than next's.

At an exhibition of somewhat heterodox art in the Manege
Building, Khrushchev points to an object and asks,
"And what is that ass with two ears?"
Answer: "But Nikita Sergeyevich, that
isn't a painting. It's a mirror."

Other jokes punctured myths of Soviet greatness. One concerned an outline for an academic lecture about elephants:

Section 1. The classics of Marxism-Leninism about the elephant.
Section 2. The USSR as the homeland of the elephant.
Section 3. Soviet elephants are the happiest elephants in the world!

However, toleration of Khrushchev could not prevent strong grumbling in stores about the absence of flour and macaroni, the long lines for bread and potatoes, of which too many were going to animals, nor shouts in shops like "They live off pies, but for us there isn't even enough bread!"

The violence that lay just beneath the surface in Moscow reminded me of the atmosphere in the United States. As in New York, I was advised not to go into certain parts of the city after dark. A serious knifing attack occurred in the part of the university building where I lived. I also witnessed a disheartening, low-level spectacle in a university hallway: Two young women were sullenly hitting each other and taking no notice of the onlookers. They looked exhausted. Maybe the fight resulted from overwork and from curses having lost their effect. And in January a murderer called Ionesyan plunged Moscow into terror for a week. He gained access to apartments by posing as an official of Moscow Gas who had to come to read the meter, then stabbing his victim. Eventually, it was said, he was caught after killing six people; but rumors had the real figure as high as seventy. The most bizarre rumor regarding this man was that he had murdered Marshal Zhukov of World War II fame on the street, and Zhukov had been secretly buried a few days later, on January 6. Actually, the victim turned out to be someone else called Zhukov.

Another rumor that survived for two years was that Khrushchev had been injured in an assassination attempt in Minsk in 1961. A friend of a friend of mine had been there at the time, and was sure that it had happened. The shooter had been caught and found insane. Someone else said that it was not Khrushchev but another quite important figure who had been attacked and killed in Minsk.

More reliably, a friend who occasionally visited the Institute of Criminal Psychology told me that maniacal murderers were quite common; the last time he had gone to the institute they had been investigating a man who walked into a restaurant and machine-gunned eighteen people. Another person recounted to me something I had earlier read about in very general terms, namely, that after the first post-Stalin amnesty of prisoners in 1954, there had been a dramatic rise in violent crime. One example was a whole trainload of freed prisoners who had terrorized every station they stopped at, stealing and raping, until at last they were brought under control and returned to their prison camp.

This person also told me a story from the same period concerning Stalin's longtime secret police chief, Lavrenty Beria. It is well known that after Stalin died in 1953, his successors soon united to arrest and execute Beria and his close cronies, who posed a real threat to their lives. They also removed lesser cronies from their positions and gave them either long prison terms or severe warnings before putting them into jobs where they had no power to do harm. One of the figures in the last category was given a lectureship in the ideology of Marxism-Leninism, about which he knew very little, at one of Moscow's teachers colleges, and also became its party secretary there.

Everyday street violence could strike. A friend of mine, a frail woman of about seventy-five, was attacked in daylight while walking. Three youths with knives held her up with a knife against her neck while she searched through her pockets. Fortunately she found only five rubles for them to rob her of. The thugs departed with ugly threats against her if she should report them to authorities.

Cabbies seemed to be particularly close to violence, as victims and perpetrators. A cab driver told me that from May to November 1963, twenty-three cabdrivers and chauffeurs had been murdered in Moscow. One cabbie was the victim of a thief, but the other twenty-two seem to have been victims of attempts to cover up various large-scale frauds that threatened to unravel. Another theory was that the murderers were jealous husbands who were ensuring that their victims did not reveal that they had taken the murderers' dissatisfied wives out to the countryside for romantic interludes. Since that time many cabbies had not ventured at night into the most dangerous areas, primarily various suburbs such as the former Academic Lanes district, where a cabby was knifed, and the road to the nearby town of Dmitrov, to the north, where another one was killed.

My source knew of no other cabbies who had died from November through February, which another driver confirmed for me later. But this one told me how three drunk students had threatened one of his colleagues, who had managed to escape, only for the students to seize the cab and drive it wildly until it plunged into the river, killing two of them.

A cabdriver of about forty confirmed the information about the murder of the twenty-three cabbies. He was certain that the rate of violent crime and rape was rising, and hauled from below his seat an iron bar that he said he kept on the passenger seat after dark. I had noticed that the police always went around in pairs, both on foot and on motorbikes.

A less drastic measure was an "earnings requirement" for cabbies, whereby they had to be able to prove that they had earned a minimum of sixty-four rubles in the previous month. One cabby I spoke with made about eighty rubles a month, though he could make more if he used his taxi to give some unofficial rides—a risky business since the recent introduction of so-called comrades' courts in the taxi bases. Comrades' courts were informally operating bodies made up in this case of taxi drivers, which had considerable powers. A driver told me that in his park over fifty cases a day were heard, and he much resented the whole scheme. It tightened controls excessively and wasted far too much of everyone's time.

In that connection he asked if I was carrying a tape recorder—he could possibly get into trouble if I recorded his comments about illegal traffic.

This cabbie volunteered that he had watched a TV presentation by the British prime minister, Alec Douglas-Home, and been much impressed. He had seemed "so cultured and intelligent."

A cabby of about forty-five confirmed the difficulty of fulfilling the earnings requirement; adding that on 64 rubles a month, with a family, he could never afford new clothes. Stalin had had the policy of lowering food prices, but Khrushchev kept on raising them, so things were getting worse. His wife made 40 rubles a month in a hotel, while he made about 90 driving. Another cabby's wife made 70 in a bottling factory, while he earned 140, "counting everything"—presumably some of the money was illegal. Many cabbies said they had previously earned more as long-distance truck drivers, but living in Moscow made it easier to get food for their families.

More than one cabdriver urged caution on me, saying that after letting a foreigner out he was sometimes stopped and asked by plainclothes KGB types where he'd picked the foreigner up and what they had talked about. He asked me to keep our conversation to myself. Another colleague described a bittersweet occasion when a passenger had "gone to collect the money" after a ride, but failed to reappear. Three days later the driver went to the factory where he had dropped him off, and asked for payment. The man apologized and promptly paid up. "At this point," the cabby said, "it would actually have felt awkward to bawl him out."

Most taxi drivers were noncommittal over whether life was improving much, though one said that Khrushchev's successor could certainly not be worse than him. Several of them agreed on the need for radical measures in agriculture. However, they held that Khrushchev's big idea of "chemicalization" through fertilizer use would bring only very slow results. This was due to peasant ignorance—specialized knowledge was needed—and the lack of suitable roads and storage facilities in the countryside. One reliable source recounted how he had recently driven around the Moscow region and seen huge piles of chemical fertilizer at every train station. These piles had stood there for months, partly because a considerable proportion of rural transport had been idle for lack of new vehicle tires, which simply could not be found, so the fertilizer could not be trucked to the farms. This was a serious problem for both truck and private car owners who lacked the right connections.

A realistically minded cabby complained bitterly about the ever-receding "radiant future" (*svetloe budushchee*) when people in other countries already had a "radiant present." He also spoke of the twenty-five-foot walls that hid the country houses of the elite along the Rublev Highway a little outside Moscow. Others mentioned these walls and also stressed the dangers of strolling along the sidewalks near the dachas on the Lenin Hills near my university building, because of the possibility of arrest for having dubious motives. He also called me "a smart guy" (*molodets*) for not accepting the Kremlin propaganda and for looking deeper for myself.

When Khrushchev turned seventy on April 15, 1964, the event elicited a torrent of phony praise from his colleagues, including the hope that he would live for "another seventy years." A level-headed cabby of forty commented, "Yes, he's already an old man," and went on to compare the four leaders he had lived under, the other three being Stalin, Malenkov, and Bulganin. "Of course the one who cared most for the people, not only in words but also in actions, was Malenkov." He had canceled the peasants' debts, giving them some hope, and had opposed Khrushchev's folly of trying to develop the barren, distant "virgin lands" in Kazakhstan.[8] Then came the widespread refrain: "Today almost all my money goes to food." However, he was quite philosophical about it, and thought that Khrushchev could well rule for quite a bit longer. Ordinary people died of physical labor or hunger, he said, but Khrushchev just "sat, rested, and ate." In any case, the next leader might be worse, not better.

One taxi driver related how he had started his career as a Seventh Day Adventist preacher in Hungary, and then in Czechoslovakia. Then he had become a Communist and had moved to the Soviet Union. Now he had given up on his religious calling, but was clearly still worrying about it.

It is tricky to generalize from the economic situation of cabdrivers to the situation of other members of the working class, because cabdrivers are not typical of the working class, even though most of them came from worker or peasant backgrounds. Generalizations about political attitudes are even trickier because cabbies tend to be individualists and therefore probably more inclined to critical thought. So, my guess at their overall views is extremely rough. Some 5 percent seemed to feel strongly enough about their anti-regime attitudes that, given half a chance, they would take some protest action. Some 75 percent were in varying degrees discontented and understood at least some of the reasons for the worst aspects of public life. About 15 percent were discontented, but hadn't started to wonder why. And some 5 percent were more or less content.

On interclass relations in 1963–1964, I sensed that just as the peasants hated the city people for their tyranny, so the workers tended to hate the intelligentsia for their privileges. It was also tragic to observe the alienation between students and the workers who were re-laying my huge building's floors. I never witnessed a greeting, let alone a conversation, between the two groups. I couldn't help thinking, "If only Russia had British-style pubs, this social gulf might be diminished, if only slightly." Instead, the Russian norm is to drink at home or in parks, where there is no meaningful social context—or closing time—to rein it in.

But my judgments were just that—based on my impressions and my specific points of contact with Russians. I had real contact only with well-educated people, and thus could only try to sense and intuit the moods of other sections of the population. I lived in the capital and visited only other big cities such as Leningrad, Kiev, and Tbilisi, places where at least a few improvements were occurring. I can't say whether similar or different improvements were occurring in smaller cities, towns, the countryside, and the huge parts of the country that were still effectively inaccessible to Westerners. I would have given a great deal to be allowed to get to know areas outside the cities.

Furthermore, one couldn't rely too much on what people said they believed; one had to bear in mind the awful emotional abyss that faced any expression of pessimism, especially on the part of those who had been kept from real contact with religion. "Internal emigration" or suicide were grim prospects. Some of these folks were decidedly curious about religion, but in my first two months I still had not met any young people who expressed religious belief openly. Later that would change.

For my Christmas 1963 letter home I collected a few more political observations, in particular regarding political controls. Khrushchev had recently forbidden the police to make payments to voluntary informers but he had also appealed to every citizen to be "a controller," which in Russian implies not just monitoring the behavior of others but also possibly reporting it to the authorities. Yet paranoid realities had not stopped the steady spread of the twist, which the authorities continued to forbid as being too erotic. Recently, rude *anekdoty* about Lenin had begun to circulate, almost all of them too lewd to print. And the university newspaper had complained that more than half of the physics students were simply skipping the compulsory course on political economy.

Finally, I pointed to the "danger of sabotaging our own efforts to end the Cold War by being overly optimistic about the tense and complex process of change in Russia. We can do a little to influence this change, but mostly we must wait patiently and hope for the best, while analyzing only with our reason."

Several times during my eight months in Russia the question arose of how critical foreigners should be in their writings about Soviet affairs. Some friends thought that recent articles by Richard Pipes and Patricia Blake were examples of Westerners going too far in their criticism. The point was not that their interpretations were unreasonable, but that they provided Soviet hard-line advisers like Leonid Il'ichev with evidence that the articles testified to the undesirable softness of the Soviet political line and current attitudes to the West. Moral support was of course welcomed by the liberal Russians mentioned in the articles, but perhaps it would be better expressed in private. I felt unsure about this, but over time I moved toward the camp of the Blakes and the Pipeses in my view that all things Soviet were fair game for analysts in the West.

When I showed my Christmas letter to Dmitry Shestakov and his wife, she protested that I had painted too dark a picture. Dmitry disagreed, and told me later in sexist fashion that his wife was even more pessimistic about the future than he was, but, being a woman, she could only rarely face up to reality and mostly needed to escape from it. He supported my general impression that a huge, dangerous gulf existed between the intelligentsia and the mass of poor people. A handful of liberal writers wrote about this, but they were far too few: Konstantin Paustovsky, Alexander Yashin, Vladimir Tendryakov, and Solzhenitsyn, one of whose plays had been in rehearsal at the Sovremennik Theater (Contemporary Theater), but had then been banned before opening night. Also, liberal writers were not persistent enough in creating waves. It was hard for them to resist the temptation of enjoying the perks they got as members of the Writers' Union, such as going for long stays to the writers' vacation houses in Peredelkino and Golitsyno, where they could live in hotel-like luxury. Peredelkino was a complex of dachas near Moscow owned by the Union of Soviet Writers and surrounded by woods, and many prominent writers lived there.

Richard Pipes's point about society's social groups struggling against each other in seeking the Kremlin's favor had relevance in understanding the standing of writers. The strategically placed intelligentsia, large swaths of it bureaucratized, had naturally done better in the fight for flats, vacation homes, and so on than the workers and peasants.

Equally distressing was the fact that some of the well-off reveled in their new comforts and fiercely defended and expanded them against incursions by the lower orders. They paid little attention to lobbying for the decollectivization of agriculture, which would have benefited most of the peasants and also might have helped Khrushchev, whose popularity had been declining quite sharply since summer 1963 because of the dreadful shortages of farm goods. Understandably, the peasants put the blame for the lack of fodder and the pressure not to slaughter their animals on the Kremlin.

In response, Khrushchev had clearly been trying to regain his popularity through, for example, gestures of détente toward the West and through the quite extraordinary wave of sympathy for the Americans in the media over President Kennedy's assassination on November 22. The reaction to the assassination reflected the real feelings of Russians. Even as a Briton, I received dozens of spontaneous, heartfelt expressions of condolence from friends and acquaintances.

However, opposition to Khrushchev within the party was noticeably growing by the turn of the year; in retrospect these signs of restiveness seemed like harbingers of his overthrow in October 1964. His Politburo colleagues forced him to make severe budget cuts in his long-standing programs for new housing and the widespread use of fertilizer in agriculture, and his defense of the collective farm system and of limiting military expenditures took on a tentative, uncertain tone. In early March came reliable secondhand reports that discussions regarding the decollectivization of agriculture were taking place at the highest levels, but they came to nothing. Khrushchev tried to regain ground through media interviews, meetings with foreign statesmen, and plans for a big foreign tour, and by keeping his Politburo rivals in the shadows.[9]

One of his weaknesses was that in his public image he fell between the stools of a distant, all-powerful, semi-divine figure such as Stalin and a genuine man-of-the-people leader such as President Lennart Meri in post-Soviet Estonia. He tried to be more like a Meri figure, but wasn't convincing: he continued to lecture the peasants, even when he was in a field, and he was still driven around in a huge, dark, curtained car and guarded by a phalanx of security men. So he lacked the dignity needed in a true leader, and I never met anyone who regarded him as such.

Another problem that undermined Khrushchev was that few officials in the higher echelons of the upper class saw the need for serious economic reform, so they didn't give him enough help and guidance in this difficult field, and he made many mistakes. But it had to be economic reform, because it was too risky to give the people a measure of political freedom. And no amount of political freedom would have produced for them the Communist world promised by Marx and Lenin, or even a united world Communist movement. So raising living standards fast was the only realistic goal. However, while rapidly building scores of residential blocks with one-family apartments fulfilled the yearning for privacy, it often aroused frustration over the quality of the product. A new joke made the rounds about a man who stepped into a brand-new apartment and tapped his neighbor's wall to ask, "Can you hear me?" "Good Lord, man," came the reply, "I can *see* you!"

What could happen with the help of some political freedom was shown in a town in the Ural mountains soon after Khrushchev delivered his second de-Stalinization speech, in 1961: A group of enlightened people, mostly teachers, got themselves elected to the town's key party and state positions and governed humanely for about a year. Then they were removed in one fell swoop by the town's conservative bureaucrats. On a more modest scale, I was told that the boards of clubs and libraries had sometimes organized a boycott of hard-line lecturers and poets. Only occasionally were liberals targeted, because few young people favored the extreme political right.

In general, the main obstacle to effecting genuine economic reform was the fact that most members of the upper class never imitated their leader by going into the collective farms, the villages, the towns, or the slums, to see them for themselves, and therefore never understood the depth and urgency of the problems to be solved if the goal of economic reform were ever to be achieved. Instead, they lived in the cocoons of their comfortable homes, segregated from the people and enjoying a multitude of privileges carefully graded according to each person's rank.

So although Khrushchev insisted almost fanatically in party speeches that rapid economic reform was absolutely essential, his impractical, even sometimes bizarre ideas for how to do this were not the joint product of discussion by well-informed Politburo members that would have improved the ideas. This was true even of the reform proposals of the economist Yevgeny Liberman, which Khrushchev had backed. But Khrushchev received little practical help, even though the Politburo should have taken fright at the emergence of more worker strikes at a Leningrad electrical factory in early 1963—which should have reminded them of the Novocherkassk massacre in June 1962—and a near-general strike for a whole week in Tula, south of Moscow, caused by major shortages of food, especially bread. (In Tula workers hung a loaf of bread over a factory gate to make their point. When the situation improved after a week, the workers returned, but things soon deteriorated again. Neither in Leningrad nor in Tula were any reprisals reportedly taken against individuals or groups.)

One friend believed that if the strikes ever became too numerous, they would be met by a Kremlin swing to aggressive nationalism. A taxi driver held that if Khrushchev's grip began to slip, he would simply gather a group of well-paid security officers around him, become increasingly ruthless, and stay in power until he died. At that point, many believed, a new power struggle would be inevitable.

Equally worrying in early 1964 was the spread of underground sedition (*kramola*) among young people. In February, Sergei Pavlov, the head of the Komsomol, reportedly gave a closed-door speech recounting that *kramola* had taken on organized forms in Saratov, Kiev, Odessa, Minsk, and Kuibyshev, and in Kuibyshev a secretive "people's socialist party" was operating. He added that Leningrad currently posed more problems than Moscow; that Vilnius contained some "bad" trends, having been linked to the literary samizdat journal edited by Alexander Ginzburg, *Sintaksis* (Syntax); and that an Odessa artist had entered a self-portrait in an exhibition that had turned out to have some obscene words at the bottom in very small letters. Pavlov declared that he would like to shoot the man.

However, Pavlov's take on Moscow soon proved overly optimistic. Shortly after he spoke, Ginzburg was back in Moscow after being imprisoned for editing *Sintaksis* and was now deeply involved in dissident activities so that he could collect documents that would allow him to create what would become a famous book about the imprisoned writers Andrei Sinyavsky and Yuli Daniel. Also, a large group of students at Moscow's Institute of International Relations—closely tied to the Foreign Ministry—were arrested. Sinyavsky and Daniel were expected to get ten years for allegedly planning terrorist acts against high-level members of the government. Komsomol leaders apparently felt that something drastic was necessary to check the rot at an institution famed for its low intellectual caliber and its members' cynicism.

In March, three students were expelled from Moscow University's Biology Department for distributing pamphlets headed "Let's Return to

Leninism!" One of the three was sent for trial, another was expelled permanently, and the third was expelled temporarily.

A visit that we English-speaking foreign graduate students paid to a district court provided one insight: A judge and a deputy prosecutor gave us their opinion that prison was getting too soft. Clearly, they said, some defendants wanted to land in prison so that they could get good free medical care and food.

Public opinion on the death penalty was quite severe—seemingly for it. I found no intellectuals who favored abolishing it, a fact aligned with cruel attitudes among almost everyone to animals and old people. One person said that the elderly "damn well should die at sixty, when they retire, and not go on living as parasites on the labor of others."

Hostile worker attitudes included an outburst overheard by a friend: "When the hell do Khrushchev and Castro do any *work*, what with all their hunting and receptions twice a day?" (In January Castro had made some remarkably critical remarks about Khrushchev on Soviet TV.) One day I listened in a bus, as a drunk shouted, "Khrushchev and the Central Committee live in luxury, while for us everything is as before. They're fascists, fascists, fascists!"

A student friend who was notably loyal to the Kremlin surprised me by recalling that whereas before the war his family of five had been able to live modestly but manageably on the income of his factory-worker father, now it was unthinkable that such a family could survive unless the wife worked too. He also told me about the extraordinary level of thievery he had observed during the war and after, and of the subsequent careers, mostly in prison, of his playmates.

The workers were also angered by Khrushchev's misuse of the media to cover up his bad behavior. For example, the previous year the foul smell in a synthetics plant in Klin that he visited had put him in a bad mood—but the party-controlled press had published a report that he had stopped and had friendly chats with workers in several different workshops.

The hard-liners saw Khrushchev's whole philosophy of attacking Stalin, pleasing the people, and putting the main emphasis on material goods as extremely dangerous to the future of party rule.

THE AGRICULTURAL CRISIS

Agricultural policy was central to Khrushchev, and to his detractors. The core issue was how to feed the country efficiently. Ideology may have preoccupied party members and some intellectuals, but the citizens were more concerned with the availability and price of food; the system for getting food into the shops was of interest to the extent that it worked, or didn't work. Meanwhile, the Kremlin needed extra cash to invest in agriculture. Certainly, some individuals were doing better than others: within three days one cabdriver told me he earned 70 rubles a month and life was getting harder, while another earned 120 and things were steadily improving! Certainly rather more goods were now available for people with money. However, the average Russian was still spending more than half his income on food, because hefty increases in prices for meat and butter that had been decreed in 1963 were still in force.

For about two-thirds of the population monthly incomes ranged from 30 to 100 rubles (1 ruble = 100 kopeks). In late 1963 and early 1964 lemons cost 35 kopeks each; oranges, 70 kopeks per pound; staples were rationed: bakeries would sell to one person no more than 4 pounds of bread, a pound of other flour products (if available—still in very short supply), and a pound of sugar. For the poorest Russian wage earners, those living on 30 rubles a month or less, a pound of butter cost 2 rubles, a quarter of a week's wages. A day's wages, 1 ruble, bought 2 pounds of apples or mandarins, 2.5 pounds of sugar, 8 pounds of white bread or potatoes, or a quarter pound of tea. Cheaper items included black or rye bread and cigarettes.

In February 1964, the British postgraduates toured the northwest USSR and found that the situation in Estonia was marginally better, with the ration for flour products at two pounds, not one. But no white bread was available in Estonia, Novgorod, or Pskov, except in some hospitals.

In March 1964, the queues for basic food products, including potatoes, became even longer. In the days before the widely celebrated Women's Day, March 8, there was a desperate shortage of cakes and pastries to celebrate the day. Also, Moscow University started having regular days when no meat of any kind was served out of solidarity, because it was not available to ordinary citizens.

Despite the marginally better situation in Estonia, in more out-of-the-way places things were little better. A South American friend living on the best collective farm in Moldavia in the southwest USSR in August

1963 told me of the long daily queues for black bread. He was "appalled" by the terrible diet and the awful housing conditions. Other friends reported similar situations in the Checheno-Ingush Autonomous Republic, in the North Caucasus, and in Mozhaisk, west of Moscow—but here at least there was milk. A cabby recounted having worked in the so-called "Virgin Lands" area in Kazakhstan in 1962. He gave a vivid description of whole districts becoming uninhabitable through administrative chaos and material shortages in equipment, roads, and food. Another cabby had worked until recently in a rural area where the food situation had become slightly better than in Moscow.

The food supply had been worsened when a number of peasants had been forced to abandon their animals and private plots of land. By March 1964, about 90 percent of taxi drivers had become talkative and unanimous in their feeling that a sharp increase in real incentives for the peasants had become an urgent necessity. About half of them realized that this would require a radical reform of the whole agricultural system. As one of them said, "Everyone realizes that the collective farm system has failed." But, he added indulgently, "It's politically difficult for Khrushchev to get rid of it."

In light of so much protest, discussion, and downright hardship, I wished to understand the profound underlying causes of the USSR's agricultural crisis. I was fortunate to get to know an outspoken retired agricultural economist then in his sixties, Ivanov, who was willing to share his opinions and experience with me. In the 1930s he had been exiled for three years for protesting against the violent collectivization of all the country's peasants. He felt that now, thirty years later, the peasants had been "alienated" from their profession for so long that they had lost their previously ingrown flair and knowledge.[10] This meant that even the most thoughtful reform program, such as that put forward by the writer Fyodor Abramov, would take a very long time to bring substantial results—all the more painful to Ivanov, because Russia enjoyed "staggering natural wealth," much of it residing in its land.

He was particularly disgusted by all the servile, wishful-thinking hot air about the promise of Khrushchev's "chemicalization" program that was currently being blown—for example, at a conference he was attending on the subject at the Academy of Agricultural Sciences of the Soviet Union. Khrushchev had conducted large-scale experiments with chemical fertilizers in 1937, and criticism had been showered down on him when, as Ivanov had predicted, the slightly increased yields nowhere near covered the increased running costs, not to mention the capital investment. As a result, many of the collective farms in the project had gone bankrupt, and, as noted, railways to the farms.

As a side story, he also told me about a Communist he had known, who had protested in 1939 that Stalin was naïve at best not to see that the "Ribbentrop–Molotov pact" was a clear ploy by Hitler. The untrustworthy Hitler would defeat the West, then turn against the Soviet Union. For expressing this view, the man had been arrested and locked up indefinitely in a prison psychiatric hospital as a madman. A few years later he committed suicide.

An Old Bolshevik friend of a friend, N. K. Ivanov, a journalist, had views similar to those of the economist Ivanov (they weren't related). This Ivanov occupied a senior position on *Izvestia*, the Soviet Union's daily newspaper of record, until a series of heart attacks led to his being given lighter work on the party's theoretical journal, *Kommunist*. By 1964 he was deeply disillusioned by both the moral decline of Communism and by the failure of the economy, as compared to its early successes. He bitterly reproached his own generation for having brought about a situation in which no one could hope to significantly change things. Earlier, the old generation either believed the party was right in all things or made itself believe this out of honorable motives. Now, the young generation, including those on the staff of *Kommunist*, understood the reality but had no faith, felt impotent, and were forced to compromise themselves. His only hope lay in the fact that the reality was now understood, and would be a basis for improvement in the future.

Obviously, the agricultural crisis had a huge effect on health. The Russians were only saved from serious malnutrition by free medical care (though not free medicines) and very low rents—and often, petty thievery. The extremely high rate of illness among Soviet students caught the attention of their British colleagues, who were lucky enough to have access to the well-supplied food shop in the U.K. embassy. No serious statistics were ever published on prices, shortages, or income distribution, or the effects of the agricultural and distribution crisis on Soviet citizens' basic health.

The shortages produced a sharp change in my approach to shopping. I had to shop for food because I greatly disliked the university's restaurant, cafeteria, and single shop. I would look at every stall or shop window I passed, and if there was no queue or only a short one, I at once bought everything offered that might conceivably satisfy my current or future needs.

Planned shopping was out. (In March, I heard that the university shop had shut down for eight days when a major embezzlement scheme came to light. No sooner had it reopened than a pipe burst and flooded it, causing a new closure.)

Some people saved money to spend on food by successfully avoiding paying for other things, such as trains, Moscow Metro trains (the rapid transit system), and theaters. They quietly jumped over barriers or slipped past carefully distracted ticket collectors. An official told me that Komsomol dances were organized on the assumption that 20 percent more people would attend than the number of tickets printed.

HOUSING TO THE RESCUE

The housing situation in Moscow had serious and deeply rooted problems, but at least a measure of upgrading was on the way. A typical cabdriver with a total family income of 99 rubles per month told me he lived in a communal apartment—one he shared with another family—in which he had 18 square yards of space for his wife, himself, and two children. The rent was free, but he had to contribute 10 rubles a month in service charges. Families living in such conditions needed to be rehoused, and real progress was being made. A steady stream of people were leaving their strife-torn communal apartments for new self-contained ones that provided 9 square yards of living space per person. In 1963, 115,000 new apartments went up in a city of over 10 million inhabitants, giving the lucky occupants some gratifying security and privacy, and a defense against "the hell of other people." But it would take twenty years for Moscow to meet the target of 9 square yards per person. For the lucky the biggest cause of grumbling was the deplorable quality of the hasty construction and the poorly installed fittings.

KATYA'S TALES

The stories told me by a new Moscow friend, Katya, shed interesting light on political developments in the Soviet Union under Stalin and Khrushchev and the ways they affected one family. Katya, thirty-six in 1963, hailed from a family of provincial intellectuals with a Bolshevik background ("Old Bolsheviks"), and admitted to being politically rather naïve. She worked as an experienced secretary in the university, earning seventy rubles a month. Her parents had both joined the party in the 1920s, but she had refused to do so because the party secretary in her division was particularly unpleasant. Her father, who had died in the war, had worked with one of the party's national leaders, Sergo Ordzhonikidze, whom he greatly liked. Her mother had been, like him, a construction engineer.

During Stalin's anti-Jewish campaign of 1948–1949, Katya had known an ethnically Russian man who had started denouncing his ethnically Jewish, though Russianized, wife. However, when the campaign ended he promptly desisted, and they lived happily together again!

In 1957 Katya's mother spoke up in disgust at a party meeting called by Khrushchev to denounce the so-called Anti-Party Group, led, Khrushchev maintained, by Georgy Malenkov, Vyacheslav Molotov, Lazar Kaganovich, and Dmitri Shepilov. This group had initially enjoyed majority support in the Politburo after Stalin's death, but had ultimately lost out to Khrushchev's maneuvering in a struggle for power. Khrushchev had then dispatched the group's leaders to minor jobs in far corners of the country. She remained disgusted by this for the rest of her life. Her bravery was due to her "Old Bolshevik" idealism and integrity, and particularly to her having known Lazar Kaganovich (1893–1991) personally while working on the construction of the building that I lived in in the early fifties, the Main Building of Moscow University (inaugurated in 1953) in the Lenin Hills. Alone among the leaders, he took an interest in it, visited it frequently and—this was rare—unofficially, and talked to people in an unassuming way, thus becoming much appreciated. My friend's father, who worked on railway development, also heard much praise of Kaganovich for his personal conduct. Katya added that much of the labor force for building the university building had been prisoners, and the number of fatal accidents was horrific. Others worked on the condition that they would be admitted as students when it was finished.

Katya shared some of her mother's political attitudes, including her indignation at the 1957 power struggle in the Kremlin and the unpleasant fate of the losers. Her mother had a high regard for the kindness and cleverness of Dmitri Shepilov, whom she met several times; for Vyacheslav Molotov as being learned and good at languages; and for Stalin's disfavored son, Vasili, who had a long and sensitive chat with her and gave her a drink when she visited him to ask for his intervention over some injustice.

Boris Pasternak's architect brother, Alexander Pasternak, with whom I became good friends, also had positive memories from his collaboration on two projects directed by Kaganovich, the design of Lenin's and Stalin's Mausoleum (for his work on this Alexander was rewarded with a trip to Germany) and also in meetings about construction of the Volga–Don Canal. Kaganovich's conduct had been "polite and efficient," in contrast to that of Genrikh Yagoda, the future head of Stalin's secret police, with whom Alexander also had to deal on occasion. Yagoda's eerie, frightening manner was that of a sadist. He always made his interlocutors feel the power he wielded over them, which he might use at any time—as he indeed did against a million or so of his fellow citizens.

Katya was a friend of the composer Mitya Tolstoy's wife. Mitya told Katya how he had been invited to write the music for the still-suppressed film of the novel *Sekretar' obkoma* (The regional party committee secretary), by the hard-liner Vsevolod Kochetov (whom I wrote about in my master's thesis), and didn't think it wise to refuse. Despite her dissatisfaction with living standards and especially travel restrictions, Katya gave good marks to Khrushchev for denouncing local "tyrants," people who could break rules and get perks for themselves. She had recently been in the Bryansk area 250 miles southwest of Moscow, where the food situation was truly alarming: bread was made of powdered peas and corn, and there were no milk products because all the cattle had been slaughtered for food. Yet the "local tyrants" had come to hunt and fish, and the ponds had been filled with specially imported fish for them to catch. Her comment: "They're the sort of people who ought to be shot."

Katya was also bewildered and indignant when endless investigative Party commissions came to her after the March 1963 crackdown, which she had attended by chance, to listen to the tapes of a fiery university debate on artistic freedom that had taken place in the wake of Khrushchev's famous blow-up against liberal artists in the Manege Building in central Moscow three months earlier. Their aim was obviously to identify and then persecute the most outspoken contributors, actions she considered wholly unreasonable.

In addition, Katya told me about the truly terrible relations that had developed between drivers and the Moscow police. The latter had clearly been instructed to take drivers' documents on some excuse and then deliver sadistically long upbraiding rants, before imposing fines or compulsory attendance at lectures. Soon after Katya told me of these episodes the authorities introduced a new system. Now the police referred many alleged offenses to the so-called Comrades' Courts in Moscow's dozen or so taxi parks.

In 1963–1964, while Khrushchev's star appeared to be fading, only gradually did Leonid Brezhnev emerge as a possible replacement. At first people knew little about him, except that he looked more friendly and relaxed than the leader. But as he rose politically after Khrushchev's ouster in 1964, Soviet citizens started to think he was no better than a *podkhalim*, an "insincere ass licker."

FOUR

Expulsion

Cultural Trends, Literary Friends, and the Sharp Edges of the Soviet State

Cultural trends in 1963–1964 followed political trends closely, with the level of freedom permitted expanding and contracting as the balance of forces in the Kremlin bounced around, depending mainly on how much Khrushchev succeeded or failed to strengthen his position. When he gained in strength, cultural policy tended to ease somewhat; when he was under attack, the reins were tightened. Gradually, however, as 1964 progressed, the graph was trending downward as some of his supporters saw him aging and also failing to set a clear political and economic path that would attract fresh support.

Intelligent Russians who befriended me or agreed to share their perceptions with me provided some of the best insights into what was really going on with their deep experience, their educated observations, and, well, their gossip.

THE PASTERNAKS

My friend Martin Dewhirst introduced me to some unusually interesting individuals, especially the family of Boris Pasternak, the celebrated author of *Doctor Zhivago*, his younger brother, Alexander, a prominent architect, and his son, Zhenia, by his first wife, Yevgeniya. Zhenia had fought in World War II and then trained to teach mechanical engineering.

I spent a lot of time with the relaxed, outgoing, hospitable Alexander. At his Moscow apartment I met his son and family, all of them charming and realistic about the current scene.

After his retirement in the 1950s, Alexander had turned his attention to working with Zhenia on the literary legacy of his famous brother, and also to writing his own memoirs.[1] He told me about a new book of Boris's collected poems that had been commissioned from on high to show that the USSR could do a better job of publishing Pasternak's works than Gleb Struve and Boris Filippov, who had published a three-volume collected works in the United States of early poems, prose works, late poems, articles, and transcriptions of talks.[2] The new book of poetry—thoroughly edited by Zhenia, Elena, and two young disciples of Boris—was a complete collected works, unlike the poetry in the Struve and Filippov volumes. A contract had been signed, Andrei Sinyavsky had written the introduction, the whole manuscript had been handed over to the publishing house in January 1963, and publication appeared to be imminent. Unfortunately, though, most of the extensive editors' notes had been vetoed by the party, and before long the book appeared to have been shelved indefinitely. The main cause may have been the reactionary surge set off by Il'ichev's and Khrushchev's March 1963 speeches.

In 1975 Zhenia was ousted from his job at the Moscow Energy Institute for his heterodox political views. Now he turned to intensive work as a literary historian and critic, editing the writings of his father and composing a memoir about him that appeared in 1997. In 2005 he and his engaging wife, Elena, published the massive eleven-volume complete collection of his father's works, which they had edited together.

In about 1963 Zhenia had just concluded that the fragments of a play that Boris had left unfinished probably could be rescued and completed by himself as a work of two or three hours' length. By April he had fashioned the fragments into a series of self-contained scenes, which a senior manager of theatrical programs thought could be viable theatrically, of course subject to the difficult issue of political clearance. Zhenia also had good reason to believe that additional material that had been confiscated from Boris by the KGB and was now in a supposedly public archive would not be released to him. He also noted that Olga Andreyev Carlisle had been wrong when she asserted in one of her books that Boris had planned a trilogy of plays. This was not the case.

Alexander thought that the regimentation of thought had been the worst single aspect of the last forty years in the USSR. He also believed that Khrushchev would stay in power until he died, partly because there was no one else powerful enough to replace him. He told me that for the present there was no prospect of *Doctor Zhivago*'s being published in the Soviet Union, nor of its author being posthumously reinstated in the Writers' Union, from which he had been expelled in 1958. Instead Alexander was directing his energy to collecting all the articles and books of literary criticism that had been written about Boris's work, and translating into Russian those written in foreign languages. He planned to place the finished collection in the archive at Boris's house in Peredelkino, near Moscow, where his widow, Zinaida, still lived.

Sadly, Zinaida was living in impoverished circumstances. She had no pension and no income, her savings were exhausted, and the new collection of Boris's poems would only bring her enough for six to twelve months when it was eventually published. Heirs only received half of what a living author would receive. Another hope was the current appeal to the Italian publisher Giangiacomo Feltrinelli, the first publisher of *Doctor Zhivago*, to send some of the Pasternak royalties he was holding to Zinaida. I later heard that this appeal had been successful, although the money would last for less than a year. Zinaida was a difficult person to help, bitter about the past as well as about falling on hard times in the present. I sensed all this when I paid her a brief visit in Peredelkino.

Abram and Stella Adelson were close friends of Alexander and his wife and had previously lived with them. They seemed to be well connected to the Communist higher-ups. Stella had worked for some time at quite a high level in the establishment, where she had met the ideologically oriented biologist Trofim Lysenko, whom Stalin made head of the Academy of Agricultural Science. Lysenko's fanaticism showed in his philo-Semitism when, in 1949, he refused to fire any Jews, despite Stalin's sweeping campaign against Jews and especially Jewish scientists. Today, Stella said, he was still, as before, living personally in filthy surroundings like a pig. Stella was also haunted by an especially close associate of Stalin, Lazar Kaganovich, whom Khrushchev had removed in an insulting way in 1957, but her recollections of him were less fond than Katya's and her mother's. He lived near the Adelsons. His wife had just died, and every time he passed them on the sidewalk he would leer at Stella. She also had vivid memories of Stalin's colleague, the international Communist leader Karl Radek (1885–1939). He had loved the sound of his own voice and delivered long monologues in front of his secretaries by way of "conversation." Later he succumbed to Stalin's Great Purge and was killed in a prison camp.

THE SOVIET STAGE

In the context of Soviet culture, the ideas and images that could be openly expressed had to adhere to the Kremlin's ideology of Marxism-Leninism. One facet of this ideology was that it was militantly antireligious, and this had to be furthered in theatrical productions. The setting of Vladimir Tendryakov's *Bez kresta!* (Without a cross!),[3] staged at Moscow's most impressive theater, the Sovremennik, was a village in which more than half the inhabitants believed in God, and by no means all of these characters were unattractive. In the play's gripping and tragic struggle between the proponents and opponents of religion, the author evoked fear and pity regarding individuals on both sides. The audience was spellbound. This shocked the authorities, who had the play taken off after only three performances. When it reappeared some weeks later, it had been stripped of its sharp edge and the audience had shrunk.

Later, in January, an adaptation of the 1920 vaudeville comedy *Lev Gurych Sinichkin* provided sharp political satire of the Communist state with Jewish overtones. The eponymous main character impersonates a party official who is inspecting the work of actors, urging them on to "genuinely *Soviet* acting" and proclaiming that "*our* dead person thrusts himself vigorously forward into life!" He asks, and then answers: "Why should Soviet people be constantly worried about their lives? The future is so clear, they should be calm." Some accordionists rehearse a satirical act before a party official who complains how tough life is "when you're given artistic matters to direct." And so on. In similar vein in a different theater, I felt empathy for many of the viewers on reading the prominent placard with the statement "A car is not a luxury, but a means of transportation" (*avtomobil—ne roskosh', a sposob peredvizheniya*).

Utrennie poezda (Morning trains) was a film with a convincing negative hero, no "party-mindedness" (*partiinost'*), and a realistic idea of a pretty girl falling for a playboy rather than a noble youth and she soon realizing her mistake and parting from him, but with no happy ending. But it was also a propaganda film, containing shots of workers frequenting deluxe stores and restaurants. This appeared intended to show ordinary people what they should expect out of life if they could extract a fair deal from the party. I wondered: where *are* these shops and restaurants? Perhaps the characters in the film wondered the same thing.

I had the good fortune to see two of the leading Russian comic actors at the height of their formidable powers. Georgy Menglet had a rubbery face that he could twist into a hundred shapes, and Igor Il'insky had the versatility to play every kind of rogue and buffoon with absolute conviction. Both of these comic geniuses gave me laugh cramps.

A notable figure in the Leningrad theater scene was the director Georgy Tovstonogov. I learned from my friend the literary scholar Misha Meilakh that he had a positive but slightly mixed reputation. He had recently put on at the Gorky Theater an innovative version of Alexander Griboyedov's famous classic of the 1820s, *Gorye ot Uma* (Woe from wit), whose theme is the satirizing of officials' stupidity and tendency to corruption. Tovstonogov encouraged the leading actors to imply subversively that the action might equally be playing out in the present. He also had printed on the stage curtains a provocative quotation from Pushkin that caused the authorities to have it taken down in favor of one from Khrushchev. But this was not good enough to satisfy the cultural police, and ultimately the curtain was blank. Tovstonogov also made a bold, unreported speech promising that he would never produce a play by either of the notoriously conservative writers Anatoly Sofronov or Alexander Korneichuk, a vow echoed by his equally famous colleague Mikhail Romm. On the other hand, he was quite widely despised for his blatant so-called "plagiarism" of the production methods of two famous directors of the past, Vsevolod Meierhold and Yuri Zavadsky.

One of Tovstunogov's protégés was the brilliant, popular actor Innokenty Smoktunovsky. Discovered by Tovstonogov in 1958, he had acted in his stage productions for two years and then switched his attention to films. He was currently playing Hamlet in a movie under production.

A great boost for the liberal intelligentsia, and for the play-going public, came in early April, when a talented group of British actors performed Shakespeare plays in Moscow and Leningrad. This was a huge success. A minor riot occurred at Moscow University's crammed theater when a mass of students had to be locked out. Doors were smashed and people were half crushed in the frenzy to get in. The British embassy also held a triumphal reception for the visitors, and a huge number of Russians were allowed to attend. Apart from numerous theater people, many liberals from the literary and other fields came en masse. One of them was the poet Bella Akhmadulina, who was self-confident as she chatted with me and invited me to call on her when she returned to Moscow.

Earlier she had appeared with the witty and popular poet and parodist Yuri Levitansky, who included a new parody of Yevtushenko for the occasion. Her own contribution was a poem about Pasternak, a longer one called "Dozhd'" (Rain), and extracts from a poem in the magazine *Yunost'* (Youth), all of them allegories whose real subject was the previous year's rows with officialdom.[4]

Vladimir Dudintsev, the writer whose anti-bureaucratic novel, *Ne khlebom edinym* (1956; *Not by Bread Alone*, 1957) had helped to launch Khrushchev's thaw in the mid-1950s and was widely published in translation in the West, spoke with a couple of my British friends and created the rather bitter impression of a not very attractive personality. He hinted that he had recently published some inferior old short stories for purely financial reasons.

In Leningrad, the Shakespeare group received an even more fabulous reception from the public, and I heard that one party went on until 3:00 a.m. in a spirit of close and uninhibited friendship.

THE OPINIONATED AND VOLUBLE RITA RAIT-KOVALEVA, TRANSLATOR

Through my friend Martin I met a prolific writer and translator, Rita Rait-Kovaleva, who was in her late fifties and lived alone. Rita was well connected to many parts of the Soviet literary scene, had views on all aspects of it, and didn't hesitate to let me know them. She had translated into Russian some stories by Kafka, which she was trying to get into print. One of them soon appeared in the journal *Inostrannaya Literatura* (Foreign literature), and she hoped to have *The Trial* published as a book; failing that she would try to get it into a literary journal.

Recently she had spent two weeks on vacation in Britain and had loved feeling herself a citizen of the world. She admitted to great political naïveté, but, although hating many things like the travel restrictions—why could her daughter not do an exchange with a British girl, and why could she herself not go and stay with William Golding?—she believed that all was slowly improving, if in fits and starts. In April it seemed she might yet get to Britain and see Golding, because she had now obtained two favorable reviews of his first novel, *Lord of the Flies* (1954) by respected writers, and these would help her get a contract to translate it. The reviews might overcome officials' obsession about the book's "pessimism."

The cultural ups and downs were, Rita felt, just temporary "family quarrels" to which foreigners gave too much significance and often ended up complicating when they wrote about them. This slowed progress and handicapped any liberals who were quoted. She much disliked Patricia Blake's article "New Voices in Russian Writing," not because of any factual inaccuracies, although she found the emphasis on Jewish writers exaggerated, but because of her deep emotional antipathy to washing dirty linen in public, especially when done by a foreigner.[5] She seemed to think that the vast majority of intellectuals were as open-minded as she (probably the middle generation was much less so), and the ultraconservative Kochetovs, Serovs, and Gribachevs would gradually be edged out. In this way, everything in the garden would become more lovely without anything much in the way of dirty linen being washed in public.

Rita was most distressed to hear that the long poem "Requiem" by the doyenne of Russian literature, the world-famous Anna Akhmatova, had appeared in the West, because its author had badly wanted it to be published at home first, and had taken pains to prevent its falling into unreliable hands.[6] She and Tvardovsky, the editor of *Novyi mir*, had been waiting for the right moment to get it into that journal. It was a real consolation to hear also that Akhmatova had been officially nominated for the Nobel Prize in Literature, because this might make publication at home easier. Rita noted at the same time that Tvardovsky still held a score of unpublished poems by Marina Tsvetayeva that had been rejected point-blank by the censors, despite some careful advance groundwork.

Although often pressing for forward progress in literature, Rita favored caution in all things. She typified the successful side of the official policy of "buying off" the intelligentsia: give them good pay, a decent apartment, perhaps a car, access to a free and comfortable vacation with a good restaurant for a few weeks twice a year, occasional foreign travel, also to non-Communist countries, higher fees than other writers for their books and articles, and gradually ease their publishing conditions. All except the most radical were fairly content with this, no matter how divergent their views on aesthetics might be. Another method of pacification was private screenings of foreign films that were kept from ordinary people, such as *Tom Jones* and Fellini's *8-1/2*.

Another of Rita's activities was encouraging young writers of real talent, who had great difficulty getting published. One of these young writers was the friendly and open Natalya Tarasenkova, some of whose short stories I read and one of which—"Poputchiki" (The companions) from her collection *Kak eto vse skazat'?* (*How to Say All of This?*, 1968)—I translated for a collection of Soviet short stories.[7]

Rita had interesting things to say about the poet Vladimir Mayakovsky, who became a fiery Communist poet and playwright and ended up committing suicide in 1930, after controls tightened. She had recently attended a lecture by the critic Vasily Katanyan at the Writers' Union about the one hundred or so errors or outright lies in the hefty book *Mayakovskiy v vospominaniyakh sovremennikov* (Mayakovsky in memoirs by his contemporaries), which came out in 1963. Katanyan produced a stream of stories about the notoriety of one of the contributors, the critic Korneliy Zelinsky, as a fabricator of reminiscences in one of his own books and in his article about Mayakovsky.[8] At another meeting where Zelinsky was being criticized along these lines, he wailed in his defense, "Well, there are a lot of misprints in my book." Someone fired back, "Your whole book is a pile of shit!"

By April, Rita had placed her translation of Kafka's *The Trial* into consideration for pre-book publication by both *Novyi mir* and another journal. Although she would have preferred the former, she felt that probably the latter would be simpler, because *Novyi mir* did not need to make life politically more complicated for itself by pushing for a European text. Rita had been helped in getting *The Trial* accepted as a book, because Grigoriy Breitburt, a Writers' Union official, loved Kafka.

On the other hand, she was absolutely furious with another journal, *Inostrannaya Literatura* (Foreign literature), for censoring some short passages in her translation of a story by Heinrich Böll. They had done this at the very last minute and without informing either her or her two young editors. Now she intended to work hard to get permission for the publication of William Golding's *The Lord of the Flies*, and, after that, an early story by Natalie Sarraute. She would do the translating.

Some good news was that the Writers' Union had at last sanctioned translations into Russian by a colleague of Rita's of William Faulkner's trilogy of novels, *The Hamlet*, *The Town*, and *The Mansion*, to be followed by other Faulkner novels. Also, Berthold Brecht's work was becoming increasingly permissible.

Rita found that the egotism of young writers such as Bella Akhmadulina and Andrei Voznesensky was affecting the quality of their work, while Yevgeny Yevtushenko's work deserved considerable contempt. When he commented to a friend of hers, "They say Dostoyevsky's good—give me something of his to read," she gave him a copy of *The Brothers Karamazov*, only to have him groan and demand something thinner! When a passer-by on a street in Leningrad asked if he was Yevtushenko, he had replied with false pathos, "I have the misfortune to be him." This reminded me of a popular joke supposedly recited by him about a widely despised writer of the older generation, Yevgeny Dolmatovsky, and himself. "I'm Yevgeny, you're Yevgeny, I'm no genius, you're no genius, I'm a shit, and you're a shit, but I of late, and you of yore."[9]

Despite Yevtushenko's apparent glibness and his being held in varying degrees of contempt in all of Soviet society's creative circles, he remained extremely popular among the rest of the educated class. Presumably this was for his pseudo-profundity, his personal subject matter, his easy comprehensibility, and his seeming anti-authoritarianism.

Rita held in greater respect the young painters whose works were not displayed in exhibitions. She had met several of them soon after Khrushchev had crudely poured scorn on them and their works on a notorious occasion in late 1962. They had brushed off his insults and remained calm and unworried, content that they could still sell their works privately and discreetly.

Rita deplored the activity of the literary underground, saying that it did more harm than good, and anyway its products were of poor quality. Creative people should keep up firm, steady pressure within the system. In her view, Leonid Il'ichev and the party leaders honestly believed their restrictions were doing the best thing for the Soviet people, a belief stemming from their ignorance of culture and the persistence of Stalin-era ways of thinking. She had hope that younger successors would prove more enlightened.

Rita much admired Vladimir Tendryakov for writing about basic human dilemmas and observed that he suffered the same sort of criticism in Russia as William Golding: he was considered too pessimistic, or not optimistic enough. Of serious concern to her was the current state of the theater and the absence of a single playwright of real standing. She had known the playwright Yevgeny Shvarts and liked him a lot for his fortitude and humor.

Evidently Rita felt obliged to keep in the good graces of the reactionary Writers' Union. One day when I visited her in her apartment there sat the Writers' Union official Grigoriy Breitburt. He was militantly against such Western magazines as *Encounter*, and I immediately decided not to engage with him. This did not stop him from claiming that *Encounter*, *Preuves*, *Der Monat*, and their Italian equivalent had been "almost completely deserted" by Europe's intellectuals, nor from denouncing *Encounter* for its American funding and political bias, the "slanders and complete misconceptions" about Soviet literature of Patricia Blake, and the magazine's "lies" about where the Russian author "Abram Tertz" (a pen name) lived: *Encounter* falsely claimed that he resided in the USSR.[10] Two years later, contrary to Breitburt's bluster, Andrei Sinyavsky, who used the pen name Abram Tertz, was arrested in Moscow and sentenced to seven years in a labor camp. (According to my "informant" Dmitry Shestakov, Breitburt was a sly, heavy-drinking homosexual who occupied a key Writers' Union post for deciding what foreign literature should be translated, and what not. This explained to me Rita's behavior and seeming agreement with some of his points.)

JOSEPH BRODSKY AND OTHER POETS

On my February 1964 visit to Leningrad I had much enjoyed an evening with my friend Misha Meilakh, a literary scholar with a strong interest in French literature (much later he went to live in French Guyana). He told me in confidence about the mounting official harassment of a twenty-three-year-old poet, Joseph Brodsky (Iosif in Russian). A protégé of the renowned poet Anna Akhmatova, a group of talented young writers had gathered around him. They were united by their respect for Brodsky, the KGB's barring of them all from publication, and their focus on Buddhism and Christianity, not politics (Brodsky was a nonpracticing Jew). Many of them performed at a recently opened poets' café in Leningrad, where a friend of mine saw Brodsky recite and found him modest, sober, and serious, like his poetry.

Recently, said Meilakh, the KGB had interrogated Brodsky for a month about a friend of his, and two articles about him had appeared in *Leningradskaya Pravda*, the second one accusing him, fantastically, of wanting to hijack a plane and fly out of the USSR. It also accused him of not having a job, and therefore being "a social parasite" and liable to arrest.

At this point he started preparing for a libel action against the paper. This caused the prosecutor's office—very likely under KGB orders—to rush through a prosecution of him for "parasitism." The trial took place in a remote suburb of Moscow and was only announced at the last moment, in early March. Nonetheless, many of Brodsky's friends got there in time to witness the pronouncement of an obviously predetermined sentence: five years of internal exile. His work book (the record of his paying work) showed that he had earned only 100 rubles in 1963. When people rose to say that he was a poet of great promise, writing apolitical poems, KGB operatives replied that this was tantamount to anti-Soviet activity. When Brodsky asked quietly whether they had read any of his poems, most said no, and the rest he embarrassed by asking where they had obtained them. Letters to the court in his defense from the eminent writers Kornei Chukovsky and Samuil Marshak were not read out, which was illegal suppression of evidence. Also, Akhmatova had written various letters before the trial. Brodsky impressed those present by his calm and modest bearing. His friends agreed that this was a case for publicity abroad as well as at home to apply pressure to the cultural dictators.[11]

Akhmatova and Tvardovsky were especially wound up over Brodsky's treatment. At a birthday party, Tvardovsky asked a conservative official, Prokofiev, what the hell he thought he was doing getting defenseless youngsters of twenty-three with no subversive tendencies exiled. When Prokofiev gave an aggressive reply, Tvardovsky seized him by the lapels and threw him out of the room. Akhmatova read some poems on the Yunost' (Youth) radio station and then with heavy irony expressed on the air her horror that the station had broadcast her work and thus had contaminated young minds with alien, formalistic, subversive writings. The whole scenario was unfortunate for both Akhmatova and Brodsky because it led some journals to postpone and even cancel publication of their poems.

Most unfortunate for Brodsky was that he was committed to a mental institution twice and did have to serve eighteen months of hard labor. Most unfortunate for the Soviet Union was that after his release Brodsky emigrated to the United States and won the Nobel Prize for Literature in 1987.

Meanwhile a completely different branch of poetry, with an ultra-conservative cast, continued to be practiced and also came into conflict with the regime. Dmitry Shestakov talked about the continuing relevance of the Slavophile-Russophile writers, who were some of the poets around the semi-underground poet Krasovitsky. Other figures were Tyurin and Sveshnikov. People of this type had jobs in museums and as translators, and tended to believe fanatically that Orthodoxy (*pravoslavie*) was the only force that could save Russia, not Christianity (*khristianstvo*), with its wretched belief in original sin. They also wrote complex and often excellent poetry, their main models being Osip Mandelshtam, murdered in captivity in the 1930s, and the futurist Aleksei Kruchyonykh, who lived a long life, from 1886 to 1968. They spent their holidays in monasteries in the north, created exceptionally fine icons, and were remarkably chauvinistic. They were strongly against Russians mixing their blood with that of any other people, and in that they were like the extreme-right-wing painter Ilya Glazunov.

However, they were swimming against the mainstream of the day, in which the moderate Russophiles, most of whom favored Christianity more than Orthodoxy, went with the flow.

Whither Morality? Right-Wing Views

In March 1964 I oddly heard all at once of several legal scandals involving homosexuals who had broken the law against pederasty (the law against homosexuality in general was often ignored). The biggest scandal reportedly involved a sizable group of people at the Moscow Music Conservatory, mostly Jews, who had been exposed in 1959 by an abused boy who told his parents what was going on. This led to hefty eight-year sentences for a number of defendants, including the well-known pianists Naum Shtarkman and Stanislav Neigauz. But Shtarkman served only eighteen months in a labor camp, and two years after his release was playing in Moscow again. Neigauz, too, served a greatly shortened sentence.

Other reported scandals were revealed concerning a large network of lesbians at the Lenin Teachers College in Moscow and a philosophy professor who had been thrown out of Moscow University for lesbian activity but then had been reinstated. In Ukraine, a senior political leader had received some sort of reprisal, as did another member of Ukraine's party presidium, who was severely demoted to the position of a local secretary somewhere in Uzbekistan.

I got some taste of right-wing views when a friend in her sixties took me to her church, one of the forty left in Moscow out of the many hundreds that had been active before the Communist takeover. Working-age people still risked losing their jobs if they were seen in church, so I was surprised to see many middle-aged people present, including men—but no young people except for two young priests and a deacon. After the service I met at my friend's place a young painter who was pleasant, strongly religious, and firmly opposed to abstract art, mainly because he saw it as "atheistic." Furthermore, he said, all the people attracted to it were sexually promiscuous. He was devoted to the art of the elderly liberal realist Russian artist Pavel Korin.

I learned that the previous year, a small church near the Tretyakov Gallery had arranged for a series of sermons on the topic "What Khrushchev Has Done for the People," which had been widely reported on. This year the church had arranged for sermons on the evils of abstract art, especially if displayed in churches. In general, the churches seemed to be bearing up under the assault that Khrushchev launched against all denominations in 1960–1961 and pretty much maintained until his ouster in October 1964. A priest I talked with in Vladimir, the ancient religious center southeast of Moscow that had been founded a millennium ago, said with apparent sincerity that it was the quality, not the quantity, of his flock that mattered.

LITERARY WIND SOCKS AND WEATHER VANES

From March 1964, liberal writers and intellectuals increasingly believed that Khrushchev's goal was to genuinely eschew crude administrative moves against them, and to rely mainly instead on self-government plus open criticism of people who went too far. This was the view of someone I became increasingly friendly with, a liberal literary critic and graduate student at the university, Volodya Skorodenko, who had many good connections. He told me emphatically that the long-running rumor that the writer Viktor Nekrasov had been expelled from the party was false, just as similar rumors about the expulsion from the Writers' Union of the elderly Ilya Ehrenburg and the young Yevgeny Yevtushenko had turned out to be a year ago. Such rumors, including the current doubtful one about the writer and singer Bulat Okudzhava, who had at last managed to get some poems printed in *Yunost'* thanks to his personal friendship with its editor, Boris Polevoi, originated with rightists who wanted to put the idea into the heads of the relevant officials. Another strong rumor was that the apartment of a leading expert on Pushkin, Yulian Oksman, had been searched by the KGB, and some of his friends had preemptively burned their riskier works. Yet another was that an influential member of the party's ruling Politburo, Frol Kozlov, had played a role in a major financial scandal in Leningrad.

The existence of a more liberal policy was confirmed, Volodya told me, by the minister of culture, Ekaterina Furtseva, who had declared that "our Ilya Grigorevich [Ehrenburg] and our Zhenia [Yevtushenko]" were very talented. She had also asked rhetorically: Who didn't make a few mistakes now and then? In accordance with Khrushchev's tastes, the great enemy was "formalism"; *Novyi mir* avoided this error and flourished. Il'ichev was regarded as being considerably to Khrushchev's right and had fallen into disfavor for having allowed the events of March 1963 to get out of control and cause bad publicity for the Soviet Union.

One example of this was the reactionary writer Sergei Mikhalkov's badly received—except in certain regions—witch-hunting speech to the Komsomol. Since the June plenum of the Party Central Committee, Il'ichev had mostly lain low, until he reappeared with a typical dose of negativism in the April issue of the party's theoretical journal *Kommunist*. This, however, stopped just short of questioning the loyalty of anyone, the most marginal case being the liberal critic Alexander Anikst. However, as a sop to the left, he criticized the arch-conservative writer Anatoly Sofronov. Also notable was that Polikarpov, Il'ichev's fellow hard-liner and subordinate in the Central Committee with special responsibility for Western culture, who hated Anikst and feared losing his job, was keeping quiet.

Indicative of the direction of the winds that were currently blowing, Volodya said, was the European Writers' Congress, which Leningrad had recently hosted. This had given new hope to the translators of Western literature, and may have been the main cause of the decision to publish Rita Rait's translation of a Kafka story. The way the regular system now worked was that the big publishing houses all had an Editorial Council on the Publication of Foreign Literature, which recommended books that then had to be approved by the relevant bureaucratic section of the Party

Central Committee. Liberals fought tactical battles on these councils over each author and work, and when at last a recommendation had been fought through, then liberals—and not only those sitting on the councils—would lobby the most relevant member of the Central Committee. When politically difficult authors like Faulkner and Kafka were at last permitted, it was usually after a blockage of several years in the Central Committee. Typically, the key factor was some special event like a general softening of the party line, or the recent Leningrad conference, or an anniversary, or the visit of a foreign author.

The liberal critic Anikst worked valiantly in this field, Volodya and Shestakov told me, calling for translations of all of James Joyce, Lawrence Durrell, and—to the horror of conservatives—D. H. Lawrence. He also gave masses of public lectures in which he propagated liberalism but also rejected suggestions that liberals should engage in organized activity. Rather, each person should work for the truth in his own sphere. Partly as a result of his advocacy in committees, Sid Chaplin was about to appear, also (after much hesitation) a Faulkner trilogy, and soon, Rita's translation of *The Trial.* One of his key opponents in this sphere was Yuri Samarin, who was wholly unprincipled, but disconcertingly knowledgeable academically. He had managed to keep Anikst off the committee that organized the visit by a troupe of British Shakespearean actors in April.

Although the well-known young poet Andrei Voznesensky appeared to be in a bit of a funk with some tame work, other liberals were on the offensive. Yevtushenko was publishing better poems. The poet Viktor Sosnora reportedly told those threatening him with non-publication to go to hell: he was a worker and his comrades would understand and support him. The officials' tone changed at once into oily servility. Anna Akhmatova, whom Volodya knew, had recently had a collection of some of her latest poems, "Beg vremeni" (The Onrush of Time), killed by a vicious internal review by the notorious Elena Knipovich, who had killed in like fashion Salinger's *The Catcher in the Rye.* (Of Knipovich Rita said that she was highly cultured and knowledgeable, and had been a close friend of the great writer Alexander Blok in the 1920s, but had been morally ruined by Stalin's cult of personality, which had turned her into a reactionary.) But this did not intimidate Akhmatova. In a rage, she abruptly removed her article, "The Duel and Death of Pushkin," from the chosen outlet, because it had imposed some illiberal changes. When the editors relented, she ignored their pleas and quickly found an alternative publisher.

Now Akhmatova had just finished compiling a two-volume collection of almost all her poems for publication, including the long work "Requiem." She hoped to push it through at the time of her upcoming seventy-fifth birthday, in June. She was surrounded with well-wishers and helpers, and stayed with the humorist Viktor Ardov when she came to Moscow. In 1965 she traveled to England to receive an honorary degree at the University of Oxford, and I was lucky enough to shake her hand. But she was aging, and died the next year at seventy-six.

Alexander Pasternak was a reliable source of views on the Soviet literary universe, albeit from his particular point of view as a member of the family that produced through Boris Pasternak one of the great Western and Russian literary uproars. In fact, when I saw him in April he was fervently hoping his sister would bring with her from England a copy of *Doctor Zhivago*.

Alexander was depressed about the apparent rejection for publication of the full collection of his brother's poems, and felt that it boded poorly for the fine analogous manuscripts of the collected poems of Osip Mandelshtam and Marina Tsvetayeva, on which dedicated people had worked hard and long.

However, he cheered up when he started to reminisce about Boris. He stressed the strong early influence on Boris of the personality of the composer Alexander Scriabin, adding that Boris had real promise as a composer himself, even though he was a rather wretched pianist. He also recalled how Boris had told the influential writer Konstantin Fedin that he would not object to a few cuts to *Doctor Zhivago* if that would get it published. This was a ploy that Lev Ozerov, the editor of the new manuscript of collected poems, was considering trying: cutting a few especially heterodox verses to improve chances that the rest would see the light of publishing day.

When the regime turned on Boris in 1958 over the publication abroad of *Doctor Zhivago*, Alexander recalled, Boris had been deserted by all his friends, except for Vyacheslav Ivanov, the son of Vsevolod Ivanov (a subject of my master's thesis), who was a professor in the Literature Department of Moscow University. His outspoken defense of Boris got Vyacheslav fired, with my supervisor, Metchenko, leading the charge. In 1964, Metchenko told a member of our British group that he had never read Pasternak's book.

In addition to Ivanov, only a few family members had remained loyal, notably Alexander and his wife, who had gone to live with Boris and his wife, Zinaida, in Peredelkino. Boris had been remarkably philosophical and unconcerned about this apparently disillusioning cowardice. A nurse was sent to live in the house for a while and keep him company in case he should contemplate suicide, but Alexander said he had never in fact contemplated this, and she soon left.

Boris had a mistress, Olga Ivinskaya, an editor, translator, and writer who had been arrested and thrown in prison in 1950, quite possibly in order to pressure Pasternak to stop his critical writings. Alexander had little time for her, nor did several other Russians I spoke with. He felt that in getting so close to Boris, she was motivated by the desire both for fame and for money. Alexander was also distressed by the persistence of the myth that the heroine Lara in *Doctor Zhivago* was chiefly modeled on Ivinskaya. In fact, he said, Lara's portrait mainly contained elements of Boris's mother, aunt, and first and second wives.

In addition, Alexander regretted the continuing influence of the eminent critic Edmund Wilson's notorious 1958 review of *Doctor Zhivago* in the *New Yorker*. The main problem with the review was Wilson's criticism of the translation, which only betrayed that Wilson decisively overrated his own unimpressive knowledge of Russian. Gleb Struve's firm rebuff of Wilson in a Russian-language journal pleased Alexander, but the article had not appeared in an English version and so had a minimal effect on the English-reading world. In Britain no reply to Wilson had appeared, because the book's accomplished translators, Max Hayward and Manya Harari, had not wanted to dignify Wilson with a response to his ignorant, inaccurate, and pretentious criticism of their translation.[12]

Alexander also reminisced about his year in the same high school class as the future writer Vladimir Mayakovsky in 1898–1899, when they were about sixteen. A rough, morose lone wolf who was to be kicked out of the school for political activity, Mayakovsky was probably closer to Alexander than to anyone else. The only moments when Mayakovsky softened—and even became quite sentimental—were when he spoke lovingly about his parents. Alexander also knew him for a short time five years later at art school, until Mayakovsky was expelled.

Looking more broadly at cultural trends, Alexander was not very optimistic about the chances for forward movement even in architecture. (An artist friend of Zhenia Pasternak's was rather pessimistic about the future for art in the Soviet Union, feeling that it now lagged far behind literature.) Real radicalism was still taboo, and the opportunities for more modest experimentation were too few for a healthy atmosphere to develop. An engaging, middle-aged, religious, and Western-oriented architect, a friend of a friend, took a similar view. He despaired at the rareness of being allowed to design anything but a tiny range of houses that had to follow a basically standard design, a practice for which, of course, no real designing was required.

In early 1964, Misha Meilakh said, Alexander Solzhenitsyn was often in the news, partly because he had written a play that Tvardovsky hoped to publish, but mainly because he had been nominated for a Lenin Prize in Literature, and Khrushchev's son-in-law Aleksei Adzhubei had stated his intention to push hard for a successful outcome. However, Adzhubei's influence had suffered a setback in March 1963, when *Izvestia*, which he edited, had sharply reduced its cultural coverage. Evidently this came in response to the reactionary surge and a direct order from an official entity that Adzhubei's cultural open-mindedness was finding too much scope for expression in the paper. Hard-liners also attacked him repeatedly by spreading dubious rumors about the imminent breakup of his marriage to Khrushchev's daughter Rada. Another problem was that Solzhenitsyn had been receiving shoals of vitriolic anonymous letters telling him to "STOP," an acronym that also stood for Stalinist Opposition.

Meanwhile, Dmitry was of the opinion that *Literaturnaya Gazeta* (Literary gazette) was going downhill. The last remaining liberal editors had left—the only even faintly liberal ones still there were Galin, Radov, and Teteryan—and the gazette criticized Solzhenitsyn as much as it dared.[13] However, hopes were still alive that Solzhenitsyn might win a Lenin Prize.

Kornei Chukovsky, one of Russia's most famous writers for children and also a translator, had escaped a bad fate under Stalin without compromising himself. By then about seventy, he came and spoke at Moscow University. He had visited Britain, and I asked him about his impressions. Several things had made a deep impact on him, for example, the fact that British students spoke two languages and were learning a third; that libraries were open twenty-four hours a day; and that everyone was able to flit over to Paris for the weekend when they felt like it. Afterwards, we had a few words and he invited me to visit him at his home in Peredelkino.

I did so in April. I was soon struck by his way of combining great affection for his guests with fierce commands that he shouted down the stairs to the kitchen. Early on he had me read out loud the last page of Isaiah Berlin's book about the two main types of human knowledge, which Berlin presented in *The Hedgehog and the Fox.* My imitation of the author's idiosyncratic way of speaking greatly amused him. Chukovsky's book on the art of translation was to reappear soon in a new edition. He was furious with an American translator of his books, Miriam Morton, for her mistakes, but was powerless to monitor her in advance.

He said that Vladimir Kornilov, Vladimir Tendryakov, and Alexander Solzhenitsyn were regular guests at his house and he liked all three very much. Each of them avoided the limelight, especially Solzhenitsyn, who asked that his identity not be revealed to other visitors. His cancer from a decade ago had proved not to be serious and was not seen as a threat for the future. His unpublished works included several stories written in the city east of Moscow, Ryazan, and also the play that the Sovremennik Theater in Moscow wanted to stage. He had given up teaching to write full-time. Chukovsky was not sure how much more he would get published, "because of those recent conflicts." He also held one of his Peredelkino neighbors, the Turkish writer Nazim Hikmet, in high esteem, both as a person and as a poet. Hikmet had been repeatedly imprisoned and was recently deceased. By contrast, Chukovsky was rather impatient with "the young poets," although he knew them socially. As a poet he liked Matveyeva the best. He himself was writing a memoir about Mikhail Zoshchenko, of whom he had been very fond.

Then he took me to see the children's library that he'd established close by, since "in our district people are seriously lacking in culture" ("*u nas v raione narod temnyi*"). Then we moved on to the Writers' House, where we bumped into an editor, I think of the magazine *Nauka i zhizn* (Science and life). Chukovsky gave a mock bow on learning that his deputy editor was Khrushchev's daughter. We also encountered a terrible woman called Skorina, a critic for the journal *Znamya* (The banner). After she left, Chukovsky was extremely rude about her and wondered why such people had always been so ready, especially in the past, to lie. He himself had never lied, and had not had to be a great hero or martyr to avoid losing his integrity.

He was astonishingly fit and mentally alert, and invited me to come again. He liked my translation of a short story by Natalya Tarasenkova. His son Nikolai was an acquaintance of an American friend of mine, and was reportedly as liberal as his father beneath a more conservative exterior.

In mid-April, the general official trend regarding literature remained mixed and unclear. The Russophiles still seemed to have the most scope, although the announcement that the Lenin Prize had been denied to Solzhenitsyn had struck them a blow. On the other hand, the second volume of Ilya Ehrenburg's autobiography had just appeared, with no cuts but instead, a "corrective" introduction by the publishers. The book was arousing intense interest among younger readers, whom the author evidently had especially in mind as his target audience. Also, a signal had been given that his collected works could proceed toward publication again after a political ban.

So the cultural authorities were tacking back and forth. The official confusion was exemplified in the treatment of a young liberal writer of short stories, Andrei Bitov. He underwent a nasty Stalinist attack in one paper, and was then defended a week later by an equally hard-line author!

It was evident to me, as an outside observer, that in the period of my Moscow sojourn from September 1963 to May 1964, Soviet society was moving toward becoming a seedbed for the emergence of samizdat and the expression of public dissent.

On the Inside, Looking Out

In general I was struck by the lack of interest in foreign affairs of the Russians I came to know. Maybe this was in part a reaction, conscious or unconscious, against the worldwide ambitions of the Communist regime and its ideology of Marxism-Leninism. After thirty-six years of Lenin and Stalin, my friends and acquaintances seemed to want the party to forget about world Communism and concentrate on giving ordinary people a decent standard of living.

Despite their ideological fatigue, many Russians were thirsty for news of outside events and popular culture in foreign countries. But their sources to gain this information were limited, and they took advantage of my knowledge of the West in order to compare it with conditions in the Soviet Union. A young taxi driver said it was "not a secret" that people lived better in the West, but he asked me how many people had their own cars, how much food and cars cost, and what the size of workers' incomes was. He noted that in the USSR almost everything was free except for food, cars, and clothes, but the problem was that no one had any money left over after buying food. In saying that as a member of the *narod*, or people, he was a joint owner of, say, the cinema that we were just passing, he seemed to be trying to convince himself that this was a better system than the West's.

One point of doubt that he and many others expressed about the economic system of the West was the West's unemployment—in the USSR everyone was guaranteed work. I explained that it often wasn't as bad as it seemed, since losing one's job could lead to finding a better one. He seemed to accept this, but stated that the recent murders of President Kennedy and Lee Harvey Oswald had made an appalling impression on Soviet people. They really didn't want the sort of freedom that allowed guns to be bought easily and the law to be flouted.

Listening to Western radio broadcasts in Russian was a way for Russians to outfox the censors and learn something about the West. Systematic nationwide jamming of broadcasts—on which the Kremlin spent large sums of money for the needed electricity—made this difficult but far from impossible. If you had a good radio, you could listen through the jamming even in Moscow. If you had only an inferior set, you could take a train about twenty minutes out of town, where jamming signals were weaker and listening became easy.

A few of my friends told me they listened regularly and gave me their views on the pluses and minuses of the stations. The most popular stations were the Voice of America and Radio Liberty, the most impartial was the BBC, the "softest"—least critical—was the French state radio, and the most anti-Soviet was the West German government station, Deutsche Welle, based in Bonn. Dmitry Shestakov reported that in his circles almost everyone listened to foreign broadcasts and was increasingly unafraid for this to be known. One complaint was that foreign broadcasters did not provide enough detailed news on Soviet domestic affairs, especially economic. Another was that boasting in detail about Western standards of living should be reduced: this aroused envy and nationalistic resentment. Voice of America was the worst offender in this. Not only well-educated people listened, and so it was felt that foreign broadcasters should pay more attention to varying the intellectual level for different audiences. For example, some of the programs on topics like philosophy and economic theory should be made simpler.

A married couple who were both scientists and taught physics at Moscow University liked the BBC best, because it was impartial without being soft. Openly anti-Soviet stations made a genuinely bad impression on them and their professional friends, and they were offended when they sensed an ulterior motive or agenda. But they stressed that they were far from typical, since they belonged to a very special, privileged social stratum because of their scientific professions. They were less starved for information about the world beyond the borders of the Soviet Union, and were more critical of what they did hear. The authorities wanted rapid progress in scientific fields that could, for example, speed up the development of military equipment. The extensive intellectual freedom they enjoyed was in effect a professional perk. They were satisfied with their pay, social prestige, work conditions, and freedom from intrusive ideology, and they were not burdened with the sort of inferiority complex vis-à-vis the West from which most Soviet people suffered. Americans might be somewhat freer to travel than they, but not much freer. In fact, many physics graduates rejected the much higher pay available in the official defense sector for the extra freedom—such as being allowed to meet foreigners—that they enjoyed as civilians.

Revealing was the meeting where my flatmate, Tolya, invited me to give a talk to students in the Geography Department about Cambridge University. The response was more than gratifying: the turnout was huge, I was showered with sensible questions, and the atmosphere couldn't have been more welcoming. Then there was the official government organization, the Society for Friendship with Foreign Countries, with branches in all the big cities, which was supposedly tasked with promoting friendship with and knowledge of other peoples. However, as I got to know two English speakers in the Moscow office it became fairly obvious that its main function was to report to the KGB on the views and activities of foreign visitors. One was Julietta Shakhbagova, who had shadowed us on our previous trip. The other, whom I met on this trip, was Elena Antonenko, who behind a cheerful, friendly exterior turned out to hold aggressively anti-Western views.

The free ten-week course on spoken English that I agreed to give at the society went well at first. I also offered the services of my economist father as an unpaid lecturer, when he made a brief stop in Moscow on his way home to Britain from India. However, the society failed to advertise his lecture, and invited just four specialists on the British economy. For these four what my father said proved to be of real value, but it was indicative of the society's paranoia that it was too frightened to advertise the lecture and draw a real audience. This was a missed opportunity for Russians to be exposed to knowledgeable Westerners.

Still, a few established Soviet figures who had been allowed to visit the West gave talks on their return home, with varied pictures of what life was like there. The mildly liberal writer Viktor Rozov was invited to give a talk at Moscow University. He found much to criticize in Britain, but he made the Russian audience of students gasp with amazement when, after praising the hard work of the British students he observed, he added that many of them saved up money to spend their summers abroad in Europe. Their ability to save this much money seemed extraordinary. In addition, the chairman of a meeting, a former editor of *Literaturnaya Gazeta*, Sergei Smirnov, recalled the years of World War II and looked forward with enthusiasm to the time when Britain and the Soviet Union would be allies again.

Returning to the Society for Friendship, another KGB representative of similar type to those named was the earlier-mentioned employee of the Foreigners' Department (Inotdel) of Moscow University, Lilya Pavlovna. The British graduate students, led by David Shapiro (who was actually a lecturer at Essex University) and myself, managed, with a few minor exceptions, to maintain reasonable relations with her. But the American group was not so lucky. In January 1964 Soviet-American relations reached a low point of hostility, ultimately due in part, I thought, to the efforts of the hard-liners in the Kremlin to derail Khrushchev's efforts to improve relations with the West and then oust him from office, as indeed happened nine months later. In the meanwhile, though, Soviet officials made a real effort to improve the situation, laying on a party for the American postgraduates and their Soviet equivalents who had recently returned from the United States. The evening passed off in a spirit of real friendliness, with the head of the Inotdel, Sergeyev, getting rather drunk.

Before long, however, the diplomatic atmosphere changed again, and, in early March, Lilya Pavlovna showed her true face. She turned nasty to the American students. Symptomatic was the incident when the Russian friend of an American graduate student was summoned to the KGB to listen to a recording of a conversation between the two of them in the American's room. The KGB issued them a stern warning.

None of this, however, prevented both American and Canadian graduate students from marrying Russian women at this time. Nor did it stop a British student, Mervyn Matthews, from getting engaged. However, he was soon expelled from the USSR and not allowed to bring his fiancée out for another five years.[14]

The seriously worsening relations of the Soviet Union with Communist China had ordinary Russians confused. The most common reaction was to fall back on feelings of Russian nationalism and prepare for a full ideological split—not to try to understand how two Communist governments could be so hostile to each other. The unsettling situation may have drawn them closer to the Kremlin. Meanwhile, ideological skeptics felt confirmed in their conviction of the falsity of dogmatic Communism, while ideological waverers moved closer to the skeptics. Jokes such as this one could be heard: "In China, Chairman Mao gets up in the morning, and the whole Chinese people gets up. At seven-fifteen the Chairman does his calisthenics, and the whole Chinese people does its calisthenics. At seven-thirty Chairman Mao goes to breakfast, and the whole Chinese people goes to work."

There were about forty Chinese students in Moscow, all or mostly in arts departments. In September 1963 the Kremlin blasted China in two major articles, which in Leningrad and Perm led to rumors of an impending war and unleashed panic buying of bread, salt, and sugar. This provoked an official statement that the rumors were false and were the product of malicious invention.

In early April, one of the most influential Soviet leaders, the Politburo member Mikhail Suslov, gave a long speech about foreign policy, which attracted an unusual amount of public attention. I was struck by the number of people I saw sitting in the Metro plowing their way through it in the newspaper. He talked about the so-called "anti-party group," and also examined in detail some of the alleged reasons for the deeper-than-ever split with the Chinese, providing along the way descriptions of unflattering Chinese political methods. These aroused interest, because they could only remind readers that similar methods were used in the Soviet Union to ensure loyalty to the regime. One common reaction to Suslov's speech was to turn to broadcasts on Western radio stations to learn more about the split in international Communism. At about the same time, the second-tier leader Leonid Il'ichev, who was reputedly liked by party workers, came to Moscow University to speak on the same themes to a closed meeting of party members.

Russians and Foreigners Together

There were many foreign students in Moscow from Africa, Asia, and Latin America. Many of these were concentrated in Patrice Lumumba University, which had been founded in 1960 with the goal of helping developing nations by educating their youth. In 1961 it had been named for Lumumba, a Soviet-friendly Congolese independence leader who had been assassinated in January 1961 in a Belgian-American plot.[15]

But Lumumba University, founded with a great deal of idealistic intentions, had a rocky start. I was eager to gain a better understanding of how Russians related to these third world students and their countries. Two of my close friends in Moscow were Kamine Tchapeyou, from French-speaking Cameroon in Africa, and Paul Singh, from English-speaking British Guyana on the northeastern coast of South America. Kamine and his nice Russian wife lived near me in the university. Paul Singh lived on the main campus of the Patrice Lumumba University in southwest Moscow.

Both Kamine and Paul had much they wanted to relate to me about their experiences and observations. There were the routine incidents of racial friction and conflict, which I had witnessed myself. Most common were scuffles for advantage in queues, and friction over girls at dances. In addition, however, far deeper tensions were in play between African students and both the university and government authorities that came down to official attempts to force Africans to toe the Soviet ideological line and align Africans with Soviet Communism. They boiled over in late 1963.

In November 1963 Kamine first told me about the officially controlled Federation of African Students in the Soviet Union. There were students from thirty-eight African countries at Lumumba, and twenty-one countries were represented in the federation. Up to this time he had been heavily involved in the organization and had worked with Soviet officials on various interethnic issues. But now, he told me, in the wake of its recent congress its committee had become dominated by Communists. Kamine became disgusted by the conformism, gutlessness, and double-dealing that came to dominate the federation. Communist domination of the federation led to an increased level of manipulation of most of the Africans, and this in turn led to the formation of an underground Pan-African Union to channel their growing resentment at the attempts to control them.

Eventually these undercurrents (perhaps with assistance from pro-Chinese elements) stimulated key African leaders to develop a secret plan to organize a big African protest demonstration on Red Square for December 18, 1963, in which they would demand that their right to independent lives should be respected. Estimates of the number of participants varied from 150 to 700, depending on the political alignment of the estimaters, including many small groups from various regions of the USSR. The demo caught the KGB completely flat-footed, because in discussing their plans on the telephone the organizers had used tribal languages, which the secret police couldn't understand. Thus the demonstrators succeeded in marching to the Kremlin's Spassky Gates, unfurling their protest banners with messages that included "Stop Killing Africans!" chanting slogans in English, Russian, and French, handing over a memorandum for the authorities, and giving interviews to the Western press without being stopped. Meanwhile, KGB agents floundered about on Moscow's most famous square, unable to get themselves organized to suppress the protesters.

This was the first unauthorized demonstration on Red Square since 1927, when Stalin crushed the last public opposition to him, led by Leon Trotsky. Where the KGB had been kept in the dark, a few Western journalists had been tipped off at the last minute, so the Africans' protest received instant worldwide media coverage the next day, December 19, 1963. This made serious reprisals against them afterward politically impossible. The African Communists in Moscow, when they had seen the action getting under way, had failed to stop it. The impossibility of instigating reprisals compounded the failure of the African Communists. Instead, in the coming days the KGB deployed unscrupulous methods to use the African Communists to exert pressure on each of the Moscow-based national associations (*zemlyachestva*) of individual African countries to denounce the demonstration. This also failed in all except two cases. Moreover, the Africans who were sent to the West to counter the effect of the media coverage met with abject failure, their numbers being small and their morale low. The Federation of African Students in the Soviet Union was largely discredited, partly because the authorities continued to reject the Pan-African Union's requests to be officially recognized.

In the wake of their Red Square demonstration and as tensions mounted in the university more broadly, the Africans soon became bolder. For example, Kamine developed the courage to raise dissident questions at professors' seminars, even though, as a result, he was chided unpleasantly for being a "rightist."

Kamine told me of another sort of tension that he had learned about in Yerevan, the capital of Armenia. Here some 8,000 Armenians who had emigrated from the USSR between the world wars decided to return—mostly from France—after the Soviet victory of 1945. They were settled together in one district. However, by now they were feeling the same sort of broadly based political pressures that exasperated the Africans (minus the racism), and 7,500 of them regretted returning. This story reminded me of a story I was told of some Russian émigrés who returned in similar circumstances from South America and were settled in Brest-Litovsk, in the Byelorusian Soviet Socialist Republic. Soon, all of the young people seventeen to twenty-five years of age asked to be allowed to return whence they came, but were repeatedly refused. One day they committed suicide en masse, in despair over their gray and joyless lives in what turned out to be captivity.

Paul Singh, who lived in Patrice Lumumba University, had a friendly personality and an all-around honesty that had made him highly trusted by his Russian friends. But some of the foreign students who lived at Patrice Lumumba University feared the 20 percent of Russians who lived among them, so didn't follow the trend of listening to foreign radio broadcasts. They feared being persecuted as "reactionaries." However, Paul had recently started daring to go to the American embassy once a week and returning with eagerly awaited free copies of *Time* magazine to distribute.

Many African students had given up on Lumumba and the USSR, and some had already returned home. According to Paul a large proportion of the rest—perhaps a majority—intended to leave at the end of the academic year. A big group of Tanganyikans had already announced that they would do this. To try to keep these numbers down, the official line toward the most vocally independent was now to be as conciliatory as possible, appoint them to various commissions, and not apply the rules strictly. At the same time, the old method of paying the dishonest to write dishonest articles continued. A continually drunk and penniless Nigerian had written an article claiming that all Lumumba students could save thirty rubles a month out of their grant of ninety. This brought a flood of protests to the rector. In fact, white bread was no longer being served in the café on the grounds that it might now be too expensive for many students to buy. Numerous protests ensued, including some complaints about the substituted gray bread that was made mostly from peas, which was inedible to all but Russians. White bread soon reappeared.

Paul estimated that 90 percent of the Lumumba students were increasingly strongly anti-Soviet, repelled by the corrupt practices used against them and the Russian people, by ordinary people's "appalling" living conditions, by the propaganda and restrictions, and by the general joylessness of life. These negative feelings were balanced on the positive side by Pan-African, pro-Chinese, or pro-liberal views. The Latin Americans held that the Chinese were pure, unbureaucratic, and revolutionary, as compared to the cynical, corrupt Soviets. In this ethnic group perhaps 80 percent were such, while 20 percent were liberal. Chinese propaganda was sedulously distributed by people who had presumably obtained it indirectly from the embassy. Its uninhibited anti-Soviet and anti-Khrushchev positions found a wide and gleeful response. Paul, one of those suspected of distributing it, had been repeatedly warned of dire consequences if he continued with this, but he had a solid group of supporters who would leave too, if he were to be expelled. However, pan-African views were much stronger than pro-Chinese ones among African students, and probably had about 80 percent backing.

The Cubans tended to be pro-Chinese. One of them asked a professor how a secretary of the Georgian Party's Central Committee could have confided in him that the Russians were colonizers of Georgia both politically and economically, and that Khrushchev was a revisionist. A friend of mine got exactly the same line, while on tour, from the first secretary of the Georgian Komsomol. He also recounted how his requests to meet a real worker were met at last with an invitation to tea from a woman with a decent room. He found out later that she was really a teacher.

The Indonesians enjoyed a reputation for political obtuseness, but most of them just blindly followed the line of President Sukarno in Jakarta. An example of that obtuseness came at the end of February, when, in an officially sponsored Soviet attempt to draw nearer to China, Chinese students were invited to speak and perform at a Camerounian party at Moscow University. Two of the Chinese gave unprovocative speeches, but then an Indonesian got up and delivered a fiery pro-Chinese, anti-Soviet oration—and spoiled the whole effect.

In mid-April two reliable sources told me that tensions at Lumumba were dangerously high, especially between Africans and Russians, despite the continuing official policy that the Russians should be as conciliatory as possible: girls were now allowed in from outside—a big concession—and teachers had greatly reduced their evening prowls to spy and eavesdrop on the foreigners. However, when individuals insisted on actions the officials disliked, or were caught organizing Pan-African Union activities, or became militantly pro-Chinese, the authorities resorted to all sorts of deception to expel them or pressure them to leave "voluntarily." Every time someone did leave, a notice announced that he had been expelled and a fake reason was given. In the current academic year this had happened on four separate occasions to British Guyanese. Each time their national association had protested so strongly, threatening a demonstration, that the notice had quickly come down. One of the four had gone to study in London, where he would furiously heckle Communists at Speakers' Corner in Hyde Park, saying, "I've lived in that society, and know at first hand how awful it is!" The Federation of African Students in the Soviet Union was now wholly discredited, at least at Lumumba, as being run by stooges. It now claimed to represent only eighteen countries, whereas earlier it was twenty-one. The one independent member of the Federation of African Students in the Soviet Union's executive committee had been thrown out on a falsified pretext.

At Lumumba's main student hostel the commandant was a former bodyguard of Khrushchev's. He was a thug and made the mistake of tearing down a picture of Stalin in a student's room. For his pains, the student hit him on the head with a glass carafe. However, harassment continued. Literature mailed from the Chinese and American embassies was routinely confiscated, to which at least one student responded by having his copy of *Time* sent to a post office box number. Komsomol meetings were halfheartedly opened to non-Soviets, but if any turned up, no real business was done and the meeting was later held elsewhere. But professors could not do much to halt the increasingly tough questions they were now getting from both left and right, questions that would have been even tougher if the students had had more access to accurate information.

Periodic violence was another feature of many third worlders' lives, a fact that encouraged them to carry knives. For example, a Ugandan who was walking with a Russian girl was attacked in the street, but used his knife to scare the attackers off. A Guyanese friend was driven with three pals into a dark alley by a taxi driver, who had refused to take them to their destination. When he hopped out to find some thugs to beat them up, my friend managed to recruit some police officers (*militsiya*) to come and protect them. However, they declined to force the driver to behave professionally, and my friend's group left. And I was in a restaurant with the same friend when he was seized and hurled aside from the Russian girl he was dancing with by a slightly drunk Azerbaijani. Understandably, he lost his temper, and I only just managed to catch his hand to prevent him from cracking the fellow on the head with a bottle. Most of the Russian bystanders were on my friend's side, and when the police came, they listened fairly impartially. Afterward, however, when my friend was recovering in hospital from his injuries I only just dissuaded him from taking the man to court.

In the hospital he encountered anti-Semitism up close. Whenever he helped an old man to walk, he was challenged with "Why'd you bother to help that old Jew?" When a Mauritian had a somewhat similar experience, he tried to defend the Jew who was the target of some thugs, and ended up being detained for some hours by the police. He was released only after he had been allowed to call Lumumba to prove his identity.

Although the early sixties were a time of troubles at Patrice Lumumba University, it has now put all this behind it, and is a thriving institution in the twenty-first century. It has many departments and a large student population of 29,000, thus emphasizing Vladimir Putin's intention of continuing to play a significant role in the developing world.

Oleg and Valentina Lenchevsky's Fate, and My Own

The first time I felt sure that I was subject to serious KGB surveillance—being followed on the street—was on December 9, 1963. After this, I was not aware of anything else until a highly suspicious incident during our early February visit to Tallinn, the capital of Estonia. The surveillance may have been triggered by a dissident friend's walking openly into our hotel in Leningrad a few days earlier and asking for me.

In Tallinn I was sitting in a bar when a man in his forties sat down next to me and started to talk about himself. As he talked he also drank, and appeared to become rather drunk. His message was that he was a telephone engineer working on the "hot line" that the United States and the Soviet Union had recently agreed to set up, for use in emergencies. There was some important secret information that he felt he needed to tell me, so that I could make sure it reached the U.S. government. Of course, I had to keep my source secret, and the KGB must not pick up on what he was telling me, or he would be in serious trouble. At this point I broke off the conversation, saying I couldn't help him. All my instincts told me that it was a carefully planned provocation, designed to find out if I was a British agent of some sort. I didn't tell anyone about the episode.

In hindsight it seemed like I may have raised a red flag of suspicion that ultimately led to my expulsion from the USSR, and that linked me to the political ordeal of two Russians whom I befriended.

As a student at Cambridge University, I had learned a lot and earned a little pocket money by occasionally acting as a guide around my home city of Cambridge. My clients were Soviet visitors invited to the U.K. by the government, and in effect my employer was the British Council. My job was to show the visitors the city's historical sights and to act as an interpreter for them with local people.

One day in 1961 the council's guest was the chief water engineer of Moscow, Oleg Lenchevsky, then in his forties. We had an exceptionally interesting day, since Oleg was keen to talk about himself and his family and to ask questions. In particular, he wanted to know if he could attend a service in King's College Chapel, whose construction was begun by King Henry VI in 1446. We entered the spacious, awe-inspiring building for the daily service, passed through the massive dividing structure that marks off the so-called ante-chapel, and sat down behind the superbly trained choir. The service was inspiring, as always, but it made an especially powerful impression on Oleg, because he was formally a Communist and had not been able to practice his faith in public since childhood.

Three weeks later I opened the paper and read that he had defected. It was all over the U.K. press. He had found it such a relief to be free of what to him were the lies of Communism that he felt he must seize the opportunity to stay in the U.K., even though it meant separating himself from his beloved family: his wife, Valentina, and his two teenage daughters. He hoped that with the help of the British government he would be able to persuade the Kremlin at least to allow Valentina to join him. I contacted him through the British Council, and from then on we saw each other from time to time and became friends.

Two years later, his efforts to get Valentina out had not borne fruit. Since she had refused official demands to denounce him as a traitor, the Soviets had punished her by forbidding her to contact him, by confiscating all his letters to her before delivery, and by trying to prevent her from getting even the humblest job. When I knew I would be in Moscow, I offered to go and see her there and convey any verbal messages. He gladly accepted my offer and gave me contact information for a friend who could take me to Valentina.

At Christmastime I went to visit this friend and we went to see Valentina. It turned out that a friend had helped her to get an unofficial job at the Romen Theater, which staged Roma (gypsy) plays; he had been able to do this because he hadn't filled in the form whose information would have precluded her being hired. She worked two shifts a day to finance her family's expenses.

We met quietly at the theater, after she finished her shift. She took me to her apartment, and we exchanged information about ourselves. She was glad to see me and to hear the messages that Oleg loved her and their daughters, was still working as hard as he could to extract at least her from the USSR, if not the girls as well, and was gainfully employed in London in his profession. She told me that she and the girls were well, although they had been deserted by most of their friends, but not all. However, she couldn't get the apartment registered in her own name, and the airman who wanted to marry her elder daughter, Lena, had been refused permission, though he hadn't given up hope. The girls were both studying satisfactorily in college. The younger one was a real bookworm, but lively, too. Although Lena was pessimistic deep down about the chances of ever being allowed to leave, and all three women were alternately resigned and optimistic about the desperate lack of postal contact with Oleg, Valentina retained a sliver of hope that she would be reunited with her husband. All sent him their warmest love.

When I met Valentina again a few weeks later, in January, I was struck by her incredible bravery and cheerfulness, despite the inevitable depression she admitted suffering. Alternately, she thought of a miracle happening and her joining Oleg abroad, and then of the impossibility of this happening and even of the KGB conceivably exiling her to Siberia. She was torn, moreover, by the needs of her girls, who couldn't manage without her right now, and would also rely on her after their marriages to help them look after their children. In addition, the prospect of going to live elsewhere and not speaking the language simply scared her. Thus with each passing year she saw more clearly the likelihood of her hopes being unfulfilled and her energies ultimately turning to trying to forget Oleg and even possibly to remarrying, although she did not think that she would. She didn't know what Oleg was thinking, or feeling, about this.

Her social life revolved around two men friends, one retired from the army, and two women friends, all of whom were long-standing friends and had remained loyal to her. One of the men had given her a little financial help. Regarding her girls, sometimes they suffered terribly from a mixture of love and bitterness regarding their father. Valentina felt that they were both basically religious, which pleased her a lot. One of them always took a holy object to exams.

Three months later, on April 22, the British embassy called and asked me to come in. There Thomas Brimelow, the number two diplomat, took me down to the soundproof room where nothing could be overheard and said that the Soviet Foreign Ministry had laid a complaint against the embassy and me, and said that I must leave the USSR within two weeks. It had accused the embassy of having sent me to Valentina in violation of an official British promise of 1961 not to have any more contact with her. The Foreign Ministry claimed that I had tried to persuade her to flee the USSR and join her husband in the U.K. The embassy had denied having sent me or knowing anything about my visits to her.

I told Brimelow that I had indeed visited her, but had not said anything so stupid, and had not given her anything except a verbal message of affection and loyalty from her husband. In light of this, Brimelow said the embassy would report to the Soviet officials and ask that the order for me to leave be rescinded. A week or so later, however, he told me that this representation had evoked no reply, so I should prepare to leave within two weeks.

I don't know how the KGB found out about my visits to Valentina, but if it was she who told them, I would understand. She was in an unenviably vulnerable position.

I told a few trusted Soviet and non-Soviet friends what had happened, and they all expressed their sympathy. Then, late on May 5, I took the train from the Belorusskiy Station to the Hook of Holland, where I boarded a ferry for home. On May 7, I arrived at the English port of Harwich, and my parents met me with their car. They were kind and understanding concerning my unexpectedly early return home. My expulsion merited only a paragraph or two in the national British press, and a longer story in the *Daily Telegraph*. The *Cambridge Daily News* sent a reporter to my parents' house, and a write-up with a photograph of me duly appeared.

My shock over being expelled was blunted by the fact that I had always regarded it as a real possibility. More upsetting was the realization that Dmitry Shestakov may very well have set me up for expulsion: The person who told me that I would have to leave the USSR within two weeks was an acquaintance of Dmitry's, to whom he introduced me at his home—clearly a Soviet official. Obviously, Dmitry had been doing some freelance work for the KGB by getting to know me and asking me questions designed to find out my interests and to ascertain whether I was working for anyone but myself—and his wife didn't approve of this. Hence her sighs when I visited them at their home.

Other Westerners in my year and previous ones had met the same fate. Of course, I was quite disturbed when I realized that my career might well be affected by the likelihood that the Kremlin would not allow me back into the country for a long time. And I hated the idea that I would not be able to see my many Russian friends. My new status as an expellee was to last for twenty-four years. But over the next few years, as I developed a strong interest in the samizdat and human rights movement that emerged at that time, I began to see that my expellee status conferred a certain compensating advantage on me: I could write freely on this subject without having to temper my views to avoid being put on a Soviet blacklist.

On the day after my arrival, I reported to the British Council and the Foreign Office in London. Then I could start meeting my British friends and relatives and relaying my adventures to them. I wrote to Oleg, who had moved to Holland.

From Moscow I had applied for a Ford Foundation fellowship to work on my doctorate under Leonard Schapiro at the London School of Economics in the coming year. The LSE had awarded me the fellowship, and I now took the chance in London to have a friendly meeting with Schapiro and to confirm that I would be coming in the fall to be one of his Ph.D. students.

FIVE

The Emergence of Dissent

Bringing Dissidents and the Emerging Human Rights Movement to the World's Attention

Settling into the London School of Economics in its building at the Aldwych and into an apartment in Kennington, just south of central London and the Thames, turned out to be quite easy. As I became more involved in the research for my thesis, I started writing not only academically oriented papers related to my thesis topic but also started to produce analyses and reports for various types of publications on the emergence of public dissent in the USSR. And soon I was also involved in the publication of a landmark volume on Lenin.

My official Ph.D. topic was the politics of Soviet literature since the death of Stalin, and after the LSE appointed me as a junior lecturer in political science in 1965, Leonard Schapiro suggested that we co-edit a volume on Lenin. I would also contribute a chapter on Lenin's attitudes to literature and the arts—which would be useful background for my research for my doctorate.[1] We planned for the book, *Lenin: The Man, the Theorist, the Leader: A Reappraisal*, to come out in 1967, the fiftieth anniversary of the Russian Revolution.[2]

Our first job was to select the authors and the topics we would ask them to write about. The planned lead time gave us more than a year to do the job, so we could assemble a strong team, including Alec Nove, Britain's leading expert on Soviet economics, who would write on Lenin as an economist; John Erickson, a senior specialist on the military, writing on Lenin's leadership in the civil war of 1918–1921; and John Keep, one of the three prime specialists in modern history (the other two being Schapiro and Hugh Seton-Watson), writing on Lenin as a tactician.

Schapiro wrote the book's introduction, providing an overview of all the more detailed chapters to follow. In it he reached a conclusion regarding Lenin that most of the authors would probably have endorsed. In 1921 Lenin's Bolsheviks not only won the civil war, one of the most significant events of the twentieth century, but he also then decided to destroy politically the fellow socialists who had helped him to victory. In addition, he set in motion the process of restricting serious discussion among the victorious Bolsheviks. Schapiro speculated, "Had he lived, he would have followed a very different course from Stalin." But, he added, "The fact is that, at this turning point in Russian history, Lenin remained a prisoner of the dominant passion which had carried him to victory (over the remnants of the monarchy) in 1917. He had failed to make the transition from revolutionary to statesman, from the battlefield to the peace conference table. A great revolutionary, he had not managed to develop the qualities required of a statesman."[3]

In my chapter, "Literature, the Arts, and the Personality of Lenin," I documented and discussed the little-known fact that Lenin had throughout his life enjoyed classical literature, some of it poetry and most of it Russian of the socially engaged variety, including some English and French works.

My Mentor, Friend, and Colleague, Leonard Schapiro

Leonard Schapiro was the man who, more than any other, provided me with unfailing intellectual support and professional guidance over the first nineteen years of my career.[4] Having spent his life from ages four to twelve in Russia helped him indirectly to become something unusual: both a true Russian intellectual and a true English scholar and gentleman.

After returning half starved from St. Petersburg to the land of his birth in 1920, a sound British education propelled him to a highly productive career. Turning down an Oxford scholarship, he read law at University College, London, winning important prizes, and joined a legal practice. He served in the military in World War II, advancing to the rank of acting lieutenant colonel in the Intelligence Corps. After the war he returned to practicing law, but also began two spare-time writing ventures: articles about international legal issues and a book on a completely different and even more demanding topic, the history of the early years of the Soviet Union: *The Origin of the Communist Autocracy: Political Opposition in the Soviet State. First Phase: 1917–1922.*

The book had been commissioned in 1951 by a committee of London's Chatham House, a research group to study international affairs. This committee was dominated by the well-known historian E. H. Carr, who had sympathies for the Soviet system, whereas Schapiro was critical of it, leading to a four-year deadlock in which Carr prevented publication of Schapiro's book by Chatham House, as originally intended. The impasse was broken in 1955 when Schapiro was appointed to a lectureship in the Government Department of the LSE, and the eminent scholar, the philosopher Karl Popper, and others helped Schapiro to have his book published by G. Bell.

Maurice Cranston, a colleague of Schapiro's and mine at the LSE, later identified a key reason why Schapiro changed his profession from lawyer to scholar: "There was a strong sense of duty which impelled Leonard to become a Sovietologist. It troubled him deeply that the West had so many illusions about the Soviet Union."

Schapiro described his book as "the story of how a group of determined men seized power for themselves in Russia in 1917 and kept others from sharing it; and of the consequences which ensued both for themselves and for their political rivals when it became evident that they enjoyed but little popular support." In writing the book Schapiro deployed a wide range of his talents: his profound understanding of Russian history and culture; his ability to make abstruse ideological controversies between Marxists intelligible to the general reader; his insight into the relationship between ideology and political practice; his meticulous regard for facts; and his readiness to make the sort of broad comparative and moral judgments that illuminate the best scholarship.

The same qualities also informed his next book, *The Communist Party of the Soviet Union* (1960), which quickly established his worldwide reputation as one of the two leading scholars in the developing field of Sovietology, alongside Merle Fainsod of Harvard. At six hundred pages, the book covered a great deal of territory, comprising a systematic history of a political party, an analytical interpretation of a novel system of government, and a history of the Soviet state since 1917. A key aspect of all three components was the party's rigid subjection of the law to itself or its leader.

Subsequently, Schapiro wrote four more books: *The Government and Politics of the Soviet Union* (1965), *Rationalism and Nationalism in Nineteenth-Century Russian Political Thought* (1967), *Totalitarianism* (1972), and *Turgenev: His Life and Times* (1978). He also edited four books and translated one, wrote some seventy chapters as contributions to edited volumes, long articles, and hundreds of reviews and articles in newspapers and magazines.

One of his conclusions: "Revolution is pitiless, shapeless, and nearly always seems to provide a cure which is worse than the disease."[5] His breadth of reading and learning in six languages was prodigious. This showed most remarkably in his literary biography of the Russian writer Ivan Turgenev (1818–1883) and in his translation of Turgenev's novel *Vesennie vody* (*Spring Torrents*, 1980). In both books the sources are heavily literary and the biography is densely documented with twenty-five pages of endnotes.

To me, one of Schapiro's most endearing features was his kindness. He would always greet me warmly when, on arriving for the day, I knocked on the door of his office at the LSE, which was one floor above the street, on the way up to my own room, which was two floors higher. It didn't matter if he was deep in a book, or reading a student paper, or writing an article. He wanted to have a chat and catch up on teaching matters and the day's news.

Leonard was never a practicing Jew or Christian, but as he grew older he discussed his religious beliefs with our mutual friend the Reverend Michael Bourdeaux. He said that he felt in tune with both religions, and he would like a service to be held after his death that would reflect this fact, and Michael readily agreed. Schapiro died in 1983 and Michael conducted the occasion at the LSE in suitable style and helped a naturally religious man on his way.

Teaching with Schapiro

Schapiro and I always taught one graduate course together, and always presided together over a weekly graduate seminar, to which we also invited selected individuals from outside LSE: experts from another department, or another university, or a nonacademic institution, or visitors from abroad. Some of the most memorable occasions were when older colleagues spoke.

For example, in the late 1970s a speaker who was then approaching ninety turned to Schapiro, who was about seventy, and said, "Young Leonard here won't remember this episode, but . . ." The room, full of people who had a vision of Leonard as being decidedly old, erupted in laughter, as Leonard happily shared the joke, his eyes twinkling in double-time and his bushy eyebrows jumping up and down.

His kindness also shined through when we co-taught Soviet politics and Russian political history from the mid-nineteenth century to the present; he invariably refrained from correcting me outright when I made a mistake, and found another way to set the record straight. Likewise with students, he encouraged them to speak up by not rebuking them if they erred.

After Khrushchev

In October 1964, one week after I started as a doctoral student at LSE, Nikita Khrushchev was ousted by his colleagues in the Politburo in a Kremlin coup. My Harvard professors and the year I had spent in Moscow had prepared me for this eventuality and it did not surprise me in the least. But the period that immediately followed was of great interest.

After the coup the collective Soviet leadership gave some signals of leniency, such as releasing a large number of Soviet citizens who were in prison for their open religious beliefs as Baptists. Eight months later, however, the leadership opted for a relatively hard-line position, both domestically and vis-à-vis the West. All this gave rise to a demand for informed analysis and commentary. When Stephen Hugh-Jones, the editor of the *Economist*'s confidential journal *Foreign Report*, sought such analysis from Schapiro, he passed on my name to Hugh-Jones. The result was that from November 1964 to March 1965 I wrote four articles for him about Kremlin politics.

I also wrote a paper on Khrushchev's fall to be presented at the annual Conference of Teachers and Research Workers on the Soviet Union in April 1965 (in 1978 the organization was renamed the National Council for Soviet and East European Research, with offices in Washington, D.C.). This is how I came to give my first academic talk to an august research body. It was well enough received for the quarterly academic journal *Survey: A Journal of East and West Studies*, edited by a leading expert on communism, Leopold Labedz, to ask to publish it in the July issue.[6] I started my article by arguing that Khrushchev's fall had not been followed by a state of equilibrium among his colleagues, because "no leader of outstanding personality" emerged to "exert a strong unifying direction." The Kremlin turned this into a virtue, hailing the collectivity of the leadership as "the greatest political asset of our party."[7] As a result, rival pressure groups skirmished with each other and induced "hesitancy and indecision in the Party's approach to many of the urgent problems bequeathed by Khrushchev." The latter's 1961 strategy of "satisfying popular demands by a rapid and steady rise in Soviet living standards" had been "both realistic and logical." However, the 1962 food price increases, followed by the severe shortages of food and other essential goods in 1963–1964, plus enormous shortfalls in consumer goods and housing, meant that he had "failed to evolve tactics suitable to his strategy." This, I judged, was the major reason for his ouster.

Other reasons were Khrushchev's cult of his own personality (an editorial in *Pravda* charged him with being a poor leader because such a one, "besides conducting, tries to play all the instruments himself"); the failure of his risky adventure of sending missiles into Cuba; his neglect of the military; and his rapprochement with the West, which precipitated a serious break with Communist China.[8] Also disliked by his colleagues was his "sweeping and undebated" vertical division of the party into political and economic sides, which he had done with the aim of helping the economy. But, as the party journal *Kommunist* later commented, this division "gave rise to so many difficulties, complications, and errors of different sorts that it was obvious, on balance, that the minuses easily outweighed the pluses."[9] Leonid Brezhnev, who later, in about 1968, took over from Khrushchev as the de facto party leader, dug this in by quoting Lenin on the subject, to wit: "We have terribly many who love to reorganize in every possible way, and these reorganizations result in such a calamity that I have never known a worse one in my life."[10]

Finally, after Khrushchev's removal, most of his cronies were dismissed or demoted, "greater democracy" became a goal, along with an "increasing role for the party" (which, however, effectively nullified the "greater democracy"), and the salient importance of Marxist-Leninist theory was stressed.

As the Kremlin's political line gradually hardened between 1965 and 1967, my contribution to *Survey* led the editors of two other specialist journals on the Communist world to ask me to write an article and two reviews: *Soviet Studies*, a journal put out by Glasgow University, and *Prob-*

lems of Communism, the journal of the U.S. Information Agency of the State Department. I also wrote articles in nonspecialist magazines.[11]

Dissent Emerges

At this time I also started writing articles on public dissent in the USSR. In 1967, *The Times* of London, approached me for the first time and asked me to contribute to a special issue on the fiftieth anniversary of the Russian Revolution. My article included references to the appearance of public dissent and ended with these thoughts:

> You get the impression in 1967 that the Soviet people are slowly waking from a long and harrowing nightmare and reasserting, strongly if incoherently, their natural humanity. Losing the fears of the night, they increasingly inquire into what has happened, defy the censorship by circulating literature underground, tell political jokes, insist on their right to go to church, search for the historical and cultural identity of their particular nationality, Slav or otherwise, and even try to think constructively about the political future. Unless the regime discerns these new aspirations and yields to them much more than it is doing at present, it is sure to meet increasingly confident and diverse forms of resistance. This would put in jeopardy [the regime's] chances of ever celebrating its centenary.[12]

I had been expecting the emergence of open dissent for a few years, and for a variety of reasons. My study of tsarist and Soviet history pointed to its happening again in the future, as it had in the last decades of the monarchy and again after Lenin took power in 1917. Then, in the 1950s, dissent and opposition had come into the open, especially in Hungary and Poland, and to a very small degree in the USSR, encouraged by Khrushchev's denunciations of Stalin in 1956 and later in 1961. Then it had again been crushed. My meeting with the Hungarian Paul Magyar in 1957 (see chapter 1) and my friendships with Russians in the early 1960s strengthened my confidence that the dam would break. As I found when I was in Moscow in 1963–1964, some of these and other Russians expressed their critical views freely among their friends, and started cautiously circulating forbidden samizdat and foreign literature.

Some key events can be identified that helped to create the atmosphere and conditions in which the human rights movement could emerge between 1965 and 1968. In the literary world, in 1958 Boris Pasternak's *Doctor Zhivago* appeared in the West. Furthermore—to the fury of the Kremlin—Pasternak won the Nobel Prize for Literature for his whole oeuvre. Then, in 1959, an essay and a stream of stories by a pair of Soviet writers using the pseudonyms Abram Tertz and Nikolai Arzhak began to come out in France and gained worldwide acclaim. Six years later the authors' real names, Andrei Sinyavsky and Yuli Daniel, were revealed when the KGB arrested them and put them on trial. They were sentenced to seven and five years, respectively, of forced labor. Later I met them both, Daniel shortly before he died in 1988 at the age of sixty-three, his life undoubtedly shortened by his ordeal in captivity.[13]

At the same time that the early Tertz-Arzhak works were appearing, a remarkable book was published in 1961 in London: "*Vesenniy list*" (A leaf of spring), by Alexander Yesenin-Volpin (1924–2016).[14] The author, who lived in Moscow, had had it smuggled out in 1959 and asked that it should appear under his own name. It contained a collection of his elegant, frankly expressed poems and his quickly written but notably original "*Svobodnyi filosofskiy doklad*" (Free philosophical treatise). This laid out clearly for the layperson his deeply felt and highly skeptical philosophy. Later in the 1960s he developed his "legalist" understanding of how citizens should view Soviet law. They should take the extensive rights granted in the constitution seriously, and hold the Soviet authorities to doing the same. This would make truth-based dissent genuinely legal. Before long, these positions became the established philosophy of the USSR's various dissident movements, and made life difficult for the KGB.

Since 1949, Yesenin-Volpin had been arrested five times for his free thoughts and free expression of them, both verbally and in writing. Most often he was forcibly interned in mental hospitals, only once serving a few years in a labor camp. However, neither form of captivity changed his behavior in the slightest. In 1972 he was pushed into emigration to the United States, where he gave powerful testimony on the Soviet regime's misuse and abuse of psychiatric "treatment" before the U.S. Senate. He taught for many years in Boston, where I felt honored to meet and correspond with him.[15]

In 1962 a book describing the near-complete perversion of Soviet biology into a pseudo-science began to circulate in samizdat, written by a molecular radio biologist of international repute, Zhores Medvedev. The rationale of this pseudo-science was the ideological importance and forceful imposition of the notion that acquired characteristics were heritable. After the fall of the Ukrainian pseudo-scientist Trofim Lysenko in 1964, when Khrushchev could no longer protect him, Medvedev's book was eventually published in the West in 1969 as *The Rise and Fall of T. D. Lysenko*.[16] The book reviewed how Lysenko's dictatorship made it almost impossible for biologists to give talks, to travel to conferences abroad, or to publish freely either at home or abroad. In 1970 Medvedev was punished for his dissent by being committed to a mental hospital.

Also in 1963 two heterodox stories by a Soviet author writing under the pen name Ivan Valerii appeared as *The Bluebottle* in London, translated anonymously by Manya Harari. It was followed in 1965 by a second book, *Ward 7: An Autobiographical Novel*, by the same author, but this time under his real name, Valery Tarsis.[17] These two manuscripts had been smuggled out of the Soviet Union. In the second book Tarsis describes in detail his harrowing experience of being interned in a psychiatric hospital for eight months after his first book appeared, and treated as if he were mentally ill. Describing the ways in which psychiatry was being systematically abused in the Soviet Union to quash dissent, the book was an education to Western society and especially its psychiatrists.

The year 1962 also saw the publication, in *Novyi mir*, of Alexander Solzhenitsyn's *One Day in the Life of Ivan Denisovich*, which revealed for the first time how forced-labor sentences for innocent people were a major though strictly secret feature of life under Stalin. And a very different and much less oppositional writer, the poet Yevgeny Yevtushenko, was allowed to tour several Western countries. In England he came to read his poetry in Cambridge, where I was studying and had the chance to speak with him in my fractured Russian. His loud delivery and melodramatic manner certainly held his audiences. But he proved to be only a regime-tolerated figure who never strayed too far off the reservation.

In June 1965 the Kremlin began to harden its policies toward dissidents. Several were arrested in Leningrad, then twenty or so in Ukraine, then Sinyavsky and Daniel in Moscow. Then, in 1966, the KGB confiscated Solzhenitsyn's archive and also persuaded its political masters to pass two new laws, articles 190-1 and 190-3 of the Criminal Code, which made it easier to prosecute secular and religious dissenters for their writings and their actions. In early 1967, Alexander Ginzburg and Yuri Galanskov—

the editors of two notable new collections of samizdat writings who had earlier held unauthorized literary readings on Moscow squares and put out collections of poetry—were arrested, along with some of their associates. Ginzburg had compiled and edited a transcript of Sinyavsky and Daniel's trial, with related documents; Galanskov had edited a collection of literary and politically oriented writings called *Feniks* (The phoenix). Their arrests were followed in 1968 by a sensational trial, many protests by dissidents, and heavy sentences.[18]

Meanwhile, the KGB crackdown since June 1965 had motivated Yesenin-Volpin and a notable young dissenter, Vladimir Bukovsky, to organize the first well-planned demonstration of protest, mainly targeting the upcoming trial of Sinyavsky and Daniel: protesters demanded that it be open to the public. The protest took place in Moscow's Pushkin Square on Constitution Day (Den' Konstitutsii), December 5, 1965, and was a huge success, with an unprecedentedly large turnout. But there were some arrests—including, just before the protest, of Bukovsky, who was committed to a mental hospital.[19] The Sinyavsky-Daniel trial was scheduled for January 1966, in Moscow. The demand that it should be open was not met, except that a few relatives of the defendants were admitted. With the help of the defense lawyers, they were able to secretly provide the materials for an extraordinarily full verbatim record of the proceedings.[20] The defendants were found guilty of writing and then spreading libelous anti-Soviet materials, and were given seven years (Sinyavsky) and five years (Daniel) of hard labor.

Over time, the December 5, 1965, demo came to be widely seen as the major event that marked the coming together of a human rights movement in the Soviet Union, a movement that lasted for twenty-five years, until the collapse of the Soviet Union. Bukovsky, released from the mental hospital in August 1966, played an important role in maintaining the movement's momentum. The demo was not his first foray into standing up for dissenters. Starting in 1960, when he was just eighteen and a student he had suffered numerous reprisals, including internments in mental hospitals that totaled nearly three years, for various dissident acts. In January 1967 he and some colleagues protested on Pushkin Square, demanding that Galanskov, Ginzburg, and their associates be released from detention and the charges against them dropped. For this they themselves were arrested. At their vehemently contested trial seven months later, where courageous lawyers presented a powerful defense based on the principles of "legalist" dissent articulated by Yesenin-Volpin, Bukovsky received a sentence of three years in a labor camp. The dissident Pavel Litvinov soon issued as samizdat a strikingly detailed transcript of the trial.[21]

As if in response to this blow struck for freedom and transparency, the Politburo decided to get rid of the inexperienced KGB head, Vladimir Semichastny, and promote in his stead an upcoming politician, Yuri Andropov, to head the KGB. It turned out to be a good choice—for the KGB: Andropov proved to be a flexible but persistent enemy of human rights; in 1974 he was elevated to the Politburo; in 1982 he succeeded Brezhnev, at the pinnacle of power, becoming the fourth general secretary of the Communist Party.

The "Legalist" Argument for Dissent outside the USSR

The legalist argument for dissent put forward by Yesenin-Volpin may have spread outside the USSR and influenced events in other Communist countries. Research shows that it has also been used, and perhaps copied, in a number of other Communist countries, notably China. In early 2012 a blind Chinese legal activist, Chen Guancheng, fled his home in the Chinese provinces and sought sanctuary in the American embassy in Beijing. Later in the year he was allowed to leave for the United States, where he gave a press conference in which he called on the Chinese Communist Party to respect its own laws that protect freedom of speech. "The problem is not that there are no laws," he said, "but they are not being well enforced." He made clear that he was not asking for the ouster of the party or even the end of one-party rule in China. Rather, he was asking that the party abide by its own laws, as well as give protection against arbitrary detention and torture. This was basically a legalist argument.[22]

The Chinese regime used similar tactics as the Soviets in trying to prevent Western journalists and scholars from analyzing and reporting on dissidents in China. Their methods were examined in a lengthy article by Jay Nordlinger, whose only mistake, in my view, was to suggest that the Chinese were tougher and more successful than their counterparts in the USSR—I don't see much difference.[23]

The Key Role of Translators

Translators were central to the success of the samizdat movement and thus to the eventual victory over repression of opinion and free speech—yet translators' role is sometimes overlooked or underrated. Without translators how would the West have known of dissident writers and writing in the Soviet Union? Furthermore, many translators, writers, and publishers took great personal risks on behalf of dissidents and their works. Three of the most important translators and Sovietologists I had the privilege to know were Manya Harari, Max Hayward, and Patricia Blake. Their contributions were enormous, and without them many valuable publications would never have appeared and the movement for freedom of speech in the USSR would have been set back significantly, or quite possibly, strangled at birth.

Manya Harari was born in 1906 in Baku, Russia, to well-to-do Jewish parents who emigrated to London in 1914. She grew up bilingual, which, coupled with a good education, enabled her to become a fine translator. She was a person of great courage and modesty who traveled widely, co-founded in 1946 and co-directed London's Harvill Press (named for Harari and Marjorie Villiers; it is now part of Harvill Secker), wrote a book of enchanting, if unfinished, memoirs, and had numerous friends in Russia and the West. She made friends through her gift for honest, sympathetic conversation and, in Russia, through giving clothes, including a fur coat, to impoverished people whom she couldn't bear to see suffering in their country's Arctic winds.[24]

The books and other works that she translated, sometimes under pseudonyms, included Pavel Litvinov's transcript of the trial of Bukovsky, works by Pasternak (*Doctor Zhivago*, which she co-translated with Max Hayward), Solzhenitsyn, and Sinyavsky, and Valery Tarsis's two books. Later a few people learned that she had smuggled Tarsis's and other manuscripts out of the USSR when she returned to London from a trip in 1961. She never spoke of this.

As the owner of Harvill Press she was able to publish her and Max Hayward's translation of *Doctor Zhivago* in September 1958; an Americanized translation was brought out by Pantheon in October. Most of the reviews were ecstatic. They also jointly translated a play by Pasternak, *Slepaya krasavitsa* (*The Blind Beauty*, 1969), and *Nezhelannoe puteshestvie v Sibir* (*Involuntary Journey to Siberia*, 1970), an engagingly written memoir by Andrei Amalrik about his and his wife's exile to Siberia.[25]

Manya continued to educate herself and broaden her understanding of the context of dissident literature and samizdat, not only through travel. On occasion she would slip into the LSE seminar on Soviet affairs run by Leonard Schapiro and me, thus deepening my connections with her. Once she asked if I could give a short presentation on Soviet censorship to a conference on oppression in the USSR, and I willingly agreed.

Patricia Blake described Harari as a "frail-looking woman of great distinction and beauty," who "was also one of the most strong-willed and principled people I have ever known." In 1959 Blake took messages from Harari and Hayward to Pasternak in the Soviet Union, who had studied their translation with enthusiasm. She reported that "he held out his arms to me with extraordinary fervor, saying 'I embrace my translators.'" Later he took the risky step of instructing that they be given a present from his royalties of $4,000 each.[26]

Max Hayward was born into a modest working-class family and grew up in a village near Sheffield in Yorkshire, from which his parents moved several times, before eventually returning. Winning scholarships to a private school and then Oxford University, he studied languages, eventually concentrating on Russian. He was a perfect complement to Harari—highly intelligent, instinctively cooperative with people whom he liked, and a supreme linguist who locked himself in a room for six weeks in 1956 to learn the remarkably difficult language of Hungarian. He wanted to better help refugees from Hungary's crushed revolution of that year. In addition, he was a superbly talented scholar of the Soviet Union, especially its literature, and also wrote with expertise about the tsarist empire. He could instantly make friends with people of all sorts in the places he visited or lived in, whether it was Oxford, New York, or, in his final decade, blessedly warm Greece.

He was also a man who never got over his feeling of being a proletarian and therefore an alien in the upper-middle-class world that he inhabited from about age thirteen onward—on occasion, he called himself a peasant, or *muzhichok*.

My own friendship with Max stemmed from meetings with him in the early 1960s, arranged by his student Martin Dewhirst. Not only did I see many of the qualities just described, but fortunately he also came to trust me. As a result he asked me, and I rashly agreed, to take on a job for which he didn't have the time, namely, editing a volume of short stories in Russian and English to be published by Penguin Books.[27]

One time when he came to dinner at our house, we were talking about languages and it came up that my wife, Kathy, spoke Turkish. Max volunteered that he too spoke some Turkish, and they proceeded to exchange some remarks in that language. It was, as things turned out, one of the fifteen tongues that he spoke with some degree of fluency.

Early in his career he worked in the British embassy in Moscow and then as a teacher of Russian at Leeds University. His modesty and self-effacement were natural and extreme, and he had little personal life but threw himself into his work. He died too early, from cancer, at the age of fifty-four. In 1979 I learned that he was in hospital in Oxford and I wanted to visit him. However, I phoned him first to see if he would like a visit, and as we chatted it became clear that he was in poor shape. He added, in an apparently fairly cheerful voice, "It won't be long now till I'll be out of here." But I feared that the implication was not a favorable one, and indeed, a few weeks later he died. His Church of England memorial service, held in Oxford, was crammed with those who celebrated Max's life.

Max wrote dozens of articles about Russian literature and writers; although he never wrote a book, Patricia Blake, who had long worked with him as a friend, compiled and published in 1984 a volume of his selected writings—about Pasternak, Sinyavsky, Solzhenitsyn, Akhmatova, and many others known and less known. Leonard Schapiro provided the collection with a thoughtful preface, and Blake herself wrote a brilliant sixty-page introduction and put together an invaluable bibliography of Hayward's exactly one hundred articles, chapters, translations, and editorships.

Blake wrote that Max brought to his work "strong analytical powers, much erudition, seriousness of purpose, and reserves of saving wit and mischief." In a widely quoted judgment, she stated that through his work, he had "acted as the custodian of Russia's literature until such time as it could be restored to its people."[28]

The renowned critic John Bayley, the author of books about Pushkin and Tolstoy, in his review of Blake's collection of Hayward's work, called Hayward

> the most distinguished linguistic scholar of his generation, and one of the most remarkable personalities in the field of Russian studies. His death . . . was a sad blow not only to scholarship but to the academic equivalent of Dr Johnson's "gaiety of nations." . . . He had

> an incomparable sense of great literature as the embodiment of a great language: he sensed it, as a colleague said, "with a perfect pitch, embracing its heartbeat.". . . His tone is always modest and rather impersonal; but the essays in this book—models of economy, detachment, and precision—are the most valuable that we possess about modern Russian and Soviet literature.[29]

Leonard Schapiro wrote of Hayward that he was "one of the few really outstanding scholars in the Russian field to have emerged" in Britain since World War II. "He had a profound knowledge of Russia and things Russian, and his judgment was unerring and penetrating, and never eccentric, wrong-headed, or sentimental."[30]

The eminent literary scholar Clarence Brown summed up what many had experienced: "His flair for friendship, his phenomenal linguistic gifts, and his virtual clairvoyance in the matter of literary trends had, I believe, the effect of eclipsing, even for his admirers, several other qualities: the cogency and acuteness of his literary discriminations, the historical depth of his acquaintance with Russian culture, and, above all, the intensity of his feeling for the moral urgency at the heart of the greatest Russian writings of this century."[31]

The third in my troika of translators, Patricia Blake, started her career working as a journalist, including a stint in Moscow as a correspondent for *Life* magazine. Starting in the early 1960s and influenced by her time in Moscow, however, she turned away from conventional journalism to study and publicize new writing in Russia. With frequent help from Hayward, she edited, published, and sometimes co-translated seven collections of different sorts, which was a major contribution to Western understanding of the Soviet Union of that time.[32] One of her most influential contributions was "New Voices in Russian Writing," which appeared in *Encounter* in April 1963. In the latter part of her life, Blake was working on a biography of Isaac Babel, the famous Jewish writer from Odessa of the 1920s and 1930s, who was murdered by Stalin's henchmen in 1940.

The Maturation of the Human Rights Movement

In 1967 detailed knowledge of the conditions in Soviet labor camps and prisons emerged for the first time. This added to the ferment that enabled the human rights movement to become a real force. Larissa Bogoraz, Yuli

Daniel's wife, publicized material provided by her husband, and in December a new dissident, Anatoly Marchenko, appeared on the scene and issued in samizdat his remarkable firsthand account of camp life, *Moi pokazaniya* (*My Testimony*, 1969).

Also striking on the individual level was Solzhenitsyn's famous letter of 1967 on a hitherto somewhat neglected theme, censorship, that bore down heavily on all the groups in the movement. Sending it to the fourth Congress of Soviet Writers, he called for the abolition of "the now intolerable oppression of censorship. . . . Not provided for by the constitution and therefore illegal, it is nowhere called by its proper name and goes under the mysterious label of 'Glavlit,'" he wrote (Glavlit was an acronym for the Russian name for the General Directorate for the Protection of State Secrets in the Press, the censorship agency founded in 1922). Because of this "survival of the Middle Ages . . . our writers are not trusted, not endowed with the right to express their cautionary judgments about the moral life of human beings and society, to interpret in their own way social problems or the historical experience which has been lived through with so much suffering in our country." The letter resonated in wide circles and many varieties of samizdat.

It also emboldened some dissidents such as Litvinov and Larissa Bogoraz to speak out publicly. In January 1968 they called on the West to condemn the secrecy of the Galanskov-Ginzburg trial, which was still under way, and to demand for themselves and all Soviet citizens the right to attend it. Immediately after the trial ended, Litvinov quietly met with relatives of the defendants who had been allowed to attend and painstakingly put together as accurate a transcript as possible, and then checked it with still other people who had been present at the trial. In this way he compiled a remarkably full and accurate account of the trial and related issues, *Protsess chetyrekh* (August 1968). It was translated by Manya Harari (as mentioned earlier) and published in English as *The Trial of the Four* in 1972.

Previously available short accounts of these materials hardly prepared the reader, I wrote in my introduction to the English edition of Litvinov's book,

> for the full magnificence, detail, and three-dimensional images of *The Trial of the Four*. Here were the full texts of letters not just from Muscovites but also from individuals and groups in Leningrad,

> Kiev, Odessa, Latvia, Novosibirsk, Gorky, and Pskov. Here were not merely the hundred-odd protest signatures of the Sinyavsky-Daniel trial, but those of more than a thousand Soviet citizens, from a variety of professions and backgrounds. Here was the evidence that intellectuals and students, writers and scientists, Crimean Tatars and Ukrainians, neo-Leninists and liberals, Christian socialists and Marxists, were all concerned about the same thing: the prevention of injustices which indicated neo-Stalinist tendencies in the regime.[33]

A month after the trial the first broad appeal for improved human rights was signed by a Crimean Tatar, an Orthodox Christian, and ten Moscow dissidents. Their letter went to many Soviet and foreign recipients.

In the later 1960s, documents on human rights produced by particular groups and movements, especially those of the Ukrainians, Balts, Baptists, Russian Orthodox, Georgians, Jews, Crimean Tatars, Meskhetians, and general defenders of human rights around the country, began to spread much further afield, but concentrating especially in Moscow, the capital of the country's broadly based movement of dissent. Also, their styles of argument and their types of documentation started to converge on a consistent message, as they followed the path prescribed by Yesenin-Volpin's "legalist" philosophy on rights. All this prepared the ground for the founding, in April 1968, of a means for the human rights movement to track and communicate its progress in a regular samizdat periodical, *Khronika tekushchikh sobytii*, which was soon to appear in English as *The Chronicle of Current Events*.[34]

SIX

The Other '68

Upheaval in the Soviet Bloc and the Chronicle of Current Events

In April 1968 I received a phone call at the LSE from the Russian service of the British Broadcasting Corporation, the BBC. The service's chief political commentator, Anatol Goldberg, asked me to come across the street to his office. When I arrived there he told me he had just received a big envelope for me from the BBC's Moscow correspondent, Denis Blakeley. He handed it over and I took it back to my office.

Khronika tekushchikh sobytii

On opening it, I found a short personal note from the physicist and dissenter Pavel Litvinov, whom I had never met but knew of from his public activity. He was a grandson of Maxim Litvinov, who served as Soviet Minister of Foreign Affairs in the 1930s and was lucky enough to die in his own bed. Some of my journalistic articles had been summarized on the BBC; Pavel had evidently heard them and decided I would be a suitable recipient for the enclosure.

The packet that he handed to me turned out to be a typewritten document of some fifteen pages in Russian, with the title *Khronika tekushchikh sobytii* (Chronicle of current events) and a masthead proclaiming, in Russian, "Human Rights Year in the Soviet Union" (the UN had designated 1968 as International Human Rights Year). No editor was named. The front page quoted Article 19 of the Universal Declaration of Human Rights: "Everyone has the right to freedom of opinion and expression; this right includes freedom to hold opinions without interference and to seek, receive, and impart information and ideas through any media and regardless of frontiers." This quotation also appeared in every one of the sixty-three subsequent typewritten issues of *Khronika* that were put out and circulated as samizdat from 1968 to 1983.[1]

This first issue featured some two dozen accounts of recent episodes of human rights violations, in a variety of fields, that had occurred in Moscow, Leningrad, Kiev, Novosibirsk, and the forced-labor camps in the Republic of Mordovia, which held many political and religious prisoners. The language was restrained and factual throughout, and the document was for publication after April 30. Among the five Soviet groups that featured in issue 1 were democrats and nationalists in the Ukraine, Estonia, and Latvia; Crimean Tatars exiled since 1944 in Uzbekistan; and Russians exercising various kinds of basic human rights.

I made copies and sent them to people I knew in several countries who had outlets—groups of activists—that I guessed would be interested. This proved to be true.

A little later, issue 2 of *Khronika* reached me by a different devious route, followed in due course over fourteen years by all the subsequent issues, sent initially to me or to others—all except for issue 59, which was seized by the KGB and could not be retrieved until after Communism collapsed, and issue 65, which was compiled, but not released until much later, out of fear of severe KGB reprisals. *Khronika*'s mission was to keep track of and report on all human rights abuses in the Soviet Union and disseminate this information domestically and internationally.

Initially, the anonymity of the editors naturally aroused concerns on the part of Western recipients about possible inaccuracy and bias, so we examined the contents very closely. After a few issues had appeared and been given this treatment, our concerns were laid to rest. My own uncertainty had never been great, because I had followed Litvinov's previous activities and writing, and noted his sharp focus on accuracy and the avoidance of bias against any dissenter's views or the government's. I assumed that he was the editor, or one of a group of editors, but I had to conceal his role in sending me the first issue.

The reliability of *Khronika* was that much more important because a number of academics and others professed skepticism regarding the authenticity of samizdat in general—whether because of their ignorance of the true feelings of many Soviet people, or out of fear of being considered anti-Soviet or "right-wing" by their colleagues, or out of a concern that they would not get visas to the USSR if they were known to take samizdat seriously. Also, some analysts remained convinced for a year or two after samizdat started appearing on a fairly regular basis that most samizdat works were in effect forgeries, produced either by KGB provocateurs trying to entrap foreigners or by émigré organizations hoping to deceive people into thinking that a serious opposition was emerging in the Soviet Union when it wasn't. Most painful of all were occasional articles claiming that certain named dissidents either were imaginary or were provocateurs. For example, in one such article the dissident author Andrei Amalrik was denounced as a provocateur.[2]

Much later it became known that the editor of issues 1 through 10 was the poet Natalya Gorbanevskaya and that the group of subsequent editors included Tatyana Velikanova, Sergei Kovalev (issues 11–17), Lyudmila Alexeyeva, Tatyana Khodorovich, Pyotr Yakir, Irina Yakir, Anatoly Yakobson, Galya Gabai, Nadezhda Emelkina, and Yuri Shikhanovich. Some issues had more than one editor.

The most revealing account I have read of *Khronika*'s emergence and early years is in the outstanding biography of Natalya Gorbanevskaya (1936–2013) by Lyudmila Ulitskaya, *Poetka: Kniga o pamyati: Natalya Gorbanevskaya* (Poet: Book in memory of Natalya Gorbanevskaya).[3] Ulitskaya quotes Pavel Litvinov's recollection: "In 1967–68 a group of the first members of the human rights movement spontaneously came together. Each one did what they could, but in the air hung the idea of a bulletin. Then Natasha [Gorbanevskaya] just said, 'I'll do it.'" To give her the desirable privacy, Litvinov then moved to a spare apartment belonging to his family, and she began work in the empty space.

Regarding the format and tone of the bulletin, Ulitskaya writes that at this time the newly formed group of dissidents, through Aleksei Kosterin and a prominent dissident, General Pyotr Grigorenko, became friendly with some of the Crimean Tatars who regularly came to Moscow from Uzbekistan, in Central Asia, where their community had been exiled in the forties, to lobby for permission to return home to the Crimea. "And they issued an information bulletin. Regularly." Gorbanevskaya promptly adopted its format and tone, thereby setting an example for others.

One factor that helped inspire confidence in *Khronika* was the speed with which its geographical and topical range expanded. Although its editors were anonymous, clearly they were trusted, and more and more groups wanted to have their material included in its issues. Thus, whereas issue 1 carried substantial reports from only five places, in issue 11 it was twenty-nine locations: in central and eastern Russia, the Ukraine (five locations), the Baltic republics, Central Asia, and from five Western and Central European countries. Most of the items from the Western and Central European countries were summaries of responses to news of the persecution of Soviet dissidents. Also included were cases in various remote places of exile in Russia; Kaliningrad, in western Russia; Kazan, in Tatarstan; and the prison in Vladimir. Some of the persecuted groups and individuals were Andrei Sakharov, Jews, the exiled Meskhetians, the Russian military, the Russian Orthodox, and the Baptists.

To get the journal translated, at first I asked sympathetic friends to translate each issue for free. I would then edit it, have copies made, and send them to interested parties, such as Amnesty International (Bruce Laird), Radio Liberty (Peter Dornan), and my friend Anthony de Meeus in Belgium. The minimal costs were borne by me and the LSE mailing system. Starting with issue 12, however, I managed to get a small payment of fifty pounds per issue from the Information Research Department of the Foreign Office in return for sending this group a few dozen copies. This enabled me to pay the translators a small sum for their work.

I also received some support for my *Khronika* translations from Amnesty International, of which I was a member. By late 1970 my friends at Amnesty were the Soviet researcher Clayton Yeo and the head of research, Zbynek Zeman, an academic historian of Czech origin. My goal in approaching them was to try, jointly with them, to persuade Amnesty to publish *Khronika* in English, which would benefit Amnesty's many groups that were helping Soviet prisoners via their families and by other means. Our efforts eventually succeeded—when we finally overcame sustained efforts to block them by Amnesty's chairman, Sean McBride, who had some pro-Soviet sympathies. Issue 16 was the first formally published issue of *A Chronicle of Current Events*; all subsequent issues appeared as booklets with names indexed in proper published form, and were available to the Amnesty groups and the public for a modest charge. Issue 16 came out in early 1971. Routledge Journals, a commercial company, soon took on the distribution for Amnesty, and before long the conscientious Marjorie

Farquharson was put in charge of the operation. From then on Amnesty paid for the translators and the circulation costs. As an Amnesty member with a paid job at the LSE, I was happy to be a volunteer editor; I edited the translations for accuracy and clarity, and added footnotes that would assist readers.

Challenges of Smuggling Samizdat Materials Out of the USSR

Getting *Khronika* and other samizdat documents and manuscripts out of the USSR was difficult and could be risky. The ease of the handoff of issue 1 of *Khronika* by Denis Blakeley to me was not typical. The individuals who took the biggest risks were the dissidents who had to initiate the process in the USSR, so their names were usually kept strictly secret. The ones who I know for sure did this at various periods were Alexander Yesenin-Volpin, Vladimir Bukovsky, Pavel Litvinov, Pyotr Yakir, Yevgeny Barabanov, and Zviad Gamsakhurdia. A complete list would, I feel sure, be considerably longer.

Some of the foreigners who accepted documents from dissidents and either risked carrying them out or persuaded diplomats to send them out were academics: Martin Dewhirst, who passed his documents to the Possev publishing house in Frankfurt; Karel van het Reve, a Dutch professor of literature; and Stephen Cohen, a professor of Russian studies at Princeton, who passed materials to Valery Chalidze, an émigré human rights advocate in New York. In Moscow there were individuals who were willing to accept and smuggle out documents: Mario Corti, who started as a nondiplomatic translator for the Italian embassy and later became an academic, writer, and researcher; and the American diplomat Martin Wenick, who collected documents, among them many Jewish ones, and passed most of them to Paul Cook, an official in Washington.

Others who accepted documents and found ways to get them out of the USSR were the translator and publisher Manya Harari (see chapter 5); Tania Mathon of Paris; the Reverend Michael Bourdeaux and Jane Ellis, who both focused on religious materials; graduate students spending a year in the USSR such as Konstantin Huytan of Canada, who had documents on psychiatric abuse sent to the Canadian embassy in London and then to me; students who made short trips to Russia, such as Stephen Glick and Dan Yaffe; and a number of tourists whose travel plans I learned about and whom I asked to pick up documents and information. Among them was my friend David Markham, a prominent actor who picked up an issue of *Khronika* from Yesenin-Volpin, but had it confiscated during a nasty search by the KGB when he was leaving the country—possibly as a result of Yesenin-Volpin's being overtalkative. Fortunately, this was the only incident of its sort that I knew of.

In addition, the movement for human rights received considerable moral and practical support from sympathetic Western journalists based in Moscow. One of the most important of these was the above-mentioned Dutch professor Karel van het Reve, who worked in Moscow as a correspondent for the newspaper *Het Parool* in 1967–1968 and became close to Andrei Amalrik, Pavel Litvinov, Larissa Bogoraz, and others. He was also the first person to get the dissident physicist Andrei Sakharov's long essay, "Thoughts on Progress, Peaceful Coexistence and Intellectual Freedom" out to the West, by translating it into Dutch and "telephon[ing] it, all ten thousand words of it, from Moscow to Amsterdam," where it was published in 1968. Evidently the phone censor "didn't know enough Dutch to understand what I was doing." The essay was published in full.[4]

The appearance of Sakharov's essay was a seminal event in the history of samizdat and of the human rights movement. Sakharov, a brilliant nuclear physicist who had been a leading light in the USSR's development of a nuclear arsenal, had come to question his life's work in favor of campaigning for disarmament and peace. In the essay he examines questions of peace, coexistence, and intellectual freedom in the context of East-West relations, arguing that they are all interrelated. These relations will be threatened if any of the three conditions are abused by either side. Thus while peace and coexistence are practiced intermittently, intellectual freedom is regrettably absent in the Soviet Union. So, Sakharov writes, Soviet dissidents should help the Kremlin in this sphere by continuing to practice Yesenin-Volpin's legalist dissent and showing that they are observing Soviet law and not trying to overthrow the system.

Although Sakharov's lack of training in law and political theory made the essay seem naïve in places, it was still a remarkable creative feat and aroused enormous interest both in the West and, through samizdat and Western radio, in the USSR. It helped to put samizdat on the map.

When Karel finished his year in Moscow he managed to bring out—

through the Dutch embassy?—a rich collection of one hundred or so samizdat documents. At my request, he sent these to my friend Peter Dornan at Radio Liberty in Munich, who used them as the foundation of the best collection of such documents in the world, to which I and others contributed about a thousand more over the next nearly twenty years. Each week, with extraordinary dedication, Dornan edited, retyped, and sent around to one or two hundred interested parties packets of half a dozen of the latest acquisitions. Retyping was necessary so that the KGB would not see a copy of the original typeface and use it to forensically track down the original typewriter—and the person who had done the typing and found a way to send the material abroad. Dornan also got help from two dedicated assistants, Mario Corti, who became a colleague, and Martin Dewhirst of Glasgow University, who worked with Dornan for a few summers. Corti later wrote a long article about the history of samizdat, which he dedicated to Dornan.[5]

Other journalists who quietly helped smuggle out samizdat and reported seriously from Moscow on dissidents, and in some cases wrote relevant books, were David Bonavia of the London *Times*; Roger Leddington and James Peipert of the Associated Press; Anthony Astrachan and Hedrick Smith of the *New York Times*; William Cole of CBS; Alfred Friendly of *Newsweek*; Robert Kaiser and Kevin Klose of the *Washington Post*; Hal Piper of the *Baltimore Sun*; David Satter of the *Financial Times*; and Frank Starr and James Yuenger of the *Chicago Tribune*. Yuenger achieved a record by picking up issue 21 of *Khronika* from Pyotr Yakir in 1971 on the day it came out, which happened to be the day he was leaving for London on vacation. He brought it to my house the same evening. I feel lucky to have known and been able to assist these journalists. On many occasions I would suddenly find myself receiving unfamiliar and unexpected samizdat documents, usually by mysterious channels.

A number of individuals worked to create their own channels for smuggling documents out: Mario Corti in Milan, Nikita Struve in Paris, Valery Chalidze from 1973 in New York, Cronid Lubarsky from 1976 in Munich, and, a little later, Maria Sinyavsky-Rozanova (Sinyavsky's wife), also in Paris. Chalidze, Lubarsky, and Sinyavsky-Rozanova were all recent arrivals from the USSR and so they had extensive circles of friends and contacts in the USSR. Of course many others were involved in this effort beyond those mentioned here, whom I knew personally. Streams of smuggled samizdat that I knew little of were the work of those involved in all the different stages of getting materials out of Ukraine, the Baltic states, Georgia, and Armenia.

August 1968: Prague—Moscow

Four months after *Khronika* was launched in the USSR, two momentous events occurred that the journal was able to cover with remarkable thoroughness. The first was the Soviet-led invasion of Czechoslovakia on August 20, 1968, by tens of thousands of troops (from the USSR and four other Eastern Bloc countries), to crush the systematic liberalization of the political, economic, and social system in that country by Alexander Dubcek and his colleagues. The second was the response to the invasion five days later in Moscow: the demonstration that was mounted by eight dissenters on Red Square to protest the invasion. They sat on a stone platform in front of St. Basil's Cathedral and unrolled banners whose Russian-language slogans included "Hands off Czechoslovakia," "Down with the Occupiers," and, in Czech, "Long Live Free and Independent Czechoslovakia" and "For Your Freedom and Ours."[6]

The eight demonstrators were Viktor Fainberg, Pavel Litvinov, Larissa Bogoraz, Konstantin Babitsky, Vadim Delaunay, Vladimir Dremliuga, Tatiana Baeva, and Natalya Gorbanevskaya, who had her baby son with her. Seven of the demonstrators were arrested. In a two-page letter to the editors of world newspapers on August 28, Gorbanevskaya, the only demonstrator then at liberty because she had two sons, described what happened: "Almost immediately a whistle blew and plainclothes KGB men rushed at us from all corners of the square. They were on duty in Red Square, waiting for a Czechoslovak delegation's departure from the Kremlin. They ran up shouting, 'They're all Jews!', 'Beat the anti-Sovietists!' We sat quietly and didn't resist. They tore the banners from our hands. They beat Viktor Fainberg in the face until he bled, and knocked his teeth out. They hit Pavel Litvinov about the face with a heavy bag, and snatched away from me a Czechoslovak flag and smashed it. They shouted at us, 'Disperse, you scum!' But we remained sitting. After a few minutes cars arrived and all except me were bundled into them."

Ten minutes later another car pulled up, and Gorbanevskaya and her baby son were collected. "In the car they beat me. Several individuals from the crowd that had gathered, people who had expressed their sympathy with us, were arrested along with us, and released only late in the evening. During the night, searches were made of the apartments of all those held, on the charge of 'group activities flagrantly violating public order.'"

The authorities then released the author, only to summon her for subsequent interrogations. She continued: "I refuse to give evidence on the organization and conduct of the demonstration, since it was a peaceful demonstration that did not disturb public order. But I did give evidence about the rough and illegal actions of the people who detained us: I am ready to testify to this before the world public."

She concluded: "My comrades and I are happy that we were able to take part in this demonstration, that we were able, if only for a moment, to interrupt the torrent of barefaced lies and the cowardly silence, to show that not all the citizens of our country are in agreement with the violence that's being used in the name of the Soviet people. We hope that the people of Czechoslovakia have learned, or will learn about this. And the belief that the Czechs and the Slovaks, when thinking about the Soviet people, will think not only of the occupiers, but also of us, gives us strength and courage." Gorbanevskaya's letter was reprinted in issue 3 of *Khronika* a couple of days later.

The demonstration had not come out of the blue. Events in Czechoslovakia had enormously encouraged Soviet dissidents, who saw that the sort of liberalization they had been campaigning for at home could in fact take place in a Communist country. As the Kremlin had increased the pressure on its ally to reverse course, various dissenters protested publicly—in speeches and in writing—demanding that it leave Czechoslovakia alone. The actual invasion on August 20–21, overwhelmingly condemned around the non-Communist world and even, vehemently, by China, only increased the dissidents' concerns and directly provoked the demonstration. Immediately after it, personal protests recorded by *Khronika* occurred in Moscow, Leningrad, Tartu, and Novosibirsk, and many people refused to sign the statements approving the invasion that they were ordered to sign at their places of work. In this way they often incurred serious reprisals. Later, *Khronika* reported on many other protests and the severe punishments meted out to most of the protesters, including in some cases forcible internment in mental hospitals.

All the demonstrators were tried over the succeeding months and were sentenced to serve time in a labor camp or to go into exile in the Gulag, or were dispatched to mental hospitals, supposedly "suffering from schizophrenia." In September 1968 Gorbanevskaya received a similar diagnosis and was put under the care of her mother. However, a year later, in August 1969, she released in samizdat her impressive record of the demonstration and of the demonstrators' trial; she and Fainberg—supposedly mentally ill—had not been put on trial but she had been able to attend it. The English translation of this work, titled *Red Square at Noon*, appeared in 1972 and received glowing reviews.[7] Not surprisingly, in her book Gorbanevskaya expressed feelings and views similar to those expressed in her open letter describing the demonstration.

In 1970 there was a court hearing to decide what to do with her. She was not present at the hearing, having been ruled non compos mentis—the exact opposite of a diagnosis she had received a month earlier. One of the charges against her was that she had been the editor of *Khronika*. None of the judges present knew whether to believe this. The court sent her for indefinite detention to the infamous prison–psychiatric hospital in Kazan, where she was held for two years.[8]

Concordance of the Chronicle

In 1970 I decided to take my work on the *Chronicle* further and compile a book that would include the full text of issues 1 to 11 as they had been put out in Moscow through the end of 1969. I decided to slice and dice the material to group it by topic and theme, instead of just reproducing the original sequence of items. I believed this would make it a more valuable resource for historians and other scholars. The topics were :

Khronika itself
The Sinyavsky-Daniel case
The Galanskov-Ginzburg trial
The invasion of Czechoslovakia and the protest demonstration that followed
The trial of the demonstrators
General Pyotr Grigorenko
Action Group for the Defense of Civil Rights
The case of the Baltic Fleet officers
The case of Anatoly Marchenko

Alexander Solzhenitsyn
The labor camps and prisons
The prison mental hospitals
The Crimean Tatars
The Meskhetians
The Ukrainians
The Jews
The Churches
The world of samizdat
Leningrad and the provinces
Stalin, Stalinists, Fascists, and Censors

I added an introduction, a foreword written by Julius Telesin (a dissident who had recently emigrated to Israel, recounting his own history of dissent), and numerous notes.[9] It was important to show the reader that an enormous amount of detail had been revealed by the various dissident movements about themselves and their places of confinement and thus to leave no room for doubt that the material was genuine. Hence, I added seventy photographs of individuals and groups that were central to the book, the title page of issue 6 of *Khronika*, and views of the exteriors of prison–psychiatric hospitals. Finally, I added a detailed map of the complex of labor camps in western Mordovia.

Over the next two years *Khronika* thrived, and the KGB decided that it must try to close the publication down. So, having gathered a lot of information about it through its network of secret agents and technical listening and visual devices, it decided to let the bulletin's compilers know that each new issue would lead straight to the arrest of one of the editors. The editors kept on with their work but were being picked off. After seeing that the threat had not been an empty one and not wanting to lose any more valuable contributors, they decided to cease publication, but they didn't cease collecting material and putting it together into issues. Eighteen months later, the Kremlin wanted to negotiate with the West on introducing policies of detente, so the party line against dissent softened somewhat. In March 1974 *Khronika* came back to life, producing all at once the four issues, 28 to 31, that it had been quietly compiling while lying low. For the next nine years, until its ultimate end in 1983, when KGB pressures became too strong, things proceeded with ups and downs, but without a break. As early as 1974 I had concluded in an article that the dissident groups were producing "gradually mounting pressures for a more plural society, for some genuine politics . . . and for the legitimation of minority nationalism. On the other hand we see a regime increasingly on the defensive, physically powerful, but . . . morally weak."[10] Both *Khronika* and its translation, the *Chronicle*, constituted an indispensable tool that created continuous pressure. In 1978 I wrote a lengthy article, "Notes from Underground," for *The Times Literary Supplement* on *Khronika*'s first fifty-one issues, which informed readers of its continuing good health.[11]

SEVEN

Two Early Giants of Soviet Dissent

Marchenko and Grigorenko

Not all dissidents who worked for human rights in the Soviet Union and published samizdat started off as writers. Two human rights giants who didn't were Anatoly Marchenko (1938–1986), a worker, and Pyotr Grigorenko (1907–1987), a much-decorated general.[1]

Anatoly Tikhonovich Marchenko (b. 1938 in Barabinsk, Siberia; d. 1986 in Chistopol prison, Tatarstan)

Anatoly Marchenko grew up in a proletarian family in the Novosibirsk Oblast in Siberia. With little education, he made a living doing manual odd jobs. One day in about 1958 he had to defend himself in a fight. All those involved were arrested and tried, but were given no chance to present their defense or tell their side of the story. Marchenko was sentenced to six years of forced labor for supposedly resisting arrest. A year or so later he escaped from the camp with a fellow inmate and headed for the Soviet border with Iran, intending to cross it. However, the two were caught and sentenced to even longer terms, for trying to go abroad without official permission. This offense landed him among other political prisoners in one of the infamous Potma forced-labor camps clustered in a secretive off-limits area in southwestern Mordovia. These people helped to educate him.

On his release in 1966, Marchenko settled in Aleksandrov and began to write a book about the USSR's massive system of labor camps and internal exile.[2] He drew on his personal experiences, and on what reliable people in the camps had told him. His book *Moi Pokazaniya* appeared in the fall of 1967 in the Soviet Union in samizdat (photocopies of his original typescript); as *My Testimony*, in the U.K. in 1969, and as *Moi Pokazaniya* in Germany in 1969.[3] The *New York Times* published extracts in the United States, which prompted a weak, off-topic response, in English, from the Soviet news agency, TASS.[4] Earlier Marchenko had written a powerful appeal a week before the invasion of Czechoslovakia in August 1968, calling on the Kremlin not to do anything as intrusive and brutal as to invade.

His book, whether in Russian or in translation, drew enthusiastic reviews wherever it appeared, not all of them written by writers or professional critics. For example, Father Sergei Zheludkov, in the Soviet Union, in an open letter to church leaders, summarized *Moi pokazaniya*'s sobering message, quoting the author's sympathetic passage on the wide variety of religious prisoners being held. He concluded: "Such is the evidence; its veracity can, if one wishes, fairly easily be checked. I present it for examination by your Christian consciences. I feel that the sincerity and spiritual strength of our Christianity are measured by our practical deeds in relation to these facts."

In April 1968 Marchenko sent a six-page summary of his book to a variety of UN, international, and domestic bodies, but, disappointingly, received no response.

I know of only one negative review of the book to appear anywhere and that was in the United States in the *New York Times* "Book Review" section of March 1, 1970. The review, written in an unrelievedly sneering tone, was the work of Harrison Salisbury, the paper's Moscow correspondent from 1949 to 1954, a putative expert on the USSR and China, and an assistant managing editor of the *Times*. Among other insulting epithets he deployed to smear and trivialize Marchenko, Salisbury described him as "melodramatic" and "ooz[ing] with self-pity," and "a rather simple young man . . . a thoroughly naïve or amazingly reckless individual."

A powerful, even scorching rebuttal was sent to the *Times* by the book's well-known and normally calm translator, Michael Scammell, but it did not see print, nor did a caustic letter from Vera Dunham, a professor of literature at Wayne State University. Leonard Schapiro and I also wrote a rebuttal, and we encountered considerable obstacles to getting even a shortened and editorially weakened version of our letter past Salisbury's hidden defenders and into print. The bowdlerized version appeared in the July 19, 1970, edition.

We challenged Salisbury's insulting descriptions of Marchenko. We continued: "Marchenko is not 'a rather simple young man . . . a thoroughly naïve or amazingly reckless individual'—nor do such phrases ring very pleasantly when he is held incommunicado, unable to reply in any way. Finally, it is quite untrue that either the publisher or Max Hayward, the author of the introduction, puts Marchenko on the same literary plane as Solzhenitsyn or Eugenia Ginzburg. Here, as elsewhere, Mr. Salisbury produces no proof—for the simple reason that there is none."

Salisbury gave a brief and ineffectual response in which he failed to reply to any of our criticisms. The reader could only come away with the impression that someone had induced him to discredit Marchenko by writing a lot of falsehoods and implausible judgments.[5]

In July 1968, an infuriated KGB had fabricated new charges against Marchenko and arrested him again, prompting five prominent dissidents to lead a widespread defense of him in a new appeal. They extolled the book and his bravery in writing it after emerging from the camps,

> deaf and suffering from bleeding intestines and severe headaches. . . . His enemies have many ways of sentencing him to a new term on any false pretext. They can do this secretly, or libel him in the press. . . . We, his friends, have only one way of helping him—publicity. As many people as possible should know of his courageous struggle and his new arrest. If you do not want to put up with this tyranny in the future, if you realize that Marchenko has been fighting for all of us and that all of us must fight for Marchenko, we ask you to defend him in the way that you yourself deem desirable.

The marriage of Larissa Bogoraz and the jailed writer Yuli Daniel had ended, and Bogoraz had formed a close relationship with Marchenko. Now she wrote a separate appeal that was based on her personal observations:

> His book . . . aroused such hatred for him in the KGB that they began to bait him like a hare: KGB agents followed on his heels for months on end—I've spotted them so often that I know many

> of them by sight. And not only in Moscow, where he works, and in Aleksandrov, where he lives. He went to visit relatives in Ryazan, but wasn't allowed to get off the train, and had to return to Moscow. Also, he was seized on the street almost immediately after his discharge from hospital. His face was smashed in as he was being pushed into a car when he came to Moscow for a literary evening.

Bogoraz urged people to read Marchenko's book and his open letters on topics of civil rights: "You will see for yourselves that Anatoly Marchenko is not a tramp or an adventurer, but a talented, original writer and publicist, and an uncompromising and courageous man. He is courageous for our sake; for each one of us. . . . As for this being the fate of one man, remember how all the foremost people of France came to the defense of Dreyfus."[6]

Marchenko himself had written earlier that in the event of future proceedings against him, if these were a choreographed show trial in which he had no chance to defend himself, "this would only emphasize the truth of what I have written."[7] However, the *Chronicle*, in issue 10, took a different angle, detailing some of the KGB's deliberate ignoring of medical reports about his dangerously weak health by sending him to a camp in the far north and making him do hard physical labor in temperatures of minus 45 to 50 degrees Celsius. The final sentence: "It is not excluded that those people on whose orders the new case has been organized are aiming for his physical destruction."

However, the plethora of domestic and foreign appeals and protests on his behalf from humanitarian, cultural, political, and religious groups carried enough weight that the KGB did not dare to kill him. Instead, they gave him a two-year sentence in the camps and continued their brutal treatment of him. In 1971 he at last emerged, now under "administrative surveillance," to enjoy a short period of relative freedom, during which he married Bogoraz and they had a son, Pavel.

Three years later, his renewed dissent brought further reprisals, leading him to demand that he be allowed to emigrate to the United States: he had received offers of work and support from Americans. The official response was a renewed arrest and another trial; his response to this was to launch a prolonged hunger strike. The authorities had repeated their insistence that he was free to leave for Israel at any time, but not for the United States. Neither side would budge. The result for Marchenko was a sentence of four years of exile in Chuna, Siberia.[8] On his arrival, he wrote a fifty-page memoir about his journey to get there, *Ot Tarusy do Chuny* (1976; *From Tarusa to Chuna*, 1980). The book included seventy pages of documents, including a transcript of his latest trial and appeals from individual dissidents.[9]

In 1986, while serving a lengthy sentence in the prison at Chistopol in the Tatar Soviet Republic, east of Moscow, Marchenko died while on a hunger strike. He had spent twenty of his forty-eight years in various forms of captivity. But death did not silence his voice. Around 1980 he had created his third book, *Zhivi kak vse* (*To Live like Everyone*, 1989), in which he explains his reflections and descriptions in the period between his two earlier books. Posthumously published in the United States, it includes a poignant foreword by Andrei Sakharov, who calls the author "one of the most remarkable people of our time."[10]

Larissa Bogoraz also contributed a somber, deeply moving ten-page afterword in which she describes her determined but ultimately fruitless efforts to learn what her husband had died from and how it had happened. She went to Chistopol with some friends to try to get information but received a long succession of blatant lies and evasions from a doctor and an official. Nonetheless, she used some accidental leaks and her own detective powers to deduce that he had been on a hunger strike for a long time before his death, which surely had greatly weakened him. Although she was his wife, her requests for his papers, other possessions and death certificate were all flatly (and illegally) turned down.

However, her party of nine did succeed in briefly obtaining the coffin. They took it to the Russian Orthodox church they had engaged for a funeral service. The priest "conducted [it] with inspiration," while "the choir of old ladies sang emotionally and with extraordinary beauty." Afterward, "the old ladies, singing, followed the coffin to the bus." Then, in a dignified ceremony, the group buried Marchenko in a cemetery.[11]

Marchenko's work inspired me to write about the labor camps in the press and in my book *Uncensored Russia*. The greatest impact was produced in January 1971 by my full-page article in *The Observer*, "Inside Russia's Concentration Camps," which included striking portraits of six current prisoners in Potma (the cluster of camps in Mordovia), selected from twenty sketched by the longtime inmate Yuri Ivanov of inmates in camp 17.a in late 1969.[12] The drawings had recently been smuggled out of the Mordovian camps to Moscow and then to London. I also included a map, brilliantly created by my friend Victor Swoboda, that showed the thirty-mile siding that joined the main railway line at Potma in Mordovia and the exact locations of the fifteen camps that were strung out along the siding. Swoboda, of Ukrainian origin, was my good colleague at London University's School of Slavonic and East European Studies. He based the map on samizdat sources and a large-scale map of the USSR created with information from photographs taken by high-altitude Western spy planes.

The article featured a mass of detailed information about the Potma camps, the subjects of the portraits, and dozens of their fellows. Most of the stories revolved around their frequent and often incapacitating hunger strikes. Sometimes, surprisingly, these were successful, as when Alexander Ginzburg was eventually allowed to marry his fiancée.

Worst off was the artist Yuri Ivanov, who had been held in captivity for all but a few years since 1947—for his dissent, for refusing to recant, and for trying to escape. Once he was arrested for "forming an organization," whose members "were not discovered." In 1969 the Englishman Gerald Brooke, who had been given a seven-year sentence for bringing in anti-Soviet literature, met him by chance, and was struck by his high morale and attractive personality. A little later I received a smuggled self-portrait done in 1974, in colored inks on a thick piece of paper. Beneath his penetrating eyes and slightly quizzical look was a short beard drawn in orange and long curly hair down to his shoulders.[13]

My article also contained extracts from an open letter by seven political prisoners that was spirited out of camp 17.a with Ivanov's portraits. Among the signers were Ginzburg and his friend Yuri Galanskov, who in 1972 died in captivity at the age of thirty-three for lack of medical care.[14] The letter of 1970 opened thus:

> Russia is entangled in a network of camps, where, despite all the international conventions signed by the Soviet Government, forced labor and cruel exploitation are the norm, where people are systematically kept hungry, and constantly humiliated, where human dignity is debased. Through these camps there passes an uninterrupted human flow . . . which sends people back to society in a physically and morally crippled state. This is the result of a deliberate penal policy, worked out by experts and expounded by them in special handbooks with a cynicism worthy of the concentration camp experts of the Third Reich.

My *Observer* article also used detailed samizdat materials from dissident Baptists, many of whose members were widely scattered in labor camps across the country. Through these materials I had been able to collect extensive information on 202 such camps, including their official designations and exact locations, and also to estimate that there might be a total of about one million camp inmates (a figure that I later reduced somewhat and that certainly came down quite a bit over the next twenty years). Of these, there were perhaps a thousand political prisoners in the Potma camps, and an unknown additional number in other places.

The response of the Soviet press, in its lone reply, did not try to seriously dispute my article, resorting instead to an ad hominem attack: "Why should what seemed to be a reputable paper publish such lies? If the British public were aware of the fact that the author was well known for his anti-Soviet views, they would be able to judge the true value of the 'factual material' he had gathered."[15] Simultaneously, I began to get calls on my home phone where I heard only heavy breathing, but nothing else. When I ignored them, they started to come in the middle of the night. So I contacted the British authorities, who put a call-screening system on my phone and also sent someone to see if any bugs had been secretly installed in my house. There weren't any.

General Pyotr Grigorievich Grigorenko (b. 1907 in Borisovka, Russia; d. 1987 in exile in New York City)

Like Marchenko, Pyotr Grigorenko was born in a village deep in the provinces, in his case, in Ukraine. After losing both parents in the First World War, Pyotr attained a minimal education and went to work with his hands in a metal-processing factory. In 1927 he became the head of the factory's Komsomol unit and soon was launched into the workers' education system. From there he entered a technological institute and then the army's Military Technology Academy. In 1931, as Stalin prepared to launch his "mass terror," Grigorenko became an officer at the age of twenty-four. After serving three years as chief of staff of a sapper battalion, in 1937 he was invited to take a two-year course in cybernetics at the prestigious Academy of the General Staff in Moscow, from which he graduated with first-class honors.

In 1939 Grigorenko saw military action in the Soviet army divisions that defeated the Japanese invaders in the Far East. Later he fought the Germans, marching all the way to the Sudetenland. Twice he was wounded, and once received an official party rebuke for talking critically about Stalin's military purges with a colleague. From 1945 to 1961 he served as head of research, then professor of cybernetics at the Frunze Military Academy in Moscow—the Soviet equivalent of America's West Point and the U.K.'s Sandhurst. In 1956 he was promoted to the rank of major-general. By this point he had received the Order of Lenin, five military awards for valor, and six medals, had earned a master's degree (*kandidatskaya*), had published seventy-eight articles, and had finished his dissertation for a Ph.D. (*doktorskaya*) on the subject of cybernetics and the military.

Along the way to these outstanding military and scholarly achievements Grigorenko also became disaffected with the party, which he criticized mildly in a 1961 speech for "the unwise and in many respects nationally harmful activity of Khrushchev and his associates."[16] Among other things he criticized the privileges that the elite enjoyed. For this he won applause from his military audience, but also a demotion by his superiors and a transfer to military work in the primitive Far East, six thousand miles from Moscow. To him this was further proof that his political position was the right one, and in 1963 he formed a secret Action Group for the Revival of Leninism whose members, as Communists believing in a pure form of Lenin's ideas, entered into quiet discussions with individual officials and also circulated anonymous leaflets. In 1964 he was expelled from the party, arrested, demoted to the ranks, and given a dishonorable discharge from the army.

Fearful of putting the popular Grigorenko on trial and causing an uproar, the authorities played their most refined and insidious card by sending him in 1964, to ward 2 of Moscow's Serbsky Institute of Forensic Psychiatry for in-patient examination. Doctors and criminal investigators demanded that he "make the confession of his political mistakes," but he refused to do so. The consequence was a month of interrogations, designed to compel him to change his mind and then blame his politically deviant behavior on the "schizophrenia" that they claimed he suffered from.

In 1969, after his release, Grigorenko published a revealing essay, "O spetsial'nykh psikhiatricheskikh bol'nitsakh ('Durdomakh')," later published in English as "Concerning the Special Psychiatric Hospitals." This recounted what he had undergone up to that time at the hands of the Soviet psychiatric establishment working with the KGB to suppress dissent.[17] The orchestrator of this ordeal, according to Grigorenko, was Professor

Daniil Lunts, a Soviet psychiatrist whom he saw "coming to work [in the Serbsky Institute] in the uniform of a KGB colonel. True, he always wore a white coat in our ward. I also saw other doctors of the institute in KGB uniforms. What relationship these KGB officers had with the Ministry of Health I did not manage to find out" (the Serbsky Institute was formally subordinate to that ministry).

Grigorenko speculated that the KGB controlled many of the Serbsky's wards, not only the ward for politicals. But even if they controlled only the political ward, "The question arises: Can psychiatric examinations in political cases be objective, if both the investigators and the psychiatrists are subordinate to a single person and are also subject to military discipline?"[18]

Prior to his Serbsky experience, Grigorenko had never thought that such a system of abuse might exist in the Soviet Union. He knew only of the notorious case of the critical writer Pyotr Chaadayev in the 1830s, who expressed dissenting views and as punishment had been officially declared insane by Tsar Nicholas I—but he had not been arrested.

When the chief investigator presented Grigorenko with the official order dispatching him to the Serbsky, he asked the official: "So, have you found a way out of your dead end?" To this, "The already much embarrassed investigator began evasively and confusingly to mumble: 'Pyotr Grigorievich, what are you saying! No, of course, this is a pure formality. You're an absolutely normal person. I don't doubt it. But your medical record has a note about a concussion, and in such cases a psychiatric exam is obligatory. Without it, the court won't accept the case.'" Grigorenko had gotten a concussion as a battleground injury.

Grigorenko went on: "When I noted that before giving such a case to anyone, you must first have an actual case, he assured me that after the psychiatric exam the investigation would continue and a case would be compiled. But to me it became increasingly clear that there would be no investigation and I would just be sent to a psychiatric clinic for the rest of my life (that's what I thought at the time)."

In ward 2 Grigorenko had eleven fellow inmates. Through his conversations with them he made predictions to himself about what fate awaited each one of them: Would they be committed to mental institutions or sent to labor camps? He predicted that only three would be committed to mental institutions, he and two others, because they were the only ones who would not "confess" and against whom the investigators had no case. A fourth one, with whom he later became friends, at first refused to recant.

But he complied after Grigorenko advised him that if he wanted to go to a camp, not an institution, he must make a false confession of guilt. And that was indeed what happened. All the rest, including the only one who was genuinely mentally ill, as Grigorenko accurately predicted, likewise found themselves in labor camps.

So the former general was duly dispatched by a court to the Leningrad Special Psychiatric Hospital for indefinite detention and treatment. His friend Boris Tsukerman wrote in a long, well-documented essay about him, "The general's illness was, apparently, extremely dangerous to those around him: he was not allowed to meet the lawyer appointed to defend him, nor to participate in the investigation or trial of his own case. Neither the general nor his relatives ever saw the verdict."[19]

In his essay Grigorenko describes the institution where he found himself for a year in some detail.[20] He starts with a page of praise for its handling of the nonpolitical inmates, who made up the great majority: "Only in five departments are there cells. In the others the wards are completely open from morning to night. Most of the patients work in workshops. One department is designed for recreation and has a radio and television. There is a library—and a very good one. . . . Moreover, books, newspapers, and magazines can be provided by relatives. Twice a week there's a movie. Locally based people can have two visits a month, and those who come from further afield can have visitors for three whole days." In addition, visitors could bring food, and "the hospital's food is more varied and tasty than what prisons provide." Butter, milk, sometimes fruits and meat (considerably more than in prisons) are included. "The medical services (I'm not afraid of exaggerating) are models. . . . You immediately see the very high level of qualification of the mid-level medical personnel (evidently the higher pay-scales here are a factor)."

But conditions in the wards for politicals were much tougher. Yet even these "are headed by doctors, and in all matters concerning the treatment of patients doctors play the decisive role." This made things bearable for him:

> Maybe it was the context of my professional life, or maybe it was the iron good health inherited from my parents that allowed me to adapt quickly to the required self-isolation from everything that didn't directly concern me . . . like the catching of a deeply disturbed person who somehow managed to escape from the warders

> and run naked around each floor of the building. . . . In this regard my stay in the hospital passed without significant damage to my psyche. The only thing I cannot forget—something that still wakes me at nights—is a wild night-time shriek mixed with the sound of a window-pane being smashed. From this I could not isolate myself. During sleep, it seems, the nerves are not protected from such sensations. But I can imagine how a person must suffer who absorbs the whole surrounding environment on his unprotected nervous system, whose defensive nervous functions are not well developed, as mine are.

Only after reading Marchenko's *My Testimony*, about the labor camps, did Grigorenko understand why mentally ill prisoners like the patients just mentioned were sent to these camps, namely, "to make the lives of the healthy people there even more unbearable," as he had experienced in the Serbsky Institute.

Grigorenko also describes the lives of people with whom he became friends in the Leningrad Special Psychiatric Hospital. One of them was Pyotr Lysak, an engineer from the provinces: "At a meeting of students he had criticized the authorities for expelling some of them for political unreliability. He wound up in this Special Psychiatric Hospital. When I arrived he had already been there for seven years. His anger about this terrible tyranny and the whole of his ruined life had flooded his mind, and every day he wrote the angriest letters, which, of course, went nowhere, but lay in his medical file to serve as the basis for his further 'treatment.'"

Grigorenko tried to convince Lysak of the futility of acting like this, "but he, a man with absolutely normal judgments on all issues, was on this one, as they say, 'unshakable.' On one occasion, Lysak said with irritation: 'You argue so unrealistically that I'm beginning to doubt if you're normal.' Then suddenly he stopped, trained a look on me that I'll never forget until I die, and quietly, very quietly, asked in a tone tinged with bitter reproach: 'Do you really think that one can spend seven years in here and remain normal?'" To this Grigorenko observed that living in such prisons is "especially awful for people with easily affected psyches, who suffer from sleep loss, and can't isolate themselves from the noise around them."

He also "met on walks a man who was most interesting to talk with, Volodya Pantin. He possessed an exceptional memory and the ability to recount episodes in an entertaining way. And he had things to recount.

Despite his relatively young age, he had already contrived to spend over ten years in captivity, most of them in camps for non-adults." Arrested on a charge of petty theft, he would probably have been released, but for an investigator who suddenly saw a way of using him to "solve" a difficult case. When Pantin repeatedly declined to give false evidence against the man concerned, the investigator burst out, "I'll have you sent off to a place where you won't forget me for the whole of your life," namely a prison hospital.

Eventually Pantin got lucky: "He happened to be in the hands of a clever, honest woman, who was able to handle his case in such a way that his psychiatric diagnosis was discarded. A doctor who behaved very well with me said that this was an exceptional case." As a rule such a discard could only be carried out by the doctor who had made the original diagnosis. But Pantin had to wait for it "for six long years."

Among the conclusions of Grigorenko's essay are these: "One should not think that among psychiatrists there are any less good qualities than there are among the members of other professions." And he rebutted the question of a doctor who asked if he placed no trust in doctors, expecting an affirmative answer. But he replied, "No, that's the one thing I'm relying on!"

However, he also wrote that "a system in which your only hope is in the honesty of doctors is worthless." And most of those in the prison's section for politicals were not honest in their practice, whatever their private opinions might have been. The result was enormous human suffering. The complete lack of information about how long you would be held caused especial heartache. Grigorenko had learned that "doctors are bound by some minimum terms. They are unknown to me. However, I know for sure that people who've committed murders are held for a minimum of five years. And people say that politicals are held to the same standard as the murderers." But if you refused to recant your views, you could be held indefinitely.

Boris Tsukerman recounts the key reason for Grigorenko's early release in 1965—at least when judged by these standards: "In due course the chief psychiatrist of the army, who, the regulations prescribe, must be presented with every army person who is suspected of having a mental illness, got to his case." On seeing the former general, he set in motion his release. Because army people were only rarely driven insane by their political beliefs, Tsukerman states, Soviet psychiatry was hardly used to handling such cases. This explained how "an honest person could occupy the position of the army's chief psychiatrist."[21]

So Grigorenko was released, but he was refused his back pay and all his documents except for a certificate of sanity, so he could not get a decent job and had to go to work as a stevedore. As the human rights movement took off over the next few years, he soon became active in it. In early 1966 he joined an ad hoc committee that planned to demonstrate on Moscow's Red Square against a threatened official turn toward Stalinism on the anniversary of Stalin's death. But the committee members were arrested and interrogated by the head of the KGB, General Vladimir Semichastny, before the anniversary day arrived. Refusing to countenance any demonstration, he blustered, "If you go onto the street with a placard reading 'Long Live the Leninist Central Committee!,' we'll still put you in lunatic asylums.'" Grigorenko also addressed and publicized a closely reasoned letter to Prime Minister Aleksei Kosygin, explaining exactly why he could not vote for him in the upcoming elections; among other things, Kosygin "sticks to what he learned from Stalin and Khrushchev: he thinks that Soviet laws do not apply to him."

Grigorenko interceded in the arrest of Marchenko, the Czechoslovakia crisis, and the arrest of the dissidents who demonstrated on Red Square against the subsequent invasion of that country on August 20. In late July he and four other Communists had written a letter to the Czechoslovak Communists and people, expressing profound admiration for the democratization of their land. Then came a prophetic sentence: "Fear has even been expressed . . . that the ruling circles of our country are planning—assuming that the development of events appears to be unfavorable from their viewpoint—to use the armed forces to halt such a development."[22]

At about this time, Grigorenko's wife, Zinaida—a party member—appealed to Brezhnev to restore her husband's rights: "P. G. Grigorenko is employed as a foreman . . . and also heads a party school as a party propagandist. There are twenty people in his group, thirteen of them Communists and seven non-Communists. It thus turns out that in one place my husband serves as a political leader, while in another he is regarded as mentally disturbed. When I asked at what point my husband had lost his sanity—since I had never noticed it—I was told by the investigators, Lieutenant Colonel Kuznetsov and Lieutenant Colonel Kantov—that my husband's political views and his dissemination of them had rendered him socially dangerous."[23]

In December 1968 Grigorenko wrote the longest and most sweeping open letter of all that he wrote, one addressed to the USSR's attorney general. First, he chided him because his ministry ought to have prevented the KGB from committing crimes. Then he turned to his own treatment:

> Already for more than three years I've been subject to continuous surveillance: constant, round-the-clock trailing of myself, my family members, and my visitors, permanent observation of my apartment by visual and other special means, the tapping of my phone, the reading of my correspondence, and the non-delivery of some letters. Twice in this time my apartment has been secretly searched.
>
> I am a Communist, and as such I hate with all my soul organs of illegal force and arbitrariness. . . . Among these is numbered in our country the KGB. I do not hide from anyone my hatred of this organization, and I consider it hostile to the people. This parasitic organization, which devours unlimited quantities of the people's wealth, in return removing the people's best sons and causing irreparable moral damage, ought to disappear from our society for ever, and the sooner the better.[24]

A few months later the KGB cleverly lured Grigorenko to Tashkent in Central Asia, where it snatched him and initiated again the whole process of tucking him away in a psychiatric prison. It was desperate to silence him, and this method had the smallest cost: there would be no trial to provoke demonstrations, the action would take place far from his friends and military colleagues in Moscow, and psychiatrists would do the hard work.

However, a major snag arose: The psychiatric commission appointed to examine him found that he was healthy enough to stand trial! And when its members couldn't be moved to change their minds, the KGB had to fall back on its last resort—transferring him to the long-discredited Serbsky Institute in Moscow. Here the doctors could be trusted to do the Kremlin's bidding, and their long report brazenly rebutted their Tashkent colleagues' findings. In addition, a trial was held in Moscow, in the general's absence, and the similarly obedient court quickly endorsed the Serbsky report. In 1972, Dr. Semyon Gluzman wrote and circulated in samizdat a brilliant comparison of the two differing psychiatric reports, which demonstrated the fraudulence of the second one, whose lead author was none other than Professor Daniil Lunts of the Serbsky Institute. This landed Gluzman with a seven-year sentence in a forced-labor camp, followed by forced exile.

This time, Grigorenko's fate was to be committed in 1969 to the infamous prison hospital, also a "special psychiatric hospital," in Chernyakhovsk, on the Lithuanian border, where he was held for three years, until September 1973. Meanwhile protests rained down on the KGB and the party from various directions. After his release he resumed his dissident activity in the face of the usual threats, and his writing continued to appear abroad: a book of his writings and supporting documents and a collection of his articles in Russian.[25] In early 1977, he released a new essay: "*Nashi budni, ili rasskaz o tom, kak fabrikuyutsya ugolovnye dela na sovetskikh grazhdan, vystupayushchikh v zashchitu prav cheloveka*" (Our everyday lives, or an account of how criminal cases are fabricated against Soviet citizens who speak out on human rights). It was published in the Munich-based Ukrainian-language journal *Suchasnist'* (*Modernism*) in 1978.

Grigorenko had also played an active part in the Helsinki Agreements. In 1975, after two years of negotiation at the Conference on Security and Cooperation in Europe, the European and North American governments signed in Helsinki the agreements that ushered in the formal concept of détente. The next year Yuri Orlov, an eminent physicist and dissident in Moscow, created the Moscow Group to Promote the Implementation of the Helsinki Agreements in the USSR, in whose work Grigorenko played an active part.[26] Since Grigorenko was starting to feel more deeply about understanding his Ukrainian heritage and improving his knowledge of the language, he began to contribute to the Ukrainian Helsinki Group when it was formed in support of the Helsinki Agreements.

In addition, in 1977 he actively helped the Moscow-based Commission on the Abuse of Psychiatry in the Soviet Union. This group had been founded by a young assistant doctor and dissident, Alexander Podrabinek, who had also written an excellent book on the topic, *Karatel'naya meditsina* (*Punitive Medicine*). It was circulated in samizdat in 1977, and published in Russian in New York in 1979 and in English in 1980.[27] Grigorenko's experiences made his relations with the group of the greatest interest to both parties.

In late 1977 Grigorenko required surgery that could not be done in the USSR but could be done in the United States. On learning this, the Kremlin saw a chance to get rid of him and offered him and his family members tourist visas. The former general, his wife, and their handicapped son, Oleg, departed on November 30. Soon after, Leonid Brezhnev had the Supreme Soviet pass a decree depriving Grigorenko of his Soviet citizenship. As they say, "Quite easily done."

The Grigorenkos' elder son, Andrei, had already emigrated to the United States in 1975 and lived in Brooklyn.[28] Pyotr—or Petro, as the Ukrainians called him—quickly underwent the operation he needed in St. Barnabas Hospital, and was discharged in four days. Now Andrei's father began the last nine years of his life living in the same city as his son. With the help of the American Crimean Tatar community, the family was installed in a modest apartment in Brooklyn, not far from Andrei and his wife. Soon he started not only to give occasional talks but also to write his detailed memoirs, which he finished in 1980.[29] In these, he describes all seventy-three years of his life to date, and gives thanks and praise to many people with whom he worked on human rights—notably Anatoly Marchenko—and also to those who helped him in other ways: his family; Tatyana Khodorovich; Tanya Zhitnikova, the wife of Leonid Plyushch, a Ukrainian victim of psychiatric abuse; Dr. Semyon Gluzman, Dr. Marina Voikhanskaya, Dr. Boris Zoubok, and Dr. Gery Low-Beer; and me.[30] The Russian edition included as an appendix a write-up, translated into Russian, of an eight-hour psychiatric exam of Grigorenko in 1978 by Dr. Walter Reich and Dr. Alan Stone. Dr. Stone is a lawyer and a past president of the American Psychiatric Association, and Dr. Reich is an eminent professor of psychiatry and international affairs at George Washington University.

The exam was meticulously prepared, with input from various related professionals. The concluding section stated: "Having carefully studied once again all the materials of the investigations, we did not detect in General Grigorenko any signs of psychiatric illnesses. . . . We also did not detect signs of any illnesses in the past. In particular, we did not find any paranoid symptoms, even in the weakest form."[31] The examination and written report were intended to reach the eyes of Soviet citizens and officials, as a refutation of the whole program of the abuse of psychiatry in the Soviet Union to hound and destroy political dissidents.

On March 17, 1979, the Grigorenkos kindly invited me and my wife, Kathy, to come to their apartment for a delicious home-cooked lunch—a very special occasion for me and Kathy. It gave me an opportunity to express to General Grigorenko in person the admiration for his courage and achievements that I felt and had done my best to convey in my many articles. He generously told me that his morale had benefited greatly from my articles. He gave me a copy of his book, which had been published in English as *Memoirs*, with a gracious inscription. Three years later, when his book appeared in Russian, he mailed us a copy with an even warmer inscription: "To our distant but true friends, Peter and Kathy Reddaway: We have forgotten nothing, and always remember you with love and gratitude. From the Grigorenko family, Petro, Zinaida, Oleg, and Andrei. 27.12.81."

In 1987 Grigorenko's extraordinary life came to an end, just short of his eightieth birthday. No other dissident that I know of, in Russia or elsewhere, had led such an extraordinary life. Somewhat like with Marchenko, the regime did not dare to just kill him, because too many people admired him.

How Many Political Prisoners Were There?

After the collapse of the USSR, many files were opened that provided new perspectives on the persecution of dissidents—and, indirectly, cast new light on the persistence and courage it had required to launch, maintain, and grow a human rights movement in the USSR.

In 1992, party archives were opened of official reports on the struggle to control political activism and dissent covering the years 1975 to 1988 that had been written by the KBG head, Yuri Andropov, and others. They contained official statistics on the number of political prisoners held in the labor camps (a small percentage of the system's total number of prisoners), especially from 1967 on, as compared to the very much larger number of ordinary criminals. The statistics also contained some information about the political prisoners interned in mental hospitals of all sorts, about dissidents who were deliberately charged with falsified offenses under criminal articles of the official code, and about anonymous dissenters whom the KGB could or could not identify.

Political prosecutions were officially defined and undertaken mainly under articles 70 and 190-1 of the Criminal Code of the Soviet Union—punishing the spreading of anti-Soviet material and "libel" of the Soviet system—and these are the statistics that were collected. The figures given by Andropov for all political prosecutions were 8,664 for 1959–1966, and 4,879 for 1967–1974. These figures, along with later similar statistics, are broken down by type of offense, and also by the trends in certain categories. For example, the rate of arrest of political dissidents increased by a factor of three in the period from 1979 to 1983, when the Kremlin ordered a serious and in some ways effective crackdown. An important role in keeping the total number of prosecutions down was played by so-called "prophylaxis"—warning talks that KGB agents delivered to dissidents. Andropov reported that in the 1967–1974 period only 4,879 people had to be politically prosecuted, because 121,406 others had been successfully intimidated through prophylaxis. In 1971–1974, "Through prophylaxis alone, 1,839 anti-Soviet groups were put out of action at the point where they were in the process of being formed." Only the brave, such as Marchenko and Grigorenko, persisted.

Official reports also give figures for the number of anonymous protests that the KGB discovered from 1975 to 1988. This varied from a low of 8,723 in 1987 to a high of 22,502 in 1981; one dissident wrote on average seven of these in a year. The KGB succeeded in identifying between 60 percent and 90 percent of the authors. An average of 5 percent of them were then sentenced to prison, while 14 percent—2,438 individuals—were committed to mental hospitals.[32]

Despite the existence of these official statistics, huge gaps remain in our knowledge of the actual scale of dissent from the 1950s on. If 2,438 writers of anonymous protests were interned in psychiatric institutions over a thirteen-year period, what was the combined total for all other categories of dissenters who were held alongside them? Unless there is some recent research out there that has not reached me, we do not know. Extremely rough, speculative estimates can be made for the number of dissidents held in the dozen or so high-security psychiatric prisons, yielding a figure of between 10,000 and 15,000 in all between the late 1950s and the late 1980s. But the number held in the hundreds of ordinary mental facilities cannot as yet even be estimated.

EIGHT

Confronting the Naysayers in the West

The emergence of the human rights movement added a new factor to the healthy ongoing debate about exactly what policies the U.K. should pursue vis-à-vis the Soviet Union. One unsettling feature of this debate, however, was that human rights violations in the Soviet Union often were trivialized or used like a poker chip. Even more unsettling was that certain individuals not only questioned the credibility and truthfulness of samizdat writings that reached the West but also challenged the basic credibility of dissidents—even the existence of men and women currently incarcerated in psychiatric hospitals and labor and prison camps in the Gulag.

An Anglo-Soviet Treaty of Friendship—Yes or No?

This debate was stimulated in February 1967 by the decision of the Labour government under Prime Minister Harold Wilson to accept in principle Prime Minister Aleksei Kosygin's proposal to conclude an Anglo-Soviet Treaty of Friendship and Cooperation. A group of academics led by Leonard Schapiro, the economist Peter Wiles, David Shapiro, and me came to the view that such a treaty would not be a good idea. What we objected to in the proposed treaty was that it contained no provisions for the recognition of human rights in the Soviet Union. We sketched a letter expressing our views to Foreign Minister George Brown and circulated it to a large number of academic colleagues, seeking their signatures or suggested amendments.[1]

We stated that we would "warmly welcome" a treaty if it were "based on a genuinely increased respect for human rights." Failure to respect human rights would be a deal breaker and nullify the treaty. In other words, we argued, "A treaty from which no practical consequences would follow could only serve to confuse real issues, and might, by erecting an empty verbal symbol, suggest the acceptance of practices which remain deeply alien to the British people."

On May 18, Foreign Minister Brown replied, in a three-page letter, that he was "fully conscious of the weight of responsible opinion expressed in your letter, and I have given most careful consideration to the points raised in it." Although the exact provisions of the treaty had not yet been agreed, he assured us that it "will not be found to justify fears" such as those expressed in our letter. Moreover, he concluded, "It must surely be right that we should take every opportunity to promote cooperation and develop friendship, provided always that we make no sacrifice of our own principles and interests." In the end, however, the differences between London and Moscow turned out to be too great, and no treaty was ever signed. Our letter may have contributed to this outcome. That is, our insistence on prioritizing human rights may have been too unpalatable to the leaders of the Soviet Union.

A somewhat similar case arose in the United States when, in February 1972, Senator William Fulbright denounced his own government for continuing to finance Radio Liberty and Radio Free Europe (RFE-RL), stations that focused mainly on domestic affairs in the USSR and East Europe, respectively. He argued that their broadcasts angered the Kremlin and the stations should be closed down to please the Soviet leaders and ease East-West tensions. This provoked much opposition as well as some support in both the United States and the U.K., where a stream of letters appeared in *The Times,* only three of them favorable to Fulbright. Among the critical ones was a letter from Leonard Schapiro, Maurice Cranston, an expert on human rights, and me (our letter appeared on March 4, 1972). We pointed out that the rich materials of samizdat were "living proof that many of the most creative Soviet citizens are ready for such free media," and that "Radio Liberty . . . has a crucial role to play for the indefinite future." We also pointed out that Fulbright's "ignorance seems to be willful," because he had refused "without explanation to accept an apparently favorable Library of Congress report on the two stations, which he himself had ordered."

D. A. N. Jones: Attacking the Dissident Messengers

Another sphere in which strong conflicts occurred in the U.K. was that of how to understand Soviet cultural life and the dissidents' role in it. As discussed in chapter 6, some observers thought that Russia was not tightly controlled and that dissidents were Stalinists who had turned 180 degrees to gain approval in the USSR and abroad. Others felt that dissidents were suspicious characters of dubious authenticity who had possibly even been invented by émigrés, the intelligence organization MI6, or the CIA and didn't actually exist. One of the main questioners of the dissidents' integrity, their literary purpose, and even their existence was the well-known literary critic D. A. N. Jones. In 1970–1971 he conducted long, furious polemics against a variety of well-qualified authors who criticized him for this view in three of the leading cultural magazines: *New Society*, *The Spectator*, and *The Listener*, the flagship publication of the BBC (British Broadcasting Corporation). Jones opened the duel with a review in *New Society* of five books by contemporary Russian authors, two of which were Andrei Amalrik's *Involuntary Journey to Siberia* and *Will the Soviet Union Survive until 1984?*[2] When the protests at his article began to be published, he defended himself in no less than six letters, one to *New Society*, two to both *The Spectator* and *The Listener*, and one to me personally. Ten letters rebutting him and his arguments were published.

Jones's principal target was the distinguished writer and historian Amalrik, who had been arrested and sentenced for his dissent for the second time in five years and was currently incarcerated in a forced-labor camp. The review starts: "Two of these books are allegedly written by one 'Andrei Amalrik,' as exposures of the failings of the Soviet Union. . . . Anyone used to reading novels will recognize the vein of solemn-faced self-parody and self-exposure, comparable with the picaresque satires of Thackeray and Thomas Mann. . . . The books are deliberate parodies of anti-Communist propaganda, malicious satires on dissident Soviet writers. . . . We have Amalrik. . . . cheating and lying and fiddling, . . . as a rogue and lay-about." The book is "the autobiography of a rat." "How can Max Hayward come to write a perfectly serious foreword to this parody, as if it were a genuine, undoctored memoir? . . . How has anyone been able to take all this nonsense seriously? . . . I do not believe that the author or authors of these books can be under arrest."

Four days before this review appeared, Jones had written a letter to *The Spectator* (December 26, 1970) expressing the same views and asking how Tibor Szamuely, the reviewer of one of Amalrik's books, *Involuntary Journey to Siberia*, in the magazine, could have regarded it as "a truthful memoir by a sincere man." In reply, Szamuely reviewed at length the reasons why Amalrik was a widely respected writer and dissident, and asked, "Can there be anything more contemptible than the sight of a member of the cozy Left-wing British intelligentsia sniggering at a brave man who has been sentenced to three years' hard labor for daring to write the truth about an inhuman tyranny?" (*The Spectator*, January 9, 1971).

I responded to Jones's review in *New Society* (January 7, 1971):

> It is unpleasant to see D.A.N. Jones parading his prejudices so nakedly in public. . . . Why did he accept these five books for review if he was not prepared to read them properly, but only to use them as a pretext for smearing as many people as possible? Why does he admit he is out of his depth but then proceed to fire off a stream of vicious judgments and false innuendoes? Why did the many favorable notices the books have received from a wide range of reviewers not make him mistrust his own hysterical responses and exercise especial care and restraint?

Amalrik and his wife were concerned with freedom and human rights in other countries, not just the USSR. Thus, I ended my letter by asking Jones whether he regarded the reports and photographs of the anti-British demonstration by Amalrik and his wife against British opposition to Biafra "as concoctions?" And was "Amalrik's filmed interview—shown on the BBC's *24 Hours* on 28 August 1970 and published in full in *The Listener*—yet another fiendish fabrication? Perhaps Jones would now visit Amalrik in his prison camp and either repeat to his face what he has written, or else—let us hope—apologize? I will gladly supply him with the address."

Jones retreated not an inch. Instead, he claimed (*New Society*, January 14, 1971) that his opinions were justified because there had been rumors that Amalrik was a KGB agent. Second, he claimed that certain episodes in Amalrik's account of his partially paralyzed father were contradictory and therefore showed him up as a liar. In doing so, he deliberately omitted

Amalrik's statement of the well-known fact that the degree of mobility of a partially paralyzed person may, from time to time, vary.

Leopold Labedz provided some background by writing in the *New Society* (January 21, 1971) that he had earlier had an exchange of letters with Jones that had gotten nowhere. He had soon seen the uselessness of debating with "a crank," when reading Jones's "exchange with David Mercer, whom Jones had attacked in *The Listener* with the ferocity of a Zhdanov over Mercer's deviations from Marxism." Labedz concluded by rejecting Jones's belief that "a police mentality is needed to get at the truth here." Rather, what was needed was "a minimum of intellectual integrity in handling the texts, some willingness to learn facts whatever one's own ideological prejudices, and an elementary ethical capacity to distinguish honest writings."

Stuart Hood also had a letter in the January, 21, 1971, issue of *New Society*, saying that he wrote "as a socialist" who had become convinced, by reading, of the genuineness of the dissident movement in the USSR. He feared that Jones was a victim of the fact that "in too many cases" study of the country had "become the preserve of conservative experts. The left should develop its own critique of Soviet affairs and its own experts; but that critique cannot be founded on emotion and ignorance."

Anthony Lewis of the *New York Times* also pitched in (*New Society*, January 28, 1971). Jones's letter had convinced him that the original review was not merely "a tasteless joke" but that Jones "may be serious." He quoted from his formerly Moscow-based colleague Henry Kamm and from a new book by another such journalist, Anatole Shub, who knew Amalrik well and had written about him.

Robert Conquest, a historian who had written extensively on Stalin's Terror of the 1930s, kicked off *The Listener* portion of the debate in the January 21 issue by referring to the foregoing polemical exchange and accusing Jones of ignorantly denying that Amalrik was even a real person. Jones, responding in the January 28 issue of *The Listener*, repeated some of his claims, only to yield a little at the end: "Robert Conquest says that I deny the existence of Amalrik. No. I'm prepared to believe that a writer called Amalrik has been sentenced in Moscow, just as I believe that Van der Lubbe was sentenced in Germany for setting fire to the Reichstag, and that George Blake was sentenced in London for spying. But I don't know how far Van der Lubbe was responsible for his actions and I don't know who George Blake was (or is) working for. I am similarly ignorant about

Amalrik." Jones in his acknowledged ignorance insults not only Amalrik but also the authors of all the letters written, who had jointly provided him with a wealth of information.

Ignoring Jones's implied insult, Conquest came back with a patient letter (*The Listener*, February 4), pointing out that Amalrik's "account of the present condition of Soviet society . . . is a serious one, and its general stand does not differ greatly from those of a whole range of recent commentators, both Soviet and non-Soviet, from Academician Sakharov to Anatole Shub." Conquest pointed out that in samizdat circles, a leading figure, Pyotr Yakir, "welcomes Amalrik's work as a perfectly serious contribution [that] has also been publicly cited as a reasonable picture of present-day Russia by French Communist writers."

I was less patient in my letter that appeared in the same issue, writing that Jones "has now dispensed his libels against Andrei Amalrik" in three journals "at a total length of 4,500 words. . . . Mr. Jones is dishonest because, among other things, he has simply ignored the concrete questions I put to him" in my letter in *New Society*. One of these concerned "Amalrik's filmed interview, which you printed in full on 17 September 1970. Here Amalrik discussed at length one of his books, the authenticity of which Mr. Jones has repeatedly denied. Mr. Jones is also hypocritical, because he proclaims his anxiety to get at the truth yet takes none of the most obvious steps needed to do so. A careful reading of not just the texts, but also the introductions, appendices, and so on to Amalrik's two books would, alone, have dispersed his libelous fantasies about them."

I continued regarding the writer's authenticity: a still unmentioned confirmation had come on December 3, 1969, when "*The Times* published a long pre-arrest letter of his, which recounted his unsuccessful negotiations with the Soviet authorities over the transfer of foreign royalties." Here Amalrik referred to "the person whom I have authorized to act on my behalf" with the publishing world. As was well known, this person was "Karel van het Reve, Professor of Literature at Leiden University and one of Amalrik's numerous foreign friends who have discussed his ideas and writings with him at great length over the years."

In conclusion, I enumerated some of the key aims of the Soviet security services involving the manipulation of Soviet citizens and foreigners. "With his 4,500 words Mr. Jones has," I suggested, "doubtless unwittingly, rendered these aims magnificent service."

This at last brought a partial recantation from Jones, though one still containing subtle jabs. Previously he had "felt certain that these books had been compiled and published in order to bring discredit upon independent and 'dissident' writers. . . . I thought the deception was obvious: in this, at least, I was deluded. I had, of course, no intention of 'libeling' a defenseless man. To tell the truth, I feel more inclined to identify with him than to sit in judgement upon him, whether or not his work be found partly or wholly 'authentic.'"

In 1976 Amalrik and his wife, Gyuzel, emigrated to the Netherlands. His life ended four years later, in 1980, when he died in a car crash.

Nicholas Bethell and David Burg: Sabotaging Samizdat

A different group of people tried to help the Kremlin, blunting the impact of samizdat by attempting to discredit it as a trustworthy source on current conditions in the Soviet Union. Nicholas Bethell, a writer on Soviet affairs, and Alexander Dolberg, an émigré from the USSR, who wrote articles and a book critical of the Soviet dissidents under the pseudonym David Burg, pursued a program of disinformation in order to undermine the credibility of dissidents and their writings. Bethell and Burg were close friends. I had first heard of Burg at Harvard's Russian Research Center, where Priscilla Johnson told me about the poor reputation he had developed while there, stemming partly from his assertions to Priscilla and others that he was Abram Tertz, the intellectual who wrote stories under that synonym while pretending to be living in Russia. In fact, Abram Tertz was the pen name used by Andrei Sinyavsky, who lived in Russia until he was unmasked, imprisoned, and eventually allowed to emigrate to France in 1973. Dolberg's falsehood fit well with the Soviet line that Tertz was in reality an émigré.

Bethell launched his career working as a scriptwriter at the BBC. On December 11, 1964, I met him for lunch in a London restaurant and, not knowing his relationship with Burg, rashly decided to warn him that Burg was unreliable, partly because he had been pretending to be Tertz. Bethell then shocked me by replying that Burg was a close friend whom he and his wife had taken with them on their recent honeymoon.

In 1965 Burg provided further proof of his tendencies by working with one of the most disreputable émigrés in London, a certain Alex Flegon from Romania. Together, as Burg confirmed in writing to my friend Abraham Brumberg, they produced the first two issues of the journal *Student*, a mixture of genuine literary material larded with dubious, provocative, and obscene items that, taken together, portrayed the Soviet underground as grossly irresponsible and distasteful.

With Bethell's help Burg managed to rise in the journalistic firmament. On November 19, 1967, he published a long article in the *Sunday Times* in which he made claims that were damaging to a respected young Russian dissident, Alexander Ginzburg, who was under arrest. Burg claimed that Ginzburg was "the leader of the Russian literary underground. . . . In 1964 he smuggled works by some young writers out of the country." These were incriminating charges for which there was no evidence and that Ginzburg had expressly denied, yet they made him more vulnerable to prosecution. Two months later the KGB had Ginzburg sentenced to five years in a forced-labor camp.

Soon Burg found a new way to compromise the incipient dissident movement in the USSR: he became the literary agent of Naum Gurevich, who under the pen name Naum Odnopozov had come to the West two years earlier claiming to be a brilliant leader of the underground. A setback to sailing under this false flag occurred when *The Guardian* revealed his deception by publishing a few extracts from notes he had written about himself in the third person for publication. These claimed that in his escape from Russia "there was clever calculation, exceptional sang-froid, and amazing will-power. And then there's his talent, great artistic talent, granted by God himself. . . . [I am] probably one of the most gifted writers of the Soviet literary underground."[3]

Two days later, undeterred by Flegon's being thus exposed as a fraud, Burg penned a 2,500-word article of some writings by the dissident author Naum Odnopozov, and published it in the London *Sunday Times* under the acknowledged pen name Naum Odnopozov.[4] This gave the reader the impression that Gurevich was an important underground writer, when *The Guardian* had already exposed him as a megalomaniacal poseur. Inevitably, however, the genuine underground was discredited in the eyes of many of the *Sunday Times*' readers who did not read *The Guardian*.

After the invasion of Czechoslovakia in August 1968, a new chapter began in the Burg-Bethell saga. On September 11 *The Times* printed on page one the text of a long, anonymous protest against the invasion supplied by Bethell, whose signatories, he claimed, were "88 of the leading Moscow progressive writers . . . many of whom are of importance in the Soviet literary world, are on the editorial boards of Moscow journals, and have their work translated and published in the West." It was addressed to "The Writers of Czechoslovakia." Written with heavy emotion in an exaggerated style foreign to the dissident movement, it included such passages as "Let them threaten us with concentration camps, let them refuse to print our best works of literature, let them torment us with spiritual and physical hunger—we shall not give up our honour or our conscience."

Burg's role was to have tried the previous day (in vain) to provide the BBC and Radio Liberty with the text of the protest and get them to agree to broadcast it to the USSR in Russian after Bethell's article appeared. Undeterred, two weeks later he took part in the BBC's 10 p.m. news program. Bringing up the "letter of the 88," he gave the names of three prominent liberal Soviet writers who, he stated, had signed the letter. Later, in early March 1969, Bethell told me in a phone call that he had never seen any list of signatories and did not know any specific names. When I asked him why, then, Burg had given three names on the BBC, he offered the empty excuse that Burg "sometimes gets carried away by his enthusiasm and exaggerates." This merely emphasized Burg's real intentions, which were to make Bethell's fabrication seem more real.

Meanwhile, Martin Dewhirst, Leonard Schapiro, and I had written letters to the *Times Literary Supplement* in which we shed grave doubt on the authenticity of Burg's "letter of the 88."[5] In three replies, Bethell tried, ineffectually, to defend the letter and his presentation of it, essentially by urging his critics to trust his judgment. In response, Schapiro and I pointed out that the anonymity of the signatories lacked credibility, given that there was "no other known instance of many well-known people signing a document and then being so frightened that they circulated it anonymously." Also, in the six months since the letter was written, not one mention of it had been made in the various samizdat documents that had carefully reported all the numerous protests against the invasion of Czechoslovakia. So presumably the letter had not been regarded by the dissidents as authentic. So Bethell and Burg were taking part in attempts to discredit samizdat. Why?

In our second letter, Schapiro and I concluded that unfortunately Bethell, in his third response, "does not answer the points in our letter of February 20 and produces no evidence to convince us that the supposed 'letter of the 88' was . . . signed by '88 of the leading Moscow progressive writers.'" At this Bethell remained silent. Six months later I went to Prague and met a Czech writer who told me a story of how he had been in Moscow when the letter's author was writing it, and had advised him to make certain changes and avoid anonymity. He also told me the author's name, which I had never heard of, and how the letter had reached Czechoslovakia and been taken by a dubious Slovak writer, Pavel Licko, to Bethell in London.

Two days later, on March 15, 1969, I had a formal lunch with Bethell and his wife at their country estate near Ascot. Here he tried yet again to get me to back off, feeding me a few extra details on the writing of the letter. But it sounded like a broken record. Also, his wife, when we went on a tour of the grounds, pointed out the small house that, she said, was being renovated so that Burg could use it. So none of Burg's activities had caused Bethell to think it might be wise to distance himself from the rash provocateur. Rather, the episode with the "letter of the 88" suggested that in essence they were two peas in a pod, with similar semi-hidden aims, and actually colluding with each other.

Bethell and Burg's efforts to discredit the samizdat movement continued. The highest-profile episode was sparked in June 1970, when the conservative Edward Heath formed a government and included Bethell as a junior minister in the House of Lords. This aroused the interest of the famously idiosyncratic fortnightly satirical magazine *Private Eye*, whose bread and butter was the exposure of scandals, corruption, and cover-ups by the government of the day.

Private Eye dug up all the nefarious activities of Bethell and Burg, who they hinted were in a homosexual relationship, and published the main stories in September and October in a couple of issues.[6] The stories exposed Bethell and Burg as apparent pawns of the Kremlin and also mocked Heath for having been naïve and careless enough to appoint one of these slippery characters to his cabinet, and to criticize them both for having translated and published Solzhenitsyn's novel *Cancer Ward* against the express wishes of its author. On the first point, Heath soon took fright and told Bethell that he must resign. In January 1971 he reluctantly agreed, telling the public that he needed to do so in order to sue *Private Eye* for libel.

By this time he had looked around for a regular job, and apparently found one as director of an emerging new NGO, Writers and Scholars International, publisher of *Index on Censorship*, whose cofounder was David Astor, editor of *The Observer*. Although it was Astor who had recruited Bethell, Astor was disturbed to learn of the *Private Eye* articles, and on January 2 consulted with me, as a contributor to *The Observer* whose judgment he trusted. I told him that although I had had nothing to do with the *Private Eye* articles, I had found them, in their often highly eccentric way, to be basically on the mark. Astor replied that Bethell had just told him that he might have to abandon Writers and Scholars International, because he was considering suing *Private Eye*. I encouraged Astor to withdraw the employment offer to Bethell, which he did. Later I endorsed his idea of appointing the translator Michael Scammell instead.[7]

On May 1, 1971, Bethell wrote to me that he had been to Moscow in January and met the author of the "letter of the 88," who was not well known abroad, and a few of the signatories, whose status Bethell also played down. Although this was changing the original story, he did not publicize the fact. Instead, he asked me yet again to take his whole story on trust and, with Schapiro, to withdraw our criticisms. We declined.

Only in July 1971 did Bethell finally decide to go ahead and sue *Private Eye*; he asked Astor to support him, but Astor said he could not. At this point *Private Eye*'s lawyers drew me and some other Sovietologists into the case by asking whether I could corroborate, in court if necessary, the contents of the magazine's articles. After discussing the situation at a lunch with the *Eye*'s charmingly eccentric editor, Richard Ingrams, at his favorite pub in Soho, I agreed to help them. They proceeded to collect an impressive battery of materials for the defense. However, in a couple of places the *Private Eye* author had gone a little too far, and had not provided ironclad proof of his allegations. Thus in June 1972 *Private Eye* decided, almost a year after being sued, to see if it could settle the case out of court. This proved surprisingly easy. In return for an ambiguously worded apology, damages of 1,000 pounds to each of the aggrieved, and a miserly 1,750 pounds for their joint costs, Bethell and Burg decided to drop their suit. This outcome, though trumpeted by Bethell as complete vindication, actually showed something different: that their case was weak, that the thrust of the articles was truthful, and that the two men were simply relieved to get at least a minimal payment out of their suit.

This episode did not improve Burg's bad reputation. As before, he could hardly ever get himself published or broadcast. The key turning point had come in 1970, when an article of his appeared in *The Observer* under the headline "From a Correspondent," in which he claimed that an officer of the Baltic Fleet had been executed for his dissent, and the information came from the latest issue of *Khronika*. Checking this out and finding no such report in *Khronika*, I raised the matter with *The Observer* editors.

After a long back-and-forth with them and Burg, I was at last able to prove that Burg's report had been invented. On October 11, *The Observer* published a short letter from me in which I corrected the two falsehoods in Burg's article, but refrained from naming him. Finally, on December 18, I wrote a five-page paper about Burg's history and this case for private use, making points presented here, and sent it around to a dozen or so editors whom I knew, to forewarn them, should Burg approach them to pitch his articles. It seemed to have the desired effect of denying him an outlet for his made-up stories.

Bethell was a different case. He wrote several successful books and many articles and gave speeches in the House of Lords and later the European Parliament, where he sat for nine years and sponsored various political campaigns, mostly in the field of foreign affairs. All this he did with only occasional elements of favor to the Kremlin. When he died in 2007, he received favorable obituaries. He had shaken off the travails of 1968–1972. Observers had forgotten about them and about his close relationship with Burg.

Plugging Channels for Dissent

Of course it was hugely important to the Soviet authorities to discredit samizdat. The approach was usually rather simple: they did not engage with the content of dissent but instead went straight to an ad hominem attack on the author.[8]

Thus they looked for ways to stop me from engaging in what they considered to be subversive activities that undermined the Soviet state. When, as I mentioned earlier, I had tried in 1963–1964 in Moscow to help the family of the defector Oleg Lenchevsky, the Kremlin falsely accused me of helping the British embassy to break an agreement it had made with the Soviet authorities. However, I didn't know that the embassy had earlier agreed with the authorities not to contact Mrs. Lenchevsky after her husband defected. Even after the embassy assured the authorities that I had known nothing of the agreement, they treated me as though I had conspired with the British Foreign Service to break an agreement and persuade Mrs. Lenchevsky to flee abroad.

From 1968 on, the standard false charge against me was produced, namely that I was "closely linked to British intelligence." *Izvestia* claimed this to explain why I had given advice to a small British group of pacifists who had gone to Moscow to demonstrate for human rights on Red Square.

In January 1971 the KGB tried a different way of intimidating me and making me curtail or stop my activities on behalf of Soviet dissidents: calling me on the telephone at home in London many times a day and in the night, and breathing heavily into the phone. It was a primitive method of harassment that came to naught after the phone company, at my request, took steps to end it.

Within the Soviet Union targets of the authorities had a harder time. A unique case occurred in 1973, when the authorities, having arrested two dissidents, Viktor Krasin and Pyotr Yakir, coerced them into recounting their hitherto largely hidden activities, including helping to arrange for a draft copy of my book *Uncensored Russia* to be checked for factual accuracy by a fellow dissident, Gabriel Superfin. This episode was then used in a couple of trials as evidence that the defendants had assisted in "the spreading of anti-Soviet libels abroad."

Westerners who reported on or wrote about the USSR had to try to strike the right balance between covering official Soviet activities and critically examining aspects of Soviet society that were in bad condition and therefore were covered up by officialdom, such as housing, the health system, cultural life, and the issues of personal freedom that dissidents mostly focused on, such as freedom of assembly, personal expression, nationality, and religion.

In 1975 the BBC Russian Service organized a discussion of these questions between my friend Jonathan Steele, a journalist on *The Guardian*, and me, moderated by a veteran broadcaster, Anatol Goldberg. Steele put forward the reasonable view that "reporters should not be either propagandists for a government point of view or for a minority dissident point of view." They should "describe a country in all its many facets."

This was all well and good, but, I pointed out, "The fact is that there has not been a single article in the British press in the last few years on any of the following subjects: Russian dissenting nationalism, the dissent of the Lithuanian Roman Catholics, Georgian nationalism, Armenian nationalism, or Ukrainian nationalism." Steele retorted that it was "impossible to check on the information being given to you by the dissidents," but I disagreed: with some persistence this could usually be done.[9]

Actually, the discussion was slightly out of focus, because I did not regard myself as a common garden variety journalist. Apart from occasional articles that I wrote on Soviet politics in general, I saw my job as doing what nobody else did on a regular basis: reporting on and disseminating as rapidly as possible the dissident information of various kinds that I obtained, through my own channels. And I had the experience to be able to thoroughly evaluate the information I received.

In the USSR, Gorbachev's reforms were by 1988 affecting attitudes not just toward Western governments, but also toward me, albeit erratically. On August 20, *Sovetskaya Rossiya*, an official newspaper, printed a routinely hostile attack on me in which I was accused of working for the U.K. government. Yet on September 19, *Pravda* printed an interview by its Washington correspondent, Vitaly Gan, that made me sound quite normal. He reported that I had said that "a situation has now arisen in which the prospects for mutually advantageous agreements between the USSR and the USA have become more real, as a result of several agreements which have been concluded. . . . This, [Reddaway] considers, is good and in tune with American interests." Gan reported that he had told me that Americans seemed to think that Soviet reforms stemmed from outside pressures, and did not realize that "we ourselves saw the compelling necessity for change. 'I think you are right,' said P. Reddaway. . . . 'The present trend in Soviet-American relations,' he said in farewell, 'is very promising.'"[10]

NINE

"The Mental State of Such People Is Not Normal"

Exposing the Political Abuse of Psychiatry

The 1970s saw a great deal of variation in the relations between the USSR and the West. Kremlin policies on dissent had always reflected the trends in foreign policy, but now this was even more the case. Relations were tense after the invasion of Czechoslovakia in August 1968, because the USSR continued to turn the screws domestically on dissidents of all shades except Russian nationalists. The latter often received less harsh treatment because they enjoyed less Western support and thus posed less of a threat. In late 1972 the Kremlin also managed temporarily to stop *Khronika* from appearing.

By 1973, however, the Soviet Union felt a growing need for access to Western grain exports and subsidized Western credits to pay for them. To get this it had to systematically reduce its isolation from the West; the policies that were necessary to achieve this came to be known collectively as détente. Negotiations to bring about the creation of the Conference on Security and Cooperation in Europe (CSCE) had been running for over a year, but in 1973 they stepped up markedly. Finally thirty-five nations—all the nations of Europe, plus the United States and Canada—signed what came to be known as the Helsinki Agreement in August 1975. It required, in effect, an easing of human rights policy in the USSR, for which the West had bargained hard.

In early 1977, however, Soviet policy toughened again. According to a leaked document from that time an unidentified spokesman at a closed meeting of the Communist Party Central Committee stated: "The editors of newspapers and journals receive numerous demands from Soviet people that, at last, firmness be shown and the dissidents silenced. It has been decided to imprison the fifty most active dissidents and deal severely with their associates. It is time to show strength and not pay attention to the West." On the subject of emigration, the spokesman said, "The Soviet Union showed its goodwill by signing the Helsinki Agreement. We know that in reality no reunification of families is taking place. Young people are using emigration for selfish purposes. Let those who challenge authority go, rather, and build the Baikal–Amur railway-line."[1] In December 1979, the Kremlin put a final end to détente by invading Afghanistan in an attempt to shore up the Communist regime that had recently been installed there.

Let us look now at one of the factors that eventually helped to lead the Kremlin to this decision.

Origins of the Political Abuse of Psychiatry

The method of dealing with dissent by having the dissenter ruled insane by psychiatrists and locked up indefinitely in a mental hospital can be traced back to the early Soviet period. Considerable evolution in the application of this method took place, however. The scale of the use of this tool was very limited until the late 1930s, and the motivation until about 1950 was actually more humane than punitive: to save the individual from imprisonment in a concentration camp and the likely prospect of death. But in the 1950s things evolved in a decidedly more negative direction under the leadership of Drs. Georgy Morozov and Daniil Lunts of the Serbsky Institute of Forensic Psychiatry in Moscow: policy became more punitive and this punitive policy became more routine

The history of psychiatric abuse from the Bolshevik revolution to about 1960 contains much of interest and is presented in chapters 2 and 3 of the first comprehensive book on the whole subject by the psychiatrist Sidney Bloch and me, published in 1977.[2] This book was the fruit of a couple of years of collaborative work in which each of us did a first draft of the aspects where we were strongest, and then gave them to the other to amend or extend. It was translated into several languages and widely reviewed. The Bukovsky documents of 1971, provided by Vladimir Bukovsky, the Working Group's varied production from that time, and a number of interviews that we conducted specially, all provided us with key sources.

(I will note here in passing that in seeking a publisher for this book I had a long chat in 1976 with Livia Gollancz, the owner of the major house Victor Gollancz. Victor, her father, had been, until 1940, a proselytizing Communist, and brought up his daughter accordingly. She had quietly but deeply disliked this, and felt satisfied, with him dead, about publishing a book critical of the USSR!)[3]

To return to Soviet history, notable early writers of autobiographical samizdat books or other materials about psychiatric abuse were Ilya Yarkov, Sergei Pisarev, Fyodor Shul'ts, and Nikolai Samsonov.

In 1955–1956, Sergei Pisarev, a former Party official, had managed to get the party's Central Committee to conduct research for what became an objective party report on the phenomenon of defining dissidents as mentally ill and incarcerating them. The document called for radical reform but remained secret and was soon quietly shelved.[4] However, Pisarev did not abandon his efforts.

A big part of the problem with the Soviets' use of politicized psychiatry was that Nikita Khrushchev wanted to tell the Soviet people and the world that Stalin's terror and oppression had by now truly ended, and no political prisoners remained in the labor camps. But how could this be true? On May 24, 1959, *Pravda* published his explanation: "We can say that now, too, there are people who fight against Communism. . . . But clearly the mental state of such people is not normal."

Khrushchev and later Yuri Andropov left the strong impression through their statements that the increased use of psychiatric internment was due not so much to phony new psychiatric theories from the late 1950s to the 1970s, nor to decisions by lower-level officials, but rather to policies coming from the highest levels. This was confirmed in 1969. In 1992 we learned that on April 29, 1969, Andropov "sent to the Communist Party Central Committee a letter laying out a plan to develop a network of psychiatric institutions and his own ideas on how to use them to defend the Soviet . . . system." There also exist in the archives secret follow-up resolutions on this subject adopted by the top party and Soviet governing bodies.[5]

Three other books exist that cover aspects of the whole subject discussed briefly above, two of them, both richly illustrated by photographs of the people discussed, by Robert van Voren. Especially in his book *Cold War in Psychiatry*, van Voren covers in great detail the issues from 1978 onward, when he reached the age of eighteen. At that point he came from the Netherlands to Britain to meet Vladimir Bukovsky. He paints vivid pictures of key figures in both the Soviet Union and the West, including Mel Sabshin and Ellen Mercer of the American Psychiatric Association; the East German psychiatrist Jochen Neumann; the Russians Anatoly Koryagin (a dissident psychiatrist) and Andrei Kovalev (an open-minded diplomat); and the Georgian Eduard Shevardnadze, who was foreign affairs minister for Mikhail Gorbachev.[6] The third book is by the Russian author Mikhail Shifrin, *Vyalotekushchie repressii* (Sluggish repressions), which appeared in four long installments in the electronic journal *Mednovosti*.[7]

There were important differences between the procedures for criminal and civil commitment to a psychiatric institution. Criminal commitment required a month of examination, usually in the Serbsky Institute. If, then, the finding was "not responsible," there was a trial in the defendant's absence at which the court briefly reviewed the Serbsky's report and the evidence of his or her anti-Soviet activity; he or she was then sent for indefinite treatment in a mental hospital. Civil commitment required only that a psychiatrist had allegedly observed an individual behaving in a "socially dangerous way" and, without a court hearing, ordered him or her to be treated indefinitely in a psychiatric hospital. The safeguards were thus minimal.

A well-known case of civil commitment was that of the biologist Zhores Medvedev, whose samizdat writings and free professional behavior had exasperated the authorities. In May 1970 a psychiatrist declared him to be mentally ill and simply sent him without a trial to a civil hospital for treatment. However, his twin brother Roy immediately raised such vigorous protests from friends and colleagues like Andrei Sakharov that after nineteen days an international outcry had erupted and he was released. The twins quickly wrote a book about the case, *A Question of Madness*, which was published in several countries and awakened many people to a previously unimagined horror.

At this time Vladimir Bukovsky, twenty-eight, ended his first-time labor-camp term of three years after serving several earlier psychiatric internments, and gave interviews to foreign journalists. These were followed by an unprecedented television interview of him on July 27, 1970, by the CBS reporter William Cole in Moscow in which Cole asked Bukovsky about details of life in the Leningrad Special Psychiatric Hospital, the punishments meted out, the untherapeutic milieu, and the callousness of the staff. Bukovsky also explained that he gradually understood how the doctors had found him to be abnormal. They deemed him and other people "to have done things which from the point of view of the authorities are crimes, but which are not criminal from the point of view of the law." With the use of this nonmedical standard, "Many people—tens, hundreds of people—have been declared insane and committed to various hospitals, mainly special ones, like those in Kazan, Leningrad, Chernyakhovsk, Sychyovka, and so on."

In January 1971 the Canadian Psychiatric Association achieved the distinction of being the first national body in the world to condemn the Soviet degradation of psychiatry. It endorsed a report from one of its sections "regarding the alleged wrongful detention in mental hospitals in the USSR of seemingly healthy individuals whose views and attitudes are in conflict with those of the regime" and denounced the abuse of psychiatry "now being perpetrated in the USSR."[8]

The Bukovsky Papers and the Buildup to the Mexico City Congress of the World Psychiatric Association

Documents that came to be known as the Bukovsky papers played an important role in stimulating serious opposition to the abuse of psychiatry in the Soviet Union. On February 18, 1971, our London-based Working Group on the Internment of Dissenters in Mental Hospitals was formed by psychiatrists and laypeople, expressly to review a letter dated January 28 from Vladimir Bukovsky, a Russian-born British human rights activist and writer, accompanying a packet of 150 pages of documents about abuses. Bukovsky had written an exceptionally balanced and thoughtful letter addressed to Western psychiatrists. He asked them to study the materials he attached—ten lengthy reports of psychiatric analyses of six dissidents—and decide for themselves whether or not the reports contained enough scientific evidence to point to the illnesses cited. Here I quote from the letter at some length:

> This phenomenon arouses justified anxiety. . . . The diagnostic reports of forensic psychiatrists which have served as the basis for the court orders provoke many doubts as regards their contents. However, only specialists in psychiatry can express authoritative opinions about the degree of legitimacy of these diagnostic reports. . . . I am sending you these documents, and also various letters and materials which reveal the personalities of these people. . . . I ask you to express your opinion on only this point: Do the above-mentioned reports contain enough scientifically-based evidence to indicate the mental illnesses described in the reports, and also to indicate the necessity of isolating these people completely from society through internment?

The group sent Bukovsky's letter to *The Times*, which ran it on March 12; a French group released it in Paris on March 10.

The documents were a remarkable collection.[9] The ten lengthy reports provided forensic psychiatric analyses of the dissidents (listed here by their initials only) P. Grigorenko, N. Gorbanevskaya, I. Yakhimovich, V. Fainberg, V. Kuznetsov, and V. Borisov, and were signed by well-known doctors of the Serbsky Institute. They were photocopies of the originals, and have been acknowledged as authentic by official psychiatrists. Finally, Bukovsky invited Western psychiatrists to consider placing the whole issue on the agenda of the World Psychiatric Association (WPA) World Congress, an international congress of psychiatrists to be held in Mexico City from November 28 to December 4, 1971.[10]

The members of the Working Group, which met at my house in London, were psychiatrists, specialists in Soviet affairs, and human rights experts. All were volunteers who wanted to become active in the cause; the group did not solicit members. Materials we received from dissenters were translated mainly by Eleanor Aitken, then sent to psychiatric organizations in Western Europe, North America, and Mexico, with the request that they study them and, if possible, respond to Bukovsky's appeal. In the U.K., a Working Group member, Alec Jenner, a professor of psychiatry, wrote a response and solicited forty-four psychiatrists to sign it, including many distinguished professors and directors of psychiatric hospitals (a similar number declined to sign, for various reasons). Jenner's letter appeared in *The Times* on September 16, 1971, and reached this conclusion:

> On the basis of evidence contained in these reports, the undersigned psychiatrists feel impelled to express grave doubts about the

> legitimacy of compulsory treatment for the six people concerned, and indefinite detention in prison-mental-hospital conditions. Four of them do not appear to have any symptoms at all which indicate a need for treatment, let alone treatment of such a punitive kind. . . . It seems to us that the diagnoses of the six people were made purely in consequence of actions in which they were exercising fundamental freedoms—as set out in the Universal Declaration of Human Rights and guaranteed by the Soviet Constitution.

The authors ended by appealing to "our colleagues throughout the world to study the voluminous materials now available, to discuss the matter with their Soviet colleagues, some of whom we know to have doubts as grave as our own, and to raise the issue . . . at international conferences such as that of the World Psychiatric Association in Mexico City from November 28 to December 4."

A somewhat similar appeal to the WPA World Congress came a month later from the eminent Moscow Human Rights Committee, which included the academician Andrei Sakharov. It called for an inquiry into "the complex of questions concerning the rights of people ruled to be mentally ill," and drew attention to "the whole tortuous procedure of treatment" in Soviet psychiatric hospitals. Other strong appeals came just before the WPA Congress from the World Federation for Mental Health and, in Moscow, the Action Group for the Defense of Human Rights. The latter wrote: "We are convinced that the opinion of the participants in your international congress will carry great authority, and that it could put an end to the practice of interning people in mental hospitals without sufficient grounds." The group had also said that Bukovsky's arrest was a direct result of his appeal to the world's psychiatrists, thereby hinting that his fate was now in their hands.[11]

Meanwhile, the Kremlin felt a desperate need to put out some sort of rebuttal to this barrage of awkward truths, and delegated a psychiatric academician, Andrei Snezhnevsky, who was the head of the Moscow School of Psychiatry, to deliver it, even though he had been quoted in 1970 in private as having commented on the case of Zhores Medvedev, "In a year's time there's going to be an international psychiatric conference in Mexico. How do you think this is going to make our delegation look?!"[12]

In delivering his rebuttal Snezhnevsky sounded like a different man from the one who had made that comment. Interviewed by *Izvestia* on

October 24, 1971, he praised the "lofty humanism" that had always distinguished Soviet psychiatry, and denounced "those absurd reports that healthy persons are put in psychiatric hospitals in the USSR." His reaction was "a feeling of deep disgust at this outrageous fabrication." The Soviet system of medical training ensured "that even rank-and-file psychiatrists in our country are highly qualified. Thus cases of the confinement of healthy persons . . . are absolutely out of the question. . . . Our colleagues abroad" who have become familiar with Soviet psychiatric care "have a very high opinion of it indeed."[13]

No Help from Mexico

After the buildup of Western protests, the congress in Mexico City was a severe letdown. Despite vigorous efforts by various individuals and groups, the devious, persistent maneuvering and special pleading by the WPA Secretary General, Dr. Denis Leigh, and his associates, designed to avoid any serious discussion or action, ended by winning the day. Much Working Group literature and many copies of the Medvedevs' book, *A Question of Madness*, were sold and distributed, and moving individual speeches were made. But the final outcome in response to the publication of the Bukovsky papers, the forty-four British psychiatrists, and many others, was a loud silence.[14]

This had two tragic results. First, it sent a clear signal to Moscow that it had little to fear from the Western psychiatric establishment. As Victor Fainberg—interned in the Leningrad psychiatric hospital and later a friend of the Working Group after his release to Britain in 1974—wrote in an appeal, "Before the congress, chaos reigned in the special psychiatric hospitals and other domains of Soviet psychiatry." Large numbers of political prisoners were prepared for release by the disoriented officials and "the authorities, with extreme reluctance, improved their living conditions." But when the authorities heard the outcome of the congress, they reacted with "the glee of a cruelty suddenly unleashed. The tortures of which the world's psychiatrists had just taken no notice, began again."[15]

Second, the congress's inaction sealed Bukovsky's fate by failing to take action on the documents he had sent to the West. His trial was scheduled to begin in Moscow in January. For his supposed "anti-Soviet agitation and propaganda" he received two years in prison, plus five years in a forced-labor camp, plus five years in internal exile. If the WPA had responded to his position with understanding, he would probably have received a light sentence or none at all.

By the end of 1971 the Working Group had established a fairly regular pattern of work. The ten psychiatrist members and ten nonpsychiatrists met about once a month. Its secretary was Helena Abram, and I was its convener. It had no regular source of income, and for several years never enjoyed a bank balance of more than 150 pounds. After a time I started to solicit donations every year or two from newspaper editor David Astor and the playwright Tom Stoppard, for whom I had earlier done a favor, and each of them would give us 200 pounds.

Generally I did a presentation of the latest information on abuses from the USSR (and sometimes other countries too, including the U.K. and the United States); the group discussed what action to take: which items to send to which bodies and individuals, on what topics to write articles or letters to the editor, and who should sign them. We also started to plan to write letters to victims of abuse in the Soviet Union, or their families, and to organize trips by group members or friends or colleagues to visit these people. Our goal was to provide moral support and material help such as clothing and possibly money; to bring information about Western activities in defense of these victims (such as the victim's adoption as a "prisoner of conscience" by an Amnesty International group); and to request further information as to any particular needs the family might have.

One of the first of these visitors was the well-known actor David Markham, a strong supporter of the Working Group, who went to see the pioneering dissident and former victim of abuse, Alexander Yesenin-Volpin. Markham and his wife took Yesenin-Volpin out to a restaurant, where the latter, determined to behave normally, chatted volubly. He also gave Markham a copy of the latest *Khronika*, but without concealing it adequately. When Markham and his wife arrived at the border they and their possessions were aggressively searched and the issue of *Khronika* was soon found and confiscated. A few nerve-racking hours later, they were released from their detention. This is the only mishap that I can remember resulting from our visits.

The Slippery Dr. Leigh

The World Psychiatric Association, whose members were national societies of psychiatrists, was run by two officers and an executive committee. The WPA had now begun to play a critical role in the Western conflicts over the political abuse of psychiatry. The actions of its secretary-general, Dr. Denis Leigh, at the Mexico congress had helped the Kremlin and hurt not only specific dissidents in Russia, but also the whole movement that was working in their behalf. Not long after Bukovsky's trial I decided to confront Denis Leigh in person, a decision prompted by an interview that the journalist John Chandos had on January 21, 1972, with Leigh, a former British Army officer, about his role in the torture of Irish Republican Army soldiers in Ireland by members of the British military. At one point in the conversation, Chandos told me, Leigh had diverged to talk about the Mexico City WPA World Congress. Leigh expressed concern for the damaging effects on East-West relations of the allegations of Soviet abuse made in Mexico, and said he doubted their validity. When Chandos responded with surprise, Leigh replied that he was not convinced of the independence and authenticity of the evidence, and suspected there had been an elaborate operation by Russia's enemies to defame Russia, perhaps with CIA involvement. But he would welcome further evidence.

On February 3, I wrote to Leigh, told him of my conversation with Chandos, and asked whether he would kindly supply copies of any inauthentic documents so that I could examine them and offer my opinion. The next day Leigh phoned me and said that Chandos had been wrong to suggest that he had said he suspected forgery. He was concerned only with the official psychiatric reports on dissidents, not with any others (he did not say why). The authenticity of these had been confirmed to him in Mexico by Soviet psychiatrists. I then asked, "What evidence do you have of inauthentic evidence or CIA involvement?" Here Leigh became uneasy, but eventually said that a "Radio Free America of Miami" had pestered the Congress secretariat, which Leigh headed, asking that the WPA Congress condemn the USSR. He thought this station might have CIA connections.

I asked him, "Do you have any other evidence that our evidence is inauthentic?"

"Well, actually, no."

Leigh then volunteered that in his opinion Bukovsky was a schizophrenic, or at any rate had been in the past. He had spoken in Mexico to a psychiatrist who had examined him in the mid-1960s and had described Bukovsky's symptoms to him. He dismissed the evidence of Bukovsky's sanity provided by my friends, who had met him in 1970 and 1971. Leigh thought that the new sentence on him was cruel, but was partly to be explained by protests like the "letter of the 44" in *The Times*, which had done more harm than good. He was pleased he had gotten the "very nice" Professor Marat Vartanyan of Moscow's Institute of Psychiatry onto the WPA's executive committee. And Snezhnevsky (in reality as bad as Vartanyan) had offered to let him inspect the Serbsky Institute from top to bottom whenever he wished. Anyway, said Leigh, the psychiatric situation in the USSR was now improving, and he cited information to this effect. But it soon turned out to be untrue.

The whole episode illustrated the fact that although Leigh had consistently claimed to be neutral, just a servant of the WPA's executive committee and its member societies, in fact he had repeatedly taken the initiative in ways that had assisted the Soviet establishment and frustrated the growing body of opinion within the WPA's member societies that condemned Soviet abuses. When pressed, he had justified his position by suggesting that it was more effective to combat the abuse—as he sometimes claimed to be doing—by maintaining a dialog with the Russians than by risking the severance of contacts. The trouble here was that, as we have seen, he had several times let slip that he did not believe that any abuse existed. So his claim to be combating it carried no conviction. More convincing was the theory that Leigh was motivated in part by an empire-building urge: he wanted to prevent the large Soviet society of psychiatrists from being ousted from "his" WPA.

In our conversation Leigh had claimed to me that the campaign against abuses was sophisticated and expensive. This notion was decidedly eccentric, since the campaign's main organizer in 1971–1972 was our small, voluntary, and impecunious Working Group, whose honorary secretary, Helen Abram, had written to Leigh in longhand because she had no typewriter.

Anger after the Congress

The WPA Congress and one of its immediate consequences, Bukovsky's savage sentence, unleashed strong condemnation by the general public in the United States for virtually the first time (editorials and letters appeared in the *Washington Post*, the *New York Times*, and a blast from I. F. Stone in the *New York Review of Books*), as well as in Germany, France, and the Netherlands. The most sustained criticism was from Moscow dissidents and Britain. The WPA Congress had the additional consequence of muting criticism from the medical profession. The American Psychiatric Association made a promising start of sorts by having a new committee study the Bukovsky documents. But this soon fizzled out into virtual silence as the APA let its interest in the subject expire.

This decline in interest may have been deliberate. The official launching with much ceremony of Western-Soviet détente during President Richard Nixon's visit to Moscow in June 1972 resulted in weakening political pressure on the USSR in a number of ways. Détente included an agreement to conduct a joint U.S.-Soviet research project into schizophrenia, and this may have quashed the APA initiative. American psychiatrists had made a formal visit to the USSR in 1967, which had resulted in a 1969 book that was generally enthusiastic about and uncritical of Soviet practices, although it did pinpoint the absence of judicial review in civil commitment. This new project followed up on this earlier one. Whatever the full explanation in 1972, the sad fact was that the powerful APA now did virtually nothing to help Soviet dissidents incarcerated in psychiatric hospitals for the next four years.[16]

Meanwhile, the Kremlin reaffirmed its strong support for the Soviet psychiatric establishment, but in the autumn of 1972 it initiated a new policy of, basically, damage control: It continued to intern little-known dissenters in mental hospitals, which would not cause damaging publicity in the USSR or abroad, but it did not dispatch any well-known, arrested dissidents to either ordinary or prison psychiatric hospitals so as to avoid the inevitable bad publicity. Instead, they were sent to labor camps.

The Kremlin did not only do damage control, but engaged on a sort of charm offensive: in November 1972 it invested Dr. Leigh and William Linford Rees, a British psychiatrist who was also the WPA president, as honorary members of the Soviet Society of Psychiatrists. The move was a provocation to the well informed, such as the members of our group and other supporters of the dissidents.

A final Kremlin commitment turned out in practice to be more of a pious intention than a real fact. After Mexico, Snezhnevsky reportedly felt uneasy and decided to have the situation in the prison psychiatric hospitals inspected and improved. According to an anonymous but authenticated samizdat document, in 1972 he followed through: "The inspectors were appalled by what they saw. Their general conclusion was: a prison is a prison, and nothing else." As a result, in February 1973 an official Ministry of Internal Affairs directive, no. 022-S, gave the order "to change the whole appearance of the hospitals from looking like prisons to looking like hospitals." However, the samizdat author stated, "Things have not got better, and according to some reports even worse." Subsequent information confirmed the latter conclusion.

Dr. Semyon Gluzman's Report

In October 1972, news reached the West that a twenty-five-year-old psychiatrist from Kiev, Dr. Semyon Gluzman, had been sentenced to seven years in a strict-regime labor camp, followed by three of internal exile. Clearly—though it was not explicitly stated—the harsh sentence was retribution for Gluzman's having written, with two colleagues, an anonymous, revelatory analysis of the case of General Pyotr Grigorenko. From the labor camp Gluzman continued his dissent in a different key, helping to organize hunger strikes of prisoners for an amelioration of their terrible conditions and writing, with Bukovsky, a remarkable twenty-page booklet, *Manual on Psychiatry for Dissidents.* This brilliant document consists of detailed advice on how a dissident should best respond to a KGB interrogator and then, if necessary, a KGB psychiatrist, in order, hopefully, to be sent to a labor camp and not forcibly interned in a psychiatric hospital.[17]

Meanwhile, the Working Group was becoming ever more active. In November 1972 Andrei Sakharov appealed to the world's psychiatrists to intercede for their young colleague Gluzman, who had been "sentenced for his professional integrity." In response, in early 1973, Dr. Gerard Low-Beer, a member of our Working Group organized in Britain a series of telegrams to Sakharov bearing multiple signatures; their purpose was to furnish ammunition for Sakharov to advocate for incarcerated dissidents within the USSR. One of the telegrams read in part: "Very disturbed about Gluzman, Grigorenko, and other such cases. World opinion now beginning to understand the problem and reaction to it increasing." These telegrams had 200 signatories—a meaningful increase over the 44 signatures on Jenner's letter of the previous year. David Clark, another Working Group member, used Sakharov's appeal to stir the Royal College of Psychiatrists into action, and, through that, other medical organizations.

However, the successful visit of Leonid Brezhnev to the United States in June 1973, the indifference of Nixon and his national security adviser, Henry Kissinger, to human rights oppression in the USSR, and the rejection, by the International Congress of Psychotherapy in Oslo, of petitions presented to it led quickly to the internment of two well-known dissidents, the Ukrainian mathematician Leonid Plyushch, and another mathematician, Yuri Shikhanovich, in mental hospitals.

This in turn provoked four urgent appeals about psychiatric abuse from Moscow, including one from Sakharov's Human Rights Committee. The latter expressed its eager desire for East-West rapprochement, but then asked bitterly: "Where will the forces be found to combat this danger if even doctors desire neither to hear nor to speak about it?"[18]

This marked the beginning of a period of serious conflict between protesters in the USSR and the West, and on the other side, the Soviet authorities, Dr. Leigh, and the WPA. In hope of diverting attention from the issue and also to blunt criticism and protest, the WPA organized an elaborate conference on schizophrenia, to take place in Yerevan and Tbilisi, in the Armenian and Georgian Socialist Republics, in October. Following the conference Western participants were invited to visit the Serbsky Institute in Moscow. On July 29 *The Observer* published a story on the WPA's conference plan and revealed that conference attendees would be addressed by prominent but compromised Soviet psychiatrists such as the head of the Serbsky Institute, Georgy Morozov.

Khronika tekushchikh sobytii had been suppressed, but Sakharov had taken up the charge with numerous public reports on dissident events, and he now continued to speak out without fear despite a high-level demand that he keep quiet. On August 12 a long and radical critique of the whole Soviet system by Sakharov was published in the Western press.[19] Solzhenitsyn and a massive wave of Western protests spoke out to support him and his causes, among them the head of the Royal College of Psychiatrists, Sir Martin Roth, who stated in a press release that the college believed "that the treatment meted out to such men as Medvedev, Gluzman, and Grigorenko is odious, repugnant, and intolerable by any civilized standards."[20] In a separate letter to the press he stated that the college had not been consulted by the WPA concerning the October schizophrenia conference in any way. All this reached a crescendo on September 10, when the world press published a release from the U.S. National Academy of Sciences warning the USSR that if harassment of Sakharov, a foreign associate member of the academy, did not cease, or if he were arrested, scientific cooperation between the two countries would probably come to an end.[21]

The Kremlin had indeed planned to arrest Sakharov in the near future, but at this threat its plan bit the dust. The National Academy's warning also nudged the APA into proposing to Snezhnevsky a serious U.S.-Soviet investigation of specific alleged abuses of psychiatry. In response to this, however, the Soviet Society of Psychiatrists' twenty-one-member executive committee published a semi-hysterical harangue on Western psychiatry that appeared in various foreign media.[22] In the West and in Moscow it only provoked new protests attacking the abuse, including for the first time an editorial in the prestigious medical journal *The Lancet*.[23]

Events such as the October conference and the Serbsky visit were part and parcel of successive maneuvers and tricks of a sort often seen before, designed to get the less independent-minded Western psychiatrists onto the record as supposedly approving of Soviet practices. Major Russian players in this campaign were Marat Vartanyan, Andrei Snezhnevsky, and Georgy Morozov. Objections to their statements came from Alfred Freedman, the president of the APA, and others.[24]

In January 1974 the Kremlin sidestepped the public relations disaster of a second sensational trial of Alexander Solzhenitsyn, after the planned one of Sakharov, by the crude device of arresting Solzhenitsyn and forcing him to board a plane that took him into exile in the West.

International Momentum for Change

In Britain and most other Western countries, the impact on the psychiatric community of the Soviet manipulations at the Yerevan-Tbilisi conference was negative to the USSR. Sir Martin Roth, of the Royal College of Psychiatrists, asked to consult with the Working Group in order to come up with a public declaration of condemnation of Soviet practices by the college. A smaller subgroup of three, in which I participated, wrote a motion that the college adopted in London in November 1973. It turned out to be a breakthrough: "The Royal College of Psychiatrists deplores the current use of psychiatry in the Soviet Union for the purpose of political repression, and condemns the activities of doctors who lend themselves to this work." The proposer and seconder, Dr. Gerard Low-Beer and Dr. Harold Merskey, both Working Group members, were supported by a number of speakers, and no one spoke against. The college then wrote to equivalent bodies in fourteen countries proposing the creation of an impartial commission of inquiry into these matters; it could be headquartered in any country.[25]

By January 1974, a powerful movement arose in France, headed by an ad hoc group that called itself the International Committee of Mathematicians to Defend Yuri Shikhanovich and Leonid Plyushch. It quickly collected 550 signatures on an appeal for the release of Shikhanovich, who had translated works by famous French mathematicians into Russian. By July he was free.

The campaign to spotlight abuse of psychiatry in the USSR dovetailed with a historic development in East-West relations: negotiations within the Conference for Security and Cooperation in Europe and the Kremlin's economics-based decision to press ahead strongly in 1973–1974 with its participation in these negotiations. Among activists in the West interest in the negotiations had increased partly because the dissidents had shown that an easing of East-West tensions would improve their situation and the prospects of freedom for many of them. Thus the negotiations helped to produce in May 1974 both a relaxation of Soviet policies on permissible citizen activity and the sudden issuance by Moscow dissidents of four issues of *Khronika*. The conference unrolled in three stages. The third stage, which came to be known as the Helsinki Final Act, was signed by thirty-five participating countries in Helsinki in August 1975.

Meanwhile, I had established fruitful relations with Michel Broué, the organizer of the International Committee of Mathematicians, in France. Broué now had to embark on a tougher path regarding Plyushch, who was being inhumanly treated at the Dnepropetrovsk Special Psychiatric Hospital, in the Ukraine, and launched a petition drive to apply pressure on the Soviet authorities. Urged on by Sakharov, the committee soon assembled almost one thousand signatories to the petition to free him, which was published at an international congress of mathematicians in Vancouver and presented to the Kremlin.[26]

In Britain, protest continued and led to the release, in October 1974, of Victor Fainberg, the first inmate of a prison psychiatric hospital to be allowed immediately to emigrate, in this case, to the U.K. Six months later a Leningrad psychiatrist, Marina Voikhanskaya, who had begun quietly assisting interned dissidents, including Fainberg, was allowed to emigrate to Britain. Then Sir Martin Roth, the president of the Royal College of Psychiatrists, intensified the interventions made by the Royal College. In

July 1975 Roth wrote to Snezhnevsky that the college wished "to protest in the strongest terms against the continued incarceration of Gluzman, Bukovsky, and Plyushch, which appears a perversion of psychiatric practice and denial of natural justice. Your refusal to take action constitutes a slur on our profession."[27]

Two new initiatives in Britain at this time increased the pressures on the Kremlin still more. First, drawing to a great extent on materials made available by the Working Group, Amnesty International published a carefully documented book (anonymously written), *Prisoners of Conscience in the USSR: Their Treatment and Conditions*, that covered a variety of topics, including psychiatric abuse.[28] It was soon translated into several languages and created a worldwide stir in wide-ranging human rights circles. The second initiative was that in September 1975 a parallel body to the Working Group, more focused on public protests, got off the ground. Chaired by Henry Dicks, a doyen of British psychiatry and a predecessor of Martin Roth as chair of the Royal College, it became an effective vehicle for keeping the cases of interned dissidents in the spotlight.

Successful Campaigns for Plyushch and Others

Meanwhile, the campaign to free Leonid Plyushch from the especially cruel prison mental hospital in Dnepropetrovsk was gathering steam, coordinated in large measure by Michel Broué's International Committee of Mathematicians (ICM). The leading Soviet campaigner was the linguist and dissident Tatyana Khodorovich, who had compiled a book of documents detailing the persecution of Plyushch.[29]

To coordinate humanitarian efforts on Plyushch's behalf in many countries, the ICM designated April 23, 1975, as International Plyushch Day. Press articles and letters to the editor proliferated in Australia, Canada, Italy, and Switzerland, as well as the USSR, Britain, Germany, and France.[30] On that day Amnesty International held a symposium in Geneva where the speakers included Fainberg, the famous Kiev writer Viktor Nekrasov, and Marina Voikhanskaya, who had recently been allowed to emigrate and hence became the first Russian psychiatrist to speak in person in the West about the Soviet system of psychiatric abuse.

The ICM now planned a landmark event that was so effective that it turned out to be the last that was needed: a rally on October 23 on behalf of Plyushch's release, held at La Mutualité, a huge Paris hall. Came the day, the hall was packed with 5,000 people, many of them French Marxists, who vociferously demanded the Marxist Plyushch's release. The speakers represented a broad spectrum of groups, from the worlds of mathematics, psychiatry, humanitarian issues, education, the law, students, and Ukrainian groups that had cosponsored the meeting. Dr. Low-Beer traveled from London to speak for the Working Group.

The next day, the French Communist Party decided that the pressure was now too strong for it to remain silent or continue to sit on the fence about taking a public position regarding Plyushch's fate. If it was to retain credibility on the left, it must at last jump on the bandwagon. The October edition of its newspaper solemnly confirmed "our total disapproval and our demand that he be freed as soon as possible."[31] The very next day, Plyushch's wife was summoned to appear in Moscow, where officials informed her that her request to emigrate with her husband had been granted.

Plyushch's actual release and emigration to France followed two months later, on January 10, 1976.[32] Later, when he had recovered from the profound physical and mental ordeal that he had known in advance would be the consequence of his steadfast refusal to recant his views, he held numerous press conferences and gave interviews in Paris, and before long accepted the Working Group's invitation to do the same in London. I also arranged for him to have a long chat with a well-known psychiatrist, John Wing, who had earlier been skeptical about the charges of Soviet abuse. This conversation, while not a formal psychiatric examination, convinced him that Plyushch was sane and had been ruled insane on the basis of a false diagnosis.

The predictable anti-Western propaganda blast from Moscow that followed the excitement surrounding Plyushch's release was even more extreme than usual. Much of this blast consisted of attacks that appeared in Soviet newspapers. However, the British Communist newspaper, the *Morning Star*, alleged that Viktor Fainberg had been interned in a Western mental hospital after his release from the Soviet one; this outrageous smear cost the incautious newspaper 750 pounds and a groveling apology.[33] A Soviet paper, *Novosti*, reported that the well-known dissident Alexander Yesenin-Volpin had "returned to the USSR with his peculiar 'views,' was here supplied with suitable work, and an allowance, and now enjoys the concessions provided in the Soviet Union for all such invalids."[34] In fact, he was, as before, teaching mathematics at Boston University.

Resettling in the West as the Fight Continues

Emigration from the Soviet Union to the West was a daunting watershed in the lives of the few dissidents allowed to leave, but they managed to land on their feet with the help of the organizations that had agitated for their release. In Britain, Working Group member David Clark was able to arrange for the psychiatrist Marina Voikhanskaya to work in Fulbourn Hospital, a mental health hospital near Cambridge, where Clark was the director. Subsequently, she decided not to spend time requalifying as a psychiatrist, but her engaging personality made her a natural to set up her own successful practice in Cambridge as a psychological therapist. She often spoke in public about the Soviet system of abuse, which she had seen up close as a psychiatrist in Leningrad. Since the authorities had not allowed her to bring her young son, Misha, and her mother with her, the Working Group organized a lengthy campaign, with much use of the media, to force them to do so. After four years the campaign succeeded.

A year after Voikhanskaya left, another young psychiatrist, Yuri Novikov of Moscow, defected in Germany in June 1977. As one of two administrators at the Serbsky Institute and also as the head of the Serbsky Institute's Information Department, he had brought new information about how the Soviet Society of Psychiatrists worked. Although he had almost no involvement in political psychiatry, he was well informed about the practice because of his close association with the Serbsky's head, Georgy Morozov, and other Serbsky colleagues. Five long interviews with him were published in the German weekly *Stern*.

On July 3, 1978, the Working Group organized a public hearing held in London before an eminent and sympathetic lawyer, Louis Blom-Cooper, QC, in defense of Alexander Podrabinek. The idea was to attract public attention to Podrabinek's case and its context—the abuse of psychiatry. Novikov testified at the hearing, providing information on how the abuse was organized. His interviews and testimony in the public hearings must have caused Morozov acute unease.[35]

Since Novikov spoke good German, he ended up working as a psychiatrist in Hamburg. Later, in 1979, he invited me to give a lecture on the functions of our Working Group to a large human rights group in Hamburg. He helped me translate my speech so that I could deliver it in German.

The pressure on the Kremlin from human rights activists continued to bring successes. In December 1976 Vladimir Bukovsky was released from the labor camp and sent straight to Britain in a same-day exchange with the Chilean government, which had agreed to send Luis Corvalan, the leader of Chile's Communist Party, who was in prison, to the USSR. Bukovsky, the source of the seminal Bukovsky Papers that had prompted so much of the subsequent successful campaigning, was now free to approach the world's psychiatrists in person—and well in advance of the WPA's next big world congress, which was to be held in Honolulu in August.

Human rights activism continued to intensify also in the USSR. In late 1976, in Moscow, the Working Commission to Investigate the Use of Psychiatry for Political Purposes came into existence under the aegis of half a dozen dissidents headed by Alexander Podrabinek, who had just written the samizdat book *Karatel'naya meditsina* (*Punitive Medicine*).[36] In the first issue of its "Information Bulletin," the group stated its credo that "the support of a large section of world public opinion is the most important factor in the struggle against the use of psychiatry for political purposes. However, there are still hundreds of prisoners of conscience in Soviet psychiatric hospitals and they are in need of defense and support. Their names are little known or not known at all, a fact which . . . enables the police and the psychiatrists to act arbitrarily."[37] Podrabinek had compiled a list of 155 known Soviet citizens in the cohort of those illegally confined in mental hospitals.[38]

The spring of 1977 saw the publication in London of *Russia's Political Hospitals: The Abuse of Psychiatry in the Soviet Union*, by Sidney Bloch and me. Since the topic was rather new, it excited great interest and was widely reviewed and discussed.[39] The timing of this publicity was good because the book and the publicity helped to prepare the ground for planned strong action at the WPA International Congress in Honolulu on behalf of victims of the abuse and of the Podrabinek commission's work in Moscow. In our book we introduced readers to the connection between psychiatry and politics in the USSR by analyzing the growth of the current perverted system: from its origins in the humane attempt to save innocent citizens from death in Stalin's concentration camps by committing them to hospitals; to the emergence of the corrupt Snezhnevsky school of psychiatric theory in the 1960s at the Moscow Institute of Psychiatry; to the proclamation of Khrushchev's doctrine in 1959 that there were no longer any citizens opposed to Communism, except for a few mentally ill people who needed treatment in hospitals. This false but convenient doctrine caused the steady spread of what one could call the Snezhnevsky-Khrushchev system of abuse.

In late 1976 I compiled a register, "Victims of Soviet Psychiatric Abuse," for inclusion in the book. On the register were people who since 1962 been forcibly locked up in a mental hospital for peacefully expressing their beliefs, listed alphabetically by name, with their birth date, nationality, residence, cause of internment, source of information, and brief summary of the case. "Cause of internment" included sociopolitical activity, attempt or desire to emigrate, nationalism, religion, and what I call inconvenience to petty tyrants. "Sociopolitical activity" was the largest group, "religion" the second largest (because the dissident Baptists were especially assiduous in collecting information), and "inconvenient" the smallest. There were 210 names on the register.[40]

Not on the register were about one hundred dissenters who had been forcibly subjected to psychiatric examination—mostly in the Serbsky Institute, where the process normally lasted a month—but then had been ruled responsible for their actions and had not been sent to a mental hospital, but rather, usually, to a labor camp. Also excluded were a further fifty-four internees about whom the information available to date was not sufficient to classify them with reasonable confidence.

If we add the 210 dissenters listed in the register to the 155 people named by Podrabinek's group, the total number known to me to have been forced to undergo in-patient psychiatric procedures from 1962 to 1976 was 365. With rare exceptions, the relatives and friends of these individuals regarded them as being in no need of psychiatric care, let alone compulsory treatment.

TEN

Dignity under Persecution

Dissent among the Ethnic Minorities

Dissent among the ethnic minorities in the USSR is a huge subject, not least because of the large number of such minorities, estimated to be as many as 186 different groups. Then there are also religious groupings. Between 1960 and 1991 I had contact with dissidents in about twenty of those groups, and from among those I shall write about the Crimean Tatars, the Jews, and the Ukrainians.[1]

My understanding of the whole subject of the USSR's ethnic minorities really began with my study of early Soviet history. I learned that Lenin and Stalin gained a crucial level of political support, or at least acquiescence, from the minorities that had broken away from Russia for a few years after the collapse of the tsarist order in 1917 by creating supposedly free national republics for the principal minorities. Having their own republics gave the minority peoples assets they had never had under the unitary imperial system: their own national parliaments, governments, courts, cultural institutions, language outlets, and so on. By 1930 Stalin had drained most of the national essence from these institutions, but they remained as shells of their former selves. It always seemed to me that, after the horrors of Stalin's regime had eventually receded into the past, the minorities would gradually seek to escape from the de facto unitary state of the USSR by breathing new national essence back into the formally independent institutions that Lenin and Stalin had given them around 1921. This is what indeed happened from 1987 on, though in varying degrees from republic to republic.

The Crimean Tatars

The first ethnic minority with which I came in contact in the context of dissent was the Crimean Tatars, the longtime inhabitants of the region that under Stalin became the Crimean Autonomous Soviet Socialist Republic. The Tatars represented a special case in the context of the trajectory of other ethnic republics because they had been ripped out of the republic originally granted to them. The disaster struck on May 18, 1944, when Stalin's thugs gave the entire Tatar population of Crimea—some quarter of a million people—twenty minutes to collect their children, old folks, and basic possessions, and then immediately deported them to the barren deserts of Central Asia. This was punishment for their supposed collaboration with the German invaders in World War II—in fact there is very little evidence that the Tatars constituted a fifth column within the USSR. According to the Tatars' painstaking calculations, by the end of 1945 this fearful act of ethnic cleansing had caused the deaths of 46 percent of their people, mainly the children and the elderly.

The national movement to return home to the Crimea took shape in 1956–1957, earlier than the formation of any other dissident group in the Soviet Union, a fact that gave them a prominent role in the growth of the whole dissident movement. Determined delegations of Tatars traveled to Moscow to register their demands. In March 1958 one of them was received by Khrushchev's right-hand man, Anastas Mikoyan, who apparently sought to appease its members but actually did nothing for them. The movement was remarkably inclusive, in many ways truly a grassroots "bottom-up" national movement. From 1957 on it sent to the Kremlin regular delegations carrying petitions and protests, many of them signed by tens of thousands of people, and also organized dozens of street demonstrations in Moscow and elsewhere.

In 1967 all this at last brought results, and they obtained a concession. An official decree removed the charge that the Tatars had collaborated with the Germans, and 12,000 were allowed to return to the Crimea. Soon, however, all 12,000 of them who had returned to their homeland were at once deported unceremoniously back to Central Asia, and seventeen of these were sentenced to prison terms. "The decree was issued not for you, but for the press, and for the foreign press at that," the deputy-chief of the Crimean police is reported to have barked. Nonetheless, their arrests and trials only spurred them to greater activity, even though this achieved no success in their main goal.

In 1964 their movement started issuing a regular samizdat newsletter, and in 1966–1967 it established fruitful relations with the emerging human rights movement in Moscow. The latter were following the example of the Tatars' newsletter when they started *Khronika tekushchikh sobytii* (Chronicle of current events).

In about 1966–1967 General Pyotr Grigorenko, a Communist, became friendly with a dissent-inclined Communist and Leninist in Moscow, Aleksei Kosterin, who was close to the exiled Crimean Tatars. This friendship is how the Tatars began to work with the broader human rights movement. In February 1968 a group of twelve leading dissidents included in its appeal "To the Consultative Conference of Communist Parties in Budapest" the sentence "We also call your attention to the fact of discrimination against small nations and the political persecution of people who are struggling for national equality, all this being particularly clear in the case of the Crimean Tatars."[2]

In return for this the Tatars leaped to the defense of their champion, Pyotr Grigorenko, when he was persecuted and then interned in a prison hospital. Emblematic was a placard they unfurled at a demonstration on Moscow's Mayakovsky Square in June 1969 that read "Free General Grigorenko!" and carried a photograph of him next to the slogan.

Among the Tatars' qualities that struck me the most was the fact that, although they had faced a barbaric policy of ethnic genocide that killed tens of thousands of innocent people, including a fearful number of defenseless children and old people, they had stayed true to the inspiring but difficult policies of nonviolence and democratic self-governance. This achievement (*podvig*) expressed the essence of what the human rights activist and historian Lyudmila Alekseyeva has called their dignity under persecution, their absence of nationalistic pride or xenophobia, their abhorrence of violence, their benevolence toward the peoples living around them, and their patience with the opinions of others.[3]

They had great difficulty, however, settling back in. Most of their dwellings had been stolen from them in their absence, and now they faced housing, land, and employment problems that officials did nothing to alleviate but actually exacerbated. Over 100,000 others remained in Central Asia. In 2014, Putin annexed Crimea to Russia, and the Tatars were, once again, persecuted severely. Their leaders were driven abroad and their institutions forcibly closed down.

To go back to 1987, despite Mikhail Gorbachev's release of virtually all political prisoners, the Tatars had still not achieved their main goal of returning home. Aysha Seytmuratova, a Crimean Tatar historian, was broadcasting daily to them on Radio Liberty and Voice of America and wrote in a private letter that they were trying to return from Central Asia on foot, because the authorities took them off trains and out of cars. However, it was "difficult for the regime to crush the Tatars, because now the people's patience has run out. Its understanding has sharply increased."[4] Four years later, after forty-seven long years, the Kremlin at last relented. Tatars started to stream back, notwithstanding the various forms of resistance put up to their resettlement by the Crimean authorities. At least they were back in the Crimean Autonomous Republic (now part of Ukraine) and able to create, though not easily, their own parliament, local councils, and cultural and media institutions.

I first learned about the Crimean Tatars' movement in 1967–1968. Initially I was curious, then I was impressed, and I persuaded the editor of *The Observer* to publish an article I wrote about them. "Exiled Tatars in Struggle with Kremlin" appeared on March 30, 1969, on the front page, with the byline "By Our Diplomatic Staff." It recounted for the first time for the Western public the story of this unknown people. It appeared with two photographs showing the police trying to break up a peaceful demonstration in Central Asia. Also, the KGB was preparing to launch a massive trial of ten Tatars in Tashkent. As the main source for my article, I used a samizdat document that had just reached me, issue no. 82 of the *Information Bulletin of the Permanent Representation of Crimean Tatars in Moscow*. One of these people had given it to Russian dissidents, who had outwitted the KGB to smuggle it from Moscow to London. When we later received the full secretly recorded verbatim account of the trial, the Alexander Herzen Foundation in Amsterdam published the entire text as an 854-page book.[5]

In 1973, *Khronika* devoted the whole of issue 31 to the Tatars, covering the dramatic events of the early 1970s. I published further articles about the Tatars, one in *The Observer*, and two chapters in books.[6] Meanwhile, other journalists, writers, and a documentary filmmaker produced a stream of materials about the history and plight of the Tatars. I had befriended Aysha Seytmuratova, who had moved to the United States in the mid-1970s, and she helped me with my writings.

The best photographic views that Western press readers saw of the Crimean Tatars came in 1974, when the *Sunday Times* devoted fourteen pages of its magazine section to the feature "The Right to Dissent," with an article by me. It included some fifty photographs of Soviet dissidents, one-fifth of whom were Crimean Tatars.[7] The most dramatic Tatar photo showed a procession of 7,000 to 8,000 Tatars in the Central Asian city of Yangi-Yul, protesting against the police killing of their compatriot Femi Aliyev in a demonstration.

A major undertaking that saw the light of day in 1980 was a 450-page book that provided a full transcript of a January 1970 trial of the much-imprisoned Tatar leader Mustafa Djemilev and the Moscow dissident Ilya Gabai.[8] Djemilev was defended by the brave lawyer Dina Kaminskaya, who asked for a not-guilty verdict. Gabai defended himself; he made a speech that when printed ran to thirty-eight pages, at the end of which he, too, asked to be found not guilty. Both were given sentences of three years in forced-labor camps, Gabai in one of ordinary regime, and Djemilev in one of strict regime.

In May 2012 I had the honor to be invited by Mustafa Dzhemilev, the president of the Crimean Tatar Parliament, or Mejlis, to the Crimea for a five-day visit to take part in the annual memorial meetings for the 100,000 Tatars who died or were killed in 1944–1945, many of them children and the elderly. I was one of more than a dozen speakers who addressed a banner-waving crowd of 30,000 Tatars at a four-hour meeting on the main square of the Crimean capital, Simferopol. After Dzhemilev, the grand mufti of the Tatars, and others had spoken, I gave my speech in Russian. I recounted that I had been invited because my respect for their people's courage had led me to start writing about their cause in Western media and books in 1969. I had been able to do this thanks to the dedicated work of their movement in sending delegates and documents to Moscow, and from there, with help from the dissidents, to the West. People I spoke to afterward were surprised and delighted to learn that such a network had been created and had functioned in the ways intended.

The Jewish Movement

The Jews, considered an ethnic minority in the USSR, were also a special case for several main reasons. First, being scattered in many regions of the country, they had no republic of their own and therefore no self-government, even a nominal one. Second, they had a diaspora twice as big as their own population within the USSR of 2.5 to 3 million, and many diaspora Jews were ready to support in one way or another the desire of a large proportion of them to emigrate. Third, in June 1970 a group of twelve "refuseniks" (Jews who had been refused emigration) became so frustrated at being repeatedly denied emigration that they organized a plan to escape abroad on a small plane that one of them would pilot. After this was aborted at the last moment, they were all arrested and two of them were sentenced to death. This gave rise to such a worldwide outcry that the authorities backed down on the death sentences a few days later.

And fourth, after a mere two years of campaigning, the Jews started to achieve something denied by the Kremlin to all other dissenting groups except the Volga Germans: namely a sizable amount of the rare commodity known as success. From 1968 to 1970 about 1,000 Jews a year were allowed to leave, and starting in 1971 this figure went up dramatically, reaching some 51,000 by 1979. Then it declined sharply to nearly zero, before leaping back up under Gorbachev to 187,000 in 1991. Thus, from 1971 on, journalists and researchers in the outside world had no shortage of informed Jews from whom to seek information.

To put the movement's launch in historical context, one could say that in late 1968 "the Jews of silence" finally lost their patience. Their community began to speak, led by a group of twenty-six Lithuanians. By 1970 they were shouting. They had been inspired by Israel's victory in the war against the Arabs in 1967 and the example given by the dissidents since 1965. An early leader, Boris Kochubievsky, expressed the message: "I am a Jew. I want to live in the Jewish state. That is my right, just as a Ukrainian has the right to live in Ukraine, a Russian to live in Russia, and a Georgian to live in Georgia. . . . I want my children to go to a Jewish school. I want to read Jewish papers. I want to go to Jewish theaters."[9]

Complicating the situation, however, the Israeli government and its most obedient supporters abroad tried to impose a specific policy on Jews in the outside world and other supporters of the "Soviet exodus." They believed that the best way to keep the exodus going was by quiet pressure on the Kremlin behind the scenes and by telling the Soviet Jewish "refuseniks" not to collaborate with other groups such as the human rights movement; thus the foreign publicity given to Jewish protests in the USSR should be modest. To try to enforce this policy to tamp down publicity, the Israeli government encouraged setting up Jewish groups in the principal target countries of emigration for the strictly limited purpose of agitating for Jews' right to emigrate—for example, the National Conference on Soviet Jewry in the United States.

Many Soviet and diaspora Jews rejected this policy as being too passive; they thought the premise that pressuring the Kremlin publicly would be counterproductive was false. So they founded their own organizations to pursue a bolder line of maximum responsible pressure and publication of information. The most successful example in the United States was the Student Struggle for Soviet Jewry, and in Britain, the Women's Campaign for Soviet Jewry, headed by Rita Eker and Margaret Rigal and assisted in crucial ways by the indefatigable Michael Sherbourne. Sherbourne, a Russian teacher, spoke Russian fluently, and he phoned Soviet Jewish refuseniks and their families every day. He pioneered the additional step of recording on tape the documents they dictated and the information they gave about themselves and others regarding KGB actions against individuals as well as everyday needs that could be met by visits from Jews in the West.

Thanks to the determined refusenik dissent in Moscow, Leningrad, the Baltic states, Ukraine, Georgia, and elsewhere, and the countless demonstrations and media protests in their support in the West, only 135 refuseniks were arrested from 1969 through 1984, and all of them received only short terms at labor camp or internal exile.[10]

For my own information about Soviet refuseniks I remained in close contact with the Women's Campaign for Soviet Jewry and the exceptionally helpful Sherbourne, who quickly wrote up each phone conversation. My public contributions on Soviet Jewry, apart from the occasional press article (the media covered the Jews quite well), were to circulate any Jewish documents I received, to document the Jewish sections of the *Chronicle of Current Events*, to add extensive commentaries to the chapter on the Jews in my book on the *Chronicle*, and to include sections on the Jews in book chapters I wrote about the full range of dissenting groups in the Soviet Union.[11]

Not surprisingly, many of the refuseniks emigrated to Israel, while many others chose the United States, Canada, the U.K., or elsewhere. Some later moved from Israel to the United States on finding conditions in Israel harder than they expected. Julius Telesin, an active member of the human rights movement, was one of those who settled in Israel in 1970. Known in Moscow as Prints Samizdatskiy (Prince Samizdat) for the assiduity of his typing and circulation of samizdat documents like the *Khronika*, he gladly accepted my invitation first to visit the U.K. and then to write the foreword to my book on the *Khronika*, in which he described in fascinating detail the principles on which the human rights movement operated and his own roles in it.[12]

Another Jew who cooperated vigorously with the movement was the well-known computer specialist Anatoly Shcharansky. Refused permission to emigrate in 1973, he became active as an interpreter between Western reporters and Russian dissidents, including Andrei Sakharov, and refuseniks. In 1976 he cofounded the Moscow group to monitor the Kremlin's observance of the Helsinki Agreements. On this activity he later commented, "My interest in helping other persecuted peoples was an important part of my own freedom—a freedom that became real only after I returned to my Jewish roots. . . . Only he who understands his own identity and has already become a free person can work effectively for the human rights of others."[13]

Arrested in 1977 and sentenced a year later on trumped-up charges as a supposed "American spy," Shcharansky behaved with remarkable courage under fearful conditions in prisons and camps for eight years, before being exchanged for a pair of real Soviet spies held in the United States. After joining his wife in Israel, he changed his first name to Natan, wrote and published a weighty autobiography, entered politics, and later became a minister in the Israeli government.[14]

Ukrainian Dissidents

The Ukrainians have had a long and complex relationship with the Russians. Starting with a common ancestry in the ninth century, they later lost territorial contact with each other, before the Ukraine ended up being incorporated into the Russian empire. In the nineteenth century, Ukrainians started developing their independent language, literature, and culture, only to have them persecuted by Moscow. In 1917–1919, however, they at last gained independence, only to have it taken away by a combination of military force and the promise of being able to operate their own republic with its own political, legal, and cultural institutions within what became the USSR. But in the 1930s Stalin reduced these institutions to an empty formality, destroyed most of the Ukrainian intelligentsia, and deliberately caused some 4 million Ukrainians, mostly peasants, to starve to death.

After a more tolerant start in the 1950s, Khrushchev developed the doctrine of the "coming together" of the Soviet nations, which was leading toward their "merging" (*sliyanie*)—but in effect this "merging" meant russification. In the early 1960s a few Ukrainian intellectuals formed a group to begin to seriously protest this policy; in the mid-sixties a much larger group was formed that included some of the previous dissenters. Both groups put heavy emphasis on the constitution's basis in the country's federal structure and its guarantee, in Article 17, of the right of republics such as the Ukrainian Soviet Socialist Republic to secede from the USSR. Members of both groups met with severe reprisals. However, numerous documents written by the individuals were translated and collected in two books edited by the Ukrainian journalist Vyacheslav Chornovil and the British academic Victor Swoboda, the latter writing under the pseudonym of Michael Browne.[15]

These works were complemented by a wide-ranging historical analysis by Ivan Dzyuba of the national rights of Ukrainians and the methods used against them by the russifiers in Moscow and elsewhere. *Internatsionalizm chy rusyfikatsiia* (Internationalism or russification? A study in the Soviet nationalities problem) started to circulate in samizdat in 1966, and appeared in the West in English in 1968.[16] A year later, at an official meeting to discuss his work, two writers accused Dzyuba of disclosing state secrets. To Dzyuba's bewildered question—what secrets were they talking about, since he had never had access to any?—one of them replied indignantly, "Is not the disclosure of our party's nationalities policy the divulgence of a state secret?"

Dzyuba and Chornovil do not use the words "nationalism" and "nationalist," but rather "national movement" and "equal national rights" in order to distinguish themselves from the armed Ukrainian nationalist opposition that fought against the Nazis and then the Soviet Communists during and after World War II, right up to 1953.

In 1965–1966 two dozen intellectuals were arrested and most of them received heavy sentences. This, coupled with the explosion of the human rights movement in Moscow in early 1968 provoked a rapid expansion of the national movement in Ukraine. In April 1968 a "letter of the 139" intellectuals and workers denounced both the Ukrainian and the Moscow trials, and commented, "In Ukraine, where violations of democracy are magnified and aggravated by distortions connected with the national question, the symptoms of Stalinism are being manifested even more overtly and grossly."[17] By this time key figures in the Ukrainian human rights movement such as Ivan Svitlychny had established close connections with *Khronika* through Lyudmila Alekseyeva, Larissa Bogoraz, and others. They also expressed their belief in the rights of groups such as Jews, Crimean Tatars, Belorusians, and Armenians, and solidarity with their struggles.

The movement was strongest in Kiev and western Ukraine, but was not confined to that part of the region. In Dnepropetrovsk, in the southeast, the chairman of the Ukrainian Writers' Union, Oles Honchar, in 1968 published his novel *Sobor* (The cathedral), whose theme is the historical depth of Ukrainian culture; it provoked furious debate in the Ukrainian media, followed by official reprisals against its supporters. "The Cathedral in Scaffolding," a profound analysis of the book by a leading intellectual dissenter, Yevhen Sverstyuk, could only be published abroad.[18]

These developments and others led to the appearance in January 1970 of a rough Ukrainian equivalent of *Khronika*, *Ukrains'kyi Visnyk* (Ukrainian herald). Four issues of this substantial publication, with greater purely intellectual content than *Khronika* offered, came out over the next year, before threats and arrests caused it to close. But this did not stop the appearance of protest documents of other sorts.

In November 1976 the Ukrainian Public Group to Assist the Implementation of the Helsinki Agreements came into existence, following the example of the Moscow group that had emerged a few months earlier.[19] Two months later it faced persecution when its leader, the writer Mykola Rudenko, and another of its ten members were arrested and later sentenced to long terms. However, the group continued to function and acquire new members for a few more years, despite continuing harassments and arrests, before the drastic clampdown on all dissent that began in 1979 more or less finished it off.

My own contribution to the impressive Ukrainian movement, which continued in various forms until the collapse of the Communist system, was similar to what I put into the Jewish movement. Apart from writing the occasional article, I compiled an annotated chapter on the Ukrainians in my book *Uncensored Russia,* added footnotes to each Amnesty International issue of *A Chronicle of Current Events*, which carried rich material from Ukraine, and wrote sections on the Ukrainian movement in book chapters about the different forms of dissent in the USSR.[20]

From 1987 on, Gorbachev's relaxation of controls allowed the movement to burst forth again. This gave overwhelming momentum to the Ukrainian referendum of December 1991 that sweepingly supported the parliament's decision to break away from the USSR and create an independent Ukrainian state.

ELEVEN

Religious Persecution, Religious Dissent

Religious dissent in the Soviet Union extended from the Lithuanian Catholics in Lithuania, to the Ukrainian Catholics, or Uniates, in western Ukraine, to the Apostolic Church in Armenia, to the Georgian Orthodox in Georgia, to the Muslims in the north Caucasus and the Tatar Republic, to the Russian Orthodox in heartland Russia and elsewhere, and to the Baptists, Pentecostals, and Seventh Day Adventists in a wide variety of places.

The level of official persecution varied considerably, with the Ukrainian Catholics and elements of the Protestant sects outlawed and the others simply harassed and persecuted in differing degrees. The Kremlin's rationale for this was the Communist doctrine that all religion was reactionary and dying out, and that soon the whole population would see the virtues of atheism. This strategy needed to be implemented by the party and a few specialized state and KGB agencies in the hope that the outside world could be fooled into thinking that religion was free in the USSR.

The Founding of Keston College

My understanding of the situation of religious dissidents in the USSR developed out of my friendship with the Reverend Michael Bourdeaux, who as a student had studied in the USSR and had undertaken research on the Orthodox Church in Russia. In 1969 we managed to promote this research on a significant scale by collaborating with Michael's friend Sir John Lawrence and my colleague and friend Professor Leonard Schapiro to form what came to be called Keston College: The Centre for the Study of Religion and Communism. Its brief was to study all religions in all Communist countries, but to study the Soviet Union in particular.[1]

Located near London in Keston, Kent, Keston was considered by the KGB to be a hostile, anti-Soviet organization, although in fact it was an apolitical research and educational group, which simply gathered, digested, and circulated the facts to anyone interested. Eventually the Keston News Service was started to facilitate this function of the college.

The number of people who were interested was quite large until the late 1980s, because scores of Soviet believers sat in prisons and camps on account of their faith, and Keston was the only body that could provide reliable information to enable interventions, prayers, and visits to the USSR on their behalf.[2] So the Keston News Service had a wide readership, while Keston's journal *Religion in Communist Lands* (later renamed *Religion, State, and Society*) appealed to more scholarly readers. This journal was edited by Xenia Howard-Johnston (later Xenia Dennen), who gave it high academic standards and ensured balance. Another important achievement by Keston was to develop an impressive and unique archive of samizdat documents and secondary materials and a library that grew to contain 8,000 books and 200 periodicals. From Keston's origins up to the present day the institution has remained wholly independent, interfaith, and international in character, despite needing to fend off occasional efforts by religious extremists or Western governments to pressure it to espouse their positions. For example, in 2001–2002 Lawrence Uzzell, who had succeeded Bourdeaux as director, led a group that wanted Keston to focus solely on current events and tried to take it over to that end. This attempt was defeated by Keston's longtime leading members.

Keston had a group of patrons who were some of the most senior religious leaders in the U.K., usually including the Archbishop of Canterbury. To direct and oversee its work on a day-to-day basis, the college appointed a council made up of individuals eminent in Keston's field—the intersection of religion and Communist regimes—usually including a bishop, a former ambassador, a former director of the Great Britain–USSR Association, and a couple of academics. The charming and knowledgeable Sir John Lawrence served as an exemplary chairman, the director was an Anglican priest, the Reverend Michael Bourdeaux, and Leonard

Schapiro and I were members.[3] Lawrence came from an Anglo-Irish and Indian background. He had served in the British embassy in Moscow during World War II and edited there the uncensored publication *Britanskiy soyuznik* (British ally). Later, as the chairman of the Great Britain–USSR Association, he shocked many of its members when, in the early 1980s, he presciently dismissed Communism in the pages of *The Times* by saying, "There's no substance in it! Communism will collapse like a house of cards, and I shall live to see it." He also edited a journal of his own, *Frontier*, which expressed his Christian humanist outlook, and wrote seven books about Russia.

Keston's three main activities—research, education, and being a clearinghouse for disseminating information—evolved in natural ways over the years. In 2007 Keston College's reduced finances forced a move to smaller premises in Oxford; its all-important archive and library were sold to Baylor University in Texas, where the Keston Center for Religion, Politics, and Society took root; and Keston College divided into two institutions, Keston-Oxford and Keston-Baylor. Keston-Oxford became the Keston Institute in Oxford, where it still flourishes on a modest scale.

My involvement in publicizing religious problems in the Soviet Union widened in spring 1976, when an Australian friend, George Boniecki, invited me to give some lectures in Australia and New Zealand on this topic and its sociopolitical context. This was a challenging assignment, but came off as an enjoyable undertaking, because although none of the participants were very knowledgeable, all were keen to learn.

Publicizing Religious Dissent

My work in the field falls into three periods: the late 1960s, 1975, and the mid-1980s.

THE 1960S: RELIGIOUS SAMIZDAT

In the first period, when Bourdeaux was publishing pioneering books and compilations of documents from persecuted Baptists and Russian Orthodox, he and I collaborated on a major article in 1968 about the harassment and imprisonment of members of the outlawed, independent section of the Baptist church. In addition, in 1968 I wrote an analysis of how the authors of the samizdat documents of the Baptists and the Orthodox argued on the basis that they were carefully observing the Soviet Constitution and laws, thus using the same method as the human rights dissidents.[4] The publications in which these articles appeared, especially the journal *Problems of Communism,* were, for many scholars, the first ones to introduce them to the existence and significance of samizdat.

The legalist viewpoint featured vividly in the writings of the main Orthodox ally of the Moscow dissidents, Anatoly Levitin. In 1965 he spoke about his articles to a meeting of prominent atheists in Moscow:

> I write there the truth. You yourselves do not say that there is any untruth in them. I protest against the barbaric persecution of religion, which expresses itself in the destruction of churches and the humiliation of believers. I protest against a situation in which the Church has been reduced to scum, and comrade Trushin, who is present, is the dictator of the Moscow Church. He, an unbeliever and a Communist, appoints and removes priests at whim. . . . All this infringes every norm and even our Stalinist Constitution. Against all this I protest in my articles, which I have circulated, am circulating, and will circulate, exercising my right to freedom of expression.

In 1971 Levitin was sentenced to a three-year term in a forced-labor camp.[5]

THE 1970S: A CHURCH SCANDAL IN SOVIET GEORGIA

In 1974 Keston received from Georgia a dossier of documents about a major scandal in the Georgian Orthodox Church. It investigated them for over a year to check out their authenticity and then asked me to write them up for the journal *Religion in Communist Lands.*[6] My article, "The Georgian Orthodox Church: Corruption and Renewal," appeared in 1975 and was summarized in *The Times.*[7]

As background, I began by noting that Georgia, in the Caucasus Mountains to the south of the Russian heartland, was one of the USSR's fifteen federated republics, and had received Christianity in the fourth century, five hundred years ahead of Russia. Only in the late eighteenth century was the country swallowed up by the Russian empire, which took away the Georgian Orthodox Church's autocephaly. The subsequent russification of the church and the other institutions was interrupted for a few years, when Georgia regained its long-lost independence in 1918 and held it until 1921.

The immediate cause of the scandal was the death of the Georgian Orthodox Church's head, Patriarch Efrem II, in April 1972. Efrem had left a written document in which he named Bishop Ilya as his preferred successor. Yet Efrem's death was followed by the immediate illegal seizure of power by the frail, corrupt Khariton Devdariani, who took the title Patriarch David V. David V then elevated Bidzina Keratishvili, a twenty-seven-year-old ex–drug dealer and convict, to a bishopric and allowed him to run the church. David V and Keratishvili were secretly in league with the KGB. The outcome of these maneuverings was the collapse or degradation of many parishes, the disappearance of the patriarchate's treasure, and the loss of public respect for the church as a whole.

These facts became known because they were laid out in an official report. The Prosecutor's Office in Georgia had appointed a senior investigator, the honest and professional David Koridze, to examine every aspect of these events. In March 1973 his lengthy report began to circulate, and later it formed the core of my *Times* article. But the party authorities took no action to deal with the scandal; instead they tried to discredit the findings published in the report. Among Koridze's recommendations for corrective action was an injunction to safeguard thirteen individuals who could testify to the accuracy of his findings. However, one of them soon died in an unexplained car crash, and another, Valentina Pailodze, was sent to a labor camp on trumped-up charges. Weighing in on the side of the party authorities in 1975 was Professor David Lang, of London, an expert on Georgian history who was a well-known apologist for Kremlin policies in Georgia. He launched an intemperate attack on my article, which led to a long back-and-forth with him in both *The Times* and in the journal *Religion in Communist Lands*.[8]

The whole scandal came to an end at last, in 1977, when the Georgian Church elected a new patriarch named Ilya II to the position he holds to this day.

1980S: COUNTERING SOVIET PROPAGANDA REGARDING RELIGIOUS FREEDOM

In the early 1980s the Soviet authorities made especially vigorous efforts to persuade the U.S. National Council of Churches and the World Council of Churches, to which the principal Soviet churches belonged, that freedom of religion was blossoming in the USSR. Their key aide in this was the Reverend Bruce Rigdon, an American minister. In 1983 he persuaded the U.S.-based *NBC News* and its executive producer for religious programming, Helen Marmor, to produce and air a two-hour documentary on the Russian Orthodox Church, with himself as the anchor and narrator. The documentary, *The Church of the Russians,* was visually beautiful, had high production values, and painted a deceptive picture of a free and flourishing church.

Then, in 1984, Reverend Rigdon organized and led a National Council "peace invasion" of the Soviet Union by 266 mainly American Christians. Before leaving on the trip, they viewed the NBC documentary, but no other films or publications that might upset its soothing impact.

These events encouraged me to investigate Reverend Rigdon's activities further. In two articles, I pointed out that neither of these events could have occurred in Britain, because Keston's information and analyses were too widely read there.[9] My most charitable explanation of the National Council's motivation in advocating for the Soviet Union's friendliness to religion was to suggest that its "natural yearning to promote world peace and closer fellowship with Soviet Christians has been manipulated by the Kremlin—to Moscow's advantage and transparent satisfaction."

Of the documentary's message I wrote:

> On the central issue of the church's relations with the state, the outcome is an extraordinary unanimity of view. The narrator, the camera, and the seven high officials of church and state who are interviewed, all tell the same story. Either explicitly or implicitly they tell the viewer that the Soviet state respects the Constitution's strict separation of church and state, does not interfere in religious affairs, and guarantees for the churches a large measure of freedom. In a variety of ways the impression is built up that the church can have as many places of worship, monasteries, priests, and seminar-

ies as it wishes, and can issue publications and make films at will, without censorship.

All this could be promulgated because not only were the materials of Keston and Michael Bourdeaux ignored, but so too were the one hundred pages of confidential reports by Vasily Furov, deputy head of the Kremlin's and the KGB's Council on Religious Affairs, which included complaisant churchmen and acted to keep the churches under tight official control. These reports came from a mole in the circles of this council and received wide circulation in much of the West. They gave chapter and verse on the strict government controls and manipulation of church groups, thus directly contradicting the message of the National Council and NBC that the churches were free. Then I spelled out some of the current facts about imprisoned Christians, including two hundred Baptists; newly sentenced Catholic priests; and the recent death in a labor camp of the revered eighty-four-year-old leader of the Adventists.

My prolonged efforts to find out exactly how the Rigdon-Marmor enterprise had taken shape did not come up with a clear answer. Bruce Rigdon told me that alternative views could not be given because the program was not long enough (at two hours). Helen Marmor explained to me weakly that the critical voices in various Russian churches were "another story" that had already been covered.

Thus it was hard to escape the impression that part of the explanation for the travesty represented by the documentary lay in some sort of a deal struck with the Soviet authorities. This conclusion was confirmed obliquely but not directly by an NBC official in private. The main consolation, it turned out, was that three years later Gorbachev had the humanity to release almost all of his country's religious and dissident prisoners in a single year.

TWELVE

Fighting on Old and New Fronts

1968 to 1983

Until the early seventies, the United States lagged far behind Britain in its responses to dissent in the Soviet Union.[1] That status changed with an important event in 1973: the arrival in New York of the prominent Moscow dissident Valery Chalidze. He had come by way of a two-week stay in London, to which I had invited him at his request, so that he could give five lectures at the London School of Economics and Political Science (LSE), where I taught. Chalidze brought with him his wife, Vera Slonim, a granddaughter of a famous former minister of foreign affairs in the USSR, Maxim Litvinov. Although the Chalidzes intended to return to the Soviet Union—they had brought minimal luggage with them—they were not truly surprised when the USSR Supreme Soviet barred their reentry by quickly depriving them of their citizenship while they were abroad. Consequently they decided to proceed on to the United States, where they were welcomed by an American Russophile, Ed Kline.

In Moscow Chalidze was a dedicated proponent of Yesenin-Volpin's "legalist" philosophy, which held that both the authorities and dissident groups should use Soviet law as the basis for action on human rights issues. Dissident groups were already doing this. This had as a consequence that Chalidze and the Human Rights Committee (Komitet prav cheloveka) that he, Andrei Sakharov, and two others had set up in 1970, did research on, for example, the legal rights of people deemed by psychiatrists to be mentally ill, who in some cases were really dissidents. The committee's members were highly esteemed in the human rights movement, even though some dissidents saw the committee as being rather academic in its approach.

In his LSE lectures Chalidze expounded this "legalist" philosophy in somewhat abstract terms, while I acted as interpreter. Although the lectures were perfectly comprehensible to the huge and captivated audience, not all of the terms used by Chalidze were easy to translate, so after the first lecture I handed over the job to a native-speaker colleague.

New Publishers, New Publications, New Channels

The American Ed Kline had inherited several clothing stores from his father, but was spending most of his time in the 1960s learning Russian and reading about Russian history and politics. Before long, he sold the stores. His studies had given birth to a strong interest in dissent, and he was delighted to help the Chalidzes to settle into an apartment near his own on the Upper East Side, and to work with Valery on supporting dissidents of various stripes. Before long, they had revived the defunct Chekhov Press to put out books of literary merit in Russian, and had set up Khronika Press to publish each issue of *Khronika* in Russian in the West, as soon as it reached them, and also the new bimonthly journal that Ed and I had founded, *A Chronicle of Human Rights in the USSR*, in English and Russian editions.[2] The journal included more materials written in the West than did the *Chronicle of Current Events*, and was compiled by Valery with help from Ed, me, and, soon, Pavel Litvinov. Pavel was Vera Slonim Chalidze's cousin and had been a pioneer of the human rights movement. He arrived in London from Moscow in 1974 en route to the United States; on meeting him, I understood at once how he had been a charismatic leader when still in his twenties, and I soon took to him myself. He went on to become a popular high school teacher in Tarrytown, New York.

These publishing efforts targeted both Western and Soviet publics. To send their publications' output to the USSR, Ed and Valery of course needed roundabout routes. So they had taken advantage of a small low-key group, the Bedford Publications Company, which had been set up by the CIA in the 1960s for the purpose of getting to readers forbidden or needed books and journals that would be confiscated by Soviet customs if they were sent by mail. Bedford was able to get materials into the USSR through various types of intermediaries traveling as academics, journalists, or students, or under diplomatic cover. I had sometimes followed Ed and Valery's example to supply my Soviet friends in Moscow, working with Bedford's representative in London, Joan Balcar. Through her I met her New York–based boss, Isaac Patch, a mild-mannered but engaging and firmly focused former diplomat who wrote an absorbing memoir after he retired from the diplomatic service.[3] Alexander Solzhenitzyn's wife told Patch that before the couple's forced exile abroad, they had regularly "received Western books through an intermediary supplied by [Bedford]."[4]

The Kline-Chalidze partnership lasted until 1983, when *A Chronicle of Human Rights in the USSR* closed down and *Khronika*, too, stopped appearing in Moscow because of KGB repression. Soon after this, Chalidze departed for Vermont to remarry, he and Vera having divorced. However, Khronika Press carried on, and Ed continued to provide information on dissent-related issues to Western media, journalists, academics, governments, and interested individuals—sometimes informally, via his personal connections.

My friendship with Ed had deepened over the years, especially after 1973, as we cooperated on many things, and I made quite frequent trips to the United States, once for a year, before I moved there permanently. Often I was lucky enough to enjoy his and his wife Jill's generous hospitality in their comfortable apartment on Manhattan's Upper East Side.

Broadcasting in Support of Dissent

Further assistance to Soviet dissent that was partially New York–based came from Radio Liberty, which broadcast daily to the USSR in some two dozen languages from New York and Munich. As mentioned earlier, it was part of a joint organization Radio Free Europe–Radio Liberty (RFE-RL), Radio Free Europe broadcasting to countries of the Eastern Bloc such as Poland and Hungary whereas Radio Liberty broadcast to the USSR. In 1967 the media revealed that the financing for the stations came from the CIA, so a switch was made to funding for the stations coming from the U.S. Congress. Despite the CIA involvement, the management had all along insisted that private-sector standards of objectivity about news coverage and reporting be observed, so nothing really changed with the departure of the handful of CIA officers. There had been one exception to the application of high journalistic standards, and it had occurred in 1956: the RFE Hungarian service had failed to quash a broadcast script implying that the United States would support an uprising against the Communist regime in Budapest to reinforce the large-scale protests that had just broken out there.

Regarding the USSR, the BBC and Voice of America, which covered the whole world, did not provide as much coverage on Soviet domestic developments as Radio Liberty did. An important part of this coverage was the systematic broadcasting of samizdat documents, edited by Peter Dornan, and rigorous analysis of them.

The complex inner workings of a large radio organization employing people of many different national origins and educational training have been well described in books by two retired longtime employees of Radio Liberty, Gene Sosin and James Critchlow.[5] Further sources of personal insights into Radio Liberty reached me from its London-based broadcaster, Victor Frank, a friend of Leonard Schapiro's; from a senior official, Bob Tuck, who mostly operated out of Munich; and from Max Ralis, head of a small audience research group based in Paris for whom I wrote a couple of reviews of individual weeks of transcribed broadcasts.

Political Abuse of Psychiatry II: WPA Redux

The long-awaited Sixth World Psychiatric Association Congress took place from August 29 to 31, 1977, when 4,000 psychiatrists from 76 national member societies assembled in Honolulu.[6] Three weeks before the start, Vladimir Bukovsky, now living in the U.K., appealed to them. He declared that the position they took on abuse would "determine the fate of hundreds of people and, in the shorter term, the fate of Soviet psychiatry itself." The abuse could be halted, he stated, through "unambiguous international condemnation," which the world congress obviously offered an excellent opportunity to accomplish.[7]

Two WPA member societies, from Britain and Australasia, had put forward resolutions to be considered at the congress, condemning the USSR by name for its abuses of psychiatry. Ultimately the Australasian one was voted on. The resolution read in full:

> That the WPA take note of the abuse of psychiatry for political purposes, and that it condemn those practices in all countries in which

> they occur, and call upon the professional organizations of psychiatrists in those countries to renounce and expunge those practices from their countries, and that the WPA implement this Resolution in the first instance in reference to the extensive evidence of the systematic abuse of psychiatry for political purposes in the USSR.

Among those who spoke in support of this position in one or another meeting were John Grigor of the Australasian group; Paul Chodoff, Jack Weinberg, and Boris Zoubok from the United States; France's Leonid Plyushch; and Britain's Marina Voikhanskaya.[8] Sidney Bloch organized a group of a dozen like-minded colleagues from various countries who met several times to decide what actions to take and what literature to have distributed at what meeting. Meanwhile, the Soviet representatives soon launched themselves into overdrive, denouncing these actions in extravagant terms, led by the volatile Eduard Babayan, a nonpsychiatrist and department head in the Ministry of Health, and Dmitry Venediktov, a nonpsychiatric doctor who was the deputy minister of health.

The WPA's voting rules allotted a national member society one vote for each 100 subscribing members. The vote on the Australasian resolution, held in strict accordance with the rules, came out as 90 votes in favor and 88 against (or 19 national societies in favor and 33 opposed).

An additional resolution, proposed by the Americans, was to set up a special WPA committee to review political abuses wherever they occurred. Although it aroused less emotion than the resolution condemning the USSR, it proved important in the longer run. While Russia and its allies opposed this one too, it passed by 121 to 66 (or by 28 to 26 national societies). In the short term, the sting of the congress resolutions caused the Soviet psychiatric establishment to continue lashing out wildly against the West and its "libelous accusations" on every possible occasion The congress also adopted unanimously a "Declaration of Hawaii," which laid out in rather general terms the ethics of psychiatry and did not refer to any specific abuses.

The year after the Sixth WPA World Congress, the American Psychiatric Association, at its congress in 1978 in Washington, D.C., gave its annual Manfred S. Guttmacher Award for the best book of the year in psychiatry to Sidney Bloch and me for our book *Russia's Political Hospitals* (published in the United States as *Psychiatric Terror*).

Later, in 1983, the key American resolution at the Sixth WPA World

Congress served as the basis for a powerful movement to expel the USSR from the WPA, which ended up being preempted by the Soviet decision to resign before it could be thrown out.

1977 to 1981: The Working Commission and the Kremlin Response

In early 1977 Alexander Podrabinek had formed the Working Commission to Investigate the Use of Psychiatry for Political Purposes as an offshoot of the Moscow Helsinki Group, which monitored official observance of the Helsinki Agreements of 1975. The Working Commission's liaison person to the Moscow Helsinki Group was the former Soviet general Pyotr Grigorenko.[9]

In the wake of the resolutions approved at the Honolulu congress, the Kremlin adopted an ambivalent policy on psychiatric abuse. It retained the official psychiatric leaders and continued to order new internments of dissidents on psychiatric grounds, albeit on a lesser scale. But at the same time it quietly released a number of long-term internees. In addition, in an effort to avoid inflaming too much the delicately poised international situation, the regime grudgingly tolerated Podrabinek's Working Commission.

In addition to its leader, the commission's most active members were Vyacheslav Bakhmin and Irina Grivnina, both computer specialists; Felix Serebrov, a self-educated worker; and Leonard Ternovsky, a doctor. From 1978 through January 1981 all the group's members were arrested and most were sentenced to either five years of internal exile or three years of forced labor. At first, each arrest was followed by a new member stepping forward to join. Members operated on the accurate assumption that they would be arrested, but did not allow this to affect the dedication of their work.

Mainly thanks to this work, the range of coverage of the abuse of psychiatry to quash dissent expanded greatly, allowing many more victims to be identified and helped. Moreover, this trend somewhat inhibited the authorities, and the total number of dissidents and independent thinkers who were interned in hospitals for their beliefs (whom we knew of) grew by only 250 between 1977 and 1983. We gained additional information on 84 of those on the 1976 list.[10]

The KGB was soon operating against the backdrop of a Kremlin that in 1979 had finally given up on the foreign policy of détente. This decision derived partly from the continuing rise of dissenting groups intent on exercising their moral rights under the Helsinki Agreements of 1975, and partly from a fear that the Olympic Games set for the USSR in summer 1980 would become a de facto platform for these groups. Suppression of the groups before the Games was seen as essential for a reactionary regime's safety, even if it came, as it did, at the expense of viable relations with the West, including a partial boycott of the Games.

So the KGB went into overdrive, accumulating a massive amount of information about the Podrabinek group, as well as all other dissidents, from its numerous official searches of members' apartments and the confiscation of loads of documentation. Following a common pattern, it also conducted numerous interrogations of witnesses connected with Podrabinek and his colleagues, and, starting in 1978, from a volunteer East German agent, Gisela Otto, a doctor in East Berlin. She had succeeded in deceiving Friedrich Weinberger, the leader of the West German activist group analogous to our London Working Group, into thinking she was on his side. Later she felt acute remorse about her deception and betrayal. In 1986 she defected to the West and in 1994, after the collapse of the German Democratic Republic, she committed suicide at the age of fifty-nine.[11]

Throughout the four years of its intensive activity—1977 to 1981—the Working Commission issued over 1,500 pages of detailed documentation, much of it also distilled and published in its official *Information Bulletin*. This appeared every six or seven weeks, featuring members' names and addresses and replete with the latest details on interned or threatened dissidents, ethically corrupt psychiatrists, and abusive practices in ordinary and prison-type mental hospitals. The group's purposes could be summed up as working to prevent inappropriate internments, helping those abusively held in hospitals to get out or to receive material and moral aid from their families, and assisting in humanizing the everyday conditions and the psychiatric treatment of the inmates of such institutions.

The Working Commission spelled out carefully the ethical and legal principles on which it operated, which flowed naturally from the legalist philosophy of Alexander Yesenin-Volpin and the human rights movement: "All the activity of the Commission is conducted openly, within the framework of the law, and is accessible to public scrutiny." At first, the group's principles included the position that it could not be absolutely certain about the mental condition of any individual without a full psychiatric evaluation. To address this, it worked with a practicing psychiatrist, Alexander Voloshanovich, who volunteered to conduct such evaluations of people who wanted them as a form of insurance against the compulsory internment or re-internment that they feared the KGB was planning for them. Voloshanovich wrote up forty detailed evaluations, each one seven or eight single-spaced pages, only one of which pointed to a mild mental illness in one individual who did not, however, require hospitalization. A copy was given to each individual and another was sent to me by a secure route, so that I could share it in confidence with the Royal College of Psychiatrists and a few other such institutions.

Although he operated "under the radar," Voloshanovich, like the commission members themselves, was subjected to strong official pressures. These eventually induced him to give a press conference describing his work. This did not alleviate his position, and before long the KGB told him that he must emigrate or he would face arrest. In 1979 he chose to move to Britain, where he cooperated with the Royal College of Psychiatrists and the Working Group (and in due course married an Englishwoman). In 1980 the Royal College of Psychiatrists made him an honorary member.

In 1979 I called Dr. David Owen, who had been the British minister of foreign affairs since 1977 and had been a medical doctor before his entry into politics. I asked Owen to consider weighing in on the Soviet authorities to protest the mistreatment of dissidents by the especially unethical means of psychiatry. He promised to do this, and issued a press release containing a brief but powerful public statement that the abuse of psychiatry in the USSR was a disgrace to the medical profession, which added to the growing Western pressure on Soviet authorities.

The Royal College of Psychiatrists also took public positions on the issue of the abuse of psychiatry for political aims. Influenced by Dr. Owen's statement and action, in 1980 it bestowed honorary memberships on the imprisoned Dr. Semyon Gluzman and, in 1983, on Dr. Anatoly Koryagin, who acted as a medical consultant to the Working Commission. It also informed Dr. Andrei Snezhnevsky, the head of the Moscow School of Psychiatry, that it would withdraw his honorary membership unless he came to London to appear before a Royal College court and was able to convince its members that he did not deserve to lose his membership. Rather than do this, in 1980 Snezhnevsky resigned his membership. Beyond this, the Royal College's Review Committee on Psychiatric Abuse, which was headed by Dr. Peter Sainsbury and on which the abuse expert Dr. Sidney Bloch served, increasingly discussed a plan whereby the college would issue a formal proposal to the WPA that the Soviet society, a national member, be expelled. This plan came to fruition in November 1981.

In Moscow, after the forced emigration of Dr. Voloshanovich, the psychiatrist Anatoly Koryagin had promptly stepped into Voloshanovich's shoes. Acting as a consultant to the Working Commission he assisted sixteen more dissidents, or potential dissidents, in the same way as Voloshanovich, writing up detailed psychiatric evaluations that gave evidence of their mental health. In 1981 the KGB threatened him with forced emigration unless he gave up his activities in support of the Working Commission. Koryagin refused to cease his activity, and in 1981 he was arrested. He refused to answer any probing questions or recant his activity in any way; a gamut of psychological torture and beating could not break him and make him recant. At his trial, charged with "anti-Soviet agitation and propaganda," he made a long, stirring speech:

> I do not ask anything of this court. Regardless of the sentence imposed on me, I state that I will never accept the situation that exists in our country, where mentally healthy people are imprisoned in psychiatric hospitals for trying to think independently. I know that long years of physical imprisonment, humiliation, and mockery await me. Fully aware of this, I embark on them in the hope that they will increase the chances for others to live in freedom. I know that a hard life, full of material deprivation, bitterness, and perhaps direct persecution by the authorities, awaits my family.

His reward was a sentence of seven years in a strict-regime labor camp, plus five subsequent years of internal exile. Later, for continuing his independent behavior while in captivity, he received two further years of forced labor, and fears for his life became real. However, despite all of this, he succeeded in writing, as an appeal to the World Health Organization and the UN Commission on Human Rights, a searing account of his imprisonment and smuggling it out to supporters, who then smuggled it further west to England. I wrote it up for the *New York Review of Books*, quoting from it at length.[12]

In his account, Koryagin described the conditions, codified by the government, during his six months in the internal prison of the Perm region's camp no. 37, and his thirty-seven days in the prison's even stricter "cooler," the location of especially harsh treatment:

> The conditions in which prisoners are held in political camps are designed to break their physical and mental health. The conditions threaten and shorten their lives. This derives in no small degree from the physical torturing of them through starvation, cold, and deprivation of sleep. Food rations are specially reduced. . . . So you always feel starved and you constantly think about your next intake of food, which of course doesn't fill you either. This feeling is so prolonged and intense that it has the effect of genuine torture. In the cooler, where every other day you only get bread and water, the torture becomes almost unbearable. During the winter months the temperature in the cells was mostly between 48 and 57 degrees. [This] made one feel frozen, even when wearing a jacket. Whenever the temperature reached 64 the warders promptly took the jacket away. The cold made it impossible to sleep. In the cooler the night becomes an endless torment. Feelings of hopelessness and frustration, outbursts of desperation and anger—these are the common emotions of prisoners in the cooler. . . . Officials try to extract from them what the KGB wants—renunciation of their beliefs in exchange for their health and their lives. I have repeatedly been punished for my firm refusal to talk with KGB officials. The last one to visit me made this unconcealed threat: "The longer you stay silent, the longer you'll stay in the prison." His revenge followed at once: fifteen days in the cooler.

An accompanying letter by nine fellow dissident inmates highlighted two reasons why they thought Koryagin was being treated with such special cruelty. First, as a doctor he had been repeatedly treating—without any equipment—prisoners who had been beaten up or otherwise physically abused by the warders. And second, more important still, the KGB was desperately trying to obtain recantations from key critics of their policy of political psychiatry, and Koryagin was their number one target. If they could break him, this would be a trump card in the USSR's current efforts to ward off what had now become the serious danger of the country's expulsion from the World Psychiatric Association at its next planned World Congress, in Vienna in July 1983.

1983: Victory

Meanwhile, in the wake of the Honolulu congress of 1977, activity in a number of Western countries had continued at a fast pace in support of Koryagin, the Working Commission, and all known victims of abusive psychiatry.[13] One result of this striking level of interest and activity was the creation of a new international organization: representatives of the London Working Group and its equivalents in France, Germany, the Netherlands, and Switzerland met in Paris in December 1980 to form a confederation named—after much debate—the International Association on the Political Use of Psychiatry, or IAPUP. On principle, it had no statute and no rules. It held occasional meetings, and produced three Information Bulletins, which replaced the bulletin of the Working Group. Its first secretary-general was Gerard Bles of France; in 1984 Catherine Kuhn of Geneva succeeded Bles; and in 1987 she was succeeded by Robert van Voren of the Netherlands.

From the start, IAPUP's principal goal was to persuade enough national member societies of the WPA to vote in favor of expelling the Soviet society from the association so that an expulsion resolution at its congress in Vienna in 1983 would succeed. Gradually the list of yes votes grew longer and as it grew the Kremlin reduced the number of new internments, but declined to cease them completely. In early 1983, however, the confrontation became unbearable in Moscow. The Soviet Society of Psychiatrists counted up the combined vote totals of these societies and realized that expulsion was inevitable. So, several months ahead of the congress, on January 31, 1983, it decided to resign from the WPA, an exit evidently considered less shameful and newsworthy than being expelled.[14] Nonetheless, it was a major victory for IAPUP and the national societies, partly because it was sure to make a powerful impact on the top Soviet political figures.

Of course, this campaign was not the only source of pressure. Other pressures included Western anger over the prolonged Soviet campaign of especially severe treatment of all forms of dissent, launched in 1979. This had led to increased arrests, physically vicious measures against some dissidents, such as Koryagin, and an almost complete ending of Jewish emigration, which had been steadily rising through the 1970s. The goal appeared to be to put an end to all freedom of speech, association, and movement.

Two years later, top Soviet political figures could be said to have yielded to the foreign pressures by choosing the soon-to-be liberal Gorbachev as their leader.

The severe policies continued under Gorbachev until late 1986. But then, after he had established his authority, Gorbachev moved to a radically liberal amnesty for political and religious prisoners. In February 1987 this brought the release of a physically and mentally grossly abused, but morally uncompromised, Dr. Koryagin, after which he immediately emigrated to the West. It also brought freedom for many other believers in human rights.

Peter Reddaway (left) and Valery Lebedev, 1961.

Medical student Boris Kudashev with his wife. Moscow, 1964.

Italian boys on the Land Rover driven around the USSR in 1961 by the author and other Cambridge students. The board reads, in Russian: "Cambridge—Moscow—Black Sea."

Leonard Schapiro, professor of political science, London School of Economics, author of a number of acclaimed books on the USSR.

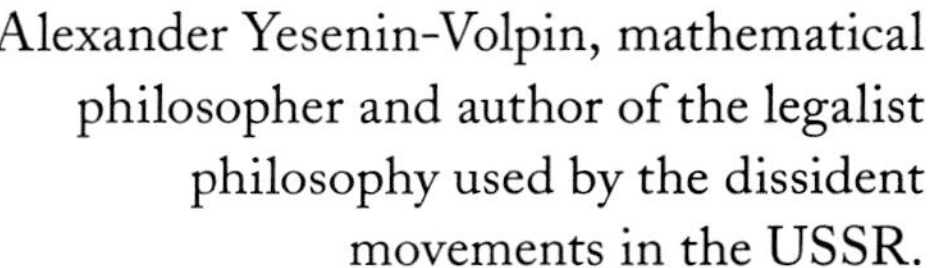

Alexander Yesenin-Volpin, mathematical philosopher and author of the legalist philosophy used by the dissident movements in the USSR.

Alexander Ginzburg with his children. He was imprisoned for two long periods for samizdat writing and other activity.

Alexander Solzhenitsyn, author of *The Gulag Archipelago.*

Vladimir Bukovsky, pioneering mainstream dissident, imprisoned in mental hospitals and labor camps for, among other acts, organizing demonstrations, 1970.

General Pyotr Grigorenko (left) and Ivan Yakhimovich, a collective farmer in Latvia, delivering a letter supporting the Czechoslovak reformers to the Czechoslovak Embassy, Moscow, July 29, 1968.

Moscow dissidents Larissa Bogoraz and Pavel Litvinov, Moscow, 1968.

Dissident Moscow poet and samizdat editor/compiler Natalya Gorbanevskaya, with her son. She was the first editor of the *Chronicle of Current Events,* Moscow, c. 1968.

Dissidents Pyotr Yakir (left) and Viktor Krasin (right) visit their colleague Pavel Litvinov in his place of exile near the Manchurian border, 1969.

Yakir (at back) and Krasin (in front of him) visit Litvinov (right) in his place of exile.

Dissident writer Anatoly Marchenko with his son during a rare period of freedom between imprisonments for writing *My Testimony* and other works, Moscow, mid-1970s.

View of fences surrounding Camp No. 36, used for political prisoners, at Kuchino in the Perm Region.

Wall of prison camp No. 1 in Dubrovlag, Mordovia.

The Moscow KGB's Lefortovo Prison for political suspects.

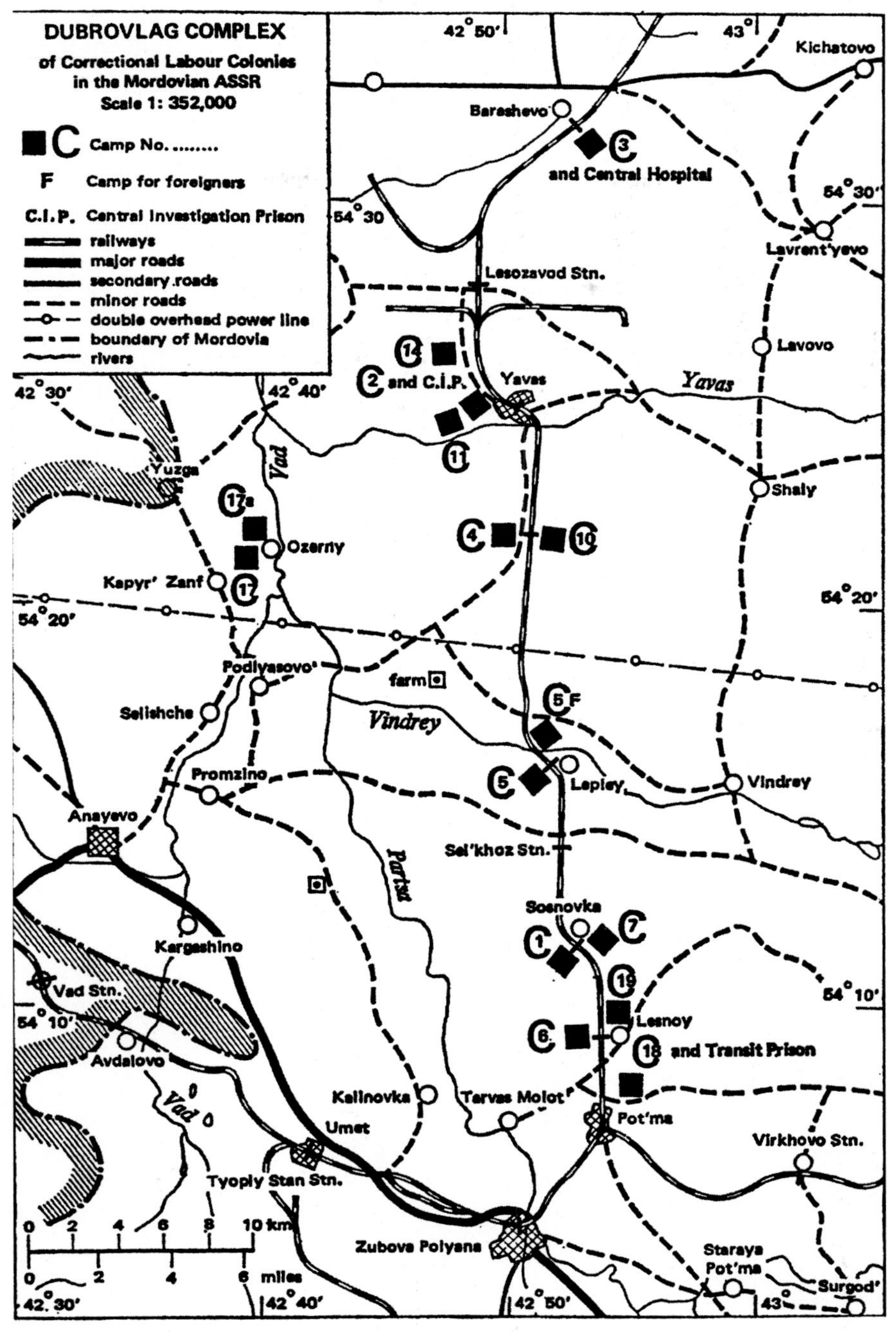

A map created by Victor Swoboda of London University showing the Dubrovlag labor camps on a 30-mile stretch of railroad in Mordovia, southeast of Moscow.

Karel van het Reve (right), creator of the Herzen Foundation for publishing books that could not appear in the USSR, with his publisher, Amsterdam, 1982.

Julius Telesin, mathematician and Jewish dissident, renowned for his prodigious circulation of samizdat, Moscow, c. 1970.

Moscow dissidents: Naum Meiman, Sofia Kalistratova, General Pyotr Grigorenko and his wife, Zinaida; Natalya Velikanova, mother of Tatiana; Rev. Sergei Zheludkov; Andrei Sakharov; and, in front, Genrikh Altunyan and Alexander Podrabinek, Moscow, c. early 1970s.

Self-portrait by long-imprisoned dissident Leningrad artist Yuri Ivanov, drawn at the Dubrovlag Camp Complex, in 1969. At the same time, he drew portraits of fellow dissidents, top row left to right: Leonid Borodin, a headmaster from Leningrad region and member of a Christian democratic group; Vyacheslav Platonov and Mikhail Sado, members of the same group and both Leningrad Orientalists; bottom row left to right, Yuri Galanskov, dissident Moscow editor of samizdat; Yuli Daniel, Moscow writer of poetry and short stories; and Victor Kalninŝ, a Latvian journalist.

Tatiana Velikanova, an editor of the *Chronicle of Current Events*, with a Japanese specialist on samizdat, Shinichi Masagaki, Moscow, 1970s.

Dr. Andrei Snezhnevsky, chief proponent of the USSR's officially approved psychiatric school and a frequent apologist for it.

The prison psychiatric hospital in Oryol, with prisoners exercising in the yards, mid-1970s.

The Serbsky Institute of Forensic Psychiatry, the apex of the system of psychiatric abuse, Moscow.

Dr. Georgi Morozov (second from left), director of the Serbsky Institute, and Dr. Nikolai Zharikov (far right), his deputy, with Finnish colleagues, 1970s.

Late 1960s, Roy Medvedev (left) and his twin brother, geneticist Zhores Medvedev, who was placed in a psychiatric hospital for his dissident writings in 1970.

Dr. Denis Leigh (center) and Prof. Linford Rees, top officials of the World Psychiatric Association, receive diplomas of recognition from the Soviet Society of Psychiatrists, London, 1972.

Pyotr Starchik, who sang dissident songs and was a member of a group opposing psychiatric abuse of the sort he underwent from 1976, with his family, mid-1970s.

Dr. Marina Voikhanskaya, dissident Leningrad psychiatrist, with her son Misha. After she emigrated in 1975, Misha was officially prevented from following her for four years.

Dissident Leonid Plyushch, mathematical philosopher and victim of psychiatric abuse, Kyiv.

Vladimir Bukovsky in the U.K. after release from a prison camp in 1976 and his exchange by the Kremlin for the leader of the Chilean Communists.

Paris public meeting demanding the release of psychiatrist Semyon Gluzman, philosopher Leonid Plyushch, and dissident Vladimir Bukovsky, 1975.

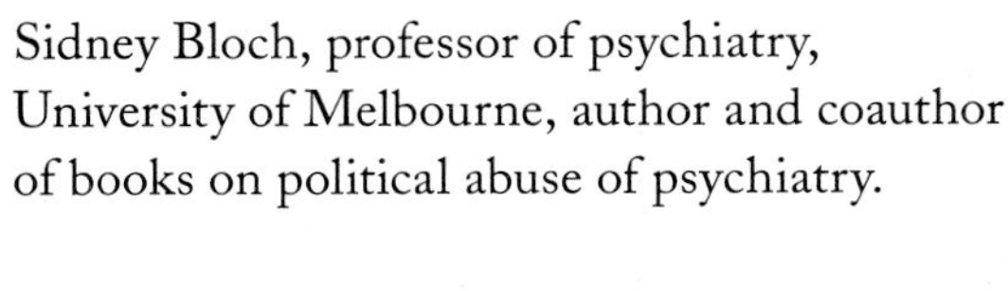

Sidney Bloch, professor of psychiatry, University of Melbourne, author and coauthor of books on political abuse of psychiatry.

Members of the Moscow commission to combat psychiatric abuse, with Dr. Gerard Low-Beer (second from right). From left: Alexander Podrabinek, Dr. Alexander Voloshanovich, and Vyacheslav Bakhmin, Moscow, 1978.

Alexander Podrabinek is arrested and taken from his home to Lefortovo Prison, Moscow, 1978.

Right to left: Three members of the Soviet group combating political abuse of psychiatry: Irina Grivnina, Dr. Anatoly Koryagin, and Felix Serebrov, as well as Serebrov's daughter, Moscow, c. 1979.

Tatiana Khodorovich (right), samizdat editor and writer, with Tatiana Velikanova, also a Moscow editor, Moscow, c. 1970.

London public meeting demanding the release of (pictured left to right) dissident Viktor Nekipelov and members of the group opposed to psychiatric abuse, Vyacheslav Bakhmin and Leonard Ternovsky. On stage, fourth from right: General Pyotr Grigorenko; sixth, wife Zinaida Grigorenko; seventh, Peter Reddaway, c. 1980.

Anatoly Shcharansky (below center), democratic Jewish leader, with fellow dissidents Ludmila Alexeyeva and Valentin Turchin (standing), Moscow, 1970s.

Moscow dissidents Zinaida Grigorenko, Ludmila Alexeyeva (about to emigrate to the U.S.), Vyacheslav Bakhmin, Ternovskaya, Alexander Podrabinek, and lawyer Sofia Kallistratova, 1977.

Mustafa Djemilev, leader of the Crimean Tatar people since the 1960s, imprisoned several times for dissident activity.

Crimean Tatar demonstration in the Crimea following the self-immolation of Musa Mamut in protest of the persecution of the Tatars. His widow walks in front, June 1978.

Moscow Jew David Khavkin's departure from Moscow airport, 1969. He is third from the left in the first row, standing, and his wife is at the far left.

Sir John Lawrence, president of Keston College, which studied the abuse of religion in Communist countries.

Rev. Michael Bourdeaux, director of Keston College, c. 1990.

ОНИ ПЕЧАТАЛИ ЕВАНГЕЛИЕ

Пидченко Виталий Иванович 1941 г. рож., прож. Харьков, пос. Песочин, ул. Новоселовская 18.

Гриценко Екатерина Ивановна 1943 г. рож., прож. Киевская обл., с. Малая Салтановка.

Пикалов Виктор Анатольевич 1950 г. рож., прож. г. Фергана, ул. Омская 18.

Тарасова Зинаида Петровна 1942 г. рож., прож. Курская обл., д. Ворощнево.

Коротун Ида Даниловна 1938 г. рож., прож. Ворошиловград, Вергунский разъезд, ул. 2 Высоцкая 10.

Кожемякина Татьяна Сафроновна 1937 г. рож., прож. Жданов, с. Талаковка, ул. „40 лет Октября" 88.

Львова Надежда Герасимовна 1946 г. рож., прож. Краснодарский край, станица Елизаветинская, ул. Дубинская 109.

ВСЕМ ХРИСТИАНАМ МИРА

ВСЕМ, КОМУ ДОРОГИ ПРИНЦИПЫ СВОБОДЫ

ЧРЕЗВЫЧАЙНОЕ СООБЩЕНИЕ ИЗДАТЕЛЬСТВА «ХРИСТИАНИН»

Спасай взятых на смерть, и неужели откажешься от обреченных на убиение?
Пр. 24, 11.

24 октября 1974 г. в районе Цесис, хутор Лигукалнс, Латвийской ССР, были арестованы 7 сотрудников нашего издательства вместе с печатным оборудованием и материалами. Это произошло в то время, когда они готовили 30 тысяч Евангелий — Новогодний подарок верующим.

Мы постоянно были готовы к этому, «ибо... нам ... Бог судил быть как бы приговоренными к смерти...» (1Кор. 4, 9). И все же такое известие принесло нам большую скорбь.

Арест наших друзей является грубым нарушением Конституции, принципов Всеобщей Декларации прав человека и всех Международных Конвенций. Более того, 5 июня 1971 г. мы офи-

Baptist appeal to the world's Christians, giving information on seven Soviet Baptists arrested for creating New Testaments on secret printing presses, 1974.

Lithuanian priest Algirdas Mocius leads a procession to the Hill of Crosses near Ŝiaulai to protest persecution of Catholics, July 1979.

Moscow dissidents, right to left: writer Andrei Amalrik; compiler of books of documents recording suppression of dissent, Pavel Litvinov; Gyuzel Amalrik, wife of Andrei; and Larissa Bogoraz, an early protester against injustice, 1968.

Herzen Foundation organizers (right to left): Jozien van het Reve; Karel van het Reve; Elisabeth Fisher; and Peter Reddaway, Amsterdam, 1975.

Cronid Lubarsky, mathematician and dissident leader in Munich after emigration in 1977, with Elena Bonner, dissident and Andrei Sakharov's wife, c. 1985.

Samizdat processors at Radio Liberty, Munich. Left to right: Martin Dewhirst, Peter Dornan, Mario Corti, c. 1980.

Valery Chalidze, physicist and dissident writer on law, later deprived of Soviet citizenship for his dissent and lived in New York, Moscow, 1970.

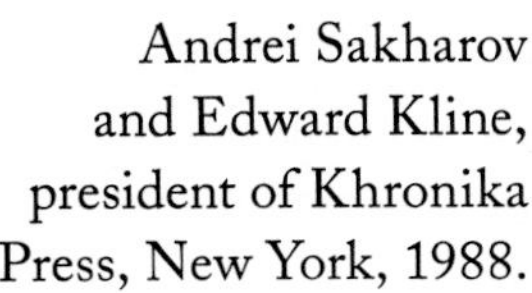

Andrei Sakharov and Edward Kline, president of Khronika Press, New York, 1988.

Andrei Sakharov with his wife, Elena Bonner, Moscow, 1974.

Tatiana Semyonova, daughter of Elena Bonner, with her dissident husband, Efrem Yankelevich, and their children. All were forced to emigrate in 1977.

Robert van Voren, the leader of the International Association on Political Use of Psychiatry, author of books on psychiatric abuse, professor at Kaunas and Tbilisi Universities.

Entrance to the prison-psychiatric hospital in Chernyakhovsk, northwest Russia, visited by U.S. psychiatrists in 1989.

Psychiatrist Boris Shostakovich (standing), at a Soviet-American seminar on the abuse of psychiatry. Behind him at far left, Dr. Viktor Fukalov, head of Chernyakhovsk Mental Prison. Next to him, Dr. Ravil Valitov, head of Kazan Mental Prison. Moscow, March 1989.

At Soviet-American seminar, Chair Yuri Reshetov (standing) talks with Dr. Alexander Churkin (right) and Dr. Nikolai Zharikov.

Dr. Semyon Gluzman (center), a Kyiv psychiatrist, with Moscow friends, Irina Yakir and Yuli Kim, c. 1989. In 1972–1982, Gluzman was imprisoned for his analysis of the documents used to imprison General Grigorenko in a psychiatric prison.

Mikahil Gorbachev, who became the leader of the Communist Party of the Soviet Union in 1985 and soon started liberalizing the political and economic systems, releasing all dissidents by 1988. From 1988 on, he lost support.

Andrei Sakharov (right), Peter Reddaway, and Charles Blitzer before a talk by Sakharov at the Wilson Center, Washington, D.C., November 1988.

Left to right, front: Dr. Anatoly Koryagin, dissident psychiatrist just released from prison for opposing psychiatric abuse; unknown; Ellen Mercer of the American Psychiatric Association (APA); John Grigor, Australian psychiatrist. Top: unknown; Boris Zoubok, Soviet psychiatrist in emigration; Peter Reddaway, at an APA congress, Toronto, 1990.

Arkady Vaksberg, Moscow journalist and author of books on, for example, the Russian Mafia, Moscow, c. 1990.

THIRTEEN

Publishing Samizdat in the West

From the start of my involvement with the free speech and human rights movement in the USSR, the publication of samizdat works—especially books and journals—in various Western countries occupied quite a lot of my time and attention. As mentioned earlier, from 1968 to 1983 I edited and in some cases also translated the *Khronika tekushchikh sobytii*. It became the English-language *Chronicle of Current Events*, as each of the sixty-three issues arrived by KGB-evading routes from Moscow. The first fifteen I published via my own samizdat system, but thereafter I handed over the printing and distribution jobs to Amnesty International for more professional handling.

Radio Liberty: Peter Dornan

Other documents that I received from various sources through different channels I mailed to the tireless Peter Dornan at Radio Liberty in Munich. He would retype, lightly edit, and then issue them weekly to some two hundred recipients in many countries. Similarly, I supplied most of the documents to Valery Chalidze, at Khronika Press in New York, and to my friend Anthony de Meeus in Brussels, Belgium, where Anthony put them out in a carefully edited journal of translations into French, the monthly *Cahiers du Samizdat*. More selectively, I did the same with Serafim Miloradovich, sending him items for publication in the weekly newspaper

Russkaya mysl' (Russian thought) in Paris, which also published occasional Armenian documents to satisfy the wishes of a small part of its readership. Documents from or about Crimean Tatars I sent to Aysha Seytmuratova after her arrival in the United States. And religious materials of all sorts I turned over to Michael Bourdeaux at Keston College, where, from a seat on the executive committee, I could help to decide on their disposition.

The Alexander Herzen Foundation: Karel van het Reve

The Herzen Foundation in Amsterdam was an important link in the chain of organizations of different kinds that published and publicized samizdat and its authors. The name of the foundation honored the Russian writer Alexander Herzen (1812–1870), a socialist and agrarian populist who edited and wrote extensively on political topics from exile in Paris. The foundation was launched in 1969 by a man who quickly became a good friend, Professor Karel van het Reve, whom I met in 1968 after his return from a sabbatical year of leave spent as the Moscow correspondent of the well-known Dutch newspaper, *Het Parool* (The word). During the year, he had become friendly with several prominent dissidents in the emerging human rights movement, including Andrei Amalrik, Pavel Litvinov, and Larissa Bogoraz.

After a speaking tour of a few Western cities designed to spread the word about the barely known subject of samizdat and its role in Soviet life, Karel came to know the tiny number of Soviet specialists who had some knowledge of this field, of whom I was one. Returning to his home to Amsterdam, he had to decide what to do with the samizdat book manuscripts he had brought back from the USSR, or had sent back via the Dutch diplomatic bag, and also, soon, the further manuscripts from dissident friends that followed.

In 1969 he resolved to set up the Alexander Herzen Foundation (Alexander Herzenstichting) in the Netherlands as a vehicle for publishing samizdat in the original language or in translation. The foundation's trustees would be Karel; a colleague of his, Professor Jan Bezemer, a historian; and I. The administrator would be Karel's wife, Jozien, and her friend Elizabeth Fisher would act as literary agent. Everyone except Elizabeth would work for free, with no personal expenses charged to the foundation. The money for printing and mailing the books would come from appeals to the Dutch public and other likely sources of funds. No contribution would be accepted from any government or the CIA. Karel's and Jozien's house would be the office.

The three trustees met once a year in Amsterdam, at the van het Reves' typical canalside dwelling beside the Amstel; it was a perfect location for quiet walks along the picturesque streets among the waterways. I would come and stay a night or two, often on my way to somewhere else, and we would decide what books to publish and not to publish, who would edit each one, which printer we would engage, and which books were of sufficiently wide interest for us to ask Elizabeth Fisher to try to sell language rights for them to other Western publishers. Karel and Jozien's daughter Jozien Jr. and their son David sometimes helped out. Several times we used the inexpensive Multilingual Printing Services in London, run by Ukrainians who had emigrated in the late 1940s.

Our meetings involved hard work, but were also fun. Karel was a professor of Russian at Leiden University who had written several authoritative books on Russian literature and was also an exacting editor of our volumes of samizdat. I remember sweating over the many hundreds of detailed footnotes that he insisted on adding for a couple of our lengthy books and having to dig out the birth and death dates of the two thousand or so individuals mentioned. But he also had an irrepressible and subtle sense of humor that he quietly unleashed every twenty minutes or so, which invariably released any tensions.

The foundation published titles itself and also found homes for manuscripts with other publishers. By itself it published about twenty volumes in the original Russian, and through other publishers, about two hundred volumes in about fifteen languages. These included a few cases where a book was published in Russian to establish the "moral copyright" when Soviet law blocked any legal copyright. The majority were translations of books by authors who had appointed our foundation as their literary agent. Often we published them in the original Russian, and then asked Elizabeth Fisher to sell the rights for other languages. All the proceeds from these sales were put into funds for the authors, some of whom collected their books' earnings when they emigrated, and others of whom asked that these sums be discreetly transferred to them or their families in the Soviet Union.

The most widely translated of our authors was Andrei Amalrik, with Pavel Litvinov in second place and Anatoly Marchenko in third. Among Amalrik's books the most popular were *Involuntary Journey to Siberia*

(Harcourt, Brace, 1970), about his sentence to internal exile, and *Will the Soviet Union Survive until 1984?* (Allen Lane, 1970), which aroused widespread interest for its bold analysis and also led some "experts" to declare that no one could write such a work except a KGB plant. Among Litvinov's, the most popular titles were *The Trial of the Four* (Longman, 1972) and *The Demonstration in Pushkin Square* (Gambit, 1979). Among Marchenko's, *My Testimony* (Dutton, 1969).

Other books of particular interest that the Herzen Foundation published in Russian included *Stikhi iz nevoli* (Poems from captivity, 1971), by the imprisoned poet Yuli Daniel; *Mysli sumasshedshego* (Thoughts of a madman, 1973), by the psychiatrically interned Pyotr Grigorenko; *Politicheskiy dnevnik* (A political diary 1964–1970, 1972), edited, as was later revealed, by the Marxist Roy Medvedev; the anonymously written *Programma demokraticheskogo dvizheniya Sovetskogo Soyuza* (Program of the democratic movement of the Soviet Union, 1970), evidently the work of a single author; *Vospominaniya tatarskogo detstva* (Memories of a Tatar childhood, 1976), by Gyuzel Amalrik, the wife of Andrei Amalrik; *Katastrofa i vtoroe rozhdenie* (Catastrophe and second birth, 1977), by the diplomat Yevgeny Gnedin about his imprisonment by Stalin; and *Tashkentskiy protsess* (The Tashkent trial, 1976), about the Crimean Tatars.

In the second half of the 1980s the Herzen Foundation wound up its affairs, as the need to publish samizdat abroad faded away and Gorbachev and his colleagues brought a good dose of freedom of publication back into Soviet intellectual life for the first time in sixty years. This lasted for nearly two decades, until the mid-2000s, when Putin reduced it again.

In 1991 Karel's Dutch colleagues decided to compile a Festschrift in his honor, which gave Jan Bezemer and me the opportunity to express our appreciation of his many samizdat initiatives, especially the founding of the Herzen Foundation.[1] In his youth he had worked underground with his wife in the anti-Nazi resistance. Here he had learned about the necessity of trust, self-reliance, discretion, flexibility, and quiet courage. These were essential if small groups of individuals were to preserve their self-respect and their lives in the face of a ruthless ruling power, and also to give society reason for hope.

When Karel and Jozien arrived in Moscow in 1967 for his sabbatical, they found Russian friends with similar tastes and values, friends who were busy creating discreet networks that operated in conditions not so different from those in the Dutch resistance a quarter century earlier.

These friends needed the help of sympathetic foreigners who would be discreet and unobtrusive and not catch the eye of the secret police, but would also give effective publicity to their dissenting writings when they left the USSR. In addition, from his own perspective Karel, as a foreign journalist, put his professional judgment on the line whenever he decided that a particular dissident was both genuine and reliable, and could therefore be used as a source, if not always by name.

On his return to the West a year later, Karel set about convincing audiences to attend his talks and listen to interviews he gave, which demonstrated that the human rights movement in the USSR was genuine and important. His personality was probably decisive in conveying his credibility: even the deepest skeptic, the sincerest "friend of the Soviet Union," the most timid academic, could not but be affected by Karel's honesty, straightforwardness, transparency, self-deprecation, and wit—in short, by his integrity and shy charm. Such a person simply could not be lying, embellishing, or distorting.

My favorite missive from him ended "I got some nice letters threatening that I will be 'executed' by the Marxist-Leninist Center in Amsterdam. I hope to see you before then. Greetings! Karel."

Unsurprisingly, the Kremlin was not slow to indulge in personal abuse, dubbing him once: "one of the CIA's most zealous agents." I chose these words as the title of my chapter about him in the Festschrift.

FOURTEEN

Dissent and Reform under Gorbachev

Uncertain Terrain

The 1980s brought earth-shaking change to the Soviet Union, while a major change in my own life placed me in an ideal spot to observe, study, and even maybe sometimes affect marginally how the West interpreted what was occurring.

In December 1985 I moved from the London School of Economics, where I had been teaching Soviet history and politics, to Washington, D.C. Here I became director of the Kennan Institute for Advanced Russian Studies, a branch of the Woodrow Wilson International Center for Scholars. In 1983–1984 I had spent a sabbatical year at this institute and found it a dynamic and stimulating place for research and intellectual exchange with both scholars and researchers in think tanks and government institutions. To be appointed to this position was an honor as well as an opening to great opportunities.

One such opportunity was an invitation to visit Japan in March 1986, so that I could meet Japanese scholars, get to know their places of work, give lectures, hand out Kennan Institute literature, and be in a position to invite some of them to Kennan activities. Japan's closest analogy to the Kennan Institute was the Institute for Slavic Research at Hokkaido University on Japan's northern island, headed by Professor Hiroshi Kimura, whom I had met in the United States a few years earlier. While spending several days on Hokkaido, I gave some lectures that were attended by twenty-five English-speaking Japanese, met informally with a dozen scholars, including Professor Tsuyoshi Hasegawa, a well-known specialist in Russian history, and got to know the area.

In Tokyo, I lectured at the Japanese Institute of International Affairs and the Foreign Ministry, conducted activities similar to those on Hokkaido, and renewed my friendship with two bright amateur scholars of the USSR, the super-lively Shin-ichi Masagaki and his quiet wife, Miiko. They wrote articles for the media, and were also strong supporters of the metalworkers' labor union. They took me to what proved to be an enjoyable lecture at the headquarters of the International Metal Federation.

My impression of the Japanese as a people was that generally they were friendly and relaxed. An exception to this was their extreme distrust of the Soviet Union, which would remain for as long as the northern Kurile Islands, seized by Moscow in 1945, were not returned to Japan.

In October 1987 I took part in a delegation of eight American scholars who attended a one-day conference in Beijing at the Institute for Soviet and East European Studies, known as CASS, on Soviet politics, economics, and foreign policy. Here my tasks were similar to those I had in Japan. On the way to Beijing we stopped in Tokyo to attend a conference on the Gorbachev regime's domestic and foreign policies.

The head of the institute was the thoughtful and friendly Xu Kui, a historian and political scientist. I also met other scholars who were intellectually serious: Li Jiangjie, a specialist in China-U.S. relations, who took me on a fascinating day-long tour of Beijing's surroundings by car; Lu Nanquan, an economist; and Ni Xiaoquan, a specialist in East-West security issues.

The Chinese participants included fifteen scholars representing seven different institutes and universities in Beijing. It was a definitely useful meeting, at which it became clear that regarding Gorbachev and the Soviet Union, there was a wider range of opinion among the Chinese than among the Americans. The main reason for this appeared to be that although many of the Chinese thought highly of Gorbachev's reforms and felt they should probably be adapted for use in China, a few hard-liners thought they went too far too fast, and should certainly not be adopted by Beijing. We were told in private that Deng Xiaoping took the latter view.

In Beijing I noted that there were fewer security concerns than in Moscow. The only alienated group appeared to be young male manual workers, whom I saw up close on my early-morning runs as they sullenly prepared for work. There were no drunks and virtually no beggars. But widespread burning of coal meant that public spaces—and also my hotel room—were covered with a layer of filth.

Enter Mikhail Gorbachev—Where From?

In March 1985 the Politburo elected Mikhail Gorbachev the general secretary of the Communist Party and the new leader of the Kremlin. This led me to write in October of that year, "It now seems possible that within a year or so the vast, lumbering Soviet Union may start to change its course."[1] Many Soviet citizens were finding the status quo unacceptable because "a lack of order . . . permeates daily existence and causes deep disquiet. . . . Crime and corruption are . . . steadily rising," along with "petty stealing, alcoholism, divorce, abortion, infant mortality, congenital defects in children, adult male mortality, and animosity between social classes." And the institutions charged with combating these trends "are regarded as increasingly corrupt or ineffective." Also, the economy was stagnant, cultural stars were defecting to the West, dissidents continued to end up in labor camps at the same rate as before (news of 117 new arrests had leaked out in the first seven months of 1985), and the Soviet troops occupying Afghanistan since 1979 had done nothing to prevent that country from being racked by civil war.

Writing in the early 1980s, the dissident Lyudmila Alexeyeva had aptly compared the permanently self-reproducing Soviet dissidents to the movements of Mahatma Gandhi in India and Martin Luther King in the United States. She also referred to opinion surveys conducted secretly by independent sociologists in 1981. These found that in large Russian cities about 20 percent of the population had democratic attitudes, a further 20 percent were anti-democratic, and the remaining 60 percent were politically inert.

As of October 1985, Gorbachev had yet to do anything about these ills, except to call vaguely, if promisingly, for "a decisive revolution in the economy" and "a profound reconstruction of the whole economic mechanism." In April 1986 he provided extremely weak leadership in Moscow's response to the nuclear tragedy at Chernobyl.

After his election as general secretary he spent eighteen months establishing his rule by dismissing a lot of mid-level party officials and finding a few strong reformers to support him in the Politburo, notably Alexander Yakovlev, a party official, and Eduard Shevardnadze, who had run Georgia for the party. By October 1986 he began actively to seek a new and firmer basis for both Communist ideology and his increasingly corrupt country. In recent years he had discussed these complex matters during long and confidential walks with Shevardnadze. Now, gradually, he eased the tight censorship and sought less hostile relations with the United Kingdom and its prime minister, Margaret Thatcher, whom he had courted even in 1984 before acquiring the top spot, and also with the United States and President Ronald Reagan.

Symptomatic of this trend was the implicit rejection of the traditional triumphal Communism that heralded Communism's worldwide victory. This came when the Party's Program in 1986 merely made a low-key reference to "mankind's movement toward socialism and communism." By May 1987, the clear aim of Gorbachev's speeches was, I wrote, "to stimulate Soviet patriotism, i.e., a concern for the country's welfare; and spreading Communism abroad is not referred to even in passing."[2] To carry out this strategy, "the vast untapped resources of socialism" must be mobilized, above all the enthusiasm of ordinary people.[3] As he explained in February 1987, "Democracy is not the opposite of order. It is order of a higher degree, based on . . . wholehearted, active participation by the whole community."[4]

Gorbachev found the greatest support in certain quarters of the intelligentsia, the media, and the foreign policy apparatus. But plenty of opposition came from other quarters of these groups and from the Communist Party and the state ministries. His dilemma was vividly exposed when he, his more conservative colleague Yegor Ligachev in the Politburo, and others clashed over how negatively or positively to evaluate the Stalin and Brezhnev periods. Of a speech that Gorbachev made at the time I wrote, "Gorbachev ended up reading a speech full of contradictions that was clearly the patchwork product of many hands."

Gorbachev's problem was his failure to grasp the country's political realities. The origins of this problem lay in the political conditioning he had received from the party and his personal experiences as a young apparatchik, which had led him to believe that if one trusted "the people," loosened political controls, increased incentives, created opportunities for political participation, strove for social justice, and conducted a more peaceful foreign policy, the people would be grateful, would work harder, would overcome bureaucratic resistance to their newly released creativity, and would "make socialism work," rather than challenge it by supporting nationalism, regionalism, anti-Communism, or multiparty democracy. Khrushchev had believed the same thing, but what both Khrushchev and Gorbachev failed (or did not want) to see was that the seeds of potential anti-Russian and anti-Communist aspirations lay within Soviet society.

In 1987 Gorbachev was in serious need of tangible achievements and turned to negotiations on arms control with the United States.[5] In October and November this was even more urgent, because the party forces that supported Ligachev eventually forced Gorbachev to go along with the expulsion of Boris Yeltsin, a radical, from the party's Central Committee, thus weakening his base. Fortunately, though, in December the U.S.-Soviet INF (Intermediate-Range Nuclear Forces) Treaty to eliminate intermediate and short-range missiles from the two countries' arsenals was successfully signed by Gorbachev and Reagan in Washington (the treaty from which President Donald Trump withdrew the United States in November 2018).

Andrei Sakharov under the Brezhnev and Gorbachev Regimes

In December 1986 Gorbachev had taken a big step forward by phoning the famous physicist and dissident Andrei Sakharov at his place of exile in Gorky and telling him that he was now free. Gorbachev summoned Sakharov back to Moscow to resume his valuable scientific work. This was the first step of a process that led to the liberation of almost all the dissidents of every stripe in 1987 and 1988, actions that received much commendation among the largely liberal Soviet intelligentsia and in circles in the West. Nonetheless, from early 1987 onward I believed that Gorbachev's radical liberalism would not be supported quickly enough by a large enough proportion of the establishment and the Soviet people for him to be able to pursue it for very long. In March 1987 I testified at a hearing before a committee of the U.S. Congress on glasnost and security in Europe. I concluded my testimony to the committee by saying, "I think it is extremely possible that if Mr. Gorbachev continues with his present policies, he will be removed within the next two or three years."[6]

My own links with Sakharov went back to the early 1970s, via my friendships with Valery Chalidze and Ed Kline in New York. Later they took place through Sakharov's wife, Elena Bonner, known as Lyusya, who in about 1980 began to come to the West for occasional medical treatment. I also had contacts through Lyusya's daughter, Tatiana Yankelevich, who had emigrated to the United States. I wrote articles about Sakharov's samizdat works, the Kremlin's harassment of him, and then his exile to the city of Gorky, which was closed to foreigners for security reasons. Here he went on incapacitating hunger strikes that were treated by the authorities with their usual cruelty.

Return to Moscow after Twenty-Four Years: Catching Up with Dissidents

My whole professional involvement with human rights dissidents and the USSR had taken place since my last glimpse of the USSR, when I was abruptly expelled in May 1964 under suspicion of having tried to influence a Soviet citizen to defect to the West. Now at last, thanks to Gorbachev, that curtain was being lifted. In January 1988, my employer at the Wilson Center, James Billington, managed to get permission for me to travel to the USSR for the first time in twenty-four years, to conduct business on Soviet exchanges for the Kennan Institute (he accomplished this by threatening reprisals if I was not admitted). Sakharov's family asked me to contact him and his wife while I was there. Arriving in Moscow, I telephoned them at their apartment, and Andrei answered the phone and pressed me to come round right away. Once there, with both Andrei and Lyusya, I quickly felt at home, first in the living room, then in the famous kitchen where hundreds of meetings with all sorts of dissidents and correspondents had taken place since the early 1970s.

Andrei told me in some detail about the first meeting, a few days earlier, of the International Foundation for the Survival and Development of Mankind. This had just been set up on Soviet initiative as a small and select forum for approved Soviet and Western intellectuals and a few politicians to discuss international affairs. He had been able at the meeting to make widely quoted statements in a short speech, in an exchange across the table with Gorbachev, and in a subsequent press conference. The list of two hundred prisoners of conscience, for whose freedom he had appealed, had been taken from him by the editor of a top Party journal, at Gorbachev's request. Sakharov realized that his participation in the foundation would be exploited by Soviet propaganda in ways that he couldn't control, but felt that he could nonetheless make a contribution through it to causes he believed in. Also, its work would perhaps strengthen Gorbachev, and this was desirable. Among other things, glasnost, which permitted open discussion of political and social issues, had made the Soviet media really exciting.

Sakharov added that as a member of the foundation's board he intended to have it sponsor a study of how to get rid of articles 70 and 190-1 of the Criminal Code, which were applied against dissidents, using liberal lawyers as consultants. Lyusya was keen that he should seek increased balance on the board, given that its chair was the establishment scientist Yevgeny Velikhov, and another board member was Yevgeny Chazov, a shameless denier of psychiatric abuse. She proposed that her husband nominate a few people like me. I expressed doubt that I would be acceptable to Velikhov.

Andrei and Lyusya were much interested in my account of recent developments in Soviet psychiatry, and also in my views on Soviet politics, telling me that they knew very little about these things. Even if Velikhov or some other scientific official knew something, he would not tell them. So I did my best in this regard.

None of Sakharov's scientific colleagues had directly apologized to him for their sins of commission or omission during his Gorky ordeal. They tended to greet him warmly, but behave as if nothing had happened.

Finally, I gave the Sakharovs greetings from Ed Kline, and Andrei asked me to tell him that he was still working on his memoirs. Andrei doubted that he would be allowed to travel to the United States, but he had just received an invitation to a conference in Yugoslavia in May, and if he applied for a visa to attend it, there would be more chance of his getting a visa for that.

LARISSA BOGORAZ AND YULI DANIEL

While in Moscow on this trip I was able to have two visits in her apartment with Larissa Bogoraz—a warm, impressive person, serious, practical, patient, strong, responsive to every woe, yet at the same time relaxed, full of humor, almost playful. Not surprisingly, prominent dissidents flocked to her home for guidance and friendship. I was fortunate enough to meet them in that relaxed setting. Sergei Kovalev came across as an intellectually and morally serious person, compassionate and patient; Alexander Lavut as a sensitive, kind listener and thinker; Sanya Daniel, Larissa's son, as a strong and decent man, with a quick mind, a broad intellectual sweep, and an attractive way of talking that commanded respect; and Malva

Landa—tiny, like a robin, with upturned face, bobbing head movements, and natural individualism—had a determined, outgoing personality. She had come partly to talk with me, knowing of my long-standing interest in Soviet dissidents. She was more radical than the others—in the mold of Podrabinek—and gave indefatigable help to people in distress. In 2018 she celebrated her one hundredth birthday.

Among the topics that came up for general discussion, one was the idea of launching a petition protesting the planned destruction of 5,000 Stalin-era case files a month that were held in the state archives. It was decided to seek both domestic and foreign signatories to this document.

Separately, Larissa told me how, encouraged by glasnost, huge numbers of seekers after justice had been descending on Moscow, with the most varied grievances. Three or four of them per week, despairing of the official bodies, found their way to her apartment. For lack of time and resources, it was, unfortunately, difficult to help more than a few of them.

Later I went to see Larissa's husband, Yuli Daniel, the poet imprisoned previously in appalling conditions, from whom she had been separated for some time. Although only sixty-two, he had suffered a debilitating stroke and considerable memory loss, causing his mind to fade in and out during conversation. He spent most of his time in bed and could hardly walk. He had, happily, one battered copy of his collection of poems *Stikhi iz nevoli* (Poems from captivity), published in Russian by the Alexander Herzen Foundation in 1971.

The same day, I started chatting with a woman of about fifty whom I met on the street, and it turned out that she was an Orthodox Christian who had been trying to emigrate for a decade but had been turned down repeatedly. Having lost touch with her sole relative abroad, an uncle, she had been unable to get a legally required invitation from him. She was divorced, somewhat educated, quite lively, lived with her twenty-year-old son, and worked in a sewing factory. Life was extremely hard and she was deeply anti-Soviet, had no hopes for perestroika, and begged me to try to find her uncle. I promised to try, and did try, but had no success. Her son and her religion were the only consolations in an intensely frustrating and poverty-filled existence. She alerted me to her church, which had a good priest, and I bought her a big bunch of flowers. Our hour together was sad, but not wholly bleak. She had been battered and was embittered, but she was not completely crushed.

ALEXANDER PODRABINEK, PYOTR STARCHIK, AND *EXPRESS-KHRONIKA*

The next day I met Alexander Podrabinek, the man who had started the Working Commission to Investigate the Use of Psychiatry for Political Purposes, which was now defunct. Pyotr Starchik, whom I met with him, had also been a member of the Working Commission, and both men were key producers of the recently founded weekly samizdat newspaper *Express-Khronika*. The paper came out in both Russian and English versions, thanks to having the Englishman John Crowfoot, who lived in Moscow, as the translator into English (I became friends with him much later, in 2003). Starchik was a gentle, burly man of about fifty who had been interned in a prison mental hospital from 1972 to 1975 for his dissent. He was also a Christian anthroposophist and a good singer with a husky voice, as I realized when he sang us a song in the mode of the famous Vladimir Vysotsky. After Starchik had performed, Podrabinek insisted that I sing some unaccompanied English songs, which I did, while he taped them.

Express-Khronika was a bulletin in the tradition of the samizdat *Khronika tekushchikh sobytii* (which appeared from 1968 to 1983), so it wasn't surprising that the phone rang regularly as news items came in from the forty cities around the USSR where the bulletin's reporters collected information on human rights issues. Podrabinek was the chief editor and Starchik and three others were editors. Their names, addresses, and phone numbers appeared in each issue. When I arrived, issue 25 had just come off the typewriter. The next day, some one hundred copies produced by the editors—typed as originals ten times, each time with ten carbon copies—would be distributed by couriers or mailed to these forty cities.

The issues were fifteen to twenty pages long. First came soberly factual news items, then a documentary section. Some of the reports carried their authors' names. Each week the entire text was read over the phone twice, once to Alexander Ginzburg in Paris and once to Cronid Lubarsky in Munich, in which cities it would be examined for key types of news, sometimes translated, then typed up again and disseminated further.[7]

So far there had been no specific threats against Podrabinek's new bulletin, but a nasty attack on it in the press amounted to the same thing. He had been forced to give up his job in an ambulance service three months before, and had also been otherwise harassed by the authorities. They seemed to be planning to charge him with "parasitism"; that is, illegally not having a paid job. Following his previous imprisonment, he was forced to live more than sixty-two miles from Moscow, but came into town frequently.

He recounted to me several snippets about the human rights movement, including the fact that the samizdat magazine *Glasnost'* was rather sloppily edited by Sergei Grigoryants, a somewhat self-important and bossy personality. Some of his assistants had defected to *Express-Khronika* to get away from him! But he still had many helpers.

Podrabinek regretted that Sakharov had become "so political" and begun supporting the Gorbachev regime, which *Express-Khronika* regarded as "wholly illegitimate": Podrabinek thought Sakharov was being used. I argued Sakharov's case, pointing out that his special status enabled him to speak out on human rights in high forums. Podrabinek conceded that his position *might* be justifiable, provided it was conditional on continuation of the currently less oppressive policies. But, said Podrabinek, Sakharov had been at his best in the years when he concentrated on defending political prisoners.

Podrabinek regarded Gorbachev as the best leader one could realistically hope for in the present situation. It would be good if he lasted, but that was very uncertain. The current policies could be reversed at any time, and then, before long, the most active dissidents would be back in camps and mental hospitals. Perestroika would not work, because Gorbachev had no source from which to draw committed, imaginative, and dynamic people to head all the institutions. The best long-term strategy for dissidents was to build up a vigorous, creative, independent public opinion, which would eventually provide Gorbachev with a good source of ideas and people to his left, thus putting him in the middle of the political spectrum. Podrabinek himself was certainly making a remarkable contribution to the furtherance of this sensible sociopolitical strategy.

IN CHURCH

The next day I went to the Russian Orthodox church recommended by my chance acquaintance on the street for the morning service. It was the sort of day Russians love: very cold, but with a bright, sparkling sun. During my first few days in Moscow the weather had been mild, which in winter makes Muscovites edgy, neurotic, and fearful of catching the flu. Now the temperature had sunk to about zero Fahrenheit, and they were happy again. The church was full of about four hundred people of various types, and they exuded a clear, calm purpose. In most of Russian life, by contrast, people have irksome or boring duties, and escape from them into alcohol, frivolity, or relaxing aimlessness. A sense of calm purpose, like the worship of God, seems rare.

The service was conducted by the parish priest, three other clergy, and half a dozen deacons and lay assistants dressed in yellow robes. A choir of about fifteen sang strongly throughout. A mezzo-soprano who must have been a professionally trained singer performed a solo. Smiles of deep emotion and contentment came into the faces of the adults when the children walked back, arms crossed on their chests, after taking communion. As they passed, the adults swiveled their heads, keen to absorb what they were watching.

The priest gave a direct and simple sermon about principles of Christian morality. His style was sincere, without either humor or rhetoric. His flock listened attentively. In general, the service was moving, focusing concentrated emotion on the worship of God, yet conveying a sense of a church no longer fixated solely on the liturgy. Now it was concerned also with members' daily needs, and the divide between clergy and congregation had shrunk.

VYACHESLAV BAKHMIN

The next day I went for lunch to the apartment of Vyacheslav Bakhmin (Slava for short), who had been a member of the erstwhile Working Commission. Now forty years old, he currently worked as a computer programmer for an electrical enterprise that had asserted its independence of the traditional ministerial system, under which ministries directly administered all enterprises, and had adopted some institutions of self-rule through elections. He expressed delight when I gave him a copy of Sidney Bloch's and my second book on this subject, *Soviet Psychiatric Abuse* (1984), which devotes the whole of a long chapter to the Working Commission's activities. He promised to share it with Alexander Podrabinek, even though the two were no longer close, partly because Slava was no longer a public dissident.

When Slava's lively wife, Tanya, said she was fond of literature and the arts, I showed her an interesting article by the nationalist Alexander Prokhanov in a recent issue of the Russian newspaper *Literaturnaya*

Rossiya (Literary Russia).[8] After reading it, she agreed with the author's condemnatory analysis of the situation in Russian culture, where the Westerners and the nationalists were so busy vilifying each other that the intelligentsia was failing to give moral and cultural guidance to ordinary people—this at a time of change when they especially needed such leadership. She and Slava stressed that the violent polemics and vicious intrigues then taking place were often related less to the ideas and values ostensibly being debated than to the ferocious fights for positions on boards, or for publication in prominent journals, or for bigger print runs of books. Slava's view of perestroika was similar to Podrabinek's: the strategy wouldn't work, because it was based on a sort of Communist liberalism that was frightening to the ruling elite, and there were far too few elite members of a new and different ilk available to be promoted into positions where they could actively support perestroika.

Nearly three years later, in December 1990, I visited Slava again, to find that he had been invited by Andrei Kozyrev, the minister of foreign affairs, to join the ministry and to head the office for humanitarian liaison. He had ties to the Russian government's Human Rights Committee, which was run by a famous dissident, Sergei Kovalev, whom he knew. It received hundreds of letters from the public in which they asked for help of various kinds, and these were being handled by a fellow dissident, Yuri Shikhanovich—but he had very few resources for seriously following up.

Also, the Moscow Helsinki Group for human rights was weak, because Kovalev was too busy with politics, Larissa Bogoraz was too unwell, and Alexander Podrabinek eschewed it as being too close to an illegitimate government.

The Communist Party, said Slava, could not win workers to its side, because it was too compromised by its corrupt past. If Gorbachev were rash enough to declare martial law, the party would be a key instrument for him to use. Only the party and the KGB had their people situated throughout the whole country, and thus able to enforce martial law. But this was most unlikely to happen. The fact was that almost all of Russia's political forces were opposed to Gorbachev.

SEMYON GLUZMAN

Fortunately, during my 1988 visit, Dr. Semyon Gluzman was in Moscow for the weekend from the Ukrainian capital, Kiev, and I met him at the

Bakhmins' apartment. As mentioned earlier, he is a humane and compassionate psychiatrist who, after serving a ten-year sentence from 1972 to 1982 for writing a twenty-page analysis showing that General Pyotr Grigorenko had never been mentally ill, found that he was barred from practicing psychiatry, and also from emigration. So he took an undemanding administrative position and put his main energies into helping people in trouble, especially political prisoners and refuseniks, and studying the relevant laws.

Gluzman didn't belong to any groups, but was good friends with a few fellow dissidents, especially Yevhen Sverstyuk, a brilliant intellectual and former political prisoner whom the KGB feared. Gluzman stressed that compared with Moscow the level of culture in Kiev was terribly low, and perestroika had made relatively little impact.

Later, in 1990, he gave me the good news that he had played a key role in setting up an expert commission of psychiatrists, one of whose tasks would be to conduct a psychiatric rehabilitation of Grigorenko (who had died in 1987 in New York City), and then promote a juridical one. He had also been commissioned by the Ukrainian minister of health to organize the Independent Psychiatric Association, which held its first congress in Kiev in December 1990. In addition, he had met with Dr. Yudin, the minister's chief psychiatrist, who had been focused on reform and in particular on banning the use of Sulphazine, a type of Soviet drug that had been used to punish dissidents in psychiatric hospitals, and was not only painful but also useless for any positive purpose.

During my 1988 visit, Gluzman took me to the apartment of Natalya Khasina, a decade-long refusenik and a physicist then in her forties who often had telephone conversations with my London Jewish friends Michael Sherbourne and Rita Eker. Natalya was an indomitable woman who worked indefatigably to help other refuseniks and steadfastly declined to give in as hundreds of her friends trickled away to Israel or the United States.

Moscow Diary

January 25, 1988. After another long chat with Jack Matlock, the U.S. ambassador, I was picked up at my hotel by a senior psychiatrist, Aron Belkin, with whom I had been establishing a relationship of close trust through correspondence and phone calls. He was employed by the state but managed to function as though he was in private practice. He knew Sidney Bloch's and my work on psychiatric abuses and wanted to keep us well informed about developments in this field. Our modus operandi had been for him to recount interesting developments in psychiatry in the USSR to me, which I then wrote up in the various articles, books, and reports for specialist groups without ever mentioning his name. This worked well, and apparently Aron never came under suspicion of spreading the information, which was highly compromising to the psychiatric establishment.

Aron took me into the cavernous, low-ceilinged, heavily guarded, semi-underground garage that housed the cars of several hundred well-off people who lived nearby. The whole place was like a fortified camp, for the good reason that stealing cars and car parts and also vandalizing cars were widespread practices in Moscow. It also had its own repair workshop. Aron sometimes socialized with a couple of highly placed politicians who lived in the area, including First Deputy Prime Minister Nikolai Talyzin. This enabled him to understand better how the whole political system worked.

Aron saw the two current political poles, center-left, headed by Gorbachev, and center-right, headed by Ligachev. He said that Prime Minister Nikolai Ryzhkov was out of his depth, and now—influenced by his advisers and multiple threats to his ministerial empire from Gorbachev's economic reforms—was leaning toward Ligachev. Aron also felt that much of the ruling class in the union republics favored Gorbachev, believing that these reforms would, whatever Gorbachev expected, actually increase the republics' autonomy from Moscow. At the same time, the sense that glasnost, democratization, and economic reform were all leading to a gradual reduction in the regime's political control over the population was increasingly alarming the party as a whole, as well as the KGB, the military, and the ministries. The growth of the extreme nationalist group Pamyat (meaning "memory") was worrying. Aron felt that his friend the nationalist writer Valentin Rasputin was moving in the direction of supporting Pamyat; Aron speculated that alcoholism might be affecting Rasputin's judgment. Despite the growth of the Pamyat movement, which most observers, including Aron, characterized as anti-Semitic, Aron regarded the Russian people in general as good, and not inherently anti-Semitic or bad.

January 26, 1988. Part of the day was taken up by an instructive chat with the *Daily Telegraph*'s Moscow correspondent, Xan Smiley, who had had a long interview with Dmitry Vasiliev, the main ideologist of the extreme nationalist group Pamyat. The experience had deeply disturbed Xan, who felt that the KGB must be somehow involved.

January 27, 1988. The main event of the day was attending an outstanding dinner-cum-meeting given at a top-class restaurant, Kropotkin 36, by Bob Bernstein, head of a delegation of the International Helsinki Federation (IHF), which sought to promote the principles of the 1975 Helsinki, or CSCE, Agreement. The reason for the event was to try to do this in Moscow through Soviet liberals.

After dinner, Bernstein, Andrei Sakharov, Lyusya Bonner, Larissa Bogoraz, and I each gave a speech. Sakharov addressed the central concerns of the IHF delegation, namely, whether or not to support the Soviet wish to hold a conference of the Commission on Security and Cooperation in Europe in Moscow. He said it would be immoral to do this until, at the very least, all the USSR's prisoners of conscience had been released, and, as a second precondition, Soviet troops had been withdrawn from Afghanistan.

The list of invitees to the meeting had been a politically contentious matter because the liberal Soviet groups typically competed with each other. Sergei Kovalev and Naum Meiman, both dissidents, sat on either side of me. Meiman, a warm and civilized man of high intelligence, was in excellent spirits, having just heard that after many years of being refused the right to emigrate, his application had at last been approved. Kovalev recounted some disturbing actions by Fyodor Burlatsky, the head of a Human Rights Commission (which surreptitiously promoted the government's interests); he was due to have a meeting with the International Helsinki Federation delegation about human rights issues in Russia. Burlatsky had tried hard to prevent three members of the federation's Moscow affiliate, Press Club Glasnost, from attending the dinner, but ultimately had been forced to relent. A similar confrontation occurred when Lev Timofeyev, a member of the press club who wrote for various news outlets, had tried to speak, only to be barred, then, after an argument, was allowed to proceed. Timofeyev argued for increased freedom of speech and impressed me as a calm but determined person with leadership qualities.

In private, Eric Siesby of Denmark, part of Bernstein's IHF group, told me that Bernstein had met the previous day with the most deeply compromised living abuser of psychiatry, the longtime head of the Serbsky Institute of Forensic Psychiatry, Dr. Georgy Morozov, in order to discuss accusations of psychiatric abuse. Morozov had reportedly behaved with aggressive truculence.

January 28, 1988. Svetlana Semyonova, whom I hadn't seen since we were good friends at Moscow University twenty-four years earlier, invited me to a delicious dinner that she prepared for us in her apartment. For her books on her favorite subject, the nineteenth-century philosopher Nikolai Fedorov, she had recently been admitted to the Writers' Union. She, too, strongly favored Gorbachev's reform program.

Among contemporary authors, she had a lively interest in liberal Russian nationalists, and knew some of them personally. She knew slightly Alexander Prokhanov, and said he was basically a hard-liner but showed occasional sparks of liberalism. She had, however, just talked at length with one of the thoroughgoing reactionaries among the nationalists, Sergei Semanov. The emergence of a viable theocracy under Khomeini in Iran had excited him, and he was extremely antifeminist. When Svetlana asked him whether women should expect to enjoy sexual intercourse he said no, they could get enough pleasure from suckling their children. He was a true believer in maintaining a traditional role for women: their involvement in three spheres: children, cooking, and religion (the German Nazis had a similar vision: *Kinder, Küche, Kirche*). Meanwhile, Svetlana's elder daughter was leaning toward one aspect of the conservative program: a student at Moscow University, she was simultaneously a secretly practicing Orthodox believer who occasionally visited a convent in Estonia.

January 29, 1988. As my driver, a graduate student, took me to the airport, he filled me in on "the appalling mess" that the education reform had got into.

I reflected on this and also on how the only members of the working class I had met were eight talkative taxi drivers. Of these, all except one had been skeptical about perestroika—both in general and as regards its effect on their standard of living. The sole stand-out was not enthusiastic, just cautiously optimistic.

A Major Attack on Gorbachev's Version of Perestroika

In March 1988 Gorbachev and Alexander Yakovlev left the country on foreign policy assignments. On March 13, the Ligachev forces took the opportunity to launch their first major attack on Gorbachev and his version of perestroika. Whereas he was restructuring and reforming the Soviet Union's institutions, the Ligachevites favored doing this in a much less radical way. They published a full-page open letter, "I Cannot Forsake My Principles," in the paper *Sovetskaya Rossiya* signed by one of their faction, a Leningrad lecturer named Nina Andreyeva. The letter argued that Gorbachev's reforms were undermining the roots of the Soviet system and should be reversed. At once Ligachev gave briefings on the letter's importance to two groups of selected journalists, and had it reprinted in dozens of local and military newspapers. Simultaneously, a rash of conservative articles on controversial topics appeared in the press.

After twenty-three days of silence on the part of the liberal Gorbachev faction, a major but anonymous reply to Andreyeva appeared in *Pravda* on April 5 that forcefully denounced those who were trying to reverse perestroika "on the sly." But the fact that it was not signed reduced its authority. Soon, however, Gorbachev gave a speech along the same lines. He also convened three successive meetings of party leaders from throughout the country for "urgent" talks on the subject of perestroika.

However, he did not fire anyone, and Ligachev, although preferring not to follow up seriously on the Andreyeva revolt, did not recant. A huge party conference was set to begin on July 1, and it was no surprise that the elections for delegates to the conference produced a clear conservative majority. At the conference, one observer said, the delegates "were ominously silent for the first sixty minutes" of Gorbachev's opening speech, even though in his comments he edged slightly toward the center, and they only "finally broke into scattered clapping when he sounded a conservative note." They were enthusiastic when he "promised not to carry out any massive purge of party officials" that could have resulted from the Andreyeva letter.[9] By contrast, Ligachev received thunderous applause after delivering a speech in which he did not criticize Gorbachev explicitly, just implicitly.

At this stage the Ligachev forces had clearly decided that Gorbachev had some strong points in foreign and domestic policy that they could support—and that they could basically contain him in a centrist position.

If he stumbled, they would step forward with their own form of conservative perestroika.

In September, however, Gorbachev managed, with adept maneuvering, to deliver some heavy blows to the Ligachev forces by pushing through the dismantling of much of the party apparatus, leaving it with only two departments and six weak commissions in place.

Moscow Diary, Part 2

Not long after my first return to Moscow since 1964, I received an invitation for another visit for the fall of 1988, from October 29 to November 2, to participate in a round-table discussion sponsored by the editors of the weekly Russian journal on current affairs, *Ogonyok,* and the American journal *Soviet Economy.*

October 27, 1988. Once installed at the Mezhdunarodnaya (International) Hotel, I called the Sakharovs, and Lyusya invited me to come around without delay. I gave her a letter from her family in the United States, and she told me that Andrei was attending a Moscow meeting of Memorial, a historical and civil rights society that he and others were working on founding. Memorial's mission was to uncover the truth about Soviet history that the Kremlin had systematically concealed.

The letter I had delivered referred to a trip that Andrei was planning to make to the States in mid-November to give a talk at the Wilson Center. Since I would be chairing this, we discussed what would be a suitable program for the visit. Lyusya told me of her and Andrei's deep concerns about certain trends in Kremlin policy, which he planned to present at the Soviet-American conference in two days' time. Lyusya also described the terrible weight that had fallen on Andrei's shoulders: he was constantly getting phone calls from people asking him to do this, travel there, write this, and so on. He got some help from Boris Altshuler—his best helper—but few people could share this work. He prepared himself scrupulously for each speech and meeting, and he was exhausted.

Lyusya and I then went to the Memorial meeting, where Andrei and the other board members were sitting on a stage discussing the organization's constitution and procedures. One physical item that had been brought from the branch of Memorial in Chernigov was a massive card index containing the names of thousands of NKVD investigators of the Stalin period; the NKVD (Narodny Komissariat Vnutrennikh Del, or People's Commissariat for Internal Affairs) was the feared internal ministry that included the secret police. In the anteroom I met various dissidents, including the man who soon became Memorial's director, the historian Arseny Roginsky; he had done four years of hard labor for compiling an always thick samizdat journal on suppressed aspects of Soviet history. He asked me to have my friends and colleagues send him as many books, journals, and documents on this subject as we could find so that he could build up the library that would be the foundation of much of Memorial's work.

At five o'clock the powerful eighty-minute documentary film *Solovki Power*, about the notorious concentration camp for political prisoners in Solovki, located on one of the Solovetsky Islands in the White Sea in northern Russia, was screened for the meeting. It is based on interviews with six survivors, historical documentary footage including shots of Stalin visiting the camp, statistics of various kinds, and views of the steep hill down which many hundreds of prisoners were thrown to their deaths after being tortured.

October 31, 1988. I visited again with my friend Aron Belkin, who spoke of growing sentiment in favor of "a strong hand" in the Kremlin "to restore order." Some people even felt that a military coup might be needed, perhaps led by General Boris Gromov. Aron was worried by all this, because if Gorbachev should be pushed aside, there was no obvious successor, and a strongman might indeed seize power.

November 1, 1988. The round-table organized by Vitaly Korotich of *Ogonyok* and Ed Hewett of the U.S. journal *Soviet Economy* lasted all day and was attended by leading dissidents and intellectuals in various fields.[10] Sakharov persuasively criticized Gorbachev for introducing "dangerous" from-above proposals for political reform and creating a new constitution, which would further centralize the whole political system and allow one person, Gorbachev, to head both the party and the government. This, said Sakharov, was "just insanity." Since the proposals did not include any direct election of legislators or any political pluralism, there would be no control over this person, who, after Gorbachev, might be a neo-Stalinist. Also, the powerful "popular fronts" in some of the union republics would have no voice. The West should criticize these failings, while supporting other aspects of perestroika.

Yuri Afanasiev, the historian Leonid Batkin, and the economists Pavel Bunich and Nikolai Shmelev made similar criticisms of Gorbachev's lack of concern for democracy and effective economic reform. As an example of the latter Shmelev pointed out that there were 15 million peasants under 3 million administrators. If you privatized agriculture, these administrators would lose their jobs. Ergo, they would not allow this reform to take place.

Sakharov's Views on Gorbachev's Reforms

In numerous speeches, such as those he gave in November 1988 and June 1989, Sakharov provided insights and analyses of what Gorbachev was trying—and ultimately failing—to do to steer the Soviet Union toward effective political reform. He spoke now to a group of interested international experts and academics, and now to his fellow Soviet citizens and their parliamentary deputies.

In November he came to Washington to give a talk at the Wilson Center. Sakharov made the same kinds of points that he had made two weeks earlier to the round-table meeting and pointed out, further, that since Stalin's day the general model of reform in the USSR had been two steps forward, one step back. For example, Gorbachev had dramatically expanded freedom for individuals and the media, but then the Nina Andreyeva article had seriously threatened these freedoms. His impression now was that Gorbachev did not have a solid reform strategy, but had merely "been improvising." I tried to draw him out on some of his other points.[11]

Gorbachev now attempted to construct a more effective basis for serious reform by creating a new legislative body, the Congress of People's Deputies. In March 1989 elections were held for deputies to the first congress, and Sakharov was among those elected. The first session opened on May 25. At the end of the scheduled votes and other business of the congress Sakharov demanded to address the deputies, and Gorbachev grudgingly allowed him to do so. In his speech he showed how the congress had been manipulated by the only person with real power, Gorbachev, who was both its chairman—no one was allowed to run against him—and also chairman of the fatally weakened Supreme Soviet (the parliament) and the head of the only somewhat less weakened Communist Party. Thus the

Congress had not been able to take power after its election in March and start representing the people's interests. "A general crisis of confidence in the nation's leadership has gripped the country," Sakharov said.

Nonetheless, Sakharov seized a last chance and appealed to the Congress to take power by adopting his brief "decree on power." If it didn't, "then there is not the slightest hope that the soviets [ruling councils] of the Union Republics, the regions, the districts, and the villages will do so. . . . Without a strong Congress and strong and independent soviets it won't be possible to implement land reform or any agrarian policy," or to overcome bureaucratic dictates, promote commercial enterprise, or fight against ecological folly.

Sakharov went on to enumerate many additional topics that needed urgent attention, leading up to his call to the Congress that it proclaim "the rule of law." At that point Gorbachev, from the chair, cut him off.[12]

What had prepared the ground for the predicament that Sakharov identified was the fact that the congress did not truly represent the public. Notable were the elections to 1,500 of the seats in the new congress in March 1989, and the fact that the other 750 were filled by the Communist party and party-dominated organizations. Of the 1,500 deputies, it turned out that only about 300 were liberals, who had in many cases beaten established conservatives, while 300 others were committed conservatives and the remaining 900 were said to be uncommitted, faceless individuals who would follow whichever way the wind blew.

Two weeks after the election, militantly nationalist but peaceful demonstrations developed in Tbilisi, the capital of Georgia. Soon, evidently following orders from anonymous hard-liners, the army dispersed them, using extremist methods: twenty unresisting people were killed while several thousands were seriously injured or poisoned by a toxic gas. An anonymous hard-line author quickly published an article in *Pravda* blaming "self-appointed leaders" for the disaster and calling for prosecutions and an all-round tightening of political controls.

Two days later, however, Gorbachev appealed for calm in Georgia and set in motion a series of skillful measures to achieve this. At the same time he inveighed against the "extreme dangerousness" of separatist actions. But intense polemics around the whole issue continued for weeks, while Gorbachev maneuvered ceaselessly to keep his opponents on both right and left off balance.[13]

Thus the first Congress of People's Deputies opened on May 25 in a tense and divisive atmosphere, which, as Sakharov showed, made any positive achievements impossible. The hard-liners blocked all the liberals' initiatives and vice versa. Meanwhile, liberals such as Yeltsin and Leonid Abalkin delivered alarmist reports on the increasingly dreadful state of the economy. And no successor to Gorbachev was in sight.

In November 1989 I summed up my view of how the world looked to Gorbachev and his associates, all of them Communists: "History is marching backwards. Nationalism and religion are rising, the socialist dominoes of Eastern Europe are falling, and a growing number of Soviet republics are in turmoil. Communist economics are an acknowledged failure, a winter of popular discontent is at hand, and much of the party's self-serving history is now a grudgingly admitted lie. The result is that the Soviet regime is going through a profound crisis of legitimacy."[14]

FIFTEEN

Upending Manufactured Schizophrenia

The political terrain roiled in the early Gorbachev years from 1987 to 1989 also saw many complex developments regarding the abuse of psychiatry. This period ended with a long, unprecedented, firsthand examination of Soviet psychiatry by a large group of American psychiatrists and other experts in which I participated.[1]

One of the signals as to where things were going came in 1987, when a few corrupt psychiatrists began to get into official trouble for their past actions. As early as 1985, Eduard Babayan, a department head in the Ministry of Health, had been dismissed from his position for "lack of principle" and other failings. Two years later, in 1987, two series of articles appeared that were much more explicit in their criticism, made possible no doubt by the liberalizing influence that Gorbachev's ally, Alexander Yakovlev, exerted over the media at that time. One series, by A. Mann, appeared in *Meditsinskaya gazeta* on May 20, 22, and 27, 1987; the other, by V. Andriyanov, appeared in *Sotsialisticheskaya industriya* on January 31, February 1, March 24, May 20, and May 30.[2]

On May 20, 1987, Anatoly Potapov, a psychiatrist who was the minister of health of the Russian Republic, summarized the reasons for the current campaign against corruption among doctors in an interview for the Andriyanov article of May 20 (the Soviet senior psychiatrist Aron Belkin told me that he, not Potapov, had actually written most of the article himself).[3]

It included this astonishing statement: "The acceptance of bribes and the practice of extortion in a number of clinics has become customary. . . . It is time the truth was told. . . . For sums of money, healthy people are changed into sick people. Evidently anything can be bought in the psychiatric hospitals in the Moscow area." The author of one of the series of articles stated: "Again and again the same group of psychiatric specialists have 'manufactured' schizophrenics out of normal persons." This healthy media trend continued for nearly a year, before the conservatives made a partial comeback in late 1987.[4]

In the West, meanwhile, the imprisoned dissident psychiatrist Dr. Anatoly Koryagin had been made an honorary member of the World Psychiatric Association's World Congress in Vienna in 1983, although the WPA leadership made Byzantine maneuverings to try to bury this fact.[5] After his release from prison in 1987 he had settled in Switzerland (he spoke some German and no English). Late that year he was awarded honorary membership of the American Psychiatric Association at its annual congress in Chicago. I was present as he delivered, to repeated applause, a dignified speech about the tough but sensible conditions on which, in his view, the Soviet Psychiatric Society should be readmitted to the WPA. At this, however, the WPA president, Costas Stefanis of Greece, made disparaging remarks to the people at his table about the speaker.[6] He subsequently turned out to be a willing instrument in the hands of the Soviet establishment, a stance that opened him up to scalding criticism from I. F. Stone.[7]

In Moscow in January 1988, Alexander Podrabinek and I briefed each other about recent developments regarding psychiatric abuse in the USSR and the West. He told me that he would be happy to be the Moscow representative of the International Association on the Political Use of Psychiatry (IAPUP) and to distribute its bulletins. Regarding conditions set by Western national members of the WPA for the Soviet Psychiatric Society to be readmitted, he strongly advocated that the Soviet society set up a monitoring commission to investigate abuses. It should contain some independent representatives of the Soviet public. Podrabinek provided a detailed analysis and list of conditions for such rehabilitation.[8]

Dr. Semyon Gluzman and I had a similar discussion about the situation in Kiev, which he said was considerably worse than in Moscow. He also told me that the coauthor of the report on General Grigorenko that he wrote in 1971, Yefim Vainman, had emigrated to the United States and was currently in St. Louis. He was a brilliant man and had passed his U.S. medical exams on the first try.

My friend the psychiatrist Aron Belkin and I turned out to have very similar views on psychiatric abuse. These were that the improvements in the situation were real, but the establishment was too deeply entrenched to let the improvements go much further. During both my January and December 1988 visits to Moscow, Aron gave me valuable information on some recent developments in Soviet psychiatry.

Andrei Snezhnevsky, the originator in the 1950s and subsequent chief enforcer of the wide-ranging Soviet doctrine and diagnosis of "sluggish schizophrenia," died in 1987. This was a blow to the doctrine, but by no means a decisive one. His grandiose theory embraced the whole of psychiatry, permeated all the relevant journals and textbooks, and was embraced by the establishment. It would take time for more rational and less ideological theories to gather force.

The ultimate overseer of policy on psychiatry was Gorbachev's more conservative Politburo colleague, Yegor Ligachev. Unfortunately he had personal ties both with the minister of health, Yevgeny Chazov, a cardiologist closely tied to the psychiatric establishment, and with the psychiatrist Anatoly Potapov. This explained why Potapov had backed away from his earlier expression of reformist ideas that Aron had helped him to formulate.

Chazov had headed the ministry's administration for twenty years prior to becoming minister. This meant running a massive organization of 750,000 officials, many of whom were responsible for the health of the members of the entire Soviet bureaucracy, estimated to be from 5 million to 10 million people. Sakharov had been right when he revealed that hospital care for the senior bureaucrats cost the state fifteen rubles per person per day, whereas in the hospitals for ordinary people the cost was less than one ruble.

Chazov had also contrived to get himself appointed to the Communist Party's Central Committee and to co-lead, with the American doctor Bernard Lown, a Soviet front organization, the International Physicians for the Prevention of Nuclear War. In addition, Chazov had been a key patron of a leader of the corrupt psychiatrists, Marat Vartanyan, coming to his defense when a brave psychiatric biologist, Viktor Gindilis, had publicly revealed some of his corruption. Then, rather than firing him, Chazov appointed Vartanyan to one of the top positions in psychiatry.

Gindilis, in a courageous two-thousand-word letter that was published in top Western scientific journals, documented Vartanyan's eye-opening record of plagiarism, corruption, and general viciousness. This was so scandalous, Gindilis noted, that the Communist Party's Disciplinary Committee felt compelled to investigate him. As a result, the committee "officially confirmed that he had grossly abused his official position and violated the norms of scientific ethics." However, because of "powerful pressure" from Vartanyan's high-up cronies, he had eventually been let off with "an administrative reprimand."[9]

As mentioned earlier, I later learned that Georgy Morozov, the head of the most prestigious psychiatric research hospital, the Serbsky Institute of Forensic Psychiatry, the previous week had behaved with remarkable arrogance before the International Helsinki Federation delegation. He said that no reforms were needed and that the USSR should be readmitted to the WPA. Aron opined that Morozov would probably stay on at the Serbsky, despite his deep corruption and his age of sixty-seven because he did favors for powerful people, avoided making enemies, and had long had supporters in high political places. In due course he would retire with honors and be replaced by his servile protégé and clone, Nikolai Zharikov. Zharikov took a step toward the top of the profession when he was chosen as the president of the Soviet Psychiatric Society at its annual congress in October 1988. The society hoped the West had forgotten the time in 1973 when he had ruled that the dissident activist Yuri Shikhanovich, widely known as an unusually sane and humane person, was psychotic. After this quack diagnosis Shikhanovich had served two years of psychiatric imprisonment.

Aron Belkin was safe because he had remained "on normal terms" with Morozov and Vartanyan and, when necessary, could get approval for delicate matters from officials who had faith in him. He also knew a few colleagues whom he trusted completely, such as Lyusya Bystretsova, a dedicated psychiatrist to whom he sent me for a thoroughly rewarding meeting, and Mikhail Buyanov, who had written an article painting an honest picture of the political corruption of psychiatry. (Buyanov later wrote a whole book on the same subject.) Aron also knew some of the half dozen liberal journalists on whom he could rely when the official controls that restrained them were eased.

Aron also told me that as a result of the recent legislation designed to remove hundreds of thousands of people from the national psychiatric register—such as those who had been given the uniquely Soviet diagnosis of "sluggish schizophrenia"—some psychiatrists were failing to diagnose schizophrenia when it was indeed present, which in certain cases had serious consequences. There had, however, still been no prosecutions of psychiatrists for deliberate misdiagnoses of dissidents for political reasons.

When, moreover, it came to deliberate lies told by the leaders of Soviet psychiatry, the practice had not been eradicated. A startling example occurred in April 1988, when Dr. Alexander Churkin, in an interview with *Corriere della Sera* that was printed on April 5, misreported the number of psychiatric patients in the USSR, claiming that there were now only 5.5 million citizens on the national psychiatric register (out of a total of some 290 million citizens). However, on April 15, *Ogonyok*, a top weekly journal, reported that the State Statistics Committee gave the figure as 10.2 million.

U.S. Psychiatrists Inspect Soviet Psychiatric Institutions

One of the most important events in the reform of Soviet psychiatry had its beginnings in 1987–1988, when the small group of reformers around Gorbachev who were promoting reform in many fields decided to make a serious effort to get the deep-seated Soviet-Western conflicts over psychiatric abuse resolved or at least alleviated. One way to do this would be to let Western psychiatrists see for themselves that reform was progressing—a daring step. To get this plan into the works, Foreign Minister Eduard Shevardnadze, a Gorbachev ally, would have to persuade the conservative Ministry of Health to release religious and political prisoners interned in mental hospitals and prepare for an inspection visit to these institutions by American psychiatrists. Not surprisingly, Yevgeny Chazov, minister of health, and the KGB and its conservative director until recently, Viktor Chebrikov, were allied in putting up a fierce resistance to this idea. Chebrikov still had a seat in the country's top institution, the party's Politburo, along with some other reactionaries.

Eventually, however, after drawn-out and tortuous negotiations in 1988, involving a variety of senior American and Soviet officials and psychiatrists, the two sides agreed on the conditions for a serious visit by American psychiatrists and others in February 1989. The Soviet reformers hoped that such a visit would lead to the WPA's allowing the Soviet Psychiatric Society to be readmitted to the WPA.[10]

During the year-long negotiations, every two or three weeks my phone would ring after dinner, and Loren Roth, the chief psychiatric negotiator for the U.S. side, would be on the line for the next hour, as we hashed out a wide range of points. His determination to reach the truth on each one, his thoroughness in covering the whole of that day's agenda, and the engaging quality of his personality made these time-consuming sessions thoroughly enjoyable. Loren was a professor of psychiatry at the University of Pittsburgh, and later rose to become one of the university's top leaders. Meanwhile, William Farrand, a high-up official in the State Department, coordinated the diplomatic angles with Roth.

Ways had to be found to apply pressure indirectly, in order to break down the consistent blocking of the U.S. goals by the Soviet health officials, led by Chazov at the Ministry of Health. So the U.S. side tried to form an alliance with the much more positive Ministry of Foreign Affairs by helping it meet one of its goals. The Kremlin's November 1987 decision to go all out to get Western agreement to hold a high-level meeting of the Conference on Security and Cooperation in Europe in Moscow in 1991 gave the Americans an opening: it led to Roth and Farrand's suddenly being offered some significant concessions regarding the visit by U.S. psychiatrists. However, once the West had agreed in late December 1988 to the CSCE meeting, the concessions began to evaporate. The bargaining hardened. In early 1989 it often seemed that the whole negotiation might collapse, but some extra trips to Moscow and stronger pressure from the Ministry of Foreign Affairs eventually saved the day.

So it was that on the morning of February 26, 1989, the U.S. psychiatric team arrived in Moscow to be met by Dr. Alexander Churkin, the chief psychiatrist of the Ministry of Health, and Andrei Kovalev, a young official of the Ministry of Foreign Affairs (he moved to the West in 2007, and we became good friends). The next day, at the American consulate, Roth gave us a briefing on our planned activities and itineraries and also explained that he had divided us into four subteams. I was on the only team that would be visiting four mental hospitals far from Moscow.

Soon the group was sorting itself into the subteams. Mine consisted of nine people, including four psychiatrists, who would spend most of the next two weeks visiting mental hospitals in various parts of the USSR. Among our four psychiatrists were the subteam's leader, Harold Visotsky, an influential academic, and also a senior State Department psychiatrist, Elmore Rigamer; and Richard Bonnie, a forensic psychiatrist at the University of Virginia. We also had two staff members of the American Psychiatric Association, Ellen Mercer and Joel Klein; a human rights expert from the U.S. embassy; and a quietly intrusive official from the Ministry of Health, Andrei Petukhov. His job was to spy on us, report our doings, prevent us from doing anything that the ministry would not like, and become friends with any of us who seemed to be sympathetic to his viewpoint. (One night in Kazan, a small group of prison officials and one member of our group got chummy and drank late into the night; subsequently our group member expressed his irritation with my refusal to trust the officials, implying that it stemmed from political bias.)

Roth explained to us that the agreement he had hammered out with his Soviet counterparts included allowing the American team members to examine some patients in Soviet psychiatric institutions. Originally the number to be examined was forty-eight, but this had dwindled to twenty-seven, as twenty-one of them had been speedily released. One of the subteams would go to the Leningrad Special Psychiatric Hospital to examine some of the twenty-seven patients, and two more subteams would do the same in Moscow. Alexander Podrabinek had helped unofficially to arrange the visits by using his unofficial contacts.

Roth then gave a general briefing on how the Soviet side had fulfilled some of its obligations under the U.S.-Soviet agreement, but not others. For example, they had agreed to provide and translate the psychiatric records of the twenty-seven patients and afford access to all of them. Now it appeared that the records and translations were not going to be provided, and twelve of the remaining patients had been released at the last minute. However, the U.S. team would maintain its pressure for the records and translations.

Then Anna Mikhailenko, a Ukrainian schoolteacher and librarian from Odessa, now sixty, who had spent several years in the Kazan prison hospital for "anti-Soviet propaganda," gave a revealing report. She had defended Ukrainian dissidents, edited reports on them for *Khronika* in Moscow, and had promoted the Ukrainian culture and language, including in schools. She had also written critical analyses of how the KGB and the court system suppressed dissent.

Mikhailenko gave a detailed description of her arrest, her refusal to recant, and her being told by the KGB investigator, "In our country your views indicate psychiatric pathology." However, subsequent examination in a mental hospital had found no reason for her to be psychiatrically interned, and she had to be sent to a hospital in Kharkov, where a more servile psychiatrist ruled that she was ill and needed treatment in the psychiatric prison in distant Kazan.

She recounted that she had been severely treated with handfuls of drugs three times a day, plus shots. Another woman received an especially powerful cocktail: "I was taking care of her because she was in a delirious state and I thought she might die. For this I was further punished. Patients are not allowed to help one another."

Mikhailenko was accompanied in the consulate by her friend Lyudmila Kuzmina, who said that she was so overdrugged in the prison that she could not eat or drink, and would have died if Anna had not come to her rescue. The two women gave us the names of patients in the prison whom we should look out for, as well as the doctors who had been especially cruel to them. No books, newspapers, or TV were allowed to most of the political prisoners. Their interests and ideas were regarded as illnesses. The goal was to reduce them to the point of having no interests or ideas. Furthermore, the material conditions were almost unbearable.

American subteams of six persons each examined all twenty-seven individuals for a whole day each. They also studied the records provided (often incomplete), talked with relatives and official psychiatrists, and made audio- and videotapes of most of the proceedings. The teams concluded that none of the twelve people who had just been released had been mentally ill, although three had minor personality problems. They had all been confined and treated for reasons evidently related to their political or religious dissent.

Of the fifteen still in a hospital, the teams concluded that five showed no signs of having been mentally ill. Ten were diagnosed as having conditions such as paranoid schizophrenia and delusional disturbances, and a few of these were dangerous. Except for the latter, none of them should have been hospitalized. Six out of the ten could only be described as having been held because of their dissent.

The prospect for change seemed to me better at Chernyakhovsk in the far northwest than at Kazan on the middle Volga. This was partly because the Chernyakhovsk administration was making considerable progress in reducing the number of people being treated, but more particularly because the new administrators were liberal and had been newly promoted, therefore, in contrast to Kazan's, being less burdened by a need to justify past practices. The new director, Viktor Fukalov, a psychiatrist, was the key figure in these processes. I found him completely open, not at all defensive, and a pleasure to talk with. He had his assistant bring us in a matter of minutes whatever documents we asked for, including the full record of General Pyotr Grigorenko, and he left us to study them alone in his office.

A bizarre incident occurred in Chernyakhovsk when I tried to take a decent photograph of one of the Grigorenko documents with my simple travel camera. An MVD guard in a watchtower that provided a view into Fukalov's office then decided to mobilize the Ministry of Health official attached to us, Petukhov, to accuse me of photographing the watchtower, which was against the law. Petukhov hounded me about this for a good twenty-four hours, picking up also on other alleged sins of mine, even though my colleagues who had been in the office with me backed me up. It was not pleasant.

When our subteam visited the hospital in Kazan where Anna Mikhailenko had been held, the conditions were less terrible than for her, because, as some of the prisoners told me, they had been given special clothing for our visit, and huge efforts had been made to clean the place and even paint a few features.

It also turned out that the transfer of the prison hospitals from the oversight of the Ministry of Internal Affairs (MVD, or the police) to that of the Ministry of Health, much trumpeted in 1988 by Minister of Health Chazov and others, was not at all what it seemed. As before, the psychiatric personnel were still MVD officers receiving MVD pay; likewise the whole guard system was still under the MVD. Thus, Ministry of Health directives in many cases had been drafted by the MVD, and were certainly carried out by MVD personnel.

Trying to find out whether the KGB still maintained a presence in the prison hospitals, I interviewed in Kazan, without warning, Major Nikolai Vdovenko, the head of the Special Department, the official who had traditionally been the KGB's representative. I just knocked on his door when walking along a corridor with the hospital's director, Lieutenant Colonel Valitov. When Vdovenko opened the door, I asked him politely if he worked for the KGB. At this, he became flustered, looked at Valitov for guidance, and then they both said no, he reported only to Valitov. Vdovenko added that he had never worked for the KGB. However, given his state of fluster, and since the only photograph hanging on the walls of his office was of Felix Dzerzhinsky, the founder of the KGB, I suspected that he and Valitov were lying.

Impact of the Visit to Psychiatric Institutions

After all our team members had returned to Moscow, a culminating meeting for joint discussion between us and a somewhat larger number of official Soviet psychiatrists was held in a lecture hall on March 10, chaired by Yuri Reshetov, a deputy minister of the Ministry of Foreign Affairs. First to address the gathering was a second-rate psychiatrist, Dr. Smulevich. He set out to explain to us that 38.1 percent of all schizophrenics suffered from sluggish schizophrenia (*vyalotekushchaya shizofreniya*), and described the symptoms, which included "anti-Soviet thinking" and "delusions of reformism." He then argued that, given the features of the disease, all dissidents could be diagnosed as suffering from sluggish schizophrenia. This extreme argument did not seem to convince many of those present—hardly even his fellow official psychiatrists.

The American psychiatrists then presented some of their thoughts about the twenty-seven patients they had examined. Dr. Keith said that the patient Alexandrov's struggle for freedom did not merit a diagnosis of schizophrenia or hospitalization. To this Smulevich replied that Alexandrov had "over-valued ideas" and a schizo-affective illness: the more he talked, the more confused his thoughts became. He had "pseudo-psychopathy," which was not the same as chronic schizophrenia. Dr. Elmore Rigamer responded that Smulevich's "terminology is confused and appears to be influenced by a desire to fit it into a category that allows broad discretion in making dispositions." Later Rigamer wrote, "The American team observed the fact that Soviet doctors do not discuss anything with their patients. Moreover, physicians *explained* nothing to their patients."

When my turn came, I gave quite a long exposition, in Russian, of the history of Soviet psychiatric abuse; I also mentioned Western abuses of psychiatry, such as having some patients stay much too long in mental hospitals. I pointed out that a fair amount of what had reached us from Soviet hospitals reflected what patients or ex-patients had said or written to fellow dissidents or Westerners. Eventually I was, in two stages, cut off by the polite chairman, Minister Reshetov.

After the joint U.S.-Soviet debriefing discussion meeting, the American psychiatrists returned home and in due course produced a 117-page report on the trip, *Report of the US Delegation to Assess Recent Changes in Soviet Psychiatry: To Assistant Secretary of State for Human Rights and Hu-*

manitarian Affairs, which was issued by the U.S. Department of State. Issued simultaneously was the Soviet response, titled "Preliminary Soviet Response to *Report of the US Delegation* . . . ," consisting of seven pages of anonymous psychiatric comments and 14 pages of legal commentary by two lawyers.[11] It painted a rosier picture than the facts warranted, both of current trends in Soviet psychiatry and the usefulness of the official psychiatric discussions that our psychiatrists had had with Soviet colleagues.

Indicative of the basically reactionary official Soviet position was the fact that the American report and the conciliatory Soviet response (designed to encourage a positive U.S. position on readmission of the Soviet Psychiatric Society to the World Psychiatric Association) were not published, or even summarized or mentioned in Russian media. Suppression of such materials was the order of the day.

In addition to the official whole group report, some subteams compiled their own reports; for example, our subteam—Dr. Elmore Rigamer, Dr. Richard Bonnie, Ellen Mercer, and I—compiled a 160-page set of reports on how we reacted to the four psychiatric hospitals we visited.[12]

I will now present my analysis first of how Soviet psychiatry looked in the aftermath of our visit, with reference to specific events during the trip,[13] and second of how it could happen that the USSR was readmitted to the WPA in October 1989, even though the APA's position was that readmission would be premature.

Our visit answered some questions and raised others. After my decades-long involvement with the issue of psychiatric abuse—my immersion in the stories and fates of many dissidents—actually seeing some of the institutions and talking with both doctors and patients of various views was a valuable experience.

The background to our trip was a situation in which the emerging reformers came up against a rigid Soviet psychiatric establishment whose officials realized that if they allowed serious reform, they would soon be swept away. For this reason, reform had been limited in its announced aims—drastically reducing the number of citizens on the psychiatric register—and even more limited in its practice, where the reduction had been rather small. Also, the most visible victims of abuse had been suddenly declared cured and released, but new cases continued to occur, and sometimes they were reported in the Russian press.

During the visit by our U.S. group the Soviet side assured us that the laws and legal measures it had passed, such as the legislation of 1988, would prevent the occurrence of the types of cases that had drawn sharp condemnation; yet the circumstances just described meant that there were no significant changes. New mental health legislation had been passed in 1988 that mandated psychiatrists' approval of civil commitments to mental hospitals, but almost all of the patients and most of the psychiatrists we asked about it were completely ignorant of what it said. (On the notice board of the Kazan Special Psychiatric Hospital we saw a memo announcing "New Developments in Legislation," where the latest item was dated 1983.) No one wanted to discuss with us a law about which they knew little or nothing.

As noted, the Soviet media published nothing about the U.S. group's findings in its big report, nor about the Soviet response to these findings. A little later, however, on June 28, 1989, *Izvestia* ran a story about the psychiatric internment of a timber yard director, Yu. I. Sobolev, which showed that the old practices were continuing. The writer stated that a police chief had told him that the local party boss, V. A. Panasenko, had said at an official political meeting that "Sobolev had been putting forward some sort of undesirable ideas. [The party boss] said that Sobolev must be taken out of circulation. [He then] phoned the psychiatrist, V. Kamalov, and explained the situation. [Dr. Kamalov] said he would write an order for hospitalization." The reporter continued: "Dr. Kamalov admits that he consigned to compulsory treatment in a mental hospital a man who was not on the psychiatric register and on whom he had never set eyes." According to the reporter, Kamalov's comment was, "What is one to do, if one is given an order?" In fact, many Soviet psychiatrists, when faced with the same situation, had, without doing anything heroic, found ways of avoiding complicity in a professional and juridical crime. For example, they would say that they did not have enough time to get involved in what was evidently a complex case.

Another case out of the many that became known in the West was that of the Ukrainian dissident Anatoly Ilchenko. He was one of the twenty-seven cases on the U.S. list for examination, twelve of whom had been quickly released before our arrival, because the authorities found they had been hospitalized for dissent. But the Ukrainians were careless and overlooked the fact that Ilchenko had been interned on a previous occasion as a dissident and his name had been reported in the West. The U.S. psychiatrists examined him and found no reason why he should be in hospital; he was at once released.

During our visit we learned that both the psychiatric personnel and the patients of the prison hospitals we visited had been severely warned by the psychiatric establishment or the KGB not to tell us anything negative about their establishments or about Soviet psychiatry as a whole. Some of the personnel ignored this stricture and spoke to us. For example, in the Kazan hospital two young psychiatrists found members of our group in our hotel and began telling them what had been concealed from us during our visit to the Kazan prison hospital. Suddenly the hospital's deputy director, Nail Idrisov, appeared and frog-marched them out of the hotel. Earlier, I had chatted with Idrisov and discerned, beneath his apparently friendly façade, a ruthless KGB mentality—similar to that of his boss, the hospital's director, Dr. Valitov.

One positive result of the U.S. visit was that it facilitated the appearance of the most radical and wide-ranging critique of Soviet psychiatry that had ever appeared in the USSR media and that broke the Soviet silence: an article by Leonid Zagalsky in the June 28, 1989, issue of the widely read *Literaturnaya gazeta*. It was the first forthright call ever made for the resignation of three long-standing top executives of the system of abuse: Dr. Georgy Morozov, Dr. Marat Vartanyan, and Dr. Alexander Churkin. Like most of their colleagues in the field of abuse, these three richly deserved not only to be forced to resign but also, in my view, to be imprisoned themselves.

Calling them servile officials and "people of the past," Zagalsky wrote: "A vast quantity of facts about the abuse of psychiatry . . . testifies incontrovertibly to the guilt of the leaders of this branch of medicine. It is with their connivance that healthy people were sent to mental hospitals, and the reputations and whole lives of these people ineradicably damaged." They had also deceived and manipulated foreign psychiatrists without scruple.

Zagalsky wrote that the officials claimed that "psychiatry has changed so much that now no one will ever be put in a mental hospital without strict criteria being met." He pointed to a few cases similar to that of Sobolev, and showed how the weak mental health legislation of 1988 had already been undermined by Ministry of Health directives. The result was that, "as in the past," despite the 1988 legislation, no one was safe from arbitrary hospitalization and excruciating treatment with the drug Sulphazine.

According to Zagalsky, when Minister of Health Chazov had been asked, in hearings held by the Supreme Soviet regarding his confirmation, whether psychiatric abuse had been ended, he gave a long, evasive answer full of distortion that did not admit that any political abuse had ever occurred. And he made no specific reference at all to the recent U.S. visit.[14]

Zagalsky quoted a comment by Dr. Churkin, the ministry's head psychiatrist, on the visit by the U.S. psychiatrists. When asked what would happen if the Americans examined hospitalized dissidents and reached conclusions different from the Soviet diagnoses, Churkin replied: "They have a right to their opinion. But it will not change the subsequent treatment of the patient."

Zagalsky also described the dirty and crowded conditions and demoralized atmosphere in Soviet mental hospitals. He recounted having accompanied a group of American psychiatrists to the Serbsky Institute, where they had been kept away from the depressing sight of the wards—a sight that was "not suitable for weak-nerved Americans." Only hardened Soviets could "endure such a spectacle." Zagalsky viewed the 1970 release of the biologist Zhores Medvedev after a few weeks, in response to a powerful Soviet and Western public campaign, as an exceptional circumstance. It had been followed by tougher policies and "the threat of serious punishment" for those who interceded for victims.

My visits to the prison hospitals confirmed the information we had received earlier from a number of sources that the problem of brutality in these institutions was acute. At Chernyakhovsk, many inmates complained to us about the cruelty of one Dr. Dmitry Podryachikov, with whom I talked twice at some length. My conversations led me to believe that he did in fact regularly intimidate patients by shouting at them and sometimes by having them severely beaten by orderlies. One patient told me he had almost died from a beating administered on Podryachikov's orders and in his presence, and several witnesses confirmed that this had happened. Later two of the doctor's colleagues indicated that they shared my impression of him.

In light of these ongoing inhumane conditions and quack theories of mental illness in the USSR, for American and other psychiatrists the most burning question in mid-1989 was whether the USSR should be readmitted to the World Psychiatric Association. Dr. Semyon Gluzman's answer was no: "I don't understand . . . how one can accept back into the WPA people who tortured in the past and do not acknowledge it today." Alexander Podrabinek, Vladimir Bukovsky, the American Psychiatric Association, and the Royal College of Psychiatrists thought the same. So did I. My position was: "The worst contribution we in the West could make to the reform of Soviet psychiatry . . . would be to soften our criticism for diplomatic reasons. The best would be to be frank and direct, just as countless people are about the shortcomings in American psychiatry."

In the event, at the WPA congress in Athens in October 1989, its leadership, in murky conditions that are still not clear, managed to push through a Soviet readmission. What is not murky at all is that the Kremlin was ecstatic at this outcome. It rewarded all its top psychiatrists by leaving them in their powerful positions, so that they could continue proclaiming their phony reforms and change virtually nothing. And so, as amazing as it may seem, even now, under President Vladimir Putin, the practice of psychiatry in the Russian Federation remains in many respects unchanged from the way it was practiced in the Soviet Union. Cases of imprisoning dissidents in mental hospitals still occur, if less often; no psychiatrists are punished, and the system is still condemned on occasion. Western efforts triumphed in 1983, but failed disastrously in 1989.

SIXTEEN

The End: RIP USSR, 1917 to 1991

The West tended to glorify Mikhail Gorbachev and see him as moving steadily forward, in the direction the West wished him to go. But despite his remarkable achievements, by spring 1990 I had become convinced that Gorbachev was politically doomed. I followed his two final years in power, and those of the Soviet Union, 1990 and 1991, with fascination and wrote a number of articles that tracked the trajectory of the leader and his far-flung Union of Soviet Socialist Republics, which was weakening dramatically as the fifteen republics asserted more and more autonomy.

I use the terms *leftist* and *rightist* in my analysis, which I define as follows: Leftists groups were made up of democrats, dissidents, intellectuals, and anti-Communists, and were supported by interested foreigners who saw them as pressing for Western ideals. Rightists were conservatives of various stripes who wanted little or no change, and included many Communists, Russian nationalists (divided between advocates for the Russian nation and advocates for the whole Soviet nation), and religious people, and some Chinese who strongly opposed anti-Stalinism of the Khrushchev ilk.

In a May 1990 article I wrote: "Gorbachev is sinking. . . . The reason . . . is that he has no popular mandate, and the blame for the Soviet Union's deepening crises is more and more being placed on him. He has taken near-dictatorial powers, but he cannot use them effectively. His authority is evaporating in the clouds of his increasingly frenetic and contradictory speeches."[1]

This judgment was later effectively confirmed by a comment from Gorbachev's interpreter Pavel Palazchenko, who came with him to Washington in about 2000. When the three of us met by chance at a reception, Palazchenko introduced me to Gorbachev by saying that although I had written many critical articles about him, they had been on the mark, because I had also taken care to refer to his unprecedented feats. Gorbachev smiled and proceeded to be utterly charming.

My viewpoint of May 1990 was rejected by some Western Sovietologists, such as Jerry Hough, a professor of political science at Duke University. After my article "Is the Soviet Union on the Road to Anarchy?" appeared in the *Washington Post* on August 20, 1989, Hough responded with a letter to the editor a week later, in the August 27 issue, where he wrote: "Never have I seen such total nonsense as that in Peter Reddaway's 'Is the Soviet Union on the Road to Anarchy?'" Hough contended that my article was "the most bizarre analysis," because "the great majority of the Russian people understand that anarchy means national disintegration, and will always accept the repression that Mr Gorbachev will use . . . to keep things under control."[2]

I did prove to be wrong in December 1992 on a somewhat related issue: the ability of the Russian Federation, created in December 1991, to hold together.[3] In May 1990, 89 percent of the citizens of the Russian Federation voted for the liberal Boris Yeltsin as their first independent prime minister. Prior to this, all prime ministers had simply done what the party told them to do. Now, Gorbachev was chairman of the USSR Supreme Soviet, but did not have the power to dictate to Yeltsin. When Yeltsin made occasional blunders, most people forgave him, because his support base was wide. Also, his chief of staff, Gennady Burbulis, struck observers as competent.

The economic situation was deteriorating rapidly and the public was clamoring for decisive measures. Yeltsin's election and impending liberal economic reforms tempted Gorbachev in the late summer to try to keep pace with his liberalism by adopting on a countrywide basis the Shatalin Plan for radical economic and political reform. Dubbed "Five Hundred Days," the plan had been developed by the economist Stanislav Shatalin and others, and had extensive input and a considerable measure of support from key union republics. The plan called for extensive privatization of the economy and liberalization of the polity.

Another plan was also on the table, one developed by two government economists, Nikolai Ryzhkov and Leonid Abalkin. This called for much less radical reform, including less privatization and less liberalization of the polity. The unanimous view of leading economists was that compromise between the Shatalin Plan and the government's Ryzhkov-Abalkin plan was not feasible and in fact would spell economic chaos. Gorbachev seemed to endorse the Shatalin Plan in public, yet he once again opted for a vacillating middle path. He evidently feared that sacking Ryzhkov and having to form a new government would be too unpopular with the rightists and the general public. This conclusion is supported by the finding of the top polling organization that his popular approval rating had sunk from 52 percent in December 1989 to a mere 21 percent in October 1990.[4]

On November 14, Marshal Sergei Akhromeyev, whom Gorbachev had made his military adviser in March, published a sensational article in which he demanded an immediate and comprehensive crackdown on Soviet society to restore the government's authority. However, when Gorbachev did nothing, Akhromeyev said no more, out of respect for the presidential office. (Nine months later, after the hard-line coup of August 1991 with which he was in full agreement had failed, he committed suicide.)

On November 16 Gorbachev made a speech in which he spoke frankly about what he called the "vacuum" and the "paralysis" of power.[5] Whenever he issued decrees, he said, "Debates begin: 'What sort of decree is this? Do we have to carry it out, or not?'" Then he commented in disgust, "This way we'll never get an executive that functions properly." To try to regain some support in the republics, half of which had been steadily accruing independent power, he embraced the idea of introducing a Union Treaty that would greatly expand the autonomy of the republics. On November 24, 1990, he published a draft, but it came two years too late. By now, too many of the various republics' inhabitants had lost all trust in Moscow's intentions, and were busy creating their own republican institutions.

Moscow, December 1990

In December 1990 I traveled to London and then to Moscow in order to interact directly with numerous firsthand observers of the scene, and a couple of active participants, who enjoyed a variety of perspectives. I had been invited to Moscow to present some lectures on psychiatry and other topics in late December as a guest of the State Historical Archives Institute, whose director, Yuri Afanasiev, knew me. The dates of my visit coincided with the fourth session of the Congress of People's Deputies, to begin on December 17, which would give me an opportunity to discuss the dynamically changing situation with ringside observers.

The Congress of People's Deputies of the Russian Federal Republic, one of the USSR's fifteen republics, had 1,060 members, some 370 of whom were Communists or Communist sympathizers, while a similar number sided with the party called Democratic Russia, which was anti-Communist. Because the resulting conflicts were so many and so deep, a new constitution for Russia had been adopted.

A number of the individuals I met with reported evidence that central authority was being challenged in multiple ways, and Gorbachev was trying to contain such developments. On December 11, I attended a conference at London University in which Galina Starovoitova, an ethnographer from Leningrad who was a respected liberal member of the USSR's Supreme Soviet, presented her insights into the imperial nature and structures of her country. On current politics her views were somewhat similar to mine, which I paraphrased as follows: "She said that in the last few weeks a creeping rightwing coup had been occurring. Gorbachev had swung sharply to the right and was systematically preparing to introduce some sort of authoritarian rule. . . . The West was guilty of blinding itself to these obvious developments. It was obsessed with supporting a man who had lost all authority."

At a seminar the next day, the journalist Andrei Fadin told us that he had interviewed a Colonel Morozov of the KGB for his newspaper, the widely respected *Kommersant*. According to Morozov, the KGB's branches in some of the republics were now wholly out of the control of Moscow. Hence it was natural that the KGB in Armenia had separated itself from its superiors and this had provoked no protests from the top: Moscow was powerless and would only have revealed this if it had protested.

On December 13, while changing planes in Frankfurt to continue on to Moscow, I met the U.S. ambassador to Russia, Jack Matlock, whom I knew quite well. Matlock, too, was bound for Moscow. He had just been in Washington to take part in talks between Foreign Minister Eduard Shevardnadze and James Baker, President George H. W. Bush's Secretary of State. Jack dismissed my fears that Gorbachev might be preparing for a decisive move to the right. According to Matlock, as I wrote, "Gorbachev was just making another feint, this time to the right. But this didn't presage any changes of substance, even if some formal changes occurred.

This was because a crackdown would never succeed. . . . Gorbachev would continue to muddle on." True, Jack went on, Gorbachev might drop Shevardnadze, who was well known to support Gorbachev's reform agenda, to appease the right, and put him in charge of running the planned Union Treaty negotiations. "This could pave the way to the only solution to everything," Jack said; "Gorbachev, Yeltsin, and the republics cooperating to create a confederation, i.e., the opposite of Gorbachev's current course." Seven days later, Shevardnadze resigned from his position as foreign minister, and turned to the Union Treaty.

When I emerged from customs at the Moscow airport on December 13, no one from the Historical Archives Institute came forward to greet me. So I wandered around through the crowd until, ten minutes later, two young women from the institute spotted me. Just then I noticed that my main suitcase had been stolen off the cart I was wheeling. We went and reported the theft to the airport's busy police station, a task that ended up taking three hours. Eventually I was able to describe what had happened to an affable detective, while a couple of drunks, slumped in penalty boxes, emitted occasional groans in the background. My guardians then deposited me in a grubby student hostel, because all of Moscow's hotel rooms had allegedly been booked by delegates to the upcoming fourth session of the Congress of People's Deputies, scheduled to begin on December 17.

The loss of my suitcase was upsetting because it contained the numerous presents that my wife and I had bought over the previous weeks to give to Moscow friends, as well as most of my clean clothes and books that I'd bought for the Memorial historical society's library. Imagine then my amazement when, three weeks later, the recovered suitcase was delivered to me, intact, at our home in Falls Church, Virginia, by the airline! Maybe the strong Samsonite suitcase with its two sturdy locks had defeated an amateur thief?

The next morning, December 14, I spoke on the phone with my host, Yuri Afanasiev, the director of the Archives Institute. He told me he was so loaded with appointments that, alas, he wouldn't be able to meet with me. However, he did share his views on political developments, saying that the basis for democratic change was weakening, because a few months ago Gorbachev had moved quietly to the right. There would probably not be any political arrests, just a general tightening and the use of intimidation. He hoped that Gorbachev would be able to muddle through, if the West would provide food aid (a need echoed by one of my other interlocutors).

Afanasiev added that a current conference organized by the five-member Inter-Regional Group of Deputies, to which he belonged and before which he had given a speech, had just managed to avoid fracturing over their different views as to what the group should be doing. However, its resolutions and his speech, which called on Gorbachev to resign and expressed fear of approaching fascism, would soon be published.

Moscow was rife with rumors and speculation—everyone was reading all available tea leaves to make predictions about imminent political events.

While in Moscow I was able to visit with Aron Belkin, the psychiatrist who had relayed to me important developments in psychiatric abuse. When I visited him in his apartment Aron told me that about 50 percent of Soviet students now wanted to leave the USSR because of their sense of alienation. A medical student who was with us spoke up to exclaim, "No more!"

Aron had contact with a Tatar Mafia group: he rendered them services such as psychiatric care, and they in return provided him with well-cooked food at no cost. This brought to mind the occasion when I had been in his car and he turned down a side street, got out of the car, and went into a dark entrance. When he came back, he was carrying a beautifully cooked chicken; the bird had come from the United States. He explained that the profits from the food business went not only to the Tatars, but also to the district party organization. Since the political trends were against the party, the organization was plowing money that might soon be confiscated from it into successful state businesses that it could simply buy when the right moment arrived. Aron added that renting a cooperative apartment in Moscow now cost 80 dollars per week, or 1,920 rubles at the black-market exchange rate, a drastic increase.

If you wanted to be able to induce taxi drivers to stop for you, Aron said, nothing was more effective than waving red half packs of Marlboro cigarettes at them. You just had to wave them vigorously and the taxi would screech to a halt. So Aron always carried some, even though he didn't smoke.

He then recounted how he had once interceded for a well-known worker of miracles, Dzhuna Davitashvili, who was in Brezhnev's circle. In 1978 a group close to Brezhnev—which included the corrupt cardiologist Yevgeny Chazov, who later turned to administering psychiatry—had been worried about the influence that she was having on Brezhnev and tried to have her put in a mental hospital. Aron went to a highly placed politician he knew, Nikolai Baibakov, the head of the State Planning Commission, who had in turn interceded with the head of the KGB, Yuri Andropov, who had saved her from this fate.

Aron also passed on what some highly placed friends had recently told him: that a decision had been taken to pursue authoritarian rule, which would involve arrests as necessary, strict discipline, and the KGB playing a key role in running the economy. In addition, agriculture would be freed of official control, and the collective farms would be allowed to disband if they wanted to.

While in Moscow I met with Paul Quinn-Judge, a reporter with the *Toronto Globe and Mail*, who told me that among his Russian contacts a major question for debate was whether General Boris Gromov would be politically neutralized, now that Gorbachev had brought him in as a top adviser. He was seen as a possible Napoleon Bonaparte—someone who could possibly seize power.

Another Russian nationalist hard-liner Paul knew, who had recently given him an interview, was Colonel Viktor Alksnis. He had argued emphatically that Gorbachev must go.

A former Gorbachev speechwriter had told Paul that Gorbachev was flustered, didn't know what to do, and couldn't wholly control where or even whether his speeches would be published. He organized a meeting with intellectuals, and mused aloud in extempore, almost dreamily, about his father and grandfather.[6] He would, Paul believed, fight on to the end and not give up. But he couldn't clamp down now; it was too late.

On a different, more personal point, Volodya and Olga Kharitonov were good friends from my Moscow University days of twenty-six years earlier and it was nice to see them again. Olga had recently visited Russian friends living in the United States and had a powerful feeling of liberation while there. Coming home had been difficult. Volodya had recently become a member of the Writers' Union, which had enabled him to take a vacation at the union's rest home on the Black Sea coast. He had been commissioned to translate works by Somerset Maugham and Dick Cheney. He was not surprised to hear that Dmitry Shestakov, who had been a great source of insights during my graduate year in Moscow in 1963, had committed suicide, but he doubted that his apparent assistance to the KGB had been the main reason.

FOURTH SESSION OF THE CONGRESS OF PEOPLE'S DEPUTIES

On the evening of December 16, the evening before the start of the fourth session of the congress, I watched a television program in which Fyodor Burlatsky, the editor in chief of *Literaturnaya Gazeta* who was a delegate to the congress, stated that in his opinion the biggest political danger was that "a center-right alliance would be created" at the Congress. He favored a center-left alliance and would argue for one as a member. On legal questions, he noted that the first reading of a new and sensible law on emigration had occurred a year ago. Since then, officials had put up huge resistance to implementing it, complaining that a "brain drain" would immediately ensue. The party had written a memo contending that 8 million citizens would emigrate, but cited no research or data to support this. *Literaturnaya Gazeta* had commissioned a genuine study, which had found that possibly 1.5 million might emigrate if the West were to admit them. The next reading of the draft law would be in January 1991. This saw it on its way to passage.

Alla Latynina, a literary critic, stated on the same show that she had a "depressing impression" from the current congress of the Russian Federation's Writers' Union. The majority of the members had been determined to put all the blame for the failures of the Soviet system on events of the last five years. To this she had replied: "Were things so great in 1985?"

My good friend Viktor Sheinis, who worked at the Institute for the World Economy and International Relations, agreed with Jack Matlock, to wit: the Army, MVD, and police were unsure of themselves and feared the dangers involved in taking radical action to restore order. Nonetheless, he also reported that his acquaintance Alexander Yakovlev, who had distanced himself somewhat from his close ally Gorbachev, had recently told people that he expected a sharp shift to the right and a few arrests soon. He was thinking of retiring, because now he retained only one nominal job, supervising the work of Boris Gromov and Boris Pugo, Gorbachev's recent appointees as top-ranking officials advising him.

Viktor also related some of his history with Yevgeny Primakov, who had recently been installed as head of one of the two constituent bodies of the Supreme Soviet. Primakov had been the director of the Institute for the World Economy and International Relations and hence Viktor's boss. Viktor's 1987 study of Soviet policy toward the third world had upset him as being too critical of that policy. They had argued about this for three hours, but Viktor stood his ground. Primakov then disapproved of Viktor's being made a member of the Soviet Academy of Science.

On the morning of December 18 I gave the first of my lectures at the Historical Archives Institute, about my understanding of Soviet politics, to about one hundred students. They paid attention and asked respectful questions for some forty minutes. Only one member of the hard right spoke up; he agreed that the right had no effective program.

In the afternoon my old friend Svetlana Semyonova and her husband took me to lunch at the restaurant of the Writers' Union, called the Central House of Writers (Tsentralny Dom Literatorov, or TsDL)—one of the best restaurants in Moscow. Svetlana had now become sharply anti-Gorbachev and was impatient with the West for not seeing the obvious fact that his day was past and the whole country needed someone like Yeltsin. The republics were gaining their independence, Svetlana said, so maybe Russia's workers and the left could put the blame for the bad things on the right and thus intimidate it into not risking an attempt to impose oppressive, chauvinistic rule on the country by force.

At the Central House of Writers I ran into Arkady Vaksberg, whom I knew from a visit he had made to the United States a few years earlier. (Arkady worked closely with Sergei Kovalev and gave him one of my articles on psychiatric abuse.) Now in his sixties, he was as lively as ever. He had long been a skillful journalist for the weekly *Literaturnaya Gazeta*: he knew just how to get around the worst of the censorship, and had used this talent to also become a successful author of books. Now he wanted to come to the States for three months to work on a new book, and I happily agreed to be a referee to help him in this regard.

He told me that his book *The Soviet Mafia*, which focused in part on its close relationship with the Communist Party, was about to come out in London. To publish it in Moscow would have been too dangerous.[7]

Arkady said he had never felt real fear until now. He had been persecuted in the past, but now a crackdown was coming. However, he would never leave his own country, which he loved with all its vices. In the evenings, the Central House of Writers was being "taken over" by "Russian patriots," who created an atmosphere of hatred around liberals and Jews, as the Nazis did in the 1930s in Germany. These "patriots" would look at liberals and Jews in a hostile way, make loud comments such as "Jews aren't needed here," "You should all be finished off," along with nasty personal remarks.

Fortunately, the waiters and other staff in the restaurant were on the side of the liberals and Jews, and did not assist the "patriots." The unpleasant atmosphere in the evenings had been described in a brilliant article by Bulat Okudzhava.[8]

Vodka was in short supply and could not be sold in the restaurant until after five p.m., but Arkady persuaded an especially nice waiter to "do his best" to bring us some. The waiter brought a bottle of vodka labeled "mineral water."

Sitting at a table near us was a well-known informer (*stukach*), Anatoly, who was trying to eavesdrop on our conversation. Anatoly worked for a joint venture called American-Soviet Cinematographers. He kept leaving the room for a few minutes of consultation.

Arkady agreed with my interpretation of how some unusual events of 1978 were an attempt to undermine Brezhnev. This was when a group of "patriots" and anti-Semites attacked the "April" group of liberal writers, which had issued some samizdat in April. Arkady included his views on this group in his book about the mafia, which I had read. The problem, Arkady said, was that the "April" group was run by not very talented writers, and was not therefore strong enough to make an impact on Brezhnev.

The son of a family-law legal scholar whom Arkady knew had just been murdered because he was active in a support club for liberal politicians, and was also a Jew. Arkady was sure that nobody would be arrested for the murder. His mother was not being told because she was too ill. Other similar cases of murder were occurring.

Arkady had been threatened directly himself, including with a physical attack, because members of the Russian Mafia had found out that his book was being prepared for publication in English abroad. Although his tendency was to keep quiet when in doubt, he now focused seriously on my idea of defending himself and planned to write a newspaper article in which he would do so vigorously. The important thing was to make his enemies aware that Arkady had friends and that they might be punished if they attacked or killed him.[9]

Literaturnaya Gazeta, a weekly, was currently being run by its deputy editor while its chief editor, Burlatsky, attended the Congress as a deputy. The paper had just received information that the Novosibirsk Institute for

Sociological Research had conducted a survey finding that the popular approval rating for Gorbachev had fallen to 3.7 percent, but the *Gazeta* might decide not to publish it.

Gorbachev would do anything to stay in power, Arkady said. He knew the danger to himself of moving more toward the rightists, who hated him for having dug their grave so brilliantly. However, Arkady saw him as already being a captive of the right, so it would mostly dictate to him, gradually forcing him to prepare the ground for the right to take over and restore authoritarianism. The main constituents of the right-wing forces were the KGB and the military, which wanted to restore order by force, first in the Russian Federal Republic and then in the fourteen other republics, if possible. But this plan might not come to pass, even though the Baltic republics were being unnecessarily provocative of the Kremlin at present, cutting off electricity to preserve minimal supplies and highlight the Kremlin's recklessness, and introducing a law on the death penalty to intimidate pro-Russian opponents of Baltic independence.

If the right—the KGB and the military—did act, it wouldn't care about foreign opinion or the situation in the republics; it would just concentrate on the main thing, using force to shore up the USSR, because it was so frustrated and so capable of acting irrationally.

Gorbachev's Communist roots were showing, Arkady believed; Yakovlev was fading, and the future of Shevardnadze was a test case. The promotion to high-level political advisory positions of the hard-line pair of Colonel Viktor Alksnis and Marshal Sergei Akhromeyev was not a spectacle put on for Gorbachev's benefit, but something more serious. Gorbachev might last a year more, while the right prepared the ground through him for it to take over in his name. Then Boris Yeltsin, and many others on the liberal side, would be arrested, while Gorbachev would have to absorb the main odium for the authoritarian takeover.

Divisions within the army, the KGB, the Ministry of Internal Affairs, and the MVD, as well as resistance from workers in the trade unions, might restrain the right, Arkady said, but if not, these entities might cause chaos and civil war. The just-appointed head of the MVD, Boris Pugo, a Latvian Communist Party official, was a nullity; the deputy head and de facto head, General Boris Gromov, also recently appointed by Gorbachev as a senior adviser, was the man who called the shots. The military would probably get Gromov into Yazov's job as defense minister and vice president and use him as their leader. He was a dynamic young veteran of the war in Afghanistan. Currently he was recruiting other veterans into the MVD. But after a coup, the right might have Gromov as minister of defense, a sort of gray cardinal, but appoint someone else as president.

Arkady held that in the new situation, Gorbachev could not foresee the consequences of his actions, wrongly thinking that he could still outwit the right and keep his freedom to maneuver. Crazily, he thought the left was plotting against him, and he was paranoid about Yeltsin. At the start of the fourth session of the Congress of People's Deputies Gorbachev had talked to Yeltsin, but Yeltsin had just nodded and looked straight ahead. In these circumstances Arkady could survive, because he was rich. But he feared for the fate of the old and the poor.

On Wednesday, December 19, I met with Vadim Birshtein, a dissident scientist who was back in Moscow after being forced by the KGB to live in the north near Murmansk for some years. He had belonged to Amnesty International and also been friendly with some Jewish refuseniks. He had been told by an anti-Semitic high official of the Academy of Science: "Your name is Birshtein. You ought to look for work in the trade sector."

Vadim said that there were lots of Jewish groups in Moscow, embracing several hundred Jews in all, campaigning to be allowed to leave the Soviet Union; one group was particularly aggressive.

Vadim told me that the new president of Georgia, the former dissident Zviad Gamsakhurdia—the first non-Communist to hold the post—had told members of the Meskhetian ethnic group not to try to resettle in Georgia from their places of exile in Central Asian that dated back to Stalin's deportation in 1944. According to Gamsakhurdia, the Muslim Meskhetians, because they were often referred to as Turks, should resettle in Turkey. In other words, although they were Georgians who had been converted to Islam in the seventeenth century, then had been deported from Georgia in 1944, he objected to their no longer being Christian.

Vadim told me that taxis were now charging eight rubles in Moscow just to go to somebody's home to pick them up. Old people could not afford this, yet they needed the service badly.

Vadim told me that Boris Men'shagin, the mayor of Smolensk under the Nazi occupation and a truly remarkable intellectual who had died in 1984, was the author of a book published posthumously, in 1988, by the YMCA in Paris. This was thanks to the efforts of Garik Superfin and Natalya Gorbanevskaya. Vadim had met Men'shagin in 1980; his friend

Natalya Grigorevna Levitskaya (whose father had died with the famous scientist Vavilov in prison in about 1940) had helped Men'shagin in his later years (his daughter lived in the United States) but had had no contact with him in the years before his death.

After 1945, Men'shagin had emigrated to the West and was living in the United States. In the 1950s, he traveled to Soviet-controlled territory in Czechoslovakia to fetch his relatives and take them to the United States, but they had already left for the United States of their own accord. He himself was taken captive and sent back to the Soviet Union. In 1984 Men'shagin fell ill in Moscow, and a doctor was ready to come and treat him, but Men'shagin said, "No, I don't want to risk his position politically in this way," and had taken the train back home to Smolensk, where he died.

Returning to the current moment, Vadim told me that the Gorbachev team was constantly sniffing around the Yeltsin camp to try to find out what initiatives Yeltsin was planning. If they succeeded in their efforts, Gorbachev quickly issued a presidential decree on that subject, so as to preempt Yeltsin. These decrees were usually vaguely worded and juridically illiterate. For example, Gorbachev had learned that Yeltsin planned to carry out a legal rehabilitation of unjustly convicted people. So Gorbachev quickly issued a decree rehabilitating all citizens who were unjustly persecuted from the 1930s to the 1950s. However, it suffered the usual defects of vagueness and legal obtuseness, with the speed involved leaving no time for research and consultation with experts.

Vadim also recounted how an enormous stone had been placed on Lubyanka Square in memory of all those who had died for political and related reasons. A meeting had been held at which one speaker had spoken for each decade that was covered. Now there was a long queue of people every day to look at the stone. Even the extreme rightist group Pamyat had held a meeting beside it. Such people avoided criticizing Stalin by calling the stone "a symbol of the victims of the Kaganoviches," Kaganovich having been a close collaborator of Stalin.

The dissident research organization Memorial had been given a large house as its headquarters, he continued, which was currently being renovated. Obtaining this house had been difficult because several wealthy cooperatives and joint ventures had also fought for it. Memorial had courted local housing and street committees run by military veterans with offers of, first, free legal advice, and second, some of the beds in local hospitals which the Moscow City Council had assigned to Memorial for former political prisoners. This second offer was an attractive one, because the medical system was in a state of collapse.

At present, Vadim said, Memorial's enormous collection of documents was held in various places, including the apartment of one of its senior members, Nikita Okhotin.

Members of Memorial had written the first draft of a law compiled by Sergei Kovalev about the rehabilitation of victims of political persecution. This law had been rejected by Russia's Supreme Soviet. There were many difficult issues, including how much compensation should be given to victims. Even though there were only about 100,000 survivors left who would probably qualify for a stipend, the proposed 140 rubles per month would cost half a million dollars a year, but these were highly inflated rubles. Also, should families of victims who had been murdered or had died be compensated? Under Khrushchev, the compensation was two months' pay at the pay rate prior to the individual's arrest. More broadly, how could one define who qualified?

While this discussion was occurring, Vadim related, a schemer called Numerov, who was over seventy and under KGB control, had been causing chaos in Memorial through various provocations. He denounced people falsely as KGB agents and claimed to have been imprisoned three times for political reasons. He had created a union of former political prisoners as competition for Memorial. And he regularly denounced Memorial, in the process stealing some of its members. Reportedly he had even been received by Margaret Thatcher and Vaclav Havel.

On Thursday, December 20, Volodya Kharitonov and I went at 9 a.m. to the Dorogomilovsky Market, where lots of good, fresh food was available at very high prices, which meant that buyers were few. The market also had open-air stands, which did not open before 10 a.m., that were co-ops. The food mostly came from wholesalers, who had bought it from peasants. The wholesalers were mafiosi, more politely called "dealers" (*tovarovedy*).

I met Konstantin Smirnov, a journalist at *Ogonyok*, a rough Soviet equivalent of *Time*, and his friend Natasha for lunch at the well-known Kropotkin 36 restaurant. There were four tables in the room. It was a perfectly delicious lunch in ideal surroundings, with excellent service. Also, everything was clean, the room was well carpeted, and the price was understandably high: sixty to seventy rubles each.

They told me that on a recent evening they had been at the Central

House of Writers. The "patriots" got drunk as usual, and started saying, louder and louder, "All the Jews should have been finished off." Fortunately, none of this was directed at Konstantin, who went by Kostia, or Natasha.

Not long before, for reasons that were unclear, *Ogonyok* had been deregistered. In September it had been officially re-registered as a commercial publication and now had money from investors to invest in companies that would hopefully survive the current recession. Seventy-six of the staff members had signed a letter of protest to chief editor Vitaly Korotich, who had quickly said that he would hive off the commercial side of the magazine. Nonetheless, the general atmosphere was very bad, and this was telling on the quality of the contents. Kostia was not sure if Korotich could turn things around. He described a new split within the editorial staff: Korotich had appointed L. A. Arapetyan as financial manager, and now Arapetyan was interfering with everyone, even phoning to Germany to check that the letters editor, Valentin Yumashev, was where he said he was! He accused Lev Gushchin, the real working head of the magazine, of embezzling the magazine's funds, but without any evidence. Arapetyan's apparent aim was to accumulate both money and power, and perhaps also political control.

According to Kostia there was clearly a trend to the right in national politics, and the possible danger of a civil war. Kostia's view was that if the right took power and control of the government, it would kill 100,000 people—and then the whole country would obey the new government.

Kostia also said that a former KGB officer had told him that Yuri Andropov had listened personally to the tapes the KGB collected on the personal phone conversations of Politburo members.

Kostia had gone shopping and bought a military fur hat. He had not been allowed into some shops, because on certain days they were only open to people from particular districts in the city who had special invitations. Kostia was feeling humiliated by this and by various everyday problems. Even though there were a thousand things that tied him to Russia, he was starting to wonder if he could bear living there any longer, even though emigration would be very difficult.

I happened to meet a driver of a polyclinic ambulance, about thirty-five, who had recently been baptized as an Orthodox Christian and attended a church whose priest was well educated. This driver had a cheerful nature, but early on in our conversation he said, "All we know how to do is to fight each other." His ambulance broke down often, and patients sometimes died as a result. He liked Moscow's mayor, Gavriil Popov, but he believed the Mafia hated him and would probably get rid of him soon. If Gorbachev should be removed by the Mafia, Russia would get a dictator and it would be terrible. Would Gorbachev last? If not, the local Communist Party and Young Communist League would grab his Orthodox church, he said, bar it up, and then, probably, burn it down. Lots of young people were now going to church, and this made Russia's new potential bosses so angry that that they were harassing the church in many ways.

THE VIEWS OF VASILY SELYUNIN

I met with Vasily Selyunin, an economist and historian who had written the economic program for the Democratic Party of Russia, founded by Nikolai Travkin. The text had been publicized in the first issue of Travkin's newspaper, *Demokraticheskaya Rossiya.*

Now Selyunin had just written a twenty-two-page analysis for the Russian Federation's parliament on how to adapt Shatalin's radical political and economic reform program, Five Hundred Days, for use by the nearly independent Russia. Among other things, Shatalin said that Russia should have its own money and its own bank.

Yeltsin had given a major speech on October 16, the most radical version of which reflected U.S. policies for the future of Russia, but added a section on the customs system that he favored.

The Russian Republic had passed a new law on Russia's economic sovereignty, saying that Russia took no responsibility for loans taken out by the USSR after June 8, 1990, the date when Russia declared its sovereignty.

As for U.S. and other Western credits granted to the federal government before then, the Russian Republic would divide these on a fair basis, but no more than that. Selyunin warned the United States and Western Europe that if Gorbachev's government should cease to exist, then these countries would lose that government's share of all the loans. He emphasized the Gorbomania that would have to be painfully walked back. In the Netherlands thousands of people had attended meetings chanting "We love Gorby, we will love him, and we're going to help him!" In the United States, he said, Paul Wolfowitz, one of President Reagan's foreign policy advisers, had presided over a similar meeting.

In November Gorbachev had issued a decree about a special regime for foreign currency to come into effect in 1991. Only 6 percent of all foreign currency earnings would be allowed to remain in the hands of the 15 republics. The rest would have to be sent to the federal government in Moscow.

On December 14, Selyunin said, Gorbachev had issued a decree demanding the fulfillment of those of his decrees that had not yet been fulfilled!

In considering how authoritarian Gorbachev's regime had now become, Selyunin reviewed the real instruments that he wielded: the Communist Party, the MVD, the KGB, and the Red Army.

THE COMMUNIST PARTY. Gorbachev had called the Soviet Communist Party "the only all-Union political organ," but it was too divided and completely lacking in prestige to be a useful power base. For example, Selyunin argued, the Central Committee of the Communist Party had ordered, through its official Alexander Dzasokhov, six documents attacking Ukrainian nationalism, because of the need to restore Soviet power in the western Ukraine, where that power had almost disappeared. But the documents had no effect.

THE MVD. The MVD's administration and members were subordinate to the pyramidal government soviets and were paid by them, and consequently were loyal to them in practice. Moreover, the MVD's special forces, known as OMON (Otryad Militsii Osobogo Naznacheniya, Special Purpose Police Unit), were not keen to be killed, as they might be if Gorbachev were to crack down. Actually, though, Selyunin argued, Gorbachev's supposed powers were not what they seemed. Formally, he had been given extra powers in March, September, November, and December—but in reality, his power had steadily diminished. A vivid example came when MVD Minister Vadim Bakatin had demanded a written decree that would have permitted the use of force, but no one, including Gorbachev, had been prepared to sign it. (It was suspected that Bakatin may have done this to get an excuse to resign from office.)

THE KGB. A third possible instrument for Gorbachev was the KGB. However, as of December 12 it was clear that Gorbachev could no longer rely on it. On that day *Pravda* printed a speech given by the director of the KGB, Vladimir Kryuchkov, and the commentary that followed.[10] Kryuchkov promised to restore the economic links that had existed under the system of a state economy, which Gorbachev had been dismantling. Furthermore, there was no more public fear of the KGB, which was simply busy trying to justify its existence. Thus Kryuchkov was probably bluffing when, two days later, he insisted that the country must be ready "to accept the possibility of bloodshed if we are to bring about order."[11]

THE ARMY. The fourth possible instrument was the army. Its head, Marshal Dmitry Yazov, had made a statement and given a press conference, saying that the army would fire on protesters without firing precautionary shots into the air first. However, 80 percent of the officer corps was against having Communist Party groups within the military controlling it (a finding of sociologists) and considered the military one of the most abused groups in Soviet society.

The federal military should, in Selyunin's view, have only two tasks—to guard nuclear sites and to guard the borders between hostile republics, to keep them apart. The Soviet military in Eastern Europe should be demobilized and brought home at once.

Selyunin said that when Ukrainian students had recently organized a nationalist demonstration, the newspaper *Kommersant* had reported that it had not been suppressed, "because the MVD was not reliable enough." In other words, Russians would not shoot Soviet citizens. In addition, the country could simply not give army leaders what they wanted, including money from the budget. The real GDP in 1991 was now predicted to be 5 billion to 5.25 billion rubles, a sum too low for all the state and private spending demands. In an interview that was published in *Izvestia*, an independent economist, Igor Birman, reported that the real Soviet military budget was now 2 billion rubles a year, or one-third of GDP .

Selyunin continued by defining how he thought the republics, to which power was steadily accruing, were currently putting their energy. First they were resisting pressures from the federal government to do things they didn't want to do. Second, they were trying to get as much money as possible out of the federal government.

In short, the two sides were very different from each other, as were the republics from each other. They all had different priorities, so their needs and efforts were diverse. Selyunin had spent two months traveling in Central Asia, where pay was much lower than in the western portion of the country, and there was a huge young generation and very few pensioners. In Estonia, it was exactly the opposite: few workers and many pensioners. So each republic should be allowed to decide its own budget, and make its own decisions about pension payments and so forth. Then they would have much more energy for dealing with important matters. However, at present the federal government was blocking the republics' initiatives as much as it could.

The Russian Republic had a draft decree that prescribed the legal conditions for buying and selling land, which Selyunin regarded as a charter. It was basically a good initiative, but had too many conditions written in. Gorbachev was demanding a referendum on it, but this was nonsense—no one would listen. As for the ideal president for the Russian Republic, this would have been Andrei Sakharov, but, alas, he had died a year ago. Sakharov had the right sort of calm demeanor, and had also drafted an excellent constitution, which had been rejected by the Supreme Soviet. Gorbachev should be sent as ambassador to the UN!

In Selyunin's view, Yeltsin would not move to the presidency. Maybe this job could be taken by Ivan Silayev, an engineer, economist, and banker, who would be an excellent choice. Yeltsin had first-class economic advisers in the persons of two of Selyunin's friends, Nikolai Petrakov and Shatalin.

That October 31, the Russian Republic had adopted its budget for 1991, which included taxes on business of 45 percent. The Republic would collect these and pass 23 percent of the total to the federal government, keeping 22 percent for itself. For defense, the republics would give the federal government only what they could afford.

The federal government still had no budget for 1991. Only God knew what would happen regarding taxes. The big hope was Yeltsin, and if not him, then someone else.

According to private sources, in both Spain and Germany Gorbachev had stated, "Yeltsin is mentally ill." Chancellor Kohl had believed this, according to the German journalist Cornelia Gerstenmaier.

Despite everything, Selyunin was quite optimistic about the future: "We are not going to just roll over and die."

On the evening of October 31, Shevardnadze suddenly resigned as foreign minister, with the warning "Dictatorship is imminent. . . . I cannot take responsibility for . . . the sufferings that await our people."[12] But it seemed as though this action had probably been agreed with Gorbachev in advance.

Nearly two months later, on Friday, December 21, I went for a run in the morning and found that milk had appeared in a shop near us, and the queue was already substantial. I also passed the Iraqi embassy, whose railings were adorned with a big picture of Saddam Hussein, smiling paternally, with a baby perched on his knee.

Mid-morning, I met up with Kostia Smirnov, the *Ogonyok* journalist, at the Riga metro station. Fortunately, the metro was still working well, as were the trolleys and the buses. I told Kostia that in the metro I had seen a woman suddenly take a vicious swipe at a boy, because he had been trying to snatch her purse. I passed him a few minutes later; he was eleven or twelve, with twinkling eyes and looking out for his next victim. Both the metro and the market featured a plethora of unlucky beggars.

The market was in a huge hall, with some 150 food stands overflowing with fresh food. However, a lemon cost a whole ruble, and a pound of meat cost 15 rubles, whereas in the Moscow city stores it would have been a maximum of 10. So there were not many buyers.

Outside in the open air were two long, straight lines of about 100 women in all, standing shoulder to shoulder, each one holding out two or three objects for sale in their hands. One woman was holding a single bra. They showed no prices. Presumably they had additional small items for sale in their pockets. There were dozens of stalls and crowds of people pushing each other, but not many purchasers.

A dozen or so of the stalls were selling fur hats, all of them staffed by people from southern regions such as Transcaucasia or Central Asia. The hats had no prices on them, and no identifying marks, even any indication of their sizes. Bargaining was almost assumed, and I thought to buy a hat, but a young dealer of about eighteen refused to go below 800 rubles for the one he was selling, which I declined. Instead, I bought two beautiful shawls—made in Orenburg, on the Kazakh border, an area famous for these items—for 280 rubles.

Just after noon, I went to the Historical Archives Institute to give my second lecture, which was on the abuse of psychiatry. Vadim Birshtein came, as did about 120 students, and it went extremely well. Later, I walked down the corridor and met Alexander (Sanya) Daniel, the son of Larissa Bogoraz and the dissident Yuli Daniel. I spoke with Larissa on the phone, and she sounded in good spirits. Sanya told me he might give lectures at the big Moscow institute where Father Alexander Men, a liberal, had lectured prior to his recent murder. Sanya would be coming to the United States toward the end of January to do research for Memorial, using Western material on dissidents.

After coffee and cookies with a faculty member, Dmitry Bezborodov, and a meeting with his superior, I gave my third and last lecture, on Soviet-Western relations, at a faculty meeting of the Department of Soviet History. There were some forty people in a small, over-crammed room. Some of the professors were not happy with what I said, not liking my critical view of the Soviet system, but Sanya, Irina Yakir, Vadim, and Svetlana Polubinskaya gave me moral support. After a talk with Irina and Sanya, I went with Svetlana to the Lubyanka stone.

THE VIEWS OF ANATOLY SALUTSKY, A RIGHT-WING CONSERVATIVE

On the evening of December 21 I had an invitation for dinner at the home of Anatoly Salutsky in a smart quarter of central Moscow called Sivtsev Vrazhek. Salutsky was a conservative writer of about sixty, whom I had met in Washington in 1989. He was the only right-wing hard-liner I spoke to at length during my visit. He belonged to the conservative nationalist group called Soyuz, or Union, which had recently been founded with the primary aim of keeping the USSR together. It also tried to push Gorbachev's government in a hard-line direction. Among its members was the conservative editor Alexander Prokhanov.

Salutsky's apartment was huge, but the area felt less safe to him than in the past, for which he blamed the Moscow city government, saying it had permitted a crime wave to develop.

Salutsky was well known for his articles in *Literaturnaya Rossiya*, *Nash Sovremennik* (Our contemporary), and other journals, had published a few books, and was also frequently on the radio and occasionally gave TV commentaries. Recently he had presented a long speech at the Russian Republic Writers' Union that had been published in *Literaturnaya Rossiya* and in which he argued for the Kremlin to adopt a less liberal cultural policy.

Salutsky believed that everything had gone well for the first two years after Gorbachev came to power. He and Yegor Ligachev got on excellently and the latter's tendency toward conservatism (of the Thatcher-Reagan variety, he said: wanting to conserve as well as progress) balanced nicely Alexander Yakovlev's radical tendency. But then Yakovlev began pushing Gorbachev hard toward radicalism, and at the same time became a Mephistopheles who schemed and intrigued immorally, trying to get Gorbachev and Ligachev to quarrel. Yakovlev was a clever, able man, but he always took things to extremes, and thus wrecked all that he touched—the media, democratization, foreign policy, ethnic relations, and so forth. He and the left and Gorbachev had been serving the interests of the so-called *teneviki* (shadow-economy dealers) who were often called the Mafia. These *teneviki* were the ultimate threat and villains for Salutsky, who cited an example of how they prospered. In 1987 a decree had laid down that any purchase costing 100,000 rubles or more must be accompanied by a report on where the money came from—but the *teneviki*, he argued, ensured that it was not implemented.

It was Ligachev who brought several planners of perestroika, including Tatyana Zaslavskaya, to Moscow, Salutsky said. He knew about them from his long years in Novosibirsk and Tomsk. Unfortunately, they turned out to be unreliable people, and began to serve the "anti-patriotic" interests of the *teneviki*. Yakovlev had cleverly placed his supporters in key positions in the media, so the media, too, had long been "anti-patriotic." They were obsessed with putting all the Soviet Union's most horrible instincts and vices on public display by, for example, making pornography available. They continuously showed food aid arriving in the USSR from the West, because this instilled the idea that capitalism was the cure-all for the country's economic problems, and until the USSR adopted capitalism, it would be humiliatingly dependent on the West. Salutsky was against all such aid because he saw it as being demeaning—and inevitably only a drop in the ocean of what was needed.

This year the harvest had been outstanding, but the peasants were understandably fed up with the country's economic and political chaos, and preferred to eat and preserve a lot of their production themselves. So the KGB just had to stop the *teneviki* from creating artificial shortages.

Evidence of manipulation of the media had been indicated in television reporting of an anti-Stalinist demonstration in Moscow on December 9: it was reported as being huge, whereas in fact only a paltry three thousand people had shown up. Also, Central Television of the USSR, the state television company, had a blacklist of most conservatives (though not Salutsky), which kept them off television the majority of the time.

One victim of this pressure was Alexei Adzhubei, Khrushchev's son-in-law. While Khrushchev was in power, Adzhubei had been a powerful and influential presence in the Soviet media—but he had also made enemies. With Khrushchev's ouster, his son-in-law became persona non grata and could get published only under a pseudonym. In 1985 he had written to Gorbachev asking to be allowed to publish articles now in the press under his own name, and to take an active part in perestroika, economic and political reform, which he strongly supported. Gorbachev had okayed the first point, but had said nothing on the second one, because, Salutsky maintained, a jealous Fyodor Burlatsky, the chief editor of *Literaturnaya Gazeta*, was presenting himself as one of Khrushchev's key advisers, unlike Adzhubei, and Gorbachev didn't want to alienate him. In reality, Adzhubei had been an adviser of Khrushchev's inner circle, whereas Burlatsky was about fiftieth in the pecking order.

Salutsky and his wife, Lyudmila, had gotten to know Adzhubei in the late 1960s, when they had both worked with him on the magazine *Sovyetskiy Soyuz* (*Soviet Union*). Through him they had quite often socialized with Khrushchev. Lyusya still worked on *Sovyetskiy Soyuz*, whose future, she said, was very uncertain.

About democratization, Salutsky opined that this had led to democrats squabbling, serving the *teneviki*, and failing to do their job properly in the cities where they had been elected. The voters were fed up with them. In a few months they would have to give up power in Moscow, Leningrad, and elsewhere. Salutsky produced further evidence of the reformers' weakness in the form of figures on planned subscription levels for various publications for 1991. All periodicals had suffered because of a sharp rise in the price of paper, which had roughly doubled all subscription rates, but the conservative ones had suffered much less severe losses than the liberal ones: *Ogonyok* was down by three-quarters—to 1 million subscribers; *Literaturnaya Gazeta* had declined similarly; yet the conservative *Nash sovremennik* (Our contemporary) and *Molodaya gvardiya* (Young guard) were down by only 30 percent. Even though the liberal *Argumenty i fakty* had not raised its price, its subscriptions were down from about 31 million to 23 million, according to the statistics Salutsky cited.

By contrast with the unpopularity of the new democracy, Salutsky said that in Tarusa, where he had a big, two-story country house (it used to belong to a famous poet, Marina Tsvetayeva), there had been no "democratic nonsense" and the town had reached a point where, in a few years, it should take off economically. A BBC team filming for the series *The Second Russian Revolution* had been impressed, Salutsky said.[13]

One thing that distinguished conservatives from democrats was that the former had been consistent. Most conservatives—men such as Ligachev, Roy Medvedev, even the Azerbaijani Geidar Aliev, and of course Salutsky himself—had been more honest and consistent, and had not succumbed to the liberal fashions that had dominated discourse since 1986. Most democrats had been inconsistent, earlier serving the "stagnation policies" of Brezhnev; and some had praised him to the skies (Salutsky quoted from a compilation of Shevardnadze's dithyrambs to Brezhnev).[14]

As for Ligachev, consistency, honesty, statesmanship, lack of intrigue and ambition, contentment with being number two, which was his natural role—these were the qualities that distinguished him, Salutsky said. Salutsky had recently finished helping Ligachev write a book that was mainly about the last five years, and was a mixture of political memoir and analysis. Holding the manuscript in his hand, he said it was a fine, serious book—unlike Yeltsin's more personal, account-settling, and shallow one. Word of it had already gotten out, and a week ago he had taken Bob Cullen, a former Moscow correspondent for *Newsweek*, to meet Ligachev and hear about the book from him. Japanese publishers were very excited about it, but so far American publishers had been slow off the mark. Presumably they regarded Ligachev as the wrong sort of conservative and as an opponent of Gorbachev. Any U.S. publisher who was interested should approach Salutsky before January 10 and come and negotiate. Ligachev planned to visit the countries where the book's prospects were best, to promote it in advance. He might come to the U.S. soon, said Salutsky.[15]

Ligachev had never been a Stalinist, because Stalin had members of his family shot. Also, Ligachev was not guilty of the official, Stalin-type actions in Tomsk in the 1970s of which he had been accused, which had led to unjust arrests. Rather the reverse: He had taken *anti*-Stalinist positions. More recently, Ligachev had steadfastly warned of the likely dangers of the policies Gorbachev had been adopting from 1987 onward, while Yakovlev intrigued against him. He acknowledged that his own mistakes included the anti-alcohol campaign of 1985–1989 and, when he was a regional chief, carrying out acts such as demoting officials if their children misbehaved, which would not have been approved at the national level. But he had retired with dignity from his party roles this past summer without displaying the sort of "dishonesty" that Shevardnadze had just shown with his resignation.

What distinguished the conservatives who had now made the Soyuz group so effective in Soviet politics—Salutsky rubbed his hands twice with relish as he exulted in how it had forced first Bakatin's resignation, then Shevardnadze's—was in part the fact that its members came from different parts of a country, which they deeply wanted to "hold together." Colonel Viktor Alksnis was Latvian, Major Petrushenko was Ukrainian, and Alexander Blokhin was a Russian. In this context Salutsky and his wife mentioned that he was a Jew and she a Cossack. Salutsky knew Alksnis and Petrushenko well and had a high opinion of them. He was also close to Ivan Polozkov, the first secretary of the Russian Communist Party, and had written speeches for him.

In November Soyuz's leaders had started threatening Gorbachev with unspecified reprisals if he did not "restore order" in the country within thirty days. But Gorbachev was a leader by nature; if he were now really to switch to right-wing policies, Salutsky felt he should stay on as leader and Soyuz should continue its support. But I sensed considerable ambivalence in Salutsky about Gorbachev, and some uncertainty about how frank to be with me on the topic. Occasionally he would let slip observations revealing exasperation, or worse, with Gorbachev, the fact that at a recent meeting with intellectuals, he had once more invited overwhelmingly leftists and no one from the right. But at other times, Salutsky seemed to go out of his way to say positive things about him as a leader. Certainly, he failed to give any convincing answers when I repeatedly pressed him on the extreme undesirability and danger of turning to authoritarianism under a leader, such as Gorbachev, who had no authority left. He did not sound convinced by his own claim that Gorbachev would be able to rebuild his authority by following rightist policies.

According to Salutsky, these policies were as follows: First and overwhelmingly most important, Gorbachev must use his power to make the media "patriotic," not "anti-patriotic." He should do this by bringing about personnel changes and creating the right political atmosphere, not by censorship. (It was not clear to me how this could in practice be done.) The depth of the anger of Salutsky and the right about Yakovlev's subversion of the media—encouraging them to become "anti-patriotic"—had no obvious limits; he kept exploding about it. Second, Gorbachev should carry out a confiscatory monetary reform to deprive the *teneviki* of much of their wealth and power. When I said the party apparatus wouldn't like this, because of its own close links with the *teneviki*, he contradicted me, saying that Polozkov had repeatedly called for this reform. But I wondered: How sincerely? Third, Gorbachev should proclaim complete freedom to decide on forms of economic activity for everyone.

Salutsky acknowledged that after the confiscatory money reform, not much private capital would be available to develop the nongovernmental sector. However, the Russian genius for collective enterprise, when freed from party and most ministerial controls, would then at last blossom in a new system that would be predominantly market socialism. Certainly, very few peasants would want to buy land and farm privately because collectivism was so strong, and also the rural infrastructure was so poor.

The new economic freedom would also make it easier than at present for industrial managers to do business across republic boundaries, and thus help counter the new plague of republic sovereignty. These managers were going to be a bigger and bigger force in politics. They wanted to be freed of most ministerial controls; thus the ministries could still be substantially curtailed.

All these measures, Salutsky said, plus the firm but judicious use of force in a few hot spots such as Moldavia and Georgia's South Ossetia, would really turn the problems around. The fad of sovereignty for the Soviet republics would soon pass.

I asked Salutsky how he interpreted Shevardnadze's sudden resignation the previous day? He said that Georgian developments made the timing of the resignation understandable: since Georgia now had an anti-Communist government under Zviad Gamsakhurdia, the Kremlin might take military action to cut him down to size, at least by annexing Georgia's regions of South Ossetia and Abkhazia. If Shevardnadze were still in the administration when that happened, he would be in an untenable position: obliged to choose either to lose all authority in Georgia, or to resign as foreign minister when the going was toughest and lose all authority in Moscow.

The writer Alexander Prokhanov had published an essay in the September issue of the "patriotic" literary journal *Nash sovremennik* (Our contemporary), in which he argued for a turn to the political right.[16] I asked Salutsky if he agreed with Prokhanov's arguments. He said that although Prokhanov was more of a statist and a Slavophile than he was, they were both in the same "broad current." Prokhanov had just asked him to become deputy editor of the USSR Writers' Union's new paper, *Den'* (Day), but he was going to turn this down. Prokhanov would continue also to edit *Sovetskaya literatura*, so he would need a real workhorse under him at *Den'*, and Salutsky enjoyed his freelance status too much to take on so time-consuming an obligation

Salutsky was a talkative, right-wing enthusiast with strong prejudices and considerable inside information on a part of the political spectrum that we knew too little about, and which now believed that its hour was at hand. He was a less sophisticated equivalent of the politically conservative American journalist team of Rowland Evans and Robert Novak. His wife was a kind hostess whose lamb pilaf and homegrown strawberries preserved in syrup fully matched Kropotkin 36's red-caviar pancakes.

DECEMBER 1990 TAKEAWAYS

First, the contrast between the near-empty state-owned stores and the laden private markets was remarkable. Teacher's Whisky of 750 milliliters cost eighty rubles on the black market—half of many people's monthly income. Even the Russian-made Stolichnaya Vodka cost fifty.

Second, everyone seemed to agree that the current political and economic situation presented no hopes for improvement, only for further decline. Some people had even ceased going to work.

Third, there was a universal yearning for all-around order. Where people divided was on how best this could be achieved.

And fourth, the world's last major empire had no longer just disintegrated at the edges in Eastern Europe. Its very heart was starting to convulse in what looked like the early stages of its death throes. How could Moscow's tentative new authoritarianism possibly hope to derail the republics' many-pronged drive for genuine sovereignty?

January to August 1991

The year 1991 saw the failure of the Kremlin's violent suppression, followed by a liberalizing trend, which in turn provoked a reactionary coup. This signaled the end of Gorbachev's tenure at the top, toppled the regime, and led to the breakup of the Union of Soviet Socialist Republics.

President George H. W. Bush ushered in the New Year by making an optimistic diagnosis of the situation in the Soviet Union in an op-ed in the *Washington Post*: "The main thing is—there's a determination to keep going down this path of reform."[17] How wrong he was. Other Western governments were equally blind, and only their Eastern European equivalents spoke up about the real situation, in particular the danger the Kremlin posed to the Baltic states—Latvia, Estonia, and Lithuania—which had all declared their independence of the USSR in 1990.

In late 1990 and early January of 1991 Gorbachev continued to proclaim right-wing initiatives that were largely ignored, and to appoint conservatives to high positions, thus confirming that his rejection of the liberal Shatalin Plan in September had marked a clear turning point that was only the start of a reactionary turn. On January 13 Gorbachev had ambiguously approved a military attack by Soviet forces on the Lithuanian parliament in Vilnius, whose aim was to suppress the country's independence by seizing the parliament and killing anyone who resisted. Thirteen people were killed, but the hundreds of Lithuanians who defended the parliament with their bodies showed no signs of dispersing. The same thing occurred in Latvia's capital, Riga, on January 20, with five more deaths. The troops were ordered by Gorbachev to retreat. All this demonstrated to the hard-liners—who anyway had no economic program and no leaders—that their central policy of an all-around crackdown on the opposition was not viable without many thousands of deaths, for which no one was ready to take responsibility. Furthermore, in the case of the Baltics such repression would mean decades of military occupation of three hostile republics. In other words, numerous costs and zero benefits.[18] In addition, large demonstrations denouncing Gorbachev, the army, and the killings broke out in dozens of cities around the country, Yeltsin spoke out forcefully, and resolutions to the same effect were adopted in many republican and city legislatures and in countries abroad, which also canceled food aid.

Gorbachev now realized at last that only a dramatic creation of a center-left coalition could save him personally, and perhaps the country too. So on April 23 he made a deft, behind-the-scenes agreement with nine republics in Novo-Ogaryovo, near Moscow, to grant numerous federal powers to them and to finalize and sign with them the still unfinished Union Treaty.[19] These memorable moves were soon aided by Yeltsin's triumphant election as president of the Russian Republic on June 12, with 57 percent of the vote compared to less than 30 percent for the hard-liners. By means of this agreement Gorbachev could cling to power and also help guide the USSR along the only road that would give it at least a chance of avoiding disaster, without provoking the right unnecessarily. The Novo-Ogaryovo agreement was the road of radical federalization and the decisive dismantling of most of the federal government's institutions with their millions of employees.

Gorbachev could now travel to London for a G-7 summit meeting, sign the START arms control agreement with President Bush in Moscow on July 31, and ignore a strong public appeal by a dozen senior figures, including top aides, that was totally disloyal to him.[20] Yet he had no real popular authority, no steady principles, no commitment to his few political allies, and no ability to select an economic reform plan and implement it, even as the abyss of his removal from office approached.

In spite of the simmering discontent and rumors, and despite some political unease, Mikhail Gorbachev and his wife, Raisa, left Moscow for their usual two-week summer vacation, arriving with family members at their luxurious mansion in Foros on the Crimean coast on August 4. Gorbachev was said to be ill with an unspecified sickness. Everything went as usual until, on Sunday, August 18, a small group of colleagues, headed by Gorbachev's chief of staff, Valery Boldin, arrived unannounced from Moscow. They represented a newly created State Committee on Emergency Rule whose members were eight hard-liners in high positions: Gennady Yanayev, Valentin Pavlov, Vladimir Kryuchkov, Dmitri Yazov, Boris Pugo, Oleg Baklanov, Alexander Tizyakov, and Vasily Starodubtsev. The committee's purpose was to launch a right-wing coup and take over the government. Basically it was a military coup, but they wanted Gorbachev to lead it. They had demanded that he, as the legally appointed president, should proclaim a state of emergency, so that the coup would become legitimate and he could rule by decree. Democratic processes would be set aside. Gorbachev was uncooperative. When Gorbachev refused, he cited the Union Treaty that was to be signed by the parties in a few days, and argued that this was his solution to the country's instability. The group responded, "Then it's time for you to resign!" After ensuring that their armed assistants had secured the mansion against any possible escape by the Gorbachev family, and had cut off their phones, they returned to Moscow later in the day to report to the committee. They adopted as informal leader Kryuchkov, head of the KGB, while the formal leader was the new president, Yanayev.

Meanwhile, Gorbachev, feeling angry and betrayed, was in no mood to yield. He waited to see what would happen next, remaining effectively under house arrest for two days.

In Moscow, the committee was thrown into disarray by Gorbachev's refusal to lead their coup and take the USSR in a hard-line direction. It could not develop an effective plan beyond declaring that he was ill and flooding the city with troops. On Wednesday, August 21, Yeltsin managed to mobilize a few thousand people to defend the White House—the House of the Government of the Russian Federation—against the expected attempt to storm it and take it over. At this point the committee saw the odds for failure as having risen too high, lost its nerve, and sent a few members off to Foros to free Gorbachev and beg his forgiveness. The coup had collapsed.

The world heaved a sigh of relief. However, as William Taubman, in *Gorbachev: His Life and Times*, acknowledges, unanswered questions remain about Gorbachev and the coup, especially concerning the possible connivance of Gorbachev himself.[21] How could Gorbachev have left Moscow when a coup was being fomented? How could he not know about it? Gorbachev's old friend Anatoly Lukyanov, a supporter of the coup, held that Gorbachev did know about it in advance "and took not a single step to stop it." His friend Eduard Shevardnadze asked a huge Moscow rally that was protesting the coup: "Is he involved in this in some way?" Prime Minister Valentin Pavlov espoused a view held by some observers (including, very tentatively, me) that by remaining in Foros in the way that he did, he could hope to emerge politically intact from the whole episode, however it eventually turned out. If the coup prospered, he could say that he had always backed it, and only his alleged illness had prevented him from acting earlier. But if it failed, he could claim to have opposed it all along—to the extent that this was physically possible for him.

Taubman wonders: Was he really as isolated at Foros as he later claimed? Reportedly he had used a telephone that wasn't cut off to call Arkady Volsky, a centrist political leader and an early associate of Andropov's and Gorbachev's, in Moscow at 6 p.m. on August 18, the day of the coup. Volsky himself reported getting this call at the time, but did not reveal what Gorbachev had said. How could Gorbachev have called him if all lines had been cut? Taubman cites two of the handful of Western scholars who think along these lines: "Historian John Dunlop writes, 'It appears that Gorbachev permitted the coup to go forward while declining to associate himself with it openly.' Amy Knight asks: Why didn't Gorbachev's 32 guards, who still had their weapons, not resist their captors? 'Did it not occur to Gorbachev to ask them for help?'"[22]

Taubman makes a plausible point in Gorbachev's defense when he writes that the coup plotters did not actually need Gorbachev's prior approval for their plan: "It was enough for them to recall his undeclared alliance with them throughout the winter and spring of 1991 to conclude that he might support their plan. All his tactical maneuvering to keep hardliners on the leash, all the contingency planning for a state of emergency that he never actually declared, all this worked too well: it convinced the plotters he was still with them, even when he was not."[23]

Gorbachev returned to Moscow on August 22 to reclaim control of the government with Yeltsin's tentative agreement, yet when he did so he did not help his own cause. He acted as though ordinary people still supported socialism and the regime, and he failed to comprehend that Yeltsin's heading of the resistance had made him the de facto number one leader. Yeltsin duly exploited these events to reduce Gorbachev's standing to an all-time low, where he could humiliate him at will. However, in an article in the October 6 issue of the *Washington Post*, Alexander Yakovlev dampened euphoria about the crushing of the coup, putting forward this view of the overall situation: "I am tempted to tell you the truth: no one is in charge."[24]

Another approach to dampening excessive euphoria about the crushing of the coup came from the liberal economist Leonid Abalkin, who warned a month after the coup: "This country hasn't changed. The people remain the same as they were a month ago, with the same culture and the same psychology. You can't change in the course of a month. It will take decades, or at least a generation."[25]

The consequences of the coup's collapse and Gorbachev's fading were numerous.[26] The entire central government was dismissed and replaced according to the Yeltsinites' prescriptions, with fewer new structures of minimal dimensions, and headed by new leaders. The republics inherited most of the powers of the old ministries. Gorbachev lost all his special powers. The military suffered a drastic reduction in size, while the KGB underwent even more devastating treatment, its few remaining powers being transferred to the republics. The legislature of the USSR was in effect abolished and new elections were held. Television and radio were freed of political controls. The Baltic republics were granted their independence, and the other republics were allowed to choose their degree of subordination to what would be a new confederated union. Most important of all, the Communist Party was suspended in most parts of the country, its property and bank accounts either confiscated or frozen, and its innumerable "cells" in almost every Soviet institution were outlawed.

On December 1, 90 percent of Ukrainians followed the lead given by their would-be president, Leonid Kravchuk, and voted for independence. This remarkable occurrence merely confirmed the spirit of what had already happened throughout most of the country.

The final confirmation came a week later, on December 8, when Yeltsin and the presidents of Ukraine and Belarus went off secretly to a resort area on the Belarus-Poland border in order to hammer out a new legal entity, in their own sort of coup. They set up a Commonwealth of Independent States and thereby in effect abolished the USSR. To write their legal document they took much of the wording from the still unsigned Union Treaty, adapting it as needed. The USSR was formally dissolved on December 25: on that day the Supreme Soviet issued a decree to that effect, and Gorbachev gave a speech on TV, announcing to the citizens of the Soviet Union that he was no longer president of the erstwhile USSR, since the latter no longer existed.

Some Conclusions

My aim in this book is to convey my memories about the USSR and individual Russians between 1958 and the end of Communism in 1991, and also to shed light on how the country evolved over these thirty years, especially politically. From early in this period I had a strong sense that the Soviet people were not as passive or conformist as they looked. Further, my expectation was that the regime, being unusually rigid, would not be able to handle the emergence of open dissent, and would sooner or later collapse.[1] And it did. In my view, three broad and deep-rooted factors contributed most to the collapse. A fourth factor helps to explain why Russian politics under Gorbachev in 1987–1991 (and later under Yeltsin and Putin) has not succeeded in facilitating solid political, economic, and social reform.

The Three Factors in the Soviet Collapse

First, from the beginning of Communist rule in 1917, the hidden curse of empire creation hung over the whole Soviet system. Until 1987 one of the pillars of the ruling totalitarian ideology was the apocalyptic myth that Communism was such a perfect system for running society that it needed to be spread by the Communist Party throughout the whole world. In practice, however, difficulties arose immediately after the revolution. To overcome the nationalistic desire for independence of the Ukraine, the lands of the Caucasus, and others, Lenin and Stalin created a largely fake federalism so that each republic could become a supposedly voluntary member of the Union of Soviet Socialist Republics, with its own superficially autonomous institutions. But these institutions were dominated by the Communists.

At the end of the Second World War, the advance of the Soviet army into a defeated Germany made possible not only the incorporation into the USSR of some of the territory newly occupied by the Soviets but also, over the next three years, the formation of a second Soviet empire outside the USSR. This one was run by national Communist parties—for example, Polish, Hungarian, East German—but in reality each party answered to Moscow and its occupying army and secret police.

The fact that these two empires had been brought into existence by the use of force, without waiting for the majority of each people to vote freely for Communism as had been predicted, rendered both of them liable to eventual collapse. This came when most of the national regimes were gradually undermined by their own people winning control of the "façade" institutions of independence that had previously been controlled by the Communists: immediately prior to the sudden collapse of Communism in Eastern Europe in 1989, and in the more gradual disintegration of the USSR between 1988 and 1991.

The second deep-rooted cause of the ultimate failure of the Communist system was the inability of the Communists to run the economy efficiently, which became apparent in the USSR with the nationalization of the entire economy except for agriculture in the 1920s, and then the quasi-nationalization of the latter through collectivization in the early 1930s. The Soviets' mismanagement of the economy provided ample opportunities for the development of a blend of stagnation and corruption in most spheres of the administration (perhaps least in the military, which, despite the requirement that it needed to be large, so that it could shore up Communist regimes, also had to innovate). As a result of growing stagnation and corruption, the Soviet economy and the standard of living fell further and further behind those of the West. The Gorbachev regime responded by embarking on radical but ill-thought-out reforms that only brought the end of Communism nearer.

The third cause is the theme of this book: the rise, despite official persecution, of independent thinking and action over a period of nearly thirty years. This had a clear precedent under the autocratic rule of the tsars, when, from about 1860 to 1907, the radical intelligentsia manifested a similar sort of independence, and with similar consequences. As for the period of "the constitutional experiment" (Geoffrey Hosking's phrase), from 1907 to 1914, it can be loosely compared to the Gorbachev years of 1986 to 1989.[2]

Under Soviet totalitarianism dissent became gradually more politicized as Andrei Sakharov and some members of the liberal intelligentsia took an increasing interest in politics. These people felt that the Party, with its bloodstained past and incompetent present, had no right to a monopoly of power. Most of them saw the anti-imperial forces in the republics as allies. Thus, under Gorbachev, democrats and nationalists formed fruitful coalitions (for example, in the federal legislature elected in 1989).

The "War of Laws"

In 1989, these three deep-rooted processes, which had been combining to unleash the anarchy of a "war of laws," led republics that were already defying the federal government in the cultural and political spheres to begin to pass laws unilaterally that asserted their sovereignty over economic resources. This compounded the existing chaos in the economy and accelerated each process still more: it helped the democrats to persuade the voting public that the Communists were no longer capable of governing; this in turn brought to power in Moscow, Leningrad, and other cities non-Communists and anti-Communists who asserted their identity and sought to protect their local economies by passing legislation that conflicted openly with the statutes of their republics and the union.

In response to this anarchy, Gorbachev and government officials repeatedly exhorted the lower levels of the bureaucracy to obey the federal government and its laws. But all their huffing and puffing achieved nothing.[3]

These points help to explain why creating a genuine civil society proved to be impossible—contrary to the opinion of some observers, such as the Russia expert S. Frederick Starr and the political scientist Gail W. Lapidus. Most theorists of civil society have seen an interdependence between civil society and the state.[4] In brief, the state grants recognition, and in return civil society makes direct inputs into the polity through, for example, political parties. Civil society has a strong interest in legal order and political stability, since disorder and revolution inevitably threaten its survival.

Yet in the USSR of 1990 the lack of any political tradition of democratic compromise, honest debate, and coalition building, and the prevalence of intrigue and diktat in traditional political culture had made the emerging pluralistic culture anything but tolerant and civilized. Moreover, government and civil associations had not built good bridges to each other, the former tending to be aggressively defensive of its old prerogatives, and the latter wary about the desirability of close cooperation with a discredited regime. Indeed, many civil associations had sensed that some sort of revolution was not so far off, and wanted to assist in the formation of a new order.

What, then, had the dissenters who, using samizdat, started to write independently of the state from the mid-1960s, achieved? In the early 1980s the fragile civil associations they had created were driven fully underground, since they lacked both an economic base and effective legal protection, the court system having gained virtually no autonomy. Thus, the will and creative ability needed for a civil society had emerged before the prerequisite for civil society's survival: an economic and legal base.

Because the state rejected the dissenters' offers to work together on social, legal, political, and economic reforms (see Sakharov's well-known essay of 1968, "Thoughts on Progress, Peaceful Coexistence and Intellectual Freedom," discussed in chapter 6), the dissenters tended to conceive their long-term goal as being the development of a civil society "from below." They believed it should be independent of the state, an instrument that would gradually roll back the state's near-total penetration of society and create islands of freedom in the manner practiced at the same time in Poland with considerable success. They projected their ideas and demands onto sections of the population and the elite through samizdat; more effectively, this material was broadcast back to the USSR by Western radio stations.

Dramatically, in 1986–1987 the ideas of the dissenters were partially adopted by the country's political leadership, and the Kremlin embarked on wide-ranging change from above. This was welcomed by "society" (*obshchestvennost'*), parts of which tried at first to work with the Gorbachev forces. Yet other parts, notably some of the national minorities, soon started to press their own "dissonant" agendas, "dissonant" because they involved moving to break up the USSR. In 1988–1989, in the "from below" scenario, the reform process began to escape from the state's control, and this led to political instability and then trended toward anarchy and revolution.

The Fourth Factor

The three factors do not fully explain why reform was so difficult to achieve, both under Gorbachev and after the USSR's disintegration in December 1991. If we look at Russia's heritage in the sphere of political culture, we find another factor: many aspects of this unfortunate heritage lived on for long years and continue to do so today. Since the eighteenth century, traditional culture has been hostile to any dismantling of the "nanny state," to the sale of land by, especially, the state, and to the establishment of a rule of law. Also, there is a widespread popular suspicion that democracy will never work in Russia. In fact, the opposition to the 1991 coup was rather weak: only Moscow, Leningrad, and the Baltic states produced determined resistance, and Yeltsin's supporters were disappointed at the passivity of most of Moscow's working class. Furthermore, under Gorbachev and after him, many key politicians were themselves recently retrofitted Communist apparatchiks who in many matters showed little true commitment to democracy or market reforms.

Thus, we should be clear-eyed that alongside real if sometimes temporary advances in politics, economics, and society since 1986, both the tenacious bequests of Communism and deep divisions in popular opinion about political and economic values survive. As a result the political landscape has often been highly confused. Even today, after eighteen years under Putin, Russia is far from being pregnant with a new order that will prove stable and conducive to lasting reform.

WORKS BY PETER REDDAWAY CITED IN THIS VOLUME, BY YEAR

1963

"Yevtushenko and Kochetov in the Soviet Literary Struggle since 1956," master's thesis, Harvard University, May 1963.

1965

"The Fall of Khrushchev: A Tentative Analysis," *Survey: A Journal of East and West Studies*, no. 56 (July 1965): 11–30.

1965

"The Great Ice Age," review of *Dissonant Voices in Russian Literature*, by Patricia Blake, *The Spectator*, January 15, 1965.

1966

"Aspects of Ideological Belief in the Soviet Union," *Soviet Studies* 17, no. 4 (April 1966): 473–83.

Review of *Lenin and the Bolsheviks*, by Adam Ulam, *The Guardian*, November 11, 1966.

1967

"Slow Awakening from a Long Nightmare," *The Times*, special issue, November 6, 1967.

1968

"Politics and Policies in the USSR," *Problems of Communism* 17, no. 2 (1968).

"Freedom of Worship and the Law," *Problems of Communism* 17, no. 4 (1968): 21–29, 96–114.

Editor, *Soviet Short Stories*, vol. 2 (New York: Penguin Books, 1968), pp. 145–69 (with parallel English and Russian texts).

1969

"The Soviet Treatment of Dissenters and the Growth of a Civil Rights Movement," in *Rights and Wrongs: Some Essays on Human Rights*, edited by Christopher R. Hill (Harmondsworth, U.K.: Penguin Books, for Amnesty International, 1969), pp. 79–120.

"Five Years in the Life of Pyotr Grigorenko," *The Listener*, February 20, 1969.

"Crimean Tatars Ask to Go Home," *The Economist*, March 29, 1969, written anonymously.

"Exiled Tatars in Struggle with the Kremlin," *The Observer*, March 30, 1969 (http://www.iccrimea.org/historical/exiled-tatars.html).

"The Soviet Defenders of Anatoli Marchenko," *The Times*, July 18, 1969.

"Leaders of Exiled Tatars on Trial," *The Times*, July 22, 1969.

"Crimes against the Tatars Being Hushed Up," *The Observer*, July 27, 1969 (http://www.iccrimea.org/historical/crimes-against-tatars.html).

"Tatar Leaders Are Gaoled," *The Times*, August 14, 1969.

1970

"The Will to Return," *New Society*, May 21, 1970.

1971

"Inside Russia's Concentration Camps," *The Observer*, January 3 1971.

"Samizdat—the Free Soviet Press," *Peace News*, May 7, 1971.

1972

Uncensored Russia: Protest and Dissent in the Soviet Union (Rockville, Md.: American Heritage Publishing, 1972).

"Lessons from a Moral Demonstration," review of *Natalya Gorbanevskaya: Selected Poems*, by Natalya Gorbanevskaya, edited by Daniel Weissbort, and *Demonstration on Red Square*, by Natalya Gorbanevskaya, *The Times*, February 17, 1972. The latter book is a compendium of materials relating to the demonstration on Red Square in August 1968 and Gorbanevskaya's 1970 trial.

Introduction to *The Trial of the Four*, edited by Pavel Litvinov, with a foreword by Leonard Schapiro (London: Longmans, 1972).

1974

"The Right to Dissent," *Sunday Times Magazine*, August 23, 1974, pp. 38–52.

"The Resistance in Russia," *New York Review of Books*, December 12, 1974.

1975

"Two True Stories: Russia," *New York Review of Books*, August 7, 1975.

"The Georgian Orthodox Church: Corruption and Renewal," *Religion in Communist Lands*, nos. 4–5 (1975): 14–23.

"Memorandum on the Georgian Church Controversy," *Religion in Communist Lands*, no. 6 (1975): 45–54.

1976

"The Development of Dissent in the USSR," in *The Soviet Empire: Expansion and Détente*, edited by William E. Griffith, pp. 57–84 (Lexington, Mass.: Aero Publishers, 1976).

1978

"Notes from Underground," *Times Literary Supplement*, June 6, 1978 (on issues 1 to 45 of the *Chronicle*).

1980

"The New Purge," *New York Review of Books*, March 20, 1980.

1983

"The Attack on Anatoly Koryagin," *New York Review of Books*, March 3, 1983.

1984

"A Question of Faith," parts 1 and 2, *The Baltimore Sun*, September 12 and 13, 1984.

"Leonard Bertram Schapiro, 1908–1983," *Proceedings of the British Academy* 70 (1984): 515–41.

"Soviet Policies on Dissent and Emigration: The Radical Change of Course since 1979," Colloquium Paper 192 (Washington, DC: Wilson Center, Kennan Institute for Advanced Russian Studies, 1984).

1985

"Waiting for Gorbachev," *New York Review of Books*, October 10, 1985.

1987

Hearing before the Commission on Security and Cooperation in Europe: Glasnost: The Soviet Policy of Openness, CSCE 100-1-10 (Washington, DC: GPO, March 4, 1987).

"Gorbachev the Bold," *New York Review of Books*, May 28, 1987.

"Images of Dissent in Soviet Propaganda," in *Contemporary Soviet Propaganda and Disinformation*, U.S. Department of State Conference Report, publication 9536 (Washington, DC: GPO, 1987), pp. 255–83.

1988

"Resisting Gorbachev," *New York Review of Books*, August 18, 1988.

"Soviet Psychiatry: An End to Political Abuse?," *Survey: A Journal of East and West Studies* 30, no. 3 (October 1988): 25–38.

1989

"Is the Soviet Union on the Road to Anarchy?," *Washington Post*, August 20, 1989.

"Life after Gorbachev: The Soviets' Grim Future," *Washington Post*, November 26, 1989.

"Should World Psychiatry Readmit the Soviets?" *New York Review of Books*, October 12, 1989.

"The Threat to Gorbachev," *New York Review of Books*, August 17, 1989.

1990

"Gorbachev, Sinking," *Washington Post*, May 27, 1990.

"Is a Civil Society Emerging in the USSR?," unpublished conference paper, December 1990 (in author's collection).

1991

"One of the CIA's Most Zealous Agents," in *Uren met Karel van het Reve: Liber amicorum* [Hours with Karel van het Reve: A book by friends] (Amsterdam: Uitgeverij G. A. van Oorschot, 1991), pp. 138–44.

"The Quality of Gorbachev's Leadership," in *Milestones in Glasnost and Perestroika: Politics and People*, edited by E. Hewett and V. Winston, pp. 431–45 (Brookings, 1991).

"The End of the Empire," *New York Review of Books*, November 11, 1991.

1993

"Russia on the Brink," *New York Review of Books*, January 28, 1993.

"Sovietology and Dissent: New Sources on Protest," *RFE/RL Research Report* no. 5 (January 29, 1993): 13–14nn. Radio Free Europe/Radio Liberty maintained a historical archive and also issued weekly reports.

1998

"The Crimean Drive for Repatriation: Some Comparisons with Other Movements of Dissent in the Soviet Union," in *Tatars of the Crimea: Their Struggle for Survival*, edited by Edward Allworth, 2nd ed. (Duke University Press, 1998).

NOTES

Chapter One: First Steps

1. W. F. Reddaway, *Documents of Catherine the Great: The Correspondence with Voltaire and the Instruction of 1767 in the English Text of 1768* (Cambridge University Press, 1931; reprint, 2012).

2. This speculation about Julietta was confirmed a few years later. I had seen a photo of my relative Frank Reddaway's grand house in the Moscow suburb of Kuntsevo. I mentioned to Julietta that I wondered whether it had later been turned into Stalin's "close dacha" in that suburb and whether it had survived. In 1969, an article in the Soviet press that attacked me stated that I had asked to be taken to the Moscow suburb of Kuntsevo, which apparently was off-limits to foreigners. The only Soviet person I had ever said anything to about all this was Julietta, so I deduced that she had reported my request to the KGB in the daily report on their charges that guides had to provide.

3. I reflected Boris's views without attribution in the first two articles I wrote about the USSR in late 1961, which were anonymously published: "Attitudes of Mind among Soviet Students," in *Inscape*, edited by Anthony Black (Cambridge University Press, 1961), pp. 10–16; and Myles Smythe (a pseudonym), "How Socialist Is the Soviet Union?," parts 1 and 2, *Cambridge Forward*, nos. 17 and 18 (1961). *Cambridge Forward* was a student journal edited by Angus Calder, who later become a noted scholar.

Chapter Two: Graduate Studies

1. In 1996 the Russian Research Center was renamed the Kathryn W. and Shelby Cullom Davis Center for Russian and Eurasian Studies, in honor of a family that supported Russian studies in the United States with extraordinary generosity.

2. Peter Reddaway, "Yevtushenko and Kochetov in the Soviet Literary Struggle since 1956," master's thesis, Harvard University, May 1963.

3. On Kochetov see ibid., p. 13n1; on Yevtushenko, see pp. 41–42n3.

4. The three articles appeared in *The Reporter.* Johnson's *Reporter* pieces were followed by a long article in *Problems of Communism.* In 1965, the MIT Press published her outstanding *Khrushchev and the Arts: The Politics of Soviet Culture 1962–1964*, which contained many documents that were useful to scholars in this field. After her marriage she published, under the name Priscilla Johnson McMillan, *Marina and Lee* (1977) and *The Ruin of J. Robert Oppenheimer: And the Birth of the Modern Arms Race* (2005).

5. Vladimir Kornilov, "The Driver," in *Pages from Tarusa: New Voices in Russian Writing*, edited and with an introduction by Andrew Field (Boston: Little, Brown, 1964), pp. 251–82. Kornilov's poem was first published in Russian as part of this collection, which originally appeared in the USSR in 1961 with different editing and a print run of 5,000 copies. It was soon withdrawn by the censors, even though it has very little political content. Kornilov was forced into silence throughout most of the Soviet period, but from about 1987 on he was able to publish more or less freely.

6. Patricia Blake, "New Voices in Russian Writing," *Encounter*, April 1963, pp. 27–38.

Chapter Three: Immersion

1. Russians commonly refer to one another by both first name and patronymic: the father's name plus a suffix indicating gender.

2. See, for example, *Nikolai Fedorov: Tvorchestvo zhizni* [Creativity of life] (1990); *Valentin Rasputin* (1987); *Tropami serdechnoi mysli: Etyudy, fragmenty, otryvki iz dnevnika* [Paths of heartfelt thought: Etudes, fragments, excerpts from a diary] (2012). For a glowing review see *Literaturnoe Obozrenie* [Literary review], no. 10 (1988).

3. Much that he told me provided a foundation for material in the pages that follow. I had reason to believe in their veracity.

4. Shulman was praised in Marzani, *Literaturnaya Gazeta*, October 1, 1963, and then reviled by Borshchagovsky, *Literaturnaya Gazeta*, October 26, 1963.

5. *Travel Notes* (Moscow, 1964) duly appeared and aroused the anger of the politically slipping Khrushchev for being too liberal. The book was quickly translated into English and appeared as Viktor Nekrasov, *Both Sides of the Ocean* (London: Cape, 1964).

6. I wrote in detail about Kochetov in my master's thesis, "Yevtushenko and Kochetov in the Soviet Literary Struggle since 1956."

7. Such prices included overcoats without fur collars for 75 rubles.

8. "The Virgin Lands Campaign was Nikita Khrushchev's 1953 plan to dramatically boost the Soviet Union's agricultural production in order to alleviate the food shortages plaguing the Soviet populace" ("Virgin Lands Campaign," *Wikipedia*, accessed March 21, 2019).

9. The Politburo of the Communist Party of the Soviet Union, founded in 1917, was the highest policymaking government authority of the USSR. From 1952 to 1966 it was officially called the Presidium but people continued to refer to it as the Politburo. Its members were elected by the Central Committee of the Communist Party.

10. This view was shared by the well-known, rather conservative writer Vladimir Soloukhin, who spent much time in rural areas.

Chapter Four: Expulsion

1. Published in English as *A Vanished Present: The Memoirs of Alexander Pasternak*, translated by Ann Pasternak Slater (Oxford University Press, 1984).

2. Gleb Struve and Boris Filippov, *Writings*, 3 vols. (University of Michigan Press, 1961).

3. Tendryakov based the play on his published story "Chudotvornaya" [The miracle worker].

4. For Levitansky's parodies, see *Den' Poezii* [Day of poetry]. For Akhmadulina's "Rain" and the poem extract in *Yunost'* see the Georgian journal *Literaturnaya Gruziya* [Literary Georgia], no. 12 (1963). "Rain" was criticized by hard-liners in Georgia, but not in Russia.

5. Patricia Blake, "New Voices in Russian Writing," *Encounter*, April 1963.

6. Anna Akhmatova (1889–1966; her real name was Anna Gorenko) was closely associated with the celebrated, politically persecuted poet Osip Mandelstam.

7. Reddaway 1968, *Soviet Short Stories*, vol. 2.

8. See Korneliy Zelinsky, *Na rubezhe dvukh epok*; Korneliy Zelinsky, *Ogonyok* (n.d.).

9. Russian: "Ya—Yevgeny, ty—Yevgeny, Ya ne geniy, ty ne geniy, Ya—govno, i ty—govno, A ya nedavno, ty davno."

10. For more on Patricia Blake, see chapter 2 of this volume.

11. See Efim Etkind, *Protsess Iosifa Brodskogo* [The trial of Joseph Brodsky] (London: Overseas Publications Interchange, 1988).

12. For a fair-minded account of this episode see Patricia Blake, introduction to Max Hayward, *Writers in Russia, 1917–1978* (New York: Harcourt Brace Jovanovich, 1983), pp. liv–lviii. Blake was a friend of Hayward's.

13. See the attack on *One Day in the Life of Ivan Denisovich* in the *Literaturnaya Gazeta*, April 4, 1964.

14. See M. Matthews, *Mila and Mervusya: A Russian Wedding* (Bridgend, Wales: Seren, Poetry Wales Press, 1999).

15. The university, much expanded, is now known as the People's Friendship University of Russia.

Chapter Five: The Emergence of Dissent

1. Further background was Adam Ulam's brilliant book *Lenin and the Bolsheviks* (London: Secker & Warburg, 1966). See also Reddaway 1966, review in *The Guardian*.

2. Leonard Schapiro and Peter Reddaway, eds., *Lenin: The Man, the Theorist, the Leader: A Reappraisal* (London: Pall Mall Press, 1967).

3. Ibid., p. 18.

4. This brief portrait of Schapiro draws on a thirty-page intellectual biography that I wrote after his death. See Reddaway 1984, "Leonard Bertram Schapiro, 1908–1983." The biography includes input from some fifteen people.

5. Ibid., p. 531.

6. Reddaway 1965, "The Fall of Khrushchev: A Tentative Analysis." At first I was indignant at the large number of cuts and changes made by *Survey*'s copyeditor, Jane Degras, but gradually I realized how much she had improved my work's readability. Thereafter I was more gracious to editors.

7. *Pravda*, editorial, November 1, 1964.

8. *Pravda*, December 5, 1964.

9. *Kommunist*, 1964, no. 16, p. 5.

10. *Pravda*, November 7, 1964.

11. Reddaway 1966, "Aspects of Ideological Belief in the Soviet Union."

12. Reddaway 1967, "Slow Awakening from a Long Nightmare."

13. For the best overview of their trial and their lives as of 1967, see Leopold Labedz and Max Hayward, eds., *On Trial: The Case of Sinyavsky (Tertz) and Daniel (Arzhak)* (London: Collins & Harvill, 1967). This is based in considerable measure on the samizdat collection edited by Alexander Ginzburg, *Belaya kniga po delu Andreya Sinyavskogo i Yuliya Danielya* [White book on the case of Sinyavsky and Yuli Daniel] (Frankfurt: Possev Verlag, 1967).

14. Alexander Yesenin-Volpin, *A Leaf of Spring*, translated by George Reavey (London: Thames & Hudson, 1961), with parallel English and Russian texts.

15. For Yesenin-Volpin's biography up to age forty-seven, see *Abuse of Psychiatry for Political Repression in the Soviet Union*, testimony of Alexander Yesenin-Volpin, September 1972, before a Hearing of a Subcommittee of the Committee on the Judiciary of the U.S. Senate, serial no. 84-417 O (Washington: Government Printing Office, 1972), pp. 1–16.

16. Zhores Medvedev, *The Rise and Fall of T. D. Lysenko* (Garden City, N.Y.: Doubleday/Anchor, 1971.

17. Valery Tarsis ("Ivan Valery"), *The Bluebottle* (London: Collins & Harvill, 1962); Valery Tarsis, *Ward 7: An Autobiographical Novel* (London: Collins & Harvill, London, 1965).

18. For the events mentioned in this paragraph, see Reddaway, *Uncensored Russia* (1972), chapters 2 and 3.

19. For a good description see V. Bukovsky, *To Build a Castle: My Life as a Dissenter* (London: Ethics and Public Policy Center, 1978), pp. 198–205 (English and Russian edition).

20. See Labedz and Hayward, *On Trial.*

21. Pavel Litvinov, *The Demonstration in Pushkin Square*, translated by Manya Harari (London: Harvill Press, 1969), pp. 47–124; see also Pavel Litvinov, *Pravosudie ili rasprava: Sbornik dokumentov* [Justice or despotism: Collection of documents] (London: Overseas Publications Interchange, 1968), pp. 56–158. On Litvinov see also Karel van het Reve, ed., *Letters and Telegrams to Pavel M. Litvinov: December 1967–May 1968* (Dordrecht: D. Reidel, 1969).

22. See Steven Mufson, "Chen Calls on China to Abide by Its Own Laws," *Washington Post*, June 1, 2012.

23. Nordlinger, "Scholars with Spine: Notes from the Field of China Studies," Initiatives for China (website), *National Review/Digital*, August 27, 2012. Nordlinger quotes the scholar Perry Link as "feeling liberated" when he was banned from entry to China, which was similar to how I felt after being banned from the USSR in 1964.

24. Manya Harari, *Memoirs 1906–1969* (London: Harvill Press, 1972).

25. Andrei Amalrik, *Involuntary Journey to Siberia*, translated by Manya Harari and Max Hayward (London: Harvill Press, 1970).

26. Max Hayward, *Writers in Russia: 1917–1978*, edited by Patricia Blake (New York: Harcourt Brace, 1983), pp. II–III.

27. See Reddaway 1968, *Soviet Short Stories*, vol 2.

28. Ibid., p. xvi.

29. John Bayley, "The Upper Depths," *New York Review of Books*, December 22, 1983.

30. Leonard Schapiro, "Max Hayward (1924–1979)," *New York Review of Books*, July 19, 1979.

31. Clarence Brown, "Max Hayward's Empire," *The Guardian*, October 20, 1983.

32. Blake's collections, some edited with Max Hayward, included *Dissonant Voices in Russian Literature* (Literary Licensing LLC, 2012), *Halfway to the Moon: New Writing from Russia* (Holt, Rinehart and Winston, 1964), *Anti-Worlds and the Fifth Ace* (Schocken Books, 1973), *Writers in Russia 1917 to 1978* (Harcourt, 1984), and Vladimir Mayakovsky, *The Bedbug and Selected Poetry*, edited and with an introduction by Patricia Blake, translated by Max Hayward and George Reavey (Indiana University Press, 1975). See also Reddaway 1965, "The Great Ice Age."

33. Reddaway 1972, introduction to *The Trial of the Four*, by Pavel Litvinov, pp. ix–x. In Russian: Pavel Litvinov, *Protsess chetyrekh* (Amsterdam: Herzen Foundation, 1971).

34. For an analysis of the development of the human rights movement that reproduces key documents, some focused on the conditions in the prisons, labor camps, and mental hospitals, see Reddaway 1969, "The Soviet Treatment of Dissenters and the Growth of a Civil Rights Movement."

Chapter Six: The Other '68

1. For the complete texts of all these sixty-three issues in English and Russian versions see https://chronicleofcurrentevents.net/2017/02/23. Amnesty International, London, published issues 16 to 64 as separate booklets. See also Reddaway 1971, "Samizdat—the Free Soviet Press," and Reddaway 1978, "Notes from Underground."

2. This was the reviewer D. A. N. Jones, whose allegations are taken apart in chapter 8.

3. Lyudmila Ulitskaya, *Poetka: Kniga o pamyati: Natalya Gorbanevskaya* [Poet: Book in memory of Natalya Gorbanevskaya] (Moscow: AST/ Redaktsiya Eleny Shubinoi, 2014), pp. 276–85. Author's translations.

4. Reddaway 1991, "The CIA's Most Zealous Agent," p. 140.

5. See Mario Corti, "The Year 1968 in the History of Samizdat," paper presented at the conference organized by the Center for the Study of East European History, "The Other '68: The Year 1968 in the Communist Bloc," Levico Terme, Italy, November 23–24, 2018, available at Cold War Radio Museum.

6. On the demonstration and its aftermath see Reddaway, *Uncensored Russia*, chapters 4 and 5.

7. See, for example, Reddaway 1972, "Lessons from a Moral Demonstration."

8. I visited this hospital in 1989 with a group of American psychiatrists, and we found it to be a deplorable institution (Gorbanevskaya was no longer imprisoned there).

9. Reddaway 1972, *Uncensored Russia*. The book was also published in American, Spanish, Portuguese, and Indian editions.

10. Reddaway 1974, "The Resistance in Russia," 1974.

11. Reddaway 1978, "Notes from Underground."

Chapter Seven: Two Early Giants of Soviet Dissent

1. This chapter draws on the many articles I wrote about dissidents in the Soviet Union from 1967 to 1988.

2. Soviet law required that former inmates of prison–labor camps settle more than one hundred kilometers (sixty-two miles) away from Moscow.

3. Anatoly Marchenko, *My Testimony*, translated by Michael Scammell (London: Pall Mall Press); Alexander Marchenko, *Moi pokazaniya*, in Russian (Frankfurt: Possev Verlag, 1969), contained additional documents about the author's fate. Note also that *The Observer* published three long extracts from the book, which caused a considerable stir. See also a later, paperback edition, Anatoly Marchenko, *My Testimony*, translated by Michael Scammell with an introduction by Max Hayward (London: Penguin Books, 1971), which also offered related documents by Marchenko and others. German, Swiss, Italian, and other editions form part of the collection of materials I have deposited in the George Washington University library.

4. See TASS, Moscow, January 6, 1972.

5. See Harrison Salisbury, "My Testimony," review of *My Testimony*, by Ana-

toly Marchenko, *New York Times*, March 1, 1970; Leonard Schapiro and Peter Reddaway, letter to the editor, *New York Times*, July 19, 1970. Scammell's and Dunham's unpublished letters are available in the archive I have donated to the George Washington University library.

6. On the sources of these quotations, see Reddaway 1969, "The Soviet Defenders of Anatoli Marchenko."

7. Ibid.

8. On the trial and his exile see Reddaway 1975, "Two True Stories: Russia," p. 3.

9. Anatoly Marchenko, *Ot Tarusy do Chuny* (New York: Khronika, 1976). The book was later published in English as *From Tarusa to Siberia* (Strathcona, 1980).

10. Anatoly Marchenko, *To Live like Everyone*, translated by Paul Goldberg (New York: Henry Holt, 1989), a combined Russian-English edition.

11. Ibid., p. 207.

12. Reddaway 1971, "Inside Russia's Concentration Camps," p. 11. Four of the foreign publications in which the article appeared were *Il Tempo*, January 17; *Weltwoche* (Switzerland), January 8; *Die Welt* (Germany), January 22; and the *New York Times*, January 13.

13. It hung on my office wall and daily gave me pleasure, until it found a new home in the library of George Washington University.

14. In 1971 Galanskov smuggled out an article in which he had some words about the West: "The Western radio-stations broadcasting in Russian publicize lawlessness and acts of crude coercion by Soviet official personnel, and thus force the state officials to take quick action. In this way the Western press and radio are fulfilling the tasks of what is at present lacking in Russia, an organized opposition, and thereby stimulating our national development."

The letter of the seven was also signed by three members of a secret Leningrad University social-Christian group of fifty-eight members and candidates in which they advocated a parliamentary system with democratic freedoms and a mixed economy. One member, a signatory of the camp letter who had been sentenced to thirteen years, was the Orientalist Mikhail Sado, born in 1937 (an imposing sketch of him was included in my *Observer* article). He asked a Swede who was about to be released to help save the group's founder, Igor Ogurtsov, also an Orientalist, who was languishing in Vladimir prison in poor health. Years later, Ogurtsov got out and managed to leave the Soviet Union for Germany. In 1992, although never acquitted of his political offense, he returned home to live and work for reform in Russia.

15. Konstantin Yuriyev, official announcement in English, TASS, January 6, 1971.

16. Reddaway 1969, "Five Years in the Life of Pyotr Grigorenko," p. 1. See also Reddaway 1970, "A Man of the Decade."

17. Pyotr Grigorenko, "Concerning Special Psychiatric Hospitals," in *Red Square at Noon*, edited by Natalya Gorbanevskaya (London: Andre Deutsch, 1972), pp. 270–79.

18. Ibid.

19. Boris Tsukerman, "The Arrest of General Grigorenko," 1969.

20. Grigorenko, "Concerning Special Psychiatric Hospitals," pp. 270–79.

21. Tsukerman, "The Arrest of General Grigorenko.". Another sign of military solidarity was the fact that during his internment some of his army friends managed to get published, in *Voennyi zhurnal* (Military journal), an article of his on the military applications of chemistry.

22. For Grigorenko's letter to the Czechs see Reddaway 1972, *Uncensored Russia*, pp. 104–05.

23. For Zinaida's letter see Reddaway 1972, *Uncensored Russia*, p. 142.

24. Reddaway 1969, "Five Years in the Life of Pyotr Grigorenko."

25. See Petr Grigorevich Grigorenko, *The Grigorenko Papers: Writings by General P. G. Grigorenko and Documents on His Case,* with introduction by Edward Crankshaw (London: C. Hurst, 1966; Boulder: Westview Press, 1966); Petr Grigorenko, *Sbornik statei* [Collection of articles], in Russian (New York: Khronika, New York, 1977).

26. On Orlov, his arrest and trial in 1977, and the history of the group, see Lyudmila Alexeyeva, ed., *Delo Orlova* [The Orlov affair], in Russian (New York: Khronika, 1980).

27. A. Podrabinek, *Karatel'naya meditsina*, in Russian (New York: Khronika, 1979); A. Podrabinek, *Punitive Medicine*, with foreword by Alexander Ginzburg (Ann Arbor: Karoma, 1980).

28. Andrei P. Grigorenko, b. 1945, was a member of his father's dissident group of 1963, for which he was temporarily arrested, and later an active member of the human rights movement. He and his mother were successful in compiling and spreading detailed information about the Chernyakhovsk prison-hospital, where Pyotr Grigorenko was held for nearly four years. Andrei was later subjected to many interrogations and beatings, which eventually led to his decision to emigrate. In New York he wrote some valuable memoirs on his dissident activities and especially on those of his friend the Crimean Tatar leader Mustafa Djemilev, whose personality he describes in some detail in Andrei Grigorenko, *A kogda my vernemsya* [And when we come back] (New York: Foundation Crimea, 1977), which includes vivid photographs of Djemilev.

29. Petr Grigorenko, *V podpol'e mozhno vstretit' tol'ko krys* [In the underground you meet only rats] (New York: Detinets, 1981); Petro G. Grigorenko, *Memoirs*, translated by Thomas P. Whitney (London: Harvill Press, 1983).

30. Grigorenko, *V podpol'e*, p. 444.

31. Ibid., p. 815.

32. Reddaway 1993, "Sovietology and Dissent: New Sources on Protest," pp. 13–14nn.

Chapter Eight: Confronting the Naysayers in the West

1. "Letter of 37 to George Brown," May 11, 1967. Among those who preferred not to sign was the eminent Oxford philosopher Isaiah Berlin, whom we knew

to be sympathetic, but who explained that he declined all such invitations on the grounds that signing could hurt his relatives and friends in the USSR. A copy of the letter and associated materials are available in the archive I have donated to the Gelman Library of George Washington University.

2. D. A. N. Jones, "Red and Black Propaganda," review of five books by Russian dissident authors, *New Society*, December 31, 1970.

3. *The Guardian*, London, January 12, 1968.

4. David Burg, *Sunday Times*, January 14, 1968.

5. The following letters appeared in the *Times Literary Supplement*: Martin Dewhirst, December 26, 1968, and February 6, 1969; Leonard Schapiro, February 20, 1969, and March 13, 1969; Peter Reddaway, February 20, 1969, and March 13, 1969; Nicholas Bethell, January 30, 1969, February 13, 1969, and March 6, 1969.

6. Auberon Waugh, *Private Eye*, September 25, 1970; Auberon Waugh, *Private Eye*, October 23, 1970.

7. *Index on Censorship* prospered, achieving the remarkable circulation for a journal of its sort of nearly 7,000 copies; it also printed the *Chronicle* for a time. For thirteen years I had the honor of serving on *Index*'s board and thus getting to know prominent figures such as Stephen Spender, Stuart Hampshire, and Edward Crankshaw.

8. For a detailed analysis of this topic see Reddaway, "Images of Dissent in Soviet Propaganda."

9. Jonathan Steele and Peter Reddaway, "Russia and the British Press—Are Our Reporters Doing Their Job?," *The Listener*, June 26, 1975.

10. Vitaly Gan interview with Peter Reddaway, *Pravda*, September 19, 1988.

Chapter Nine: "The Mental State of Such People Is Not Normal"

1. Soviet spokesman, *Chronicle of Current Events*, issue 44, Amnesty International edition, 1977, p. 185.

2. Sidney Bloch and Peter Reddaway, *Russia's Political Hospitals: The Abuse of Psychiatry in the Soviet Union* (London: Gollancz, 1977); U.S. edition: Sidney Bloch and Peter Reddaway, *Psychiatric Terror: How Soviet Psychiatry Is Used to Suppress Dissent* (New York: Basic Books, 1977); Russian-language edition: *Diagnoz, inakomyslie: kak sovetskie psikhiatry lechat ot politicheskogo inakomysliia* [Diagnosis, dissent: how Soviet psychiatrists treat political dissent] (London: Overseas Publications Interchange, 1981). References in this chapter are to the British edition, *Russia's Political Hospitals*.

3. The moving spirit behind the successful Left Book Club, Victor Gollancz, was mightily relieved when Hitler invaded the USSR in 1941, thus destroying his 1939 pact with Stalin. But he remained strongly on the left, as can be seen from his *Russia and Ourselves* (London: Gollancz, 1941).

4. The report was never circulated unofficially, but was published in London as samizdat. See Sergei Pisarev, "Soviet Mental Prisons," *Survey: A Journal of East and West Studies*, no. 77 (1970): 175–80.

5. I. Sichka, "Tayny Lubyanki" [Secrets of the Lubyanka], *Komsomol'skaya Pravda*, January 11, 1992, p. 10, quoted in Reddaway 1993, "Sovietology and Dissent," pp. 12–16.

6. Robert van Voren, *On Dissidents and Madness: From the Soviet Union of Leonid Brezhnev to the 'Soviet Union' of Vladimir Putin* (Amsterdam: Rodopi, 2009); Robert van Voren, *Cold War in Psychiatry: Human Factors, Secret Actors* (Amsterdam: Rodopi, 2010).

7. See *Mednovosti*, October 18, 22, 25, and 28, 2017.

8. Canadian Psychiatric Association, *Survey: A Journal of East and West Studies*, no. 81 (1971): 113.

9. Eleanor Aitken, a cofounder of our group, and I translated into English the documents Bukovsky sent for circulation in 150-page packets. The group later produced a detailed analysis of the reports in booklet form. See Cornelia Mee (pen name of Eleanor Aitken), *The Internment of Soviet Dissenters in Mental Hospitals* (London: Working Group on the Internment of Dissenters in Mental Hospitals, 1971).

10. On Bukovsky's appeal to Western psychiatrists, see Bloch and Reddaway, *Russia's Political Hospitals*, pp. 80–81.

11. For extracts from these documents see ibid., pp. 83, 85, 281.

12. Zhores Medvedev and Roy A. Medvedev, *A Question of Madness* (New York: W. W. Norton, 1979), p. 63.

13. For a translation of the interview see Bloch and Reddaway, *Russia's Political Hospitals*, p. 84, 93.

14. For a detailed discussion of the WPA World Congress, see ibid., pp. 82–93.

15. *The Times*, May 7, 1974.

16. See Bloch and Reddaway, *Russia's Political Hospitals*, pp. 289–94 (on the APA from 1967 to 1976), 284–89 (for more detail on the Kremlin's stance on the psychiatric establishment).

17. For more on Gluzman's analysis of Grigorenko, his camp protests, and his manual with Bukovsky see ibid., pp. 234–38. For a 1974 letter written by Gluzman to his parents see ibid., appendix 4. For the full text of *Manual on Psychiatry for Dissidents*, with an introduction by the writer Viktor Nekrasov, see *Survey: A Journal of East and West Studies*, Summer–Autumn 1975, pp. 176–98. For the most comprehensive collection of Gluzman's writings in English see Semyon Gluzman, *On Soviet Totalitarian Psychiatry* (Amsterdam: International Association on the Political Use of Psychiatry, 1989), which includes the major works discussed in this chapter plus two articles on psychiatry and a letter of 1989 to Western colleagues explaining why it would be a terrible moral mistake to let the Soviet Psychiatric Society back into the WPA after it had been essentially kicked out in 1983.

18. On the appeal of Sakharov's committee, see Bloch and Reddaway, *Russia's Political Hospitals*, pp. 301–02.

19. On Sakharov's lengthy statement see *Washington Post*, August 12, 1973.

20. See Martin Roth, *The Times*, September 4, 1973.

21. For the U.S. National Academy of Sciences statement see Bloch and Reddaway, *Russia's Political Hospitals*, pp. 307–08.

22. See, for example, *The Guardian*, September 29, 1973; Bloch and Reddaway, *Russia's Political Hospitals*, pp. 309–10, appendix 3. It is a classic document of its genre.

23. See *The Lancet*, October 13, 1973.

24. For the text of a Freedman statement signed also by others see *New York Times*, November 5, 1973; Bloch and Reddaway, *Russia's Political Hospitals*, pp. 314 (Freedman statement), 311–320 (on the WPA World Conference and the Serbsky visit) .

25. Ibid., p. 320 (full text of motion); Royal College of Psychiatrists, press release, November 14, *The Guardian*, November 17, 1973 (summary of press release).

26. See Reddaway 1974, *Chronicle of Current Events*, no. 10, 1974.

27. On the Shikhanovich and Plyushch cases and Roth's protest of July 1975, see Bloch and Reddaway, *Russia's Political Hospitals*, pp. 320–28.

28. Amnesty International, *Prisoners of Conscience in the USSR: Their Treatment and Conditions* (London: Amnesty International Publications, 1975). The book was written anonymously by my friend Clayton Yeo.

29. For rich details on the Plyushch case and for some of his articles see Tatyana Khodorovich, ed., *The Case of Leonid Plyushch*, with an introduction by Peter Reddaway (London: C. Hurst, 1976). Also, in a separate thirty-page analysis Khodorovich wrote, "His brain has been ruled *socially dangerous*. . . . Imprisonment in a camp . . . would not neutralize the danger from it. After all, there he could associate with *normal* people and have friends. . . . However, the mad-house is reliable, without term, and sound-proof. Nowadays not even a straight-jacket is needed: a few injections of some neuroleptic drug are enough to 'straighten out' any rebellious brain, and muffle it in inertia and silence." For this Khodorovich excerpt about Plyushch see Bloch and Reddaway, *Russia's Political Hospitals*, p. 302.

30. For example, a letter from Australia was signed by 88 mathematicians, a telegram from Toronto by 153 scientists, psychiatrists, and jurists, and among 12 signatories from Rome was a member of the Central Committee of the Italian Communist Party. See more details in Bloch and Reddaway, *Russia's Political Hospitals*, p. 331.

31. *L'Humanité*, October 25, 1975.

32. On Shikhanovich, Plyushch, the ICM, and Plyushch's release see Bloch and Reddaway, *Russia's Political Hospitals*, pp. 330–35.

33. See *Morning Star*, February 5, 1976; *Morning Star*, February 23, 1976.

34. E. Gorbunov, *Sowjetunion Heute* (Cologne), February 1, 1976. Gorbunov was the medical correspondent for the Soviet paper *Novosti*.

35. See Novikov's five-part interview in the weekly *Der Stern*, parts 1–5, March 23 to April 27, 1978. On the Blom-Cooper hearings and Podrabinek's case see Bloch and Reddaway, *Soviet Psychiatric Abuse: The Shadow over World Psychiatry*, vol. 2 (London: Gollancz, 1984), pp. 101–02.

36. A. Podrabinek, *Karatel'naya meditsina*, in Russian (New York: Khronika,

1979); A. Podrabinek, *Punitive Medicine*, with foreword by Alexander Ginzburg (Ann Arbor: Karoma, 1980).

37. See *Chronicle of Current Events*, no. 46.

38. On Bukovsky's release and the Working Commission see Bloch and Reddaway, *Russia's Political Hospitals*, p. 339.

39. See ibid.

40. Bloch and I devoted a chapter of *Russia's Political Hospitals* to examining the five groups in more detail; the numbers of victims in prison mental hospitals as opposed to ordinary ones; why some were sent to one type rather than the other; whether dissidents placed in mental hospitals differed from those placed in camps; and why the psychiatric "gambit" had not been used more often. See Bloch and Reddaway, *Russia's Political Hospitals*, chapter 9.

Chapter Ten: Dignity under Persecution

1. Regrettably, this strict selection means omitting the Georgians and Estonians, whom I got to know and love well in the 1990s and 2000s, and about whom I shall write in a separate publication.

2. For more on the history of the Crimean Tatars see Edward Allworth, ed., *Tatars of the Crimea: Their Struggle for Survival*, 2nd ed. (Duke University Press, 1998). See also Reddaway 1998, "The Crimean Drive for Repatriation: Some Comparisons with Other Movements of Dissent in the Soviet Union." For the full text of the appeal see Reddaway, *Uncensored Russia*, 1972, pp. 86–88.

3. Ludmilla Alexeyeva, "Mustafa Jemiloglu: His Character and Convictions," in Allworth, *Tatars of the Crimea*, pp. 206–25, especially p. 223.

4. Aysha Seytmuratova, personal letter, October 1987.

5. *Tashkentskiy protsess: Sud nad desyat'yu predstavitelyami krymskotatarskogo naroda (1 iyulya – 5 avgusta 1969 g.): Sbornik dokumentov s illyustratsiyami* [Tashkent trial: the trial of ten representatives of the Crimean Tatar people (July 1–August 5, 1969); collection of documents with illustrations], with 21 photos (Amsterdam: Alexander Herzen Foundation, 1976). I was a cofounder of the foundation, in 1969.

6. See Reddaway 1969, "Crimes against Tatars Being Hushed Up"; Reddaway 1969, "Crimean Tatars Ask to Go Home"; Reddaway 1969, "Leaders of Exiled Tatars on Trial"; Reddaway 1969, "Tatar Leaders Are Gaoled"; Reddaway 1970, "The Will to Return." For the *Khronika* items from 1968 to 1969, see Reddaway 1972, *Uncensored Russia*, pp. 249–69; see also *Chronicle of Current Events*, issue 31 (May 1974), devoted to Crimean Tatar issues; Ann Sheehy and Bohdan Nahaylo, *The Crimean Tatars, Volga Germans, and Meskhetians*, report 6 (London: Minority Rights Group, 1971). See also Christina Paschyn, director, *A Struggle for Home: The Crimean Tatar*s, documentary film (Mediadante and Paschyn Productions, 2015).

7. Reddaway 1974, "The Right to Dissent."

8. On the Dzhemilev-Gabai trial see M. Serdar, ed., *Shest' dnei—Belaya kniga* [Six days—the white book] (New York: Fond Krim, 1980).

9. Boris Kochubievsky quoted in Reddaway 1972, *Uncensored Russia*, p. 298.

10. On the details of Jewish arrests see Reddaway 1984, "Soviet Policies on Dissent and Emigration: The Radical Change of Course since 1979," p. 57.

11. See Reddaway 1972, *Uncensored Russia*; Reddaway 1976, "The Development of Dissent in the USSR," pp. 57–84.

12. Telesin, "Foreword of an Eyewitness," in Reddaway 1972, *Uncensored Russia*, pp. 43–51.

13. Natan Shcharansky, *Fear No Evil* (New York: Random House, 1988), p. xxii.

14. Ibid. Another even broader review of the history of Soviet Jews and refuseniks, written from a somewhat less independent viewpoint, is Martin Gilbert, *The Jews of Hope* (New York: Viking, 1985).

15. For Ukrainian dissident documents see Vyacheslav Chornovil, ed., *The Chornovil Papers* (New York: McGraw-Hill, 1968), and Michael Browne, ed., *Ferment in the Ukraine: Documents by V. Chornovil, I. Kandyba, L. Lukyanenko, V. Moroz and others*, with an introduction by Michael Browne (London: Macmillan, 1971). The documents were sent abroad by a key figure, Ivan Svitlychny. See especially Browne's introduction, pp. 1–28.

16. Ivan Dzyuba, *Internationalism or Russification? A Study in the Soviet Nationalities Problem* (London: Weidenfeld & Nicolson, 1968).

17. Quoted in Reddaway 1972, *Uncensored Russia*, p. 281.

18. For extracts of Yevhen Sverstyuk, "The Cathedral in Scaffolding," see *Ukrainian Review*, no. 3 (1970): 22–48.

19. Ukrainian Helsinki group, *Chronicle of Current Events*, issue 43 (December 1976), Amnesty International edition, pp. 31–33.

20. See, for example, Reddaway 1976, "The Development of Dissent in the USSR."

Chapter Eleven: Religious Persecution, Religious Dissent

1. For an excellent study of Keston College see Mark Hurst, *British Human Rights Organizations and Soviet Dissent, 1965–1985* (London: Bloomsbury, 2016). See also Mark Hurst, "The Birth of the Last Utopia: Is Keston Really a 'Human Rights' Group?" *Keston College Newsletter*, no. 21 (2015), pp. 17–25. This newsletter is so nicely produced that it looks more like a journal than a newsletter. Hurst is now a lecturer in human rights at the University of Lancaster, U.K.

2. These supporters of the persecuted formed the backbone of the college's finances, which also benefited from foundation grants.

3. Bourdeaux was the author of pioneering books on various denominations in the USSR and the winner of the renowned Templeton Prize for Progress in Religion for his outstanding work. See Michael Bourdeaux, *Patriarch and Prophets: Persecution of the Russian Orthodox Church Today* (London: Macmillan, 1969); Michael Bourdeaux, *Religious Ferment in Russia: Protestant Opposition to Soviet Religious Policy* (London: Macmillan, 1968); Michael Bourdeaux, *Land of Crosses: The Struggle for Religious Freedom in Lithuania, 1939–1978* (Augustine Publishing Co., 1979).

4. Michael Bourdeaux and Peter Reddaway, "Church and State and Schism: Soviet Baptists Today," *Survey: A Journal of East and West Studies*, no. 66 (January 1968): 48–66; reprinted in M. Hayward and W. C. Fletcher, eds., *Religion and the Soviet State: A Dilemma of Power* (London: Pall Mall Press, 1969), pp. 105–41; see also Reddaway 1968, "Freedom of Worship and the Law."

5. Anatoly Levitin quoted in Reddaway 1972, *Uncensored Russia*, pp. 319, 321–26.

6. Reddaway 1975, "The Georgian Orthodox Church: Corruption and Renewal."

7. Clifford Longley, "New Evidence in Georgian Church Affair," *The Times*, March 15, 1976.

8. See discussion of Lang and this controversy in Reddaway 1975, "Memorandum on the Georgian Church Controversy."

9. Reddaway 1984, "A Question of Faith."

Chapter Twelve: Fighting on Old and New Fronts

1. The one exception to this was in 1968, when the journal *Problems of Communism*, based in Washington, D.C., published a large quantity of samizdat documents, along with analyses of them. The journal's editor, Abraham Brumberg, had a strong interest in the subject, and I became close friends with him. He and his wife, Josie, a film expert, were generous hosts and gave many dinners that brought together a stimulating variety of Washingtonians and out-of-town visitors. For the samizdat documents and the analyses, see *Problems of Communism* 17, nos. 4 and 5 (1968).

2. Khronika Press was located at 505 Eighth Avenue, New York, NY 10018. *Chronicle of Human Rights in the USSR* was usually eighty to ninety pages long.

3. Isaac Patch, *Closing the Circle: A Buckalino Journey around Our Time* (Wellesley, Mass.: Wellesley College Printing Services, 1996).

4. Mrs. Solzhenitsyn is quoted in Gene Sosin, *Sparks of Liberty: An Insider's Memoir of Radio Liberty* (Pennsylvania State University Press, 1999), p. 282.

5. See ibid.; James Critchlow, *Radio Hole-in-the-Head: Radio Liberty: An Insider's Story of Cold War Broadcasting* (American University Press, 1995).

6. For a detailed account of the congress, see Sidney Bloch and Peter Reddaway, *Soviet Psychiatric Abuse: The Shadow over World Psychiatry* (London: Victor Gollancz, 1984), pp. 45–71. Sidney Bloch, a psychiatrist, was a participant in the congress.

7. Bloch and Reddaway, *Soviet Psychiatric Abuse*, p. 46.

8. Bloch and Reddaway, *Soviet Psychiatric Abuse*, pp. 45–71.

9. The best sources on the Working Commission are ibid., pp. 72–109, and Robert van Voren, *Cold War in Psychiatry: Human Factors, Secret Actors* (Amsterdam: Rodopi, 2010), pp. 148–50, 164–71.

10. See chapter 8 for my analysis of the statistics as of 1976.

11. On Gisela Otto, see van Voren, *Cold War in Psychiatry*, pp. 155–73. Van Voren makes extensive use of material in Sonja Suess, *Politisch missbraucht? Psy-*

chiatrie und Staatssicherheit in der DDR [Politically misused? Psychiatry and national security in the GDR] (Berlin: Links Verlag, 1998), pp. 639–48. Van Voren and Suess found extensive materials on Otto and Weinberger in the Stasi (East German Secret Police) archives. Van Voren then questioned Weinberger at length. In the mid-1990s Weinberger and his group left the International Association on the Political Use of Psychiatry, a confederation of activist groups. Suess found that although there was no systematic abuse of the Soviet type in the German Democratic Republic, there was occasional abuse, in manifold forms that differed somewhat from those used in the USSR. See also Helmut Bieber, review of *Politisch missbraucht?*, by Sonja Suess, *Mental Health Reforms*, no. 2 (1999): 15–17.

12. Reddaway 1983, "The Attack on Anatoly Koryagin." The following passages are based on that report.

13. For more detail on events from 1977 to 1983 see Bloch and Reddaway, *Soviet Psychiatric Abuse*, chapters 5 and 6.

14. On the Soviet society's resignation from the WPA see ibid., chapter 7.

Chapter Thirteen: Publishing Samizdat in the West

1. *Uren met Karel van het Reve: Liber Amicorum* [Hours with Karel van het Reve: Festschrift] (Amsterdam: Uitgeverej G. A. van Oorschot, 1991). The following account is based on my contribution to the Festschrift, "One of the CIA's Most Zealous Agents" (pp. 138–144).

Chapter Fourteen: Dissent and Reform under Gorbachev

1. Reddaway 1985, "Waiting for Gorbachev."

2. See Reddaway 1987, "Gorbachev the Bold."

3. Mikhail Gorbachev, concluding speech to a Central Committee conference, reported in *Pravda*, January 30, 1987. Quoted in Reddaway 1987, "Gorbachev the Bold."

4. Mikhail Gorbachev, speech, *Pravda*, February 26, 1987.

5. Reddaway 1987, "Gorbachev the Bold."

6. Reddaway 1987, *Hearing before the Commission on Security and Cooperation in Europe: Glasnost: The Soviet Policy of Openness*, p. 33.

7. Lubarsky had been a fairly early dissident in Moscow, and had served a prison sentence of four years until the KGB persuaded him to emigrate in 1976. With help from me and others he set up a service in Munich providing detailed information on all types of imprisoned dissidents. Later he edited a journal, *Strana i mir* (Our country and the world), that ran long articles by dissidents on sociopolitical topics.

8. Alexander Prokhanov, "Culture Is a Temple, Not a Battlefield," *Literaturnaya Rossiya*, no. 3 (1988).

9. Gary Lee, *Washington Post*, June 29, 1988.

10. For a write-up of the round table, see David Remnick, *Washington Post*, November 2, 1988, and David Remnick, *Washington Post*, November 6, 1988. For a fuller report see "Supporters and Opponents of Perestroika," *Soviet Economy* 4,

no. 4 (October–December 1988): 275–318; for a shorter version see "Perestroika: kto protiv?" [Perestroika: Who is against it?], *Ogonyok*, no. 50 (December 1988): 10–14.

11. See Andrei Sakharov and Peter Reddaway, "On Gorbachev: A Talk with Andrei Sakharov," *New York Review of Books*, December 22, 1988.

12. For a full text of Sakharov's June 1989 speech, see "A Speech to the People's Congress," *New York Review of Books*, August 17, 1989.

13. On the Tbilisi massacre and the period that followed see Reddaway 1989, "The Threat to Gorbachev."

14. Reddaway 1989, "Life after Gorbachev: The Soviets' Grim Future."

Chapter Fifteen: Upending Manufactured Schizophrenia

1. This chapter draws heavily on Reddaway 1988, "Soviet Psychiatry: An End to Political Abuse?," and Robert van Voren, *Cold War in Psychiatry: Human Factors, Secret Actors* (Amsterdam: Rodopi, 2010), pp. 317–28.

2. For more on the two series of articles see van Voren, *Cold War in Psychiatry*, 319–24.

3. For more on Potapov's statement see ibid.

4. On the partial conservative comeback see ibid., pp. 324–26.

5. On WPA maneuvering, see ibid., pp. 267–72.

6. On Koryagin and Stefanis, see ibid, pp. 238–39, esp. n182.

7. See I. F. Stone, "Another Betrayal by Psychiatry?," *New York Review of Books*, December 22, 1988.

8. Alexander Podrabinek, "Soviet Psychiatry: A Message from Moscow," *New York Review of Books*, December 8, 1988, with an introduction by Peter Reddaway.

9. Extracts from Gindilis's letter were printed in two top scientific journals. See Viktor Gindilis, *Nature*, February 16, 1989; Viktor Gindilis, *The Lancet*, February 18, 1989.

10. Van Voren, *Cold War in Psychiatry*, pp. 371–72.

11. See *Report of the US Delegation to Assess Recent Changes in Soviet Psychiatry*, *Schizophrenia Bulletin* 15 (supplement), no. 4 (July 12, 1989): 1–82; on the "Preliminary Soviet Response," see "Psychiatric Abuses Persist in Russia," *Washington Post*, August 22, 1989.

12. Dr. Elmore Rigamer and others, unpublished report, in author's collection. This report was not published.

13. See also Reddaway 1989, "Should World Psychiatry Readmit the Soviets?"

14. Churkin quoted in TASS, July 10, 1989.

Chapter Sixteen: The End: RIP USSR, 1917 to 1991

1. Reddaway 1990, "Gorbachev, Sinking."

2. Hough followed up his letter with a lengthy feature article in *The Guardian* in which he argued that Gorbachev "is more secure in power and more consistent in the use of it than many westerners imagine." See Jerry Hough, "Man of Iron," *The Guardian*, February 20, 1991.

3. This was when I believed that the spectacular breakup of the USSR into fifteen independent states a year earlier would lead to further breakup inside the biggest of them, the Russian Federation (RF). As things transpired, the Chechen Autonomous Republic was the sole defector from the RF and, as a result, it could be brought back into the country by massive military force in the civil war of 1999–2002.

4. Reddaway 1991, "The Quality of Gorbachev's Leadership," pp. 436–37.

5. Gorbachev's speech was published in *Pravda* of November 16, 1990.

6. On Gorbachev's musing, *Sovetskaya kul'tura*, December 1, 1990.

7. Arkady Vaksberg, *The Soviet Mafia* (New York: St. Martin's Press, 1992).

8. Bulat Okudzhava, *Moskovskiye novosti* [Moscow news], December 23, 1990.

9. Evidently Vaksberg never published this article.

10. *Pravda*, December 12, 1980.

11. Vladimir Kuzichkin, a KGB officer who defected in 1982, in his book written in 1989 and published in 1991, posed the question "Does the KGB have a future?" His prescient answer: "It is doubtful, because in order to survive, the current regime is having to make more and more concessions to opposition elements. One of these concessions will surely be the disbanding of the KGB." Eighteen months after he wrote, popular demand was calling for this. See Vladimir Kuzichkin, *Inside the KGB* (New York: Pantheon, 1991).

12. For more from the speech and on its ramifications, see Peter Reddaway and Dmitri Glinski, *The Tragedy of Russia's Reforms: Market Bolshevism against Democracy* (Washington: U.S. Institute of Peace Press, 2001), p. 196.

13. Norma Percy, producer, *The Second Russian Revolution*, 8 parts, BBC, broadcast from May 31, 1991.

14. Salutsky recommended to me Roy Medvedev's "brilliant" article in *Pravda*, December 21, 1990.

15. Ligachev did come to the United States in 1991 to promote his book. See Yegor Ligachev, "Speeches of Egor Kuz'mich Ligachëv at the Kennan Institute," Occasional Paper 247 (Washington: Kennan Institute for Advanced Russian Studies, Fall 1991). See also Yegor Ligachev, *Inside Gorbachev's Kremlin: The Memoirs of Yegor Ligachev* (New York: Pantheon, 1993).

16. Alexander Prokhanov, *Nash sovremennik*, September 1990.

17. George H. W. Bush, *Washington Post*, December 28, 1990.

18. See Mikhail Gorbachev, *Pravda*, January 22, 1991.

19. The six republics that refused to sign the Novo-Ogaryovo agreement were Estonia, Latvia, Lithuania, Georgia, Armenia, and Azerbaijan.

20. Valentin Varennikov and others, "A Call to the People," *Sovetskaya Rossiya* and *Moskovskaya pravda*, July 23, 1991, called for mass political action to halt the dismemberment of the USSR, and provided the first sketch of a national-conservative political program. Among its signatories were two deputy government ministers, General Valentin Varennikov and General Boris Gromov; Alexander Prokhanov; and Valentin Rasputin.

21. William Taubman, *Gorbachev: His Life and Times* (New York: W. W. Norton, 2017). On the coup see chapter 17; on Gorbachev's role see pp. 616–18.

22. Ibid., p. 617.
23. Ibid., p. 618.
24. Alexander Yakovlev, *Washington Post*, October 7, 1991, p. A1.
25. Leonid Abalkin, *Washington Post*, September 21, 1991.
26. Reddaway 1991, "The End of the Empire."

Some Conclusions

1. See Reddaway 1967, "Slow Awakening from a Long Nightmare."
2. See Geoffrey Hosking, *The Russian Constitutional Experiment* (Cambridge University Press, 1973), chapter 9.
3. This account of the "war of laws" draws on Reddaway 1991, "The End of the Empire."
4. As I argued early in 1990. See Reddaway 1990, "Is a Civil Society Emerging in the USSR?"

SUBJECT INDEX

Academy of Agricultural Sciences of the Soviet Union, 63, 71
Action Group for the Defense of Human Rights, 170
Action Group for the Revival of Leninism, 139
Afghanistan invasion by Soviets (1979), 165
African students, 92–97
Agricultural crisis, 62–65, 108
Alexander Herzen Foundation, 3, 188, 216–19, 227
Alexander Nevsky Lavra (monastery-cathedral-cemetery complex), 16
American Psychiatric Association, 175, 178, 207, 243, 256
American-Soviet Cinematographers, 266
Amnesty International, 2, 123–24, 172, 180, 195, 215, 268
Anglo-Soviet Treaty of Friendship and Cooperation, 150–52
Anti-Party Group, 66
Anti-Semitism, 43, 71, 98, 233, 265–66

Baptists, 107, 119, 123, 138, 184, 196, 198, 202
Baylor University, 198
Bay of Pigs attack (1961), 33, 34
BBC, 2, 89, 120, 152, 158, 206
Bedford Publications Company, 204–05
The Bell (magazine), 37
Berlin Wall, 26
Bez kresta! [*Without a cross!*] (Tendryakov), 72
Black market, 11, 15, 262, 283
The Blind Beauty (Pasternak), 114
The Bluebottle (Valerii, pen name of Tarsis), 111
Bolshoi Theater, 13
The Brothers Karamazov (Dostoyevsky), 77

Cabdrivers, 53–55, 60, 62–63, 65, 88, 97, 235, 262, 268

Cahiers du Samizdat (journal), 215
Cambridge University, 1, 9–10
Canadian Psychiatric Association, 168
Cancer Ward (Solzhenitsyn), 159
The Captive Mind (Milosz), 28
Catastrophe and second birth (Gnedin), 218
The Catcher in the Rye (Salinger), 83
The cathedral (Honchar), 194
Censorship, 39, 42, 75–76, 109, 115, 118, 265
Central House of Writers, 265, 270–71
Chekhov Press, 204
China: dissidents in, 113; and Gorbachev reforms, 221; and Soviet invasion of Czechoslovakia, 128; Soviet relations with, 6, 91–92; students from, 96
Christianity, 23–25, 78, 80, 133. *See also* Baptists; Russian Orthodox Church
The Chronicle of Current Events [*Khronika tekushchikh sobytii*], 120–31; author's role in, 2, 129–31, 204, 215; concordance of, 129–31; and Crimean Tatars, 187; founding of, 119, 121–23; smuggling out of Soviet Union, 124–27; and Soviet Jews, 191
A Chronicle of Human Rights in the USSR (journal), 204, 205
Churches: in *The Chronicle of Current Events*, 130; and demise of Soviet Union, 271–72; in Georgia, 21–22, 24, 199–200; and Khrushchev, 81; and Soviet propaganda on religious freedom, 201–02. *See also* Russian Orthodox Church; *specific churches*
CIA, 152, 204–05, 217, 219
Civil society, 291–92. *See also specific organizations*
Cold War in Psychiatry (Van Voren), 167
Columbia University, 3
Commission on the Abuse of Psychiatry in the Soviet Union, 146
Common Sense about Russia (Conquest), 28
Commonwealth of Independent States, 288
The Communist Party of the Soviet Union (Schapiro), 105–06
Communist Youth League. *See* Young Communist League
"The Companions" (Tarasenkova), 76
Concentration camps, 43, 46, 158, 165, 238
Conference on Security and Cooperation in Europe, 146, 164, 179, 234, 247
Congress of People's Deputies, 264–72
Congress of Soviet Writers, 118
Corruption, 73, 159, 199, 222, 242, 244–45, 290
Crimean Tatars, 119, 121–22, 130, 185–89, 194, 216, 218
Cuban Missile Crisis (1962), 5, 33–34, 108
Cuban Revolution (1958), 35
Cuban students, 96
Cybernetics, 138–39
Czechoslovakia invasion by Soviet Union (1968), 127–29, 157–58

Daedalus journal, 28
Death penalty, 61
Democratic Party of Russia, 272
The Demonstration in Pushkin Square (Litvinov), 218
Der Monat (magazine), 78
De-Stalinization, 34, 50, 59
Deutsche Welle (radio station), 89
Dialectical materialism, 18
Dissonant Voices in Soviet Literature (Blake), 36
Dnepropetrovsk Special Psychiatric Hospital, 179, 180

Dnieper River, 24
Doctor Zhivago (Pasternak), 71, 84, 85, 110, 114
"The Driver" (Kornilov), 35

Economic reforms, 59, 231–33, 258–59, 292
Electroshock therapy, 12
Emmanuel College, 14
Encounter journal, 36, 78, 117
The Entry of the Slavs into Christendom (Vlasto), 10
Ethnic minorities, 185–95. *See also specific ethnic groups*
European Writers' Congress, 82
Express-Khronika (newspaper), 228–29
Expulsion: of author from Soviet Union, 47, 99, 101–02; of Matthews from Soviet Union, 91; of Soviet Society of Psychiatrists from WPA, 213; of Yeltsin from Central Committee, 224

Federation of African Students in the Soviet Union, 93, 94, 97
Food shortages, 62–65, 108, 276
France: Armenian immigrants in, 94; Bukovsky's sentencing criticized in, 175; dissident movement in, 110; Sinyavsky's emigration to, 156; Soviet psychiatric abuse condemned by, 179–81, 213
Frank Knox Fellowships, 29
From Tarusa to Chuna (Marchenko), 136
Frontier (journal), 198
Frunze Military Academy, 139
Fulbourn Hospital, 182

General Directorate for the Protection of State Secrets in the Press (Glavlit), 118
George Washington University, 3, 4
Georgia: church scandal in, 199–200; history of, 23–24; Land Rover trip to Soviet Union (1961), 21–24; and Meskhetians, 268; smuggling samizdat out of, 127; sovereignty of, 282
Georgian Orthodox Church, 23, 196, 199–200
Glasnost, 224, 226–27
Glavlit (General Directorate for the Protection of State Secrets in the Press), 118
Gorbachev: His Life and Times (Taubman), 286
Gorky Institute of World Literature, 45
Gorky Theater, 73
Gorye ot Uma (Griboyedov), 73
The Government and Politics of the Soviet Union (Schapiro), 106
Great Britain–USSR Association, 198
The Guardian, 2

The Hamlet (Faulkner), 77
Harvard University, 1, 29–35
Harvill Press, 114
The Hedgehog and the Fox (Berlin), 87
"The Heirs of Stalin" (Yevtushenko), 34
Helsinki Agreements (1975), 146, 164–65, 179, 192, 208, 209
Hermitage palace and museum, 15
Het Parool (newspaper), 125, 216
Historical Archives Institute, 261, 265, 276
Hokkaido University, 220
Homosexuality, 43, 78, 80–81, 159
Hospitals. *See* Psychiatric abuse for political purposes; *specific institutions*
How Russia Is Ruled (Fainsod), 30
"How Socialist Is the Soviet Union?" (Reddaway), 27
How to Say All of This? (Tarasenkova), 76

Human rights movement: and *Chronicle of Current Events*, 120–31; emergence of, 109–13; maturation of, 117–19. *See also specific organizations*
Hungarian Revolution, 7

I. F. Stone's Weekly, 36
IAPUP (International Association on the Political Use of Psychiatry), 213, 243
ICM (International Committee of Mathematicians), 179–80
Independent Psychiatric Association, 232
Index on Censorship (Writers and Scholars International), 159
Indonesian students, 96
Information Research Department (Britain), 123
Inostrannaya Literatura (journal), 74, 76
"Inside Russia's Concentration Camps" (Reddaway), 136
Institute for Slavic Research at Hokkaido University, 220
Institute for Soviet and East European Studies, 221
Institute for the World Economy and International Relations, 264
Institute of Criminal Psychology, 52
Institute of International Relations (Moscow), 60
Institute of Slavic and Balkan Studies, 45
Intermediate-Range Nuclear Forces (INF) Treaty (1987), 224
International Association on the Political Use of Psychiatry (IAPUP), 213, 243
International Committee of Mathematicians (ICM), 179–80
International Congress of Psychotherapy, 177
International Foundation for the Survival and Development of Mankind, 225
International Helsinki Federation, 234, 245
Internationalism or russification? A study in the Soviet nationalities problem (Dzyuba), 193
International Metal Federation, 221
International Physicians for the Prevention of Nuclear War, 244
Internatsionalizm chy rusyfikatsiia [*Internationalism or russification? A study in the Soviet nationalities problem*] (Dzyuba), 193
Involuntary Journey to Siberia (Amalrik), 114, 152, 153, 217–18
Ireland, author's Russian language studies in, 6–9
Israel, emigration to, 130, 135, 190–92
"Is the Soviet Union on the Road to Anarchy?" (Reddaway), 258
Izvestia (newspaper), 64, 161, 253, 274

Japanese Institute of International Affairs, 221
Jews: and demise of Soviet Union, 265–66, 271; and dissident movement, 190–92, 194; emigration to Israel, 130, 135, 190–92; and human rights movement, 119; and Lysenko, 71; and Moscow Music Conservatory scandal (1964), 80. *See also* Anti-Semitism
Jvari Church, 21–22

Kak eto vse skazat'? [*How to Say All of This?*] (Tarasenkova), 76
Karatel'naya meditsina [*Punitive Medicine*] (Podrabinek), 146, 183
Katastrofa i vtoroe rozhdenie [*Catastrophe and second birth*] (Gnedin), 218
Kaunas University, 4

Kazan Cathedral, 16
Kazan Special Psychiatric Hospital, 253
Kennan Institute for Advanced Russian Studies, 3, 220, 225
Keston Center for Religion, Politics, and Society, 198
Keston College, 3, 196–98
Keston Institute in Oxford, 198
Keston News Service, 197
KGB: and African student protest, 94; author investigated by, 45, 98, 101–02; and *Chronicle of Current Events*, 121, 125–26, 130; and Crimean Tatars, 188; and demise of Soviet Union, 260, 263, 267–68, 271, 273–74, 278, 285, 287; and dissident movement, 110–11, 113; and Georgian Orthodox Church, 200; under Gorbachev, 233–34; and Grigorenko, 139–40, 144–46, 148–49; Johnson's notebooks confiscated by, 31; and Keston College, 197; under Khrushchev, 1, 5; and Land Rover trip (1961), 14–15, 23, 25–26; and Marchenko, 134–35; at Moscow Pedagogical State University, 42; and NTS, 36–37; Pasternak's notes confiscated by, 70; and poets, 78–79; and psychiatric abuse for political purposes, 208–12, 246, 248, 250, 254; recruitment campaigns, 49–50; and religious persecution, 202; Solzhenitsyn's archives confiscated by, 111; spying on students at Moscow State University, 40–41, 90–91; and Sverstyuk, 232; USSR–Great Britain Society secretly run by, 40; writers investigated by, 82
Khronika Press, 204, 205, 215
Khronika tekushchikh sobytii. See The Chronicle of Current Events
Khrushchev's Russia (Crankshaw), 28
Kiev, Land Rover trip to (1961), 24–25
King's College, 14, 99
Kommersant (newspaper), 274
Kommunist journal, 64
Komsomol. *See* Young Communist League
Krestovyi Pass, 24
Kurile Islands, 221

Labor camps: author's research on, 136, 138; Bukovsky in, 113, 183; Czechoslovakia protestors sentenced to, 129–30; Daniel in, 110, 112; Gorbachev's use of, 222; Grigorenko in, 141; Khrushchev's use of, 6, 166; Levitin in, 199; Marchenko in, 132, 133, 136, 142; number of political prisoners in, 148–49; Pailodze in, 200; and psychiatric abuse, 175–76; refuseniks in, 191; Shtarkman in, 80; Sinyavsky in, 78, 110, 112; Solzhenitsyn on, 6, 111; Yesenin-Volpin in, 110
Land Rover trip to Soviet Union (1961), 14–27; in Georgia, 21–24; in Kiev, 24–25; in Leningrad, 15–17; in Lvov, 25–26; in Moscow, 17–20; in Uzhgorod, 26
Latin American students, 96
A leaf of spring (Yesenin-Volpin), 110
Lenin: The Man, the Theorist, the Leader; a Reappraisal (Reddaway & Schapiro eds.), 2, 103–04
Leningradskaya Pravda (newspaper), 79
Leningrad Special Psychiatric Hospital, 141–42, 168, 248
Leningrad University, 33
Lenin Library, 41
Lenin's tomb, 13, 67
Lenin Teachers College, 80
Lev Gurych Sinichkin (vaudeville comedy), 72

The Listener (magazine), 152, 154
Literaturnaya Gazeta, 86, 254
London School of Economics, 1–2, 30, 103–19, 203
Lord of the Flies (Golding), 75, 76
Lvov, Land Rover trip to (1961), 25–26

Mafia, 262, 265–66, 272, 278
The Mansion (Faulkner), 77
Manual on Psychiatry for Dissidents (Gluzman & Bukovsky), 176
Marxism-Leninism, 11, 18, 52, 59, 72, 88, 108
Meditsinkskaya gazeta, 242
Memorial (organization), 237–38, 261, 269–70, 276
Memories of a Tatar childhood (Amalrik), 218
Mental hospitals. *See* Psychiatric abuse for political purposes
Meskhetians, 119, 123, 130, 268
Military Technology Academy, 138
Moi pokazaniya [*My Testimony*] (Marchenko), 118, 133, 142, 218
Molotov-Ribbentrop Pact (1939–1941), 35, 64
Morning Star (newspaper), 181
Moscow: author's visit (1960), 10–13; author's visit (1961), 17–20; author's visit (1963), 38–68; author's visit (1988), 225–35; author's visit (1990), 259–83; crime in, 52–53; housing in, 65
Moscow Energy Institute, 70
Moscow Group to Promote the Implementation of the Helsinki Agreements in the USSR, 146
Moscow Human Rights Committee, 170, 177, 203, 231
Moscow Institute of Psychiatry, 183
Moscow Music Conservatory, 80
Moscow Pedagogical State University, 12, 19, 42
Moscow School of Psychiatry, 170
Moscow State University: author's studies at, 1, 13, 29, 38–68; Department for Foreigners (Inotdel), 40–41, 91
Museum of the History of Religion and Atheism, 16
MVD (Ministry of Internal Affairs), 250, 264, 267, 268, 273, 274
Mysli sumasshedshego [*Thoughts of a madman*] (Grigorenko), 218
My Testimony (Marchenko), 118, 133, 142, 218

National Academy of Sciences (U.S.), 177–78
National Conference on Soviet Jewry, 191
National Council of Churches (U.S.), 201, 202
NBC News, 201, 202
Ne khlebom edinym (Dudintsev), 74
Neo-Leninism, 49
New Society (magazine), 152, 153
New York Review of Books, 2, 3
New York Times, 3, 133
Nezhelannoe puteshestvie v Sibir [*Involuntary Journey to Siberia*] (Amalrik), 114, 152, 153, 217–18
NKVD, 238
Not by Bread Alone (Dudintsev), 28
"Notes from Underground" (Reddaway), 131
Novgorod, Land Rover trip to (1961), 17
Novocherkassk massacre (1962), 60
Novosibirsk Institute for Sociological Research, 266–67
Novosti (newspaper), 181
Novyi mir (magazine), 47, 75, 76, 111
NTS (Narodno-Trudovoi Soyuz), 36–37

The Observer (newspaper), 2
Ogonyok (magazine), 271
OMON (Otryad Militsii Osobogo Naznacheniya, Special Purpose Police Unit), 273
One Day in the Life of Ivan Denisovich (Solzhenitsyn), 6, 34, 43, 111
The Origin of the Communist Autocracy (Schapiro), 105
Orthodox Church. *See* Georgian Orthodox Church; Russian Orthodox Church
"O spetsial'nykh psikhiatricheskikh bol'nitsakh ('Durdomakh')" (Grigorenko), 139
Ot Tarusy do Chuny [*From Tarusa to Chuna*] (Marchenko), 136

Pamyat movement, 233–34, 269
Pan-African Union, 93, 94, 96
Patrice Lumumba University, 92–93, 95, 98
Peace News, 2
People's Labor Union, 36
Peredelkino complex, 57
Perestroika, 227, 229, 231–32, 235–39, 278–79
Permanent Exhibition of Economic Achievements (Moscow), 17
Peterhof palace, 12, 15
Poems from captivity (Daniel), 218, 227
Poetka: Kniga o pamyati: Natalya Gorbanevskaya [*Poet: Book in memory of Natalya Gorbanevskaya*] (Ulitskaya), 122
Poets, 35, 59, 74–76, 78–80, 87, 111–12, 122
Politburo, 1, 5–6, 59, 66, 107, 113, 222–23
"Poputchiki" [The Companions] (Tarasenkova), 76
Pravda, 34, 163, 166
Press Club Glasnost, 234
Preuves (magazine), 78
Prisoners of Conscience in the USSR (Amnesty International), 180
Prison hospitals, 143, 187, 250, 254–55
Private Eye (magazine), 159–60
Problems of Communism (journal), 108–09, 199
Propaganda, 55, 73, 95–96, 152, 171, 201–02, 225, 248
Protsess chetyrekh [*The Trial of the Four*] (Litvinov), 118–19, 218
Psychiatric abuse for political purposes, 164–84, 206–14, 242–56; author's role in investigating, 2–3, 12–13, 226, 246–56, 276; Commission on the Abuse of Psychiatry in the Soviet Union, 146; and dissident movement, 111, 146–47; origins of, 165–68; smuggling documentation out of Soviet Union, 124; U.S. psychiatrists inspecting Soviet institutions, 12–13, 246–56; Working Commission to Investigate the Use of Psychiatry for Political Purposes, 2–3, 183, 208–14; Working Group on the Internment of Dissenters in Mental Hospitals, 168, 169, 172, 176. *See also* World Psychiatric Association
Punitive Medicine (Podrabinek), 146, 183
Pushkin Museum of Fine Arts, 15

A Question of Madness (Medvedev & Medvedev), 167, 171

Radio Free America, 173
Radio Free Europe, 151, 205–06
Radio Liberty, 2, 89, 123, 126, 151, 158, 188, 205–06, 215–16
Rationalism and Nationalism in Nineteenth Century Russian Political Thought (Schapiro), 106

Reddaway, Peter: at Cambridge University, 9–10; career overview, 1–4; expulsion from Soviet Union, 47, 99, 101–02; at Harvard University, 29–35; KGB surveillance of, 98–102; at London School of Economics, 103–19; at Moscow State University, 1, 13, 29, 38–68; psychiatric hospital inspections by, 246–56; Russian language studies, 1, 6–9; trip to Soviet Union (1960), 10–13; trip to Soviet Union (1961), 14–27; trip to Soviet Union (1963), 38–68; trip to Soviet Union (1988), 225–35; trip to Soviet Union (1989), 246–56; trip to Soviet Union (1990), 259–83

Red Square at Noon (Gorbanevskaya), 129

Refuseniks, 190–92, 232, 268

Religion in Communist Lands (journal), 197, 199, 200

Religious persecution and dissent, 196–202

"Requiem" (Akhmatova), 75, 84

The Rise and Fall of T. D. Lysenko (Medvedev), 111

Roads in Soviet Union, 20–21

Routledge Journals, 123

Royal College of Psychiatrists, 176–80, 210, 256

Russian Academy of Sciences, 45

The Russian Financial System (Reddaway), 7

Russian Orthodox Church, 198, 201–02, 229–30

Russian Research Center (Harvard), 30, 32

Russia's Domestic Security Wars (Reddaway), 3

Russia's Political Hospitals: The Abuse of Psychiatry in the Soviet Union (Bloch & Reddaway), 183, 207

Russkaya mysl' (newspaper), 216

St. Antony's College, Oxford, 29

St. Basil's Cathedral, 13

Samizdat: emergence of, 88; publication in West, 2, 215–19; religious, 198–99; sabotage by Bethell and Burg, 156–61; smuggling out of Soviet Union, 124–27. *See also specific publications*

Serbsky Institute of Forensic Psychiatry, 139–40, 142, 145, 165, 167, 169, 174, 177, 182, 184, 235, 245, 255

Sintaksis (journal), 60

Slepaya krasavitsa [*The Blind Beauty*] (Pasternak), 114

Sluggish repressions (Shifrin), 167

"Sluggish schizophrenia" diagnosis, 244, 246, 251

Smolensk under Soviet Rule (Fainsod), 30

Smolny Institute, 16

Smuggling samizdat out of Soviet Union, 124–27

Sobor [*The cathedral*] (Honchar), 194

Society for Friendship with Foreign Countries, 90, 91

Solovki Power (film), 238

Sotsialisticheskaya industriya (journal), 242

Sovetskaya Rossiya (newspaper), 163

Soviet Academy of Science, 265

The Soviet Mafia (Vaksberg), 265

Soviet Psychiatric Abuse (Bloch & Reddaway), 230

Soviet Psychiatric Society, 243, 245–46, 252

Soviet Society of Psychiatrists, 175, 178, 182, 213

Soviet Studies (journal), 108

Sovremennik Theater, 57, 87

The Spectator (magazine), 152, 153

Spring Torrents (Turgenev), 106

START arms control agreement (1991), 284

State Committee on Emergency Rule, 285
State Russian Museum (Leningrad), 15
Stikhi iz nevoli [*Poems from captivity*] (Daniel), 218, 227
Student (journal), 156–57
Student Struggle for Soviet Jewry, 191
Suchasnist' (journal), 146
Survey: A Journal of East and West Studies, 107

TASS, 133
Taxi drivers. *See* Cabdrivers
Theatrical works, 72–74
Thoughts of a madman (Grigorenko), 218
"Thoughts on Progress, Peaceful Coexistence and Intellectual Freedom" (Sakharov), 125, 292
Time magazine, 95, 97
The Times, 2, 109
To Live like Everyone (Marchenko), 136
Totalitarianism (Schapiro), 106
The Town (Faulkner), 77
Translators, 114–17
Tretyakov Gallery (Moscow), 16
The Trial (Kafka), 74, 76, 83
The Trial of the Four (Litvinov), 118–19, 218
Turgenev: His Life and Times (Schapiro), 106

Ukraine: dissident movement in, 111, 121, 123, 191–95; Dnepropetrovsk Special Psychiatric Hospital, 179, 180; independence of, 287–88, 289; smuggling samizdat out of, 127
Ukrainian Helsinki Group, 146
Ukrainian Public Group to Assist the Implementation of the Helsinki Agreements, 194
Uncensored Russia (Reddaway), 2, 136, 162, 195
UN Commission on Human Rights, 211
Union Treaty, 259, 261, 284–85, 288
Universal Declaration of Human Rights (UN), 121
U.S. Information Agency, 109
USSR–Great Britain Society, 13, 15, 17, 22, 40, 198
Utrennie poezda (film), 72
Uzhgorod, Land Rover trip to (1961), 26

"Vasili Terkin" (Tvardovsky), 43
Vesennie vody [*Spring Torrents*] (Turgenev), 106
Vesenniy list [*A leaf of spring*] (Yesenin-Volpin), 110
Voice of America, 89, 188, 206
Volga-Don Canal, 67
Vospominaniya tatarskogo detstva [*Memories of a Tatar childhood*] (Amalrik), 218
Vyalotekushchie repressii [*Sluggish repressions*] (Shifrin), 167

Ward 7: An Autobiographical Novel (Tarsis), 111
Washington Post, 3, 258
Western radio broadcasts, 44, 89, 205–06
Will the Soviet Union Survive until 1984? (Amalrik), 152, 218
Without a cross! (Tendryakov), 72
Women's Campaign for Soviet Jewry, 191
Woodrow Wilson International Center for Scholars, 220
Working Commission to Investigate the Use of Psychiatry for Political Purposes, 2–3, 183, 208–14
Working Group on the Internment of Dissenters in Mental Hospitals, 168, 169, 172, 176
World Council of Churches, 201

World Federation for Mental Health, 170
World Health Organization, 211
World Psychiatric Association (WPA), 168–77, 183, 206–13, 243, 245–46, 252
Writers and Scholars International, 159–60
Writers' Union, 35, 57, 71, 76–78, 81, 235, 263–65

The Yershov Brothers (Kochetov), 31
Young Communist League (Komsomol), 13, 18, 39, 272

Zhivi kak vse [*To Live like Everyone*] (Marchenko), 136

NAMES INDEX

Abalkin, Leonid, 241, 259, 287
Abram, Helena, 172, 174
Abramov, Fyodor, 63
Adelson, Abram, 71
Adelson, Stella, 71
Adzhubei, Aleksei, 86, 279
Afanasiev, Yuri, 239, 259, 261–62
Aitken, Eleanor, 169, 310n9
Akhmadulina, Bella, 74, 77, 303n4
Akhmatova, Anna, 75, 78, 79, 83–84, 116, 303n4
Akhromeyev, Sergei, 259, 267
Alekseyeva, Lyudmila, 187, 194
Alexeyeva, Lyudmila, 122, 222
Aliyev, Femi, 189
Alksnis, Viktor, 263, 267
Altshuler, Boris, 237
Amalrik, Andrei, 114, 122, 125, 152–56, 216, 217, 218
Amalrik, Gyuzel, 156, 218
Andreyev, Nikolai, 10
Andreyeva, Nina, 236, 239
Andriyanov, V., 242
Andropov, Yuri, 2, 113, 148–49, 166, 263, 271, 286
Anikst, Alexander, 82, 83
Antonenko, Elena, 90
Arapetyan, L. A., 271
Ardov, Viktor, 84
Arkhipov, Tolya, 39–40, 90
Arzhak, Nikolai (pen name of Daniel), 110
Astor, David, 159–60, 172
Astrachan, Anthony, 126

Babayan, Eduard, 207, 242
Babel, Isaac, 117
Babitsky, Konstantin, 127
Baeva, Tatiana, 127
Baibakov, Nikolai, 263
Bakatin, Vadim, 273, 277
Baker, James, 260
Bakhmin, Tanya, 230–31
Bakhmin, Vyacheslav, 208, 230–31
Baklanov, Oleg, 285
Balcar, Joan, 205

Barabanov, Yevgeny, 124
Batkin, Leonid, 239
Bayley, John, 116–17
Belkin, Aron, 232–33, 238, 242, 244, 245, 262–63
Bergson, Abram, 31
Beria, Lavrenty, 52
Berlin, Isaiah, 32, 86–87, 308n1
Berman, Harold, 33
Bernstein, Bob, 234
Bethell, Nicholas, 156–61, 309n5
Bezborodov, Dmitry, 277
Bezemer, Jan, 216, 218
Billington, James, 225
Birman, Igor, 274
Birshtein, Vadim, 268–70, 276
Bishop, Tony, 37
Bitov, Andrei, 88
Black, Anthony, 301n3
Black, Mrs., 30
Blake, Patricia, 36, 57, 75, 78, 114, 115, 116, 117, 305n32
Blakeley, Denis, 120, 124
Bloch, Sidney, 2, 165, 207, 210, 230, 233, 314n6
Blok, Alexander, 83
Blom-Cooper, Louis, 182
Bogoraz, Larissa, 117–18, 125, 127, 134–35, 136, 194, 216, 226–27, 231, 234, 276
Boldin, Valery, 285
Böll, Heinrich, 76
Bonavia, David, 126
Boniecki, George, 198
Bonner, Elena "Lyusya," 224–25, 226, 234, 237
Bonnie, Richard, 247, 252
Borisov, V., 169
Bourdeaux, Michael, 3, 106, 124, 196–97, 202, 216, 313n3
Brandt, Willy, 32
Brecht, Berthold, 77
Breitburt, Grigoriy, 76, 78
Brezhnev, Leonid, 2, 6, 47, 68, 108, 146, 177, 224–25, 262
Brimelow, Thomas, 32, 101
Brodsky, Joseph, 78–80
Brooke, Gerald, 137
Broué, Michel, 179, 180
Brown, Clarence, 117
Brown, George, 150, 151
Browne, Michael (pen name for Swoboda), 193, 313n15
Brumberg, Abraham, 156, 314n1
Brumberg, Josie, 314n1
Brzezinski, Zbigniew, 32
Bukovsky, Vladimir, 112, 113, 114, 124, 166, 167–71, 173–75, 180, 183, 206, 256, 310n9
Bulganin, Nikolai, 55
Bunich, Pavel, 239
Burbulis, Gennady, 258
Burg, David (pen name for A. Dolberg), 156–61
Burlatsky, Fyodor, 234, 264, 266
Bush, George H. W., 283, 284
Buyanov, Mikhail, 245
Bystretsova, Lyusya, 245

Calder, Angus, 301n3
Camus, Albert, 48
Carlisle, Olga Andreyev, 70–71
Carr, E. H., 105
Castro, Fidel, 33, 61
Catherine the Great, 8, 10, 24
Chaadayev, Pyotr, 140
Chalidze, Valery, 124, 126, 203–04, 205, 215, 224
Chandos, John, 173
Chaplin, Sid, 83
Chazov, Yevgeny, 226, 244, 246, 247, 250, 255, 262
Chebrikov, Viktor, 246
Chen Guancheng, 113
Cheney, Dick, 263
Chernenko, Konstantin, 2

Chodoff, Paul, 207
Chornovil, Vyacheslav, 193, 313n15
Chukovsky, Kornei, 48, 79, 86–87
Churkin, Alexander, 246, 247, 254, 255
Clark, David, 176, 182
Cohen, Stephen, 124
Cole, William, 126, 168
Conquest, Robert, 28, 154, 155
Cook, Paul, 124
Corti, Mario, 124, 126
Corvalan, Luis, 183
Couriss, Elizaveta, 7, 8–9
Couriss, Nikolai, 6–7, 8–9
Crankshaw, Edward, 28, 309n7
Cranston, Maurice, 105, 151
Critchlow, James, 206
Croan, Melvin, 31, 33
Crosland, Anthony, 32
Cross, Tony, 46
Crowfoot, John, 228

Daniel, Sanya, 226, 276–77
Daniel, Yuli, 2, 60, 110, 112, 117–18, 129, 134, 218, 226–27, 276
David V (patriarch), 200
Davis, Kathryn W., 302n1
Davis, Shelby Cullom, 302n1
Davitashvili, Dzhuna, 262
Degras, Jane, 304n6
Delaunay, Vadim, 127
Dementiev, A. G., 48
Deng Xiaoping, 221
Denikin, Anton, 7
Deutscher, Isaac, 32
Devdariani, Khariton, 200
Dewhirst, Martin, 2, 4, 28–29, 34, 36–37, 69, 115, 124, 126, 158, 309n5
Dicks, Henry, 180
Djemilev, Mustafa, 189, 308n28
Djilas, Milovan, 44
Dolberg, Alexander, 156
Dolmatovsky, Yevgeny, 77
Dornan, Peter, 123, 126, 206, 215–16
Dostoyevsky, Fyodor, 77
Douglas-Home, Alec, 54
Dremliuga, Vladimir, 127
Dubcek, Alexander, 127
Dudintsev, Vladimir, 28, 74
Dunham, Vera, 133, 307n5
Dunlop, John, 286
Durrell, Lawrence, 83
Dzasokhov, Alexander, 273
Dzerzhinsky, Felix, 250
Dzhemilev, Mustafa, 189
Dzyuba, Ivan, 193

Efrem II (patriarch), 200
Ehrenburg, Ilya, 81, 82, 88
Eker, Rita, 191, 232
Eliot, T. S., 19
Ellis, Jane, 124
Elvin, Mark, 35–36
Emelkina, Nadezhda, 122
Erickson, John, 104

Fadin, Andrei, 260
Fainberg, Viktor, 127, 129, 169, 171, 179, 181
Fainsod, Merle, 29, 30, 33, 34, 105
Farquharson, Marjorie, 123–24
Farrand, William, 247
Faulkner, William, 77, 83
Fedin, Konstantin, 48, 84
Fedorov, Nikolai, 45, 235
Feltrinelli, Giangiacomo, 71
Figgis, Anthony, 14, 20
Filippov, Boris, 70
Finn, Patrick, 14
Fisher, Elizabeth, 216, 217
Flegon, Alex, 156, 157
Florovsky, Georges, 32
Frank, Victor, 206
Freedman, Alfred, 178, 311n24
Friendly, Alfred, 126
Fukalov, Viktor, 249–50
Fulbright, William, 151

Furov, Vasily, 202
Furtseva, Ekaterina, 82

Gabai, Galya, 122
Gabai, Ilya, 189
Gachev, Georgy, 45
Galanskov, Yuri, 111–12, 118, 129, 137, 307n14
Gamsakhurdia, Zviad, 124, 268
Gan, Vitaly, 163
Gerstenmaier, Cornelia, 275
Gilbert, Martin, 313n14
Gindilis, Viktor, 244, 245, 316n9
Ginzburg, Alexander, 60, 111–12, 118, 129, 137, 157, 228, 304n13
Ginzburg, Eugenia, 134
Glazunov, Ilya, 80
Glick, Stephen, 124
Gluzman, Semyon, 145, 147, 176–78, 180, 210, 231–32, 243, 255, 310n17
Gnedin, Yevgeny, 218
Goldberg, Anatol, 120, 162
Golding, William, 75, 76
Gollancz, Livia, 166
Gollancz, Victor, 166, 309n3
Goodman, Bob, 29–30
Gorbachev, Mikhail, 3, 163, 167, 188, 195, 214, 218, 220–41, 257–61, 263, 267, 268, 269, 272–74, 283–88, 291, 293, 315n3, 316n2
Gorbachev, Raisa, 285
Gorbanevskaya, Natalya, 122, 127–28, 129, 169, 268, 306n8
Gorbunov, E., 311n34
Granin, Daniil, 49
Griboyedov, Alexander, 73
Grigor, John, 207
Grigorenko, Andrei, 147, 308n28
Grigorenko, Pyotr, 122, 129, 138–48, 169, 176, 177, 187, 208, 218, 232, 243, 250, 308n21, 308n28, 310n17
Grigorenko, Zinaida, 144
Grigoryants, Sergei, 229
Grivnina, Irina, 208
Gromov, Boris, 238, 263, 264, 267, 268, 317n20
Guevara, Che, 35
Gurevich, Naum, 157
Gushchin, Lev, 271

Haimson, Leopold, 28
Hampshire, Stuart, 309n7
Harari, Manya, 85, 111, 114–15, 118, 124
Hasegawa, Tsuyoshi, 221
Havel, Vaclav, 270
Hayward, Max, 28, 29, 36, 85, 114, 115–17, 134, 152, 304n13, 305n32, 306n3
Heath, Edward, 159
Herzen, Alexander, 216
Hewett, Ed, 238
Hikmet, Nazim, 87
Hill, Elizabeth, 8, 9
Hitler, Adolf, 64, 309n3
Honchar, Oles, 194
Hood, Stuart, 154
Hosking, Geoffrey, 291
Hough, Jerry, 258, 316n2
Howard-Johnston, Xenia, 197
Hugh-Jones, Stephen, 107
Hurst, Mark, 313n1
Huytan, Konstantin, 124

Idrisov, Nail, 254
Ilchenko, Anatoly, 253–54
Il'ichev, Leonid, 35, 57, 70, 77, 82, 92
Il'insky, Igor, 73
Ilya, Bishop, 200
Ilya II (patriarch), 200
Ingrams, Richard, 160
Ionesyan (serial killer), 52
Irteneva, Natalya Ferdinandovna, 12–13, 19–20, 42–43
Ivanov, Mr. (economist), 63
Ivanov, N. K., 64
Ivanov, Vsevolod, 84
Ivanov, Vyacheslav, 84

Ivanov, Yuri, 136, 137
Ivinskaya, Olga, 85

Jenner, Alec, 169–70
John XXIII (pope), 48
Johnson, Priscilla, 31–32, 156, 302n4
Jones, D. A. N., 152–56, 306n2
Joravsky, David, 28
Joyce, James, 83

Kafka, Franz, 76, 83
Kaganovich, Lazar, 66, 67, 71, 269
Kaiser, Robert, 126
Kalb, Marvin, 32–33
Kamalov, V., 253
Kaminskaya, Dina, 189
Kamm, Henry, 154
Katanyan, Vasily, 76
Katayev, Valentin, 32
Katya (Moscow friend), 65–67
Keenan, Edward, 31, 32
Keep, John, 104
Keith, Dr., 251
Kennedy, John F., 5–6, 33, 34, 58, 89
Keratishvili, Bidzina, 200
Kharitonov, Ella, 46
Kharitonov, Olga, 263
Kharitonov, Volodya, 45–46, 263, 270
Khasina, Natalya, 232
Khodorovich, Tatyana, 122, 147, 180, 311n29
Khrushchev, Nikita, 1, 5–6, 7, 29, 33, 34, 35, 62–65, 66, 70, 77, 81, 107–08, 139, 166, 183–84, 193, 224, 270, 302n5, 303n8
Kimura, Hiroshi, 220–21
Kissinger, Henry, 33, 177
Klein, Joel, 248
Kline, Ed, 203, 204, 205, 224, 226
Klose, Kevin, 126
Knight, Amy, 286
Knipovich, Elena, 83
Kochetov, Vsevolod, 30–31, 48, 67, 302n6
Kochubievsky, Boris, 190
Kohl, Helmut, 275
Koridze, David, 200
Korin, Pavel, 81
Korneichuk, Alexander, 73
Kornilov, Vladimir, 35, 87, 302n5
Korotich, Vitaly, 238, 271
Koryagin, Anatoly, 167, 210, 211–12, 213, 214, 243
Kosterin, Aleksei, 122, 187
Kosygin, Aleksei, 6, 144, 150
Kovalev, Andrei, 167, 247
Kovalev, Sergei, 122, 226, 231, 234, 265, 270
Kozlov, Frol, 82
Kozyrev, Andrei, 231
Krasin, Viktor, 162
Krasovitsky (poet), 80
Kravchuk, Leonid, 287
Kruchyonykh, Aleksei, 80
Kryuchkov, Vladimir, 273, 285
Kudashev, Boris, 13, 17–19, 43–45, 301n3
Kuzichkin, Vladimir, 317n11
Kuzmina, Lyudmila, 249
Kuznetsov, V., 169

Labedz, Leopold, 28, 32, 107, 154, 304n13
Laird, Bruce, 123
Lakshin, Vladimir, 48
Landa, Malva, 226–27
Lang, David, 200
Lapidus, Gail W., 291
Latynina, Alla, 264
Lavut, Alexander, 226
Lawrence, D. H., 83
Lawrence, John, 197–98
Lebedeva, Svetlana, 42
Lebedev, Valery, 12–13, 19, 42–43
Leddington, Roger, 126
Leigh, Denis, 171, 173–74, 175, 177
Lenchevsky, Oleg, 99–102, 161
Lenchevsky, Valentina, 99–102

Lenin, Vladimir, 18, 103–04, 185, 290
Leonhard, Wolfgang, 32
Levitan, Isaak, 16
Levitansky, Yuri, 74, 303n4
Levitin, Anatoly, 199
Levitskaya, Natalya Grigorevna, 269
Lewis, Anthony, 154
Li Jiangjie, 221
Liberman, Yevgeny, 59
Licko, Pavel, 159
Lieven, Dominic "Chai," 7
Lieven, Pavel, 7, 8
Ligachev, Yegor, 223, 224, 233, 236, 237, 244, 317n15
Link, Perry, 305n23
Litvinov, Maxim, 120, 203
Litvinov, Pavel, 113, 114, 118–19, 120–21, 122, 124, 125, 127, 204, 216, 217
Low-Beer, Gerard, 147, 176, 178, 181
Lowenthal, Richard, 32
Lown, Bernard, 244
Lu Nanquan, 221
Lubarsky, Cronid, 126, 228, 315n7
Lukyanov, Anatoly, 286
Lumumba, Patrice, 93
Lunts, Daniil, 140, 145, 165
Lysak, Pyotr, 142
Lysenko, Trofim, 71, 111

Magyar, Paul, 7, 11, 109
Malenkov, Georgy, 55, 66
Mandelshtam, Osip, 80, 84, 303n6
Mann, A., 242
Mann, Thomas, 152
Mao Zedong, 6, 92
Marchenko, Anatoly, 118, 129, 132–38, 142, 147, 217, 306n3
Maretskaya, Vera, 46
Markham, David, 125, 172
Marmor, Helen, 201, 202
Marshak, Samuil, 79
Maryamov, A. M., 48
Masagaki, Miiko, 221
Masagaki, Shin-ichi, 221
Mathon, Tania, 124
Matlock, Jack, 232, 260–61, 264
Matthews, Mervyn, 91
Maugham, Somerset, 263
Mayakovsky, Vladimir, 76, 85, 305n32
McBride, Sean, 123
Medvedev, Roy, 167, 317n14
Medvedev, Zhores, 110–11, 167, 170, 177, 255
Mee, Cornelia (pen name of Aitken), 310n9
Meeus, Anthony de, 123, 215
Meierhold, Vsevolod, 73
Meilakh, Misha, 73, 78, 86
Meiman, Naum, 234
Men, Alexander, 276
Menglet, Georgy, 73
Men'shagin, Boris, 268, 269
Mercer, David, 154
Mercer, Ellen, 167, 248, 252
Meri, Lennart, 58
Merskey, Harold, 178
Metchenko, Aleksei, 41, 84
Mikhailenko, Anna, 248–49, 250
Mikhailovsky, Boris, 41
Mikhalkov, Sergei, 82
Mikoyan, Anastas, 186
Miller, Boris, 37
Miloradovich, Serafim, 215
Milosz, Czeslaw, 28
Molotov, Vyacheslav, 41, 47, 66
Moore, Barrington, Jr., 34
Morozov, Georgy, 165, 177, 178, 182, 235, 245, 254, 260
Morton, Miriam, 87

Nathans, Ben, 4
Neigauz, Stanislav, 80
Nekrasov, Viktor, 47, 81, 180, 302n5
Neumann, Jochen, 167
Nevsky, Alexander, 17

Ni Xiaoquan, 221
Nicholas I (tsar), 140
Nixon, Richard, 175, 177
Noel-Paton, Duncan, 14, 19, 26
Nordlinger, Jay, 305n23
Nove, Alec, 32, 103–04
Novikov, Yuri, 182, 311n35

Odnopozov, Naum (pen name of Gurevich), 157
Ogurtsov, Igor, 307n14
Okhotin, Nikita, 270
Oksman, Yulian, 82
Okudzhava, Bulat, 82, 266
Ordzhonikidze, Sergo, 66
Orlov, Yuri, 146, 308n26
Oswald, Lee Harvey, 89
Otto, Gisela, 209, 314–15n11
Ovechkin, Valentin, 35, 48
Owen, David, 210
Ozerov, Lev, 84

Pailodze, Valentina, 200
Palazchenko, Pavel, 258
Panasenko, V. A., 253
Pantin, Volodya, 142–43
Pasternak, Alexander, 13, 66–67, 69–71, 84–86
Pasternak, Boris, 13, 69–71, 84–85, 110, 114, 115, 116
Pasternak, Elena, 70
Pasternak, Yevgeniya, 70
Pasternak, Zhenia, 70–72, 85
Pasternak, Zinaida, 71, 85
Patch, Isaac, 205
Paustovsky, Konstantin, 48, 57
Pavlov, Sergei, 60
Pavlov, Valentin, 285, 286
Pavlovna, Lilya (last name unknown), 40–41, 91
Peipert, James, 126
Petrakov, Nikolai, 275
Petrovna (maid for Natalya Irteneva), 12–13, 19
Petukhov, Andrei, 248, 250
Piper, Hal, 126
Pipes, Richard, 28, 29, 33, 57
Pisarev, Sergei, 166, 309n4
Plyushch, Leonid, 147, 177, 179, 180–81, 207, 311n27
Podgorny, Nikolai, 6
Podrabinek, Alexander, 146, 182, 183, 184, 208, 209, 228–29, 230, 231, 243, 248, 255–56
Podryachikov, Dmitry, 255
Polevoi, Boris, 82
Polubinskaya, Svetlana, 277
Popov, Gavriil, 272
Popper, Karl, 105
Potapov, Anatoly, 242, 244
Primakov, Yevgeny, 264–65
Prokhanov, Alexander, 230, 235, 317n20
Pugo, Boris, 264, 267, 285
Putin, Vladimir, 3, 98, 188, 218, 256, 293

Quinn-Judge, Paul, 263

Radek, Karl, 72
Rait-Kovaleva, Rita, 74–78, 82
Ralis, Max, 206
Rasputin, Valentin, 45, 233, 317n20
Reagan, Ronald, 223
Reavey, George, 304n14, 305n32
Reddaway, Frank, 8, 301n2
Reddaway, Peter W. F., 301
Rees, William Linford, 175
Reich, Walter, 147
Repin, Ilya, 16
Repin, Sergei, 16–17
Reshetov, Yuri, 251
Rigal, Margaret, 191
Rigamer, Elmore, 247, 251, 252, 316n12
Rigdon, Bruce, 201, 202
Roginsky, Arseny, 238
Romm, Mikhail, 73

Roth, Loren, 247, 248, 311n27
Roth, Martin, 177, 178, 179–80
Rozov, Viktor, 91
Rublev, Andrei, 16
Rudenko, Mykola, 194
Rywkin, Michael, 31, 32
Ryzhkov, Nikolai, 233, 259

Sabshin, Mel, 167
Sado, Mikhail, 307n14
Sainsbury, Peter, 210
Sakharov, Andrei, 123, 125, 136, 155, 167, 170, 176, 177–79, 192, 203, 224–25, 229, 234, 237, 238, 239–41, 244, 275, 291
Salinger, J. D., 83
Salisbury, Harrison, 133–34, 306n5
Salutsky, Anatoly, 277–83, 317n14
Samarin, Yuri, 83
Samsonov, Nikolai, 166
Sarraute, Natalie, 76
Satter, David, 126
Scammell, Michael, 133, 160, 306n3, 307n5
Schapiro, Leonard, 2, 28, 30, 102, 103–07, 115, 116, 117, 133, 150, 151, 158, 160, 197–98, 206, 304n4, 307n5, 309n5
Scriabin, Alexander, 84
Selyunin, Vasily, 272–73, 274, 275
Semanov, Sergei, 235
Semichastny, Vladimir, 113, 144
Semyonova, Svetlana, 45, 235, 265
Serebrov, Felix, 208
Seton-Watson, Hugh, 104
Seytmuratova, Aysha, 188, 189, 216
Shakhbagova, Julietta, 17, 21–22, 90, 301n2
Shapiro, David, 91, 150
Shatalin, Stanislav, 258, 272, 275, 284
Shcharansky, Anatoly, 192
Sheinis, Viktor, 264–65
Shepilov, Dmitri, 66
Sherbourne, Michael, 191, 232
Shestakov, Dmitry, 46–47, 48, 57, 78, 80, 83, 89, 101–02, 263
Shevardnadze, Eduard, 167, 223, 246, 260, 261, 267, 275, 286
Shifrin, Mikhail, 167
Shikhanovich, Yuri, 122, 177, 179, 231, 245, 311n27
Shmelev, Nikolai, 239
Sholokhov, Mikhail, 48
Shtarkman, Naum, 80
Shub, Anatole, 154, 155
Shulman, Marshall, 47, 302n4
Shul'ts, Fyodor, 166
Shvarts, Yevgeny, 78
Siesby, Eric, 234
Singh, Paul, 93, 95–96
Sinyavsky, Andrei, 2, 60, 70, 78, 112, 114, 116, 129, 156
Sinyavsky-Rozanova, Maria, 126
Skorodenko, Volodya, 81, 82, 83
Slater, Ann Pasternak, 303n1
Slonim, Vera, 203
Smiley, Xan, 233–34
Smirnov, Konstantin "Kostia," 270–71, 276
Smirnov, Sergei, 91
Smith, Hedrick, 126
Smoktunovsky, Innokenty, 73
Smulevich, Dr., 251
Smythe, Myles (pen name for Peter Reddaway), 301n3
Snezhnevsky, Andrei, 170–71, 174, 175–76, 178, 183–84, 210, 244
Sobolev, Yu. I., 253, 254
Sofronov, Anatoly, 73, 82
Soloukhin, Vladimir, 303n10
Solzhenitsyn, Alexander, 6, 34, 43, 47, 57, 86, 87–88, 111, 114, 116, 118, 130, 159, 177, 178
Sosin, Gene, 206, 314n4
Sosnora, Viktor, 83
Spender, Stephen, 309n7
Stalin, Joseph, 1, 6, 54, 64, 66, 71, 86, 138, 185, 186, 193, 290

Stalin, Vasili, 66
Starchik, Pyotr, 228–29
Starodubtsev, Vasily, 285
Starovoitova, Galina, 260
Starr, Frank, 126
Starr, S. Frederick, 291
Steele, Jonathan, 14, 23, 27, 162
Stefanis, Costas, 243
Stevenson, Anne, 35–36
Stone, Alan, 147
Stone, I. F. "Izzy," 35–36, 175, 243
Stoppard, Tom, 172
Struve, Gleb, 70, 85
Struve, Nikita, 126
Suess, Sonja, 314–15n11
Sukarno, 96
Superfin, Gabriel (Garik), 162, 268
Suslov, Mikhail, 92
Sverstyuk, Yevhen, 194, 232
Sveshnikov (poet), 80
Svitlychny, Ivan, 194, 313n15
Swoboda, Victor, 137, 193
Szamuely, Tibor, 153

Talyzin, Nikolai, 233
Tarasenkova, Natalya, 76, 87
Tarsis, Valery, 35, 111, 114
Taubman, William, 286
Tchapeyou, Kamine, 93, 94
Telesin, Julius, 130, 192
Tendryakov, Vladimir, 57, 72, 77–78, 87, 303n3
Ternovsky, Leonard, 208
Tertz, Abram (pen name of Sinyavsky), 78, 110, 156
Thatcher, Margaret, 223, 270
Timofeyev, Lev, 234
Tizyakov, Alexander, 285
Tolstoy, Count, 9
Tolstoy, Leo, 20
Tolstoy, Mitya, 67
Topchiy, Elena, 15–16, 17
Tovstonogov, Georgy, 73
Travkin, Nikolai, 272
Trump, Donald, 224
Tsukerman, Boris, 141, 143
Tsvetayeva, Marina, 75, 84
Tuck, Bob, 206
Turgenev, Ivan, 106
Tvardovsky, Alexander, 43, 47–48, 50, 75, 79, 86
Tyurin (poet), 80

Ulam, Adam, 29, 31, 304n1
Ulitskaya, Lyudmila, 122
Uzzell, Lawrence, 197

Vainman, Yefim, 243–44
Vaksberg, Arkady, 265–68
Valerii, Ivan (pen name of Tarsis), 111
Valitov, Dr., 250, 254
Van het Reve, Jozien, 216–17, 218
Van het Reve, Karel, 3, 124, 125–26, 155, 216–19
Van Voren, Robert, 167, 314–15n11
Varennikov, Valentin, 317n20
Vartanyan, Marat, 174, 178, 244, 254
Vasiliev, Dmitry, 234
Vdovenko, Nikolai, 250
Velikanova, Tatyana, 122
Velikhov, Yevgeny, 226
Venediktov, Dmitry, 207
Villiers, Marjorie, 114
Visotsky, Harold, 247
Vladimir, Prince, 24
Vlasto, Alexis, 10
Voikhanskaya, Marina, 147, 179, 180, 182, 207
Voloshanovich, Alexander, 209–10, 211
Volsky, Arkady, 286
Voznesensky, Andrei, 77, 83
Vysotsky, Vladimir, 228

Weinberg, Jack, 207
Weinberger, Friedrich, 209, 315n11
Wenick, Martin, 124
Wiles, Peter, 150

Wilson, Edmund, 85
Wilson, Harold, 150
Wing, John, 181
Wolfowitz, Paul, 272

Xu Kui, 221

Yaffe, Dan, 124
Yagoda, Genrikh, 67
Yakhimovich, I., 169
Yakir, Irina, 122, 277
Yakir, Pyotr, 122, 124, 126, 155, 162
Yakobson, Anatoly, 122
Yakovlev, Alexander, 223, 236, 242, 264, 267, 287
Yanayev, Gennady, 285
Yankelevich, Tatiana, 225
Yarkov, Ilya, 166
Yashin, Alexander, 57
Yazov, Dmitry, 274, 285
Yeltsin, Boris, 224, 241, 258, 261, 267, 269, 275, 285, 287
Yeo, Clayton, 123, 311n28
Yesenin-Volpin, Alexander, 35, 110, 112, 113, 119, 124, 125, 172, 181, 203, 209, 304nn14–15
Yevtushenko, Yevgeny (Zhenia), 30–31, 34, 74, 77, 81, 82, 111
Young, Mr., 10
Yudin, Dr., 232
Yuenger, James, 126
Yumashev, Valentin, 271

Zagalsky, Leonid, 254, 255
Zaks, Boris, 48
Zavadsky, Yuri, 73
Zelinsky, Korneliy, 76
Zeman, Zbynek, 123
Zharikov, Nikolai, 245
Zheludkov, Sergei, 133
Zhitnikova, Tanya, 147
Zhukov, Marshal, 52
Zoshchenko, Mikhail, 87
Zoubok, Boris, 147, 207